Wrong-Doing, Truth-Telling

MICHEL FOUCAULT

WRONG-DOING, TRUTH-TELLING

The Function of Avowal in Justice

EDITED BY Fabienne Brion AND Bernard E. Harcourt

TRANSLATED BY Stephen W. Sawyer

THE UNIVERSITY OF CHICAGO PRESS

UCL PRESSES UNIVERSITAIRES DE LOUVAIN

Michel Foucault (1926–84) is one of the most significant social theorists of the twentieth century, his influence extending across many areas of the humanities and social sciences.

Fabienne Brion is professor in the School of Law at the Catholic University of Louvain.

Bernard E. Harcourt is the Julius Kreeger Professor of Law at the University of Chicago and *directeur d'études* at the École des hautes études en sciences sociales.

Stephen W. Sawyer is chair and associate professor of history at the American University of Paris.

The University of Chicago Press, Chicago 60637
The University of Chicago Press, Ltd., London
© 2014 by The University of Chicago
All rights reserved. Published 2014.
Printed in the United States of America

23 22 21 20 19 18 17 16 15 14   1 2 3 4 5

ISBN-13: 978-0-226-25770-9 (cloth)
ISBN-13: 978-0-226-92208-9 (e-book)
ISBN-10: 0-226-25770-3 (cloth)
ISBN-10: 0-226-92208-1 (e-book)
DOI: 10.7208/chicago/9780226922089.001.0001

Library of Congress Cataloging-in-Publication Data
Foucault, Michel, 1926–1984, author.
[Mal faire, dire vrai. English]
Wrong-doing, truth-telling : the function of avowal in justice / Michel Foucault ; edited by Fabienne Brion and Bernard E. Harcourt ; translated by Stephen W. Sawyer.
pages cm
Includes index.
ISBN 978-0-226-25770-9 (cloth : alkaline paper) — ISBN 978-0-226-92208-9 (e-book) 1. Justice. 2. Truth. 3. Confession (Law). 4. Law—Philosophy. I. Brion, Fabienne, editor. II. Harcourt, Bernard E., 1963– editor. III. Sawyer, Stephen W., 1974– translator. IV. Title.
K241.F7F6813 2014
340′.114—dc23   2013037748

♾ This paper meets the requirements of ANSI/NISO Z39.48-1992 (Permanence of Paper).

This work, co-published by the Presses universitaires de Louvain and the University of Chicago Press, is the result of a collaboration between the School of Criminology of the Université catholique de Louvain and the University of Chicago.

Contents

Dr. Leuret, avowal, and the therapeutic operation.   •   The supposed
effects of truth-telling about oneself and of knowledge of the self.   •
Characteristics of avowal.   •   The spread of avowal within Western
Christian societies: individuals bound to their truth and obligated in
their relationships to others through the truth told.   •   A historical-
political problem: how the individual binds himself to his truth and to
the power that exerts itself upon him.   •   A historical-philosophical
problem: how individuals are bound by forms of veridiction.   •
A counterpoint to positivism: a critical philosophy of *veridictions*.   •
The problem of "who is being judged" in penal institutions.   •   Penal
practices and technologies of government.   •   Governing through
truth.

THIRD LECTURE *91*
April 29, 1981

Hermeneutics of the text and hermeneutics of the self in early
Christianity. • Veridiction of the self in pagan antiquity. •
The Pythagorean examination of conscience: purification of self
and mnemotechnics. • The Stoic examination of conscience: the
government of the self and the remembering of codes. • The Stoic
expositio animae: medicine of passions and degrees of liberty. •
Penance in early Christianity. • The problem of reintegration. •
Penance as a status that manifests a particular state. • The meanings
of *exomologēsis*. • A life in the form of avowal, an avowal in the form
of life. • A ritual of supplication. • Beyond the medical or judicial,
the model of the martyr. • Veridiction of the self and mortification of
the self. • From the public manifestation of the self as sinner to the
verbalization of the self: temptation and illusion.

FOURTH LECTURE *125*
May 6, 1981

Practice of veridiction in monastic institutions of the fourth and fifth
centuries: the *Apophthegmata patrum* and the writings of Cassian. •
Monasticism: between the life of penance and philosophical existence. •
Characteristics of the direction of conscience in ancient culture. •
Characteristics of the direction of conscience in monasticism: an
obedience that is continuous, formal, and self-referential; humility,
patience, and submission; the inversion of the relationship to
verbalization. • Characteristics of the examination of conscience in
monasticism: from action to thought. • Mobility of thought and
illusion. • *Discrimen* and *discretio*: avowal and the origin of thought. •
Veridiction of the self, hermeneutics of thought, and the rights-bearing
subject.

FIFTH LECTURE   *163*
May 13, 1981

SIXTH LECTURE   *199*
May 20, 1981

of crime for the criminal. • Accident, probability, and indices of criminal risk. • Veridiction of the subject and the breach in the contemporary penal system.

Editors' Preface

In 1981, Michel Foucault delivered a course of lectures at the Catholic University of Louvain. He titled them *Mal faire, dire vrai: Fonction de l'aveu en justice*. We have decided to translate this as *Wrong-Doing, Truth-Telling: The Function of Avowal in Justice*.*

* We have translated the title *Mal faire, dire vrai* as *Wrong-Doing, Truth-Telling* to capture Foucault's preoccupation, at the time he delivered these lectures, with the broad category of truth-telling and his incipient interest in *parrhēsia*. "Truth-telling" is the term that has been used in the English editions of Foucault's later Collège de France lectures to translate the expression *"dire-vrai."* See Michel Foucault, *The Courage of Truth: The Government of Self and Others II: Lectures at the Collège de France, 1983–1984*, English series ed. Arnold I. Davidson, trans. Graham Burchell (New York: Palgrave, 2011), p. 1 (translating *"ce thème de la* parrēsia, *du dire-vrai"* as "the theme of *parrhēsia*, truth-telling"). We opted for "truth-telling" rather than "speak true" or "telling true" for several reasons. First, "speak true" is almost too literal, since translating *"vrai"* as "true" in this context misses, for instance, the common usage of the expression *"a dire vrai,"* on which Foucault was playing in part. "Truth-telling," it turns out, has a more similar range of connotations. It is also not as jarring to the English ear as "speak true." Moreover, "truth-telling" is the most common English translation for Nietzsche's concept of *Wahrsagen*, one that Foucault repeatedly refers to in his writings, including in the inaugural lecture to these Louvain lectures, to specifically define *"dire-vrai"* (see p. 20). To be sure, using the term "truth" for *"vrai"* converts a word that has both an adverbial element (a kind of telling) and an objective element (saying something that is true) into a pure noun (in French, a *substantif*, carrying the idea of a substance). Foucault, naturally, is not refer-

He also led a research seminar on the genealogy of the early-twentieth-century penal policy known as *la défense sociale*, or "social defense," a preventive approach to criminal justice policy pioneered by the Belgian lawyer and professor of criminal law Adolph Prins at the turn of the twentieth century.[1] In addition, Foucault granted three interviews: the first with the philosopher André Berten, a second with the magistrate Christian Panier and the philosopher Pierre Watté, and a third with two Belgian criminologists, Jean François and John De Wit.[2]

The historical context of Foucault's invitation to Belgium was significant. He was invited by the School of Criminology within the Faculty of Law at the Catholic University of Louvain at the initiative of Françoise Tulkens, a faculty member who taught criminal law and had a reputation for being a staunch penal abolitionist.[3] At the time she invited Foucault, Tulkens was closely following the work of the Belgian Commission for the Revision of the Penal Code,[4] and was profoundly critical of it.[5] She believed that the proposed revisions would do nothing to address a fundamental problem that plagued penal law and sentencing: namely, that the classical theory of criminal responsibility and more modern notions of dangerousness, rather than substituting or ameliorating each other, compounded each other and, in a vicious circle, had begun to "offer one another mutual support."[6] The proposed reforms, Tulkens believed, simply amplified the problem by coupling positivism with legalism, science with law. They broke

---

ring to a substantive truth, to "the truth." But given Foucault's more elegant style of naming and writing, and usage in the later lectures, we decided to use the more idiomatic expression "truth-telling," expecting fully that the reader will be attuned to the ambiguity and playfulness in the grammar.

The translation of *"aveu"* in the title and text also presents a challenge. In French, the dominant connotation of *"aveu"* tends to be in the legal context, both civil and penal, and involves a juridical confession; the dominant connotation of *"confession,"* in French, tends to be in the religious context and involves the Catholic confession. By contrast, in English the dominant connotation of "confession" is evenly split between the juridical and religious contexts, and the term "avowal" refers to the more general notion of an admission or acknowledgment. It is this broader notion of acknowledgment, especially of wrong-doing, that Foucault elaborates in the Louvain lectures, and accordingly it is to this broader idea that we refer in this translation. A genealogy of avowing goes beyond a genealogy of the confession — as Foucault's discussion of Homer's *Iliad*, of Sophocles' *Oedipus Rex*, and of the Stoic examination of conscience, among others, make clear. Foucault too had the option of using the term *"confession"* and, in a limited number of occasions in the Louvain lectures, actually did so; in those instances we have used the English translation "confession." In the title and in the text where Foucault himself used the term *"aveu,"* however, we have decided to privilege the term "avowal" over "confession."

neither with the classical doctrine of deterrence nor with the doctrine of social defense.[7]

It was no secret that Foucault had allied himself with radical jurists on a number of occasions.[8] This time too he accepted Tulkens's invitation. Following the precedent of another colloquium organized that same year by the Center for Criminological Research, also at the Catholic University of Louvain, entitled "Does the Notion of Dangerousness Still Mean Anything?,"[9] Foucault's course of lectures and research seminar would contribute to the debate on penal reform by seeking to undermine the foundations of the doctrine of social defense. The strategy was two-pronged: the lectures would trace a genealogy of the type of subject the doctrine of social defense presupposed,[10] and the seminar would trace a genealogy of the accompanying apparatus: the institutions, practices, and discourses of social defense.[11] The decision, at first glance paradoxical, to conduct both the lectures and the seminar under the aegis of the School of Criminology and the Center for Criminological Research had been carefully thought through. It sought to undermine the criminological discourse that was the very basis for the doctrine of social defense, and at the same time motivate criminologists to serve as "the critical conscience of the criminal law."[12] That, succinctly, was the context.

As for the text, Foucault's course is comprised of an inaugural lecture and six additional lectures. The subject matter, he said, was to sketch a "history of avowal as a form of linkage and relationship between veridiction and jurisdiction in penal practices from its origins to the present,"[13] a history limited to the "problem of penality."[14] The first two lectures focus on prelaw Greece. The first raises the question of the relationship between agonistic combat, what is considered true, and what is considered just; the second focuses on the knowledge (*savoir*) and truth-seeking of the tyrant. The next two lectures concern the medieval and Christian world, which Foucault would associate with "the problem of avowal, confession, and inquiry."[15] The final two lectures, on the modern and contemporary world, are dedicated to "the problems of avowal, examination, and expertise."[16] Throughout, the perspective is that of "a political and institutional ethnology of truth-telling [*le dire vrai*] or truthful speech [*la parole vraie*]."[17] It is a question not of trying to determine the conditions that any assertion must fulfill to count as either true or false, but rather of analyzing the relation between truth games and games of power, where truth is seen as a weapon and discourse as an assembly of polemical and strategic facts.

Although Foucault's lectures at Louvain were of critical importance to the intellectual and political struggles that his hosts were waging at the time, the significance of the lectures naturally goes well beyond that. Two questions delineate the field of inquiry: first, what are the practices that shape the question of truth with respect to criminality and the criminal; and, second, how does one speak the truth about oneself insofar as one has something for which to reproach oneself? Beyond criminality and the criminal, these questions introduce a new object into the game of true and false: the relation to oneself. By joining the problem of the relationship that the individual bears to his wrong-doing to the power of truth, the Louvain lectures complete Foucault's genealogy of the carceral, which henceforth unfolds along the three axes of knowledge, power, and the subject. But they also signal the recentering of the work to come on the question of subjectivity and on the historicity of the subject.

Viewed in isolation, the structure of *Wrong-Doing, Truth-Telling* resembles a Möbius strip. In the inaugural lecture, Foucault announces that the problem that preoccupies him has two aspects. The first is political: "knowing how the individual finds himself tied, and accepts to be tied, to the power exerted over him."[18] The second is philosophical: "knowing how subjects are effectively tied within and by the forms of veridiction in which they are engaged."[19] The former perpetually recalls the latter, and the latter the former. Depending on the reader's point of view, the history of the processes of veridiction and jurisdiction that Foucault outlines seems to expose, on the one hand, the contingency of the procedures designed to produce juridical truth and, on the other, the historicity of any philosophy that postulates truth as a function of the jurisdiction of a subject capable of distinguishing the true from the false.

Viewed as part of Foucault's larger work, the lectures seem at first glance to confirm the hypothesis that his later writings reflect a "transition from the political to the ethical."[20] In practice, the vehicle for this transition would be the avowal, defined as "a verbal act through which the subject affirms who he is, binds himself to this truth, places himself in a relationship of dependence with regard to another, and modifies at the same time his relationship to himself."[21] In theory, the vehicle would be the notion of an obligation to truth, which has two aspects: first, "the obligation to believe, admit, or postulate, whether it be in the order of religious faith or in the order of accepting scientific knowledge; and, second, the obligation to know the truth of ourselves, as well as to tell, manifest, and authenticate it."[22]

There are, however, immediate objections to this hypothesis. Much like the lectures given elsewhere that same year — "About the Beginning of the Hermeneutics of the Self" at Berkeley and Dartmouth,[23] and "Subjectivité et verité" at the Collège de France[24] — *Wrong-Doing, Truth-Telling* paves the path to a transition, but a different one: a transition away from the hard version to the soft version of governance in Western liberal democracies, if it is the political aspect of this problematic that interests us. One could equally well describe this as a transition from the genealogy of the criminal to a genealogy of the modern subject, of the desiring subject.[25] Alternatively, one could describe it as a passage from genealogy to alethurgy, if what interests us is its philosophical dimension. Nevertheless, from the earliest to the latest writings, Foucault opposes the courage of truth to the power of truth. From the very first to the very last works, his philosophy binds together politics and ethics.

In this, Georges Canguilhem was undoubtedly right: there is no rupture between the Foucault of knowledge-power and the Foucault of ethics.[26] Foucault himself reminded us of this in 1984 when he cautioned his auditors at the Collège de France that "to depict [his] research as an attempt to reduce knowledge [*savoir*] to power so as to make of knowledge the mask of power in terms of structures where the subject has no place, is nothing more than a caricature, pure and simple."[27] In our contemporary societies, government functions not only through repression but through the formation of *ēthea* into which individuals constitute themselves as moral subjects of their conduct. Without this subject, there is the possibility neither of docility nor of *voluntary* servitude, but — and this is equally important, especially for Foucault — there is also not the possibility of the art of "reflective indocility," nor the "art of voluntary unservitude."[28]

As Canguilhem so aptly put it, it was only "normal, in the properly axiological sense, that Foucault would undertake the elaboration of an ethics."[29] Between knowledge and power, *Wrong-Doing, Truth-Telling* slots in the subject like a wedge. If governing operates through the formation of *ēthea* into which individuals constitute themselves as subjects of their conduct, then "the ability to loosen one's hold on oneself"[30] is the ethical condition of possibility for the forms of political resistance to which Foucault's philosophy invites us. But these lectures demonstrate, as well, that the notion of a conscience transparent to itself is no more than one modality of the subject. In this sense, to loosen the hold on oneself is also to unburden oneself of the fiction of that starting point of knowledge and to begin to see in the subject of the philosophical tradition and of scientific discourse an avatar of the imaginary relation humans bear to the conditions of their existence.

∷∷

Of *Wrong-Doing, Truth-Telling*, the informed reader had known only of the existence of five of the lectures. These had been originally transcribed, poorly, in the form of a typed transcript that could be found in the Foucault archives at the IMEC—a typescript based on audio cassettes that are now considered lost. That typed transcript remained unpublished, naturally, because it did not contain the final lecture and also because it contained numerous evident errors.

Subsequent research within the School of Criminology succeeded in unearthing a copy of the original handwritten manuscript of the inaugural and first lectures, as well as thirteen U-Matic tapes that had been used to make an audiovisual recording of the lecture series, originally produced by the university's audiovisual center at the request of the School of Criminology. The U-Matic tapes contained the six public lectures, but not the inaugural lecture.

As a result, we had the following sources at our disposal for establishing the text of the lecture series:

- for the inaugural lecture, a copy of the original handwritten manuscript and a copy of the typed transcript;
- for the first lecture, a copy of the original handwritten manuscript and an audiovisual recording, as well as the typed transcript;
- for the second, third, fourth, and fifth lectures, audiovisual recordings and typed transcripts;
- and for the sixth lecture, an audiovisual recording only.

The text of the inaugural lecture was therefore established on the basis of the original handwritten manuscript; in order to render the reading more fluid, some of the lists were transformed into paragraphs. The six lectures that follow are based on the audiovisual recordings, which preserve Foucault's publicly spoken words. Whenever possible, we have filled gaps in the recordings caused by changes of U-Matic tape by including the relevant passages from the original typed transcripts, corrected for evident errors.

For the French edition we decided, in consultation with Daniel Defert and François Ewald, to follow the editorial choice established during the edition of the Collège de France lectures of providing a literal transcription of the lectures. Naturally, the passage from oral to written form inevitably involves some impositions: we introduced punctuation and paragraph breaks, and, whenever it seemed necessary, we removed unnecessary redundancies or repetitions, completed interrupted phrases, and corrected inadvertent grammatical slips. We indicated each time a passage was illegible or inaudible. We noted in the margin any conjectural additions or interpretations, as well as the interactions with the auditors in the lecture hall. To render the published text of the inaugural lecture more fluid and readable, the spatial disposition of the written manuscript—which at times took the form of indented lists or single-sentence paragraphs—was modified. For the French edition, we benefited greatly from the precious help offered by Daniel Defert, François Ewald, Françoise Tulkens, and Jean-Michel Chaumont, members of the scientific committee established to oversee the French edition. We are deeply grateful for their advice and counsel, and their generosity in time and spirit.

For the English translation, we decided to remain close to the original spoken word in order to convey fully Foucault's thought processes, convictions, qualifications, and at times hesitations. We have worked closely with our translator, Stephen W. Sawyer, professor and chairman of the History Department at the American University of Paris and editor of the English edition of the *Annales: Histoire, Sciences Sociales*, to ensure a translation that is entirely faithful to the theoretical interventions in Foucault's work.

The critical apparatus—the notes at the end of each chapter and the course context—provide bibliographical references and biographical details, identify other texts in which Foucault examined similar themes, and offer interested readers directions for further research. All quotations in the text have been identified and, wherever necessary, completed. Their citation details have been provided in the endnotes as well for reference. Foucault most often translated Greek and Latin texts himself to emphasize certain key aspects of the particular passages. As a result, we have translated his translations, rather than using in text the official English translations. We have, however, provided references to the official English editions wherever they are available. Daniel Wyche, Gabriel Mathless, and Christopher Berk at the University of Chicago provided invaluable assistance in this regard, and we are deeply grateful to them.

The appendix includes translations of the three interviews granted by Foucault during his visit to Louvain. The text of the first interview, with André Berten, dated May 7, 1981, is based on an audiovisual recording made by the university's audiovisual center at the request of the School of Criminology. The text of the second interview, with Christian Panier and Pierre Watté, dated May 14, 1981, is a translation of the version published in *Dits et Écrits* that has never yet appeared in English. The text of the third interview, with Jean François and John de Wit, dated May 22, 1981, is established on the basis of a typed transcript (based in turn on an audio recording that is now considered lost) found among Jean François's personal archives. The version presented here differs from the version published in *Dits et Écrits*, which consisted of a French translation of a Dutch adaptation of the interview (which had itself been translated from French into Dutch and published in a Dutch journal).

This edition of the Louvain lectures has been authorized by the family of Michel Foucault: his brother Denys Foucault, sister Francine Fruchaud, and nephew, Henri-Paul Fruchaud. We have made every possible effort to live up to the confidence they have shown in us.

Fabienne Brion and Bernard E. Harcourt[31]

[NOTES]

1. The research papers conducted in the seminar that Foucault directed were collected, edited, and published by Françoise Tulkens in *Généalogie de la défense sociale en Belgique* (Brussels: Story-Scientia, 1986). Françoise Tulkens also reedited and introduced one of the principal texts associated with the doctrine of "social defense," Adolph Prins, *La défense sociale et les transformations du droit pénal* (Geneva: Médecine et Hygiène, coll. Classiques Déviance et Société, 1986 [originally published Brussels: Misch et Thron, 1910]). For background and context on Prins, see Pasquale Pasquino, "Criminology: The Birth of a Special Knowledge," pp. 235–50 in Graham Burchell, Colin Gordon, and Peter Miller, eds., *The Foucault Effect: Studies in Governmentality* (Chicago: University of Chicago Press, 1991).

2. These three interviews with Foucault have been retranslated and reproduced in the appendix to this English edition. The French edition of *Mal faire, dire vrai* includes as its appendix the first interview with André Berten, dated May 7, 1981, and the third interview with Jean François and John De Wit, dated May 22, 1981. The second interview, with Christian

Panier and Pierre Watté, dated May 14, 1981, can be found in French in Michel Foucault, *Dits et Écrits 1954–1988*, Vol. 4 (1980–88), no. 359, pp. 747–52 (Paris: Gallimard, 1994).

3. Tulkens would eventually become vice president of the European Court of Human Rights in Strasbourg. In addition to Tulkens, other notable penal abolitionists of the period in Belgium included Michel van de Kerchove (*Le droit sans peines: Aspects de la dépénalisation en Belgique et aux États-Unis* [Brussels: Publications des facultés universitaires St. Louis, 1987]) and Foulek Ringelheim (ed., *Punir mon beau souci: Pour une raison pénale* [Brussels: Presses de l'Université Libre de Bruxelles, 1984]). Ringelheim twice dialogued with Foucault: the first time in 1973, before *Discipline and Punish* ("A propos de l'enfermement pénitentiaire," interview with A. Krywin and F. Ringelheim, *Pro Justitia: Revue politique de droit* 1, nos. 3–4; *La prison*, October 1973, pp. 5–14;, reproduced in Michel Foucault, *Dits et Écrits*, vol. 2 [1970–75], pp. 435–45 [Paris: Gallimard, 1994]); the second time in December 1983 ("Qu'appelle-t-on punir? Entretien avec Michel Foucault," in Ringelheim, ed., supra, pp. 34–46; the transcript of this second interview was entirely reviewed and corrected by Foucault on February 16, 1984, four months before his untimely death).

4. Regarding the commission's work, see Commission pour la révision du Code pénal, *Rapport sur les principales orientations de la réforme* (Brussels: Éditions du Moniteur, 1979).

5. Regarding Françoise Tulkens' critical position vis-a-vis the commission's work, see Tulkens, "Introduction au thème du séminaire," in Tulkens, ed., *Généalogie de la défense sociale en Belgique*, p. 7; and, in more detail, Françoise Tulkens, "La réforme du code pénal: Vers quelle stratégie de changement?" in Ringelheim, ed., *Punir mon beau souci: Pour une raison pénale*, pp. 380–403.

6. Michel van de Kerchove, "Culpabilité et dangerosité: Réflexions sur la clôture des théories relatives à la criminalité," in C. Debuyst, ed., *Dangerosité et justice pénale: Ambiguïté d'une pratique* (Geneva: Médecine et Hygiène, 1981), p. 299.

7. On this point, see Françoise Tulkens, "Introduction au thème du séminair," in F. Tulkens, ed., *Généalogie de la défense sociale en Belgique*, p. 7. For a detailed treatment of the historical context and situation in Belgium, see Foucault, *Mal faire, dire vrai*, p. xi, n. 6.

8. See Colin Gordon, introduction to Michel Foucault, *The Essential Works of Foucault, 1954–1984: Power*, vol. 3, ed. James D. Faubion, series ed. Paul Rabinow, trans. Robert Hurley and others (New York: The New Press, 2000), p. xxx.

9. The work of this colloquium, organized under the direction of Christian Debuyst, then professor at the Center of Criminology at the Université Catholique de Louvain, was published. See Christian Debuyst, ed., *Dangerosité et justice pénale: Ambiguïté d'une pratique*.

10. See Tulkens, "Introduction au thème du séminaire," p. 5; and Jean François, "Aveu, vérité, justice et subjectivité: Autour d'un enseignement de Michel Foucault," *Revue interdisciplinaire d'études juridiques*, no. 7, 1981, pp. 163–82.

11. See Tulkens, "Introduction au thème du séminaire," pp. 5–13.

12. Françoise Tulkens used this expression; the probable reference was to Manfred Brusten who, in 1981, assigned to criminology this precise function. On this point, see generally Brusten, "Vers une criminology sous tutelle étatique?" *Déviance et Société* 5 (1981), no. 2, p. 177.

13. Foucault, *Wrong-Doing, Truth-Telling*, Lecture of April 22, 1981, p. 30.

14. Ibid., p. 29.

15. Ibid., p. 31.

16. Ibid., p. 31.

17. Ibid., p. 28.

18. Foucault, *Wrong-Doing, Truth-Telling*, Inaugural Lecture, p. 19.

19. Ibid.

20. Michel Foucault, "Le souci de la vérité," interview with François Ewald, *Magazine littéraire*, no. 270 (May 1984), in Foucault, *Dits et Écrits 1954–1988*, vol. 4 (1980–88), no. 350, pp. 668–78 (Paris: Gallimard, 1994), p. 676.

21. Foucault, *Wrong-Doing, Truth-Telling*, Inaugural Lecture, p. 17.

22. Interview with Jean François and John De Wit, May 22, 1981, p. 256.

23. Michel Foucault, "About the Beginning of the Hermeneutics of the Self," ("Subjectivity and Truth" and "Christianity and Confession," lectures given at the University of California, Berkeley, October 20 and 21, 1980, and at Dartmouth College, November 17 and 24, 1980), ed. Mark Blasius, *Political Theory* 21 (May 1993), no. 2, pp. 198–227.

24. Michel Foucault, *Subjectivité et vérité: Cours au Collège de France, 1980–1981*, ed. Frédéric Gros (Paris: Gallimard/Seuil, forthcoming).

25. On the concept of "the desiring subject," see Michel Foucault, *The History of Sexuality, Volume 2: The Use of Pleasure*, trans. Robert Hurley (New York: Vintage Books, 1990), pp. 5–6.

26. Georges Canguilhem, "On *Histoire de la folie* as an Event," in Arnold I. Davidson, ed., *Foucault and His Interlocutors*, trans. Ann Hobart (Chicago: University of Chicago Press, 1997), pp. 28–32.

27. Michel Foucault, *Le courage de la vérité: Le gouvernement de soi et des autres II. Cours au Collège de France, 1984*, ed. Frédéric Gros (Paris: Gallimard/Seuil, 2009), p. 10; English edition, *The Courage of Truth*, pp. 8–9.

28. Michel Foucault, "Qu'est-ce que la critique? [Critique et *Aufklärung*]," lecture delivered at the Société française de philosophie, May 27, 1978), *Bulletin de la Société française de philosophie* 84 (1990), p. 39; English translation, "What Is Critique?" pp. 41–82 in Michel Foucault, *The Politics of Truth*, Sylvère Lotringer, ed. (Los Angeles: Semiotext[e], 2007), p. 47.

29. Georges Canguilhem, "On *Histoire de la folie* as an Event," p. 32.

30. Foucault, "Le souci de la vérité," p. 675.

31. For the French edition, Fabienne Brion established the text and notes for the lectures of April 28, May 6, and May 13, 1981; Bernard Harcourt established the text and notes for the lectures of April 22, April 29, and May 20, 1981; and the text and notes of the inaugural conference, as well as the editorial work, rereading, and corrections of the French edition were the product of collaboration by Fabienne Brion and Bernard Harcourt.

For the English edition, Stephen Sawyer translated the inaugural conference, the six lectures, and the three interviews; Bernard Harcourt established the notes (with the assistance of Daniel Wyche, Gabriel Mathless, and Christopher Berk), the editors' preface (with the assistance of Fabienne Brion and Lyubomir Uzunov), and "The Louvain Lectures in Context" (with the assistance of Daniel Nichanian), and also performed the editorial work.

INAUGURAL LECTURE

April 2, 1981

Dr. Leuret, avowal, and the therapeutic operation. • The supposed effects of truth-telling about oneself and of knowledge of the self. • Characteristics of avowal. • The spread of avowal within Western Christian societies: individuals bound to their truth and obligated in their relationships to others through the truth told. • A historical-political problem: how the individual binds himself to his truth and to the power that exerts itself upon him. • A historical-philosophical problem: how individuals are bound by forms of veridiction. • A counterpoint to positivism: a critical philosophy of *veridictions*. • The problem of "who is being judged" in penal institutions. • Penal practices and technologies of government. • Governing through truth.

In a work on the moral treatment of madness published in 1840, a French psychiatrist by the name of Leuret explained the method he used to treat one of his patients.[1] Treated and cured, he insisted. Mr. A. suffered from delirium of persecution and hallucinations. One morning Leuret led him to the lavatory and stood him under a shower. A lengthy exchange began, which I will summarize. The doctor asked the patient to recount in detail his delirium.

Doctor Leuret: "There is not one word of truth in all of this. What you are saying is sheer madness, and it is because you are mad that we are keeping you at Bicêtre."

The patient: "I don't think I'm mad. I know what I saw and heard."

The doctor: "If you want me to be happy with you, you must obey, because everything I am asking of you is reasonable. Will you promise never to think of your delusions and never to speak of them again?

The patient promised, with some hesitation.

Doctor Leuret: "Up to now, you have been unable to keep your word. I cannot count on your promises. So, you will receive a shower until you avow that everything you have said is pure madness."

The ice-cold shower fell upon his head. The patient admitted that his imaginings were nothing more than madness and that he would make an effort. But he added: I am admitting it "because I am forced to."

Another ice-cold shower.

"Yes sir, everything I told you was sheer madness."

"You were mad then?" asked the doctor.

The patient hesitated: "I don't think so."

A third freezing shower.

"Were you mad?"

The patient: "Is it madness to see and hear?"

"Yes."

So the patient finally stated: "There were no women who insulted me, and no men who persecuted me. All of it is madness."

I will not continue. As you may imagine, by dint of applying shower after shower and through one avowal after another, the patient was finally cured. Since he had recognized that he was mad, he could no longer be so.

This is very clearly an idea that one finds throughout the history of psychiatry. One cannot simultaneously be mad and be conscious of the fact that one is mad; perceiving the truth drives away the delirium. And among all of the therapies that were applied to madness throughout the centuries, one finds thousands of attempts or tricks that were imagined to make the patient aware of his own madness. But Leuret was looking for something else. Or rather, he was looking to obtain this result in a very particular way. He was not at all attempting to persuade the patient. At the deepest level, he did not care in the least what happened inside the patient's consciousness. He wanted a specific act, an affirmation: "I am mad." Avowal* was the decisive element in the therapeutic operation.[2]

---

* Editors' note: Throughout this translation, we have chosen to translate *aveu* as avowal. See Editors' Preface, p. 2 n. *.

: : :

I have been struck by this passage by Leuret for some time. Its immediate historical context can be established easily enough. The famous law of 1838 had recently been passed in France establishing cooperation between an administrative power that decided on the obligatory imprisonment of certain mentally ill patients and the medical authority that was granted the responsibility for confirming, treating, and ultimately curing the illness.[3] It is clear that Leuret accorded the patient's "avowal" an important role. The patient himself had to seal the certificate that imprisoned him. Following the doctor and the prefect, the patient was the third voice that confirmed his own madness. At the same time, through this avowal, he gave himself over to a medical action that was to set him free. This was an absolutely logical piece in the system of therapeutic confinement: "I give you the right to lock me up; I am giving you the possibility of healing me." This is the meaning of the avowal of madness: avowal signs the asylum contract.

But Leuret's gesture seemed interesting to me for other reasons as well. This scene took place during a period when the treatment of the mad was being organized along the same lines as medical practice, when medical practice obeyed the dominant model of pathological anatomy: For the doctor to understand the truth of the illness, he needed to listen, not to the words of the patient, but to the symptoms of the body. And yet, compared to this scientific norm, the doctor's demand for an avowal on the part of the patient seems very strange — as if the medico-administrative logic that had made avowal so necessary introduced a practice that was foreign to the demands of psychiatric knowledge and that could grant it authority, as much in the eyes of the administration as in the eyes of medicine.

Indeed, a strange element with a long history inserted itself at this moment. I am not only thinking of the place and the form it had taken in judicial and religious institutions. I am thinking of old meanings or values that remained within it, and the origins of which we know so little. Just behind the avowal sought by Leuret, one feels tightly the connection, so often recognized, between purity and truth-telling (only the pure can tell the truth; an ancient theme that one finds in the necessity of virginity and in the necessity of continence in order to receive the word of God). Thus, one may recognize as well the theme that truth-telling purifies (and that evil is extracted from the body and the soul of the one who purges it through avowal). Or even the idea that to speak the truth about something annuls, erases, or wards off this very truth (my soul is cleansed or whitened if it avows its darkness).

There is, then, a long history of avowal behind this particular case of avowal demanded by Leuret. There are long-held beliefs in the powers and the effects of "truth-telling" in general and, in particular, of "truth-telling about oneself." [. . .] Yet one thing strikes me as unique and astonishing: Lord knows how many times myths, legends, stories, and tales—or anything else we generally consider "untrue"—have been subjected to ethnological study. But after all, isn't truth-telling also embedded in the dense and complex tissue of ritual? It too has been accompanied by numerous beliefs, and accorded strange powers. So perhaps there is an entire ethnology of truth-telling to be pursued.

But in Leuret's practice, you sense that there is more than the mere weight of such a troubled past. The requirement of avowal also introduced a new problem. While the medicine of the period tended to lay out and consider case by case the symptoms that constituted something like the natural language of illness, while the medical world tended to grant the right to true discourse solely to doctors who analyzed and interpreted the language of symptoms, in this case Leuret introduced between the illness and the doctor the discourse of the patient and the question of what was true and false for the patient. He not only set forth the obligation of the sick patient to tell the truth; he also posed as an essential question for his therapy the relationship of knowledge that the patient had with himself. To ground his practice, establish his therapeutic intervention, and open up the possibility of healing, the doctor needed the patient to formulate a discourse of truth about himself. From Leuret not only to Freud but also to a whole set of practices, it is easy to recognize the vast development which remains with us to this day.

In any case, it is out of this peculiar scene, at the crossroads between a distant tradition and a recent practice, that the idea came to me to study "the obligation of truth-telling about oneself." I will begin by proposing a brief analysis of what may be understood by avowal (an analysis of the "speech act"). Then I will sketch an overview of the historical and philosophical problems that it seems to me tie together the practice of avowal. Finally, I will come to the reason why I am here: the practice of avowal in judicial* and especially penal institutions.

---

* Editors' note: The term *judiciare* has a broader scope in French than the term "judicial" does in English because, in France and other civil law jurisdictions, it includes such figures

: : :

A French dictionary states that avowal is a written or oral declaration through which one admits having said or done something. It adds, as an example, avowing a fault. It seems to me that we can retain from this definition the following general framework; that is, in avowal, the one who speaks affirms something with regard to himself. But as soon as one moves slightly deeper, this definition no longer seems sufficient. On the one hand, it says far too little about the act of avowal itself. To declare, even solemnly or ritually, that one did or said something is not sufficient to constitute an avowal. If I declare that I have a specific profession, it is not an avowal. I may recognize publicly that I have pronounced certain words, but this would not necessarily be an avowal either. Must one turn then toward the content of the affirmation, toward the nature of what has been affirmed, as the example in the dictionary suggests? In that case, if I were a drug trafficker, the declaration of my profession would be an avowal. Or, for example, recognizing something I had said would be an avowal if what I said was a lie. But now, this is no doubt asking too much, and it leads to an overly narrow definition. After all, I may avow my age or my love, a sickness or suffering. In short, avowal is something more than a simple declaration, but it is something other than the declaration of a fault committed* by the speaking subject.

Let us return to Leuret and the avowal he hoped to obtain:

1. Leuret was not seeking the avowal of a fault. Perhaps it was something unknown or invisible? No, because the patient was obviously mad. He had demonstrated his madness throughout the interrogation and Leuret was already convinced of it. The avowal did not advance his understanding one bit. What separates an avowal from a declaration is not what separates the unknown from the known, the visible from the invisible, but what might be referred to as a certain cost of enunciation. Avowal consists of passing from the untold to the told, given that the untold had a precise meaning, a particular motive, a great value. Thus, for

---

as examining magistrates who conduct investigations. Much of the investigatory function—what Foucault refers to as *enquête*—is part of the judicial procedure. Throughout this translation, we will nevertheless use the term "judicial" to translate *judiciare*, with the expectation that reader will understand the slight difference in the scope of judicial procedures in France.

* This word (*commise*) was deciphered from an abbreviation. It may also be *connue* (known).

Mr. A., not to say that he is mad or to refuse this declaration was to give grounds for his request to leave. Or, in another situation, when someone declares his love, it is an avowal if this declaration runs the risk of being costly.[4]

2. But this is not all. There was an important moment in the scene between Leuret and his patient when the latter said: "Fine, yes, because you have forced me, I admit that I am mad"—a statement that was sheer common sense because under the shower, the freezing shower, he was indeed forced. And it is the doctor's response that is rather nonsensical because he retorts: "That is not sufficient for me. I will impose another shower on you so that you recognize in full liberty that you are mad." This is a well-known pretension on the part of a power that seeks to constrain those it forces to be free. And yet, in the strictest sense, an avowal is necessarily free. The inquisitors of the Middle Ages knew this very well: for the declarations pulled out through torture to qualify as an avowal, they had to be renewed after the torture. Why must an avowal, even when it is obtained through force, be considered free in order to take on its moral, juridical, and therapeutic effects? The reason is that avowal is not simply an observation about oneself. It is a sort of engagement, but an engagement of a particular type. It does not obligate one to do such and such a thing. It implies that he who speaks promises to be what he affirms himself to be, precisely because he is just that. There is an inherent redundancy in avowal that appears clearly, for example, when we avow our love for someone. If it were merely a question of observing a de facto situation, the "I love you" would be a pure and simple affirmation. If it were a question of promising one's love, it would be a promise or a vow that could be sincere or not, but it could be neither true nor false. But when the sentence "I love you" functions as an avowal, it is because one passes from the realm of the unspoken to the realm of the spoken by voluntarily constituting oneself as a lover through the affirmation that one loves. One who avows a crime, in a sense, commits to being the author of the crime. By that I mean he not only accepts the responsibility, but he also establishes this acceptance on the fact that he did commit the crime. In an avowal, he who speaks obligates himself to being what he says he is. He obligates himself to being the one who did such and such a thing, who feels such and such a sentiment; and he obligates himself because it is true. Leuret's patient commits to being mad. Not to claim that . . . [undecipherable].

3. But this is not yet sufficient to characterize avowal. When Leuret's

patient finally says, "Fine, yes, I am mad," he is *giving in*. He says what he had not wanted to say, but in saying it, he gives himself over to the power the doctor sought to exercise over him. He accepts it. He submits. This is, moreover, what the doctor understands and seeks, who then takes immediate advantage of it to say: "So now you will obey me." In the strictest sense, avowal can only exist within a power relation and the avowal enables the exercise of that power relation over the one who avows. These things are obvious when these power relations are institutionally defined: as in the case of judicial avowal, or confession within the Catholic Church. But it is all the same in relationships that are far more fluid and mobile. For the declaration "I love you" to be an avowal, the other must be able to accept, refuse, break out in laughter, slap the person, or say, "I will speak about this with my husband." In short, avowal incites or reinforces a power relation that exerts itself on the one who avows. This is why all avowals are "costly."

4. Finally, avowal has one characteristic, which is no doubt the most singular and difficult to discern. When Leuret makes his patient avow "I am mad," of course, he does not suppose that he will cease to be mad just because he has said this. Rather, he wants to constrain him into accepting his status as mad. And yet he considers that the mere fact of stating this will modify the relationship between the patient and his madness, his way of being mad, and therefore his illness. In the same way, if the criminal who avows is not judged in the same way as the one whose crime was established by proof and testimony, it is because avowal is supposed to modify his relationship to his crime. To avow one's love means to begin to love in another way; otherwise, it is simply informing the other of one's sentiments. While avowal ties the subject to what he affirms, it also qualifies him differently with regard to what he says: criminal, but perhaps susceptible to repent; in love, but it has now been declared; ill, but already conscious and detached enough from his illness that he himself can work toward his own healing.

Let us say then, to summarize all this, that avowal is a verbal act through which the subject affirms who he is, binds himself to this truth, places himself in a relationship of dependence with regard to another, and modifies at the same time his relationship to himself.

: : :

Avowal is thus a rather strange figure within language games. And yet it has had a deep cultural reach and a considerable institutional legacy in our society since antiquity. Does one find it to the same extent in other societies and civilizations? A proper response would require a much lengthier investigation, so I cannot answer this question. But if we restrict ourselves to "our" societies—to Western Christian societies—it seems to me that, without much in the way of speculation, one could speak of a massive growth of avowal: not necessarily a continuous growth, but by stages and thrusts, with stops and rapid accelerations. This growth tended—and this is undoubtedly one of the traits of our societies—to tie the individual more and more to his truth (I mean, to the obligation to tell the truth about oneself), to make this truth-telling function in one's relationships to others, and to commit oneself through this truth which is told. I do not mean that the modern individual ceases to be bound to the will of the other who commands him; but more and more, this connection overlaps and is tied to a discourse of truth that the subject is led to maintain about himself.

I would like to indicate but a few aspects of this process of growth by sketching out a somewhat presumptuous overview.

First, there was an institutional extension. The number of institutions that called for avowal came to encompass the realms of justice, of medicine, and of psychiatry (personal relations).

Second, there was an extension within the institutions: in Christianity, for example, through penance (not before the fixed confession); then, in the thirteenth century, once a year; and then each month; later, every eight days; and then the examination of one's conscience and the direction of one's conscience.

Third, there was the extension of this field: Christian confession and the direction of conscience (more is said, different things are said; the grain is not the same).

Fourth, there were the great phases of avowal. There was extrainstitutional development through the more or less simultaneous birth (broadly speaking) of the sacrament of penance, of the Inquisition, and of the inquisitorial procedure in judicial institutions, all of which marked another big advance in the forms of avowal. One could cite the corollary development in the sixteenth and seventeenth centuries of the direction of conscience in Catholic countries, of tales of conversion in Protestant countries, and of an entirely new literature that gave a privileged place to avowal. And this is to say nothing of avowal in the nineteenth and twentieth centuries.*

I believe that there is an important historical problem here. Why was there such an obsession with asking and soliciting discourses of truth? To this question, in the context of scientific discourses, one generally responds—or looks for a response—in the realm of economic and social necessity. Truth may well be indispensable to productive technologies. Is that the right answer? I have no idea. But when it is a question of this strange truth that the individual must produce about himself, it does not seem plausible—or at least not obvious—that an answer can be found in that realm. I think that one must try to understand why we so wanted to tie the individual to his truth, by his truth, and by his own enunciation of his own truth. Knowing how the individual finds himself tied, and accepts to be tied, to the power exerted over him is a juridical, political, institutional, and historical problem. I think it is a juridical problem as well, but it is especially an institutional, political, and historical problem to know how in a given society the individual binds himself to his own truth. Such is the historical framework within which I would like to situate my research on avowal.

[But] there is also a more philosophical aspect. Second, [then], it seems to me also that avowal and its practice pose philosophical problems, and that it is possible to imagine studying avowal in the context of a critical enterprise.

What I mean is the following. Avowal bears a strange relationship to the problem of truth. Avowal is a strange way of truth-telling. In a sense, it is always true (if it is false, it is not an avowal). And the consequences both for the speaker and for the audience are entirely different from those that an assertion such as "the sky is blue" might have, for example. It constitutes a certain way of telling, a certain mode of veridiction.† We know very well that when someone states something, one must distinguish what is announced from the act of enunciation. In the same way, when

---

* In the manuscript, these four paragraphs take the form of a series of lists.

† Translator's note: We have translated *véridiction* as "veridiction" throughout this book. Since Foucault is employing a neologism, we have decided to maintain the same neologism in English in order to maintain the two essential parts: the Latin root *ver-* for truth, and *diction* for speaking, pronouncing, or telling.

someone asserts a truth, one must distinguish the assertion (which is true or false) from the *act* of truth-telling, from the veridiction (the *Wahrsagen*, as Nietzsche would say).

If critical philosophy is a philosophy that starts not from the wonderment that there is being, but from the surprise that there is truth, then we can clearly see that there are two forms of critical philosophy. On the one hand, there is that which asks under what conditions—formal or transcendental—there can be true statements. And on the other, there is that which investigates the forms of veridiction, the different forms of truth-telling.[5] In the case of a critical philosophy that investigates veridiction, the problem is that of knowing not under what conditions a statement is true, but rather what are the different games of truth and falsehood that are established, and according to what forms they are established. In the case of a critical philosophy of veridictions, the problem is not that of knowing how a subject in general may understand an object in general. The problem is that of knowing how subjects are effectively tied within and by the forms of veridiction in which they engage.[6] In this case, the problem is not that of determining historical accidents, external circumstances, the mechanisms of illusions or ideologies, or even the internal economy of errors or failures in logic that could have produced the falsehood. The problem is to determine how a mode of veridiction, a *Wahrsagen*, could appear in history and under what conditions. If, from the point of view of the true, history can only explain the existence or the disappearance of falsehood, from the point of view of veridiction, history can explain the appearance of a truth-telling. Well, you understand, no doubt, that the objective of a critical philosophy of veridictions is not to constitute a "general police" of the true, or to constitute a set of instruments* that is general enough to fix the formal conditions according to which these statements could be true. Rather, it is a question of defining modes of veridiction in their plurality, of searching for the forms of obligation through which each mode binds the subject of truth-telling, of specifying the areas to which they apply and the fields of objects they bring to light and finally the relationships, connections, interferences that are established between them. In a word, in this critical philosophy it is not a question of a general economy of the true, but rather of a historical politics, or a political history of veridictions.

---

* The word "instrument" is difficult to decipher, and we offer it as a hypothesis.

It is in this general framework that I would situate—by way of essays, fragments, or other more or less aborted attempts—what I have tried to develop in different domains. I have not tried to know whether the discourse of psychiatrists or that of doctors was true, even though this is an entirely legitimate problem. I did not try to determine which ideology the criminologists' discourse obeyed—even if this too would be an interesting problem. The problem that I wanted to pose was different: it was the task of investigating the reasons for and the forms of the enterprise of truth-telling about things such as madness, illness, or crime.

We often speak of the recent domination of science or of the technical uniformity of the modern world. Let's say that this is the question of "positivism" in the Comtian sense, or perhaps it would be better to associate the name of Saint-Simon to this theme. In order to situate my analysis, I would like to evoke here a *counter-positivism* that is not the opposite of positivism but rather its counterpoint. It would be characterized by astonishment before the very ancient multiplication and proliferation of truth-telling, and the dispersal of regimes of veridiction in societies such as ours.

:::

But I have not forgotten that I am here at the invitation of the Law School and at the invitation of the School of Criminology. All of this is, no doubt, far from the more precise reflections that you might have hoped for. I do think, however, that it was appropriate and honest to reveal immediately, even through these overly general propositions, the unfortunately narrow limits of my lectures. I do not come to you as a jurist, and I do not have a precise professional designation—please do not ask me whether I am a historian or a philosopher. But I come to you with a problem, or rather with a bundle that is held together, in a more or less clumsy manner, by the following question: What is the place and what is the role of *Truth-telling*[7] in judicial practice?

It would hardly be news to you if I told you that this practice—which has as its functions, depending on the regime or the body, to dictate the law or decide its application, to resolve a litigation or declare a condemnation—in short, this institution, which gives the impression of working in the prescriptive or decisional realm, consumes and fashions, uses and produces, incites and enunciates a considerable amount of "truth-telling," of different veridictions. Whether it is a question of the procedures of inquiry or of the statement of facts in a judgment, of recourse to witness testimony or to expert opinion, of oral arguments or declarations of guilt, of interpreting the law or taking into account the state of morals or economic facts, judicial practice grants truth-telling considerable importance, under remarkably diverse forms. And yet the adjustment between these different veridictions is far from obvious. Since the nineteenth century, for example, the introduction of psychiatric expertise in penal affairs has given rise to a series of problems and difficulties in which the right to punish became so entangled that not only have its decisions become difficult to make, but even its foundations and final justifications threaten to elude it. Let's just say, without being too aggressive, that truth does not make law's life any easier, and especially not penal law.

It is in the context of this general problem—truth-telling and judging—that I would like to study the problem of avowal. I would like to study it based on the following problem, which I will be able to illustrate with the help of [two] scenes.* The first is a chariot race in the *Iliad*. One of the two competitors commits an irregularity. When the other complains, the judge proposes a purgative oath. The offender prefers not to submit himself to the test. He loses. Is this the equivalent of an avowal? Perhaps. But what is interesting is that he does not need to avow: it has the same effects without having the form. Moreover, it does not take place within the procedure itself. [Compare this old scene to the following in a French tribunal a few years ago.]† A man is accused of five rapes.

The judge asks: "Have you tried to reflect on your case?"

---

* With regard to these two scenes, Foucault's manuscript originally bears the number 2, which he crossed out and replaced by the number 3. A sheet of paper was inserted; undoubtedly a reminder about a third possible scene. On that sheet, Foucault wrote:

Scene of the inquisitorial procedure from the seventeenth century:
—inquest [*enquête*]
—torture
—avowal (?)
—then second interrogation to obtain the avowal.

† In Foucault's manuscript this sentence, which makes the link between the scene from Homer's *Iliad* (which Foucault would develop in the next lecture on April 22, 1981) and the contemporary scene of the man accused of sexual assaults (which Foucault would develop in his sixth and final lecture on May 20, 1981), was crossed out, probably due to Foucault's apparent intention to add, during the inaugural lecture, a discussion of the inquisitorial scene from the seventeenth century (which Foucault would also develop in his final lecture on May 20, 1981).

Silence.

"Why, at twenty-two years of age, did you start to be so violent? You must make an effort of analysis. Only you have the key to yourself. Explain yourself to me."

Silence.

A member of the jury then speaks up: "Come on, defend yourself!"[8]

Here the scene is the reverse of the one I presented earlier. An avowal of the fault is insufficient. The offender must explain who he is. We need to know in order to judge his truth—his truth stated by the experts, and also by himself.

By taking a very wide time frame, we see that there is not only a considerable expansion in the role of avowal. In fact, there is far more: an immense mutation in which there is a shift from a penal judgment of one's acts to a strange judicial action whose object, whose principle of rationality and of measure, is the truth manifested by the whole individual. This is the transformation that I would like to study: the problem of "who is being judged" in penal institutions.

But I wouldn't want to analyze this problem solely from the perspective of the realm of judicial institutions and penal practices. I would like to take up a hypothesis that I have already announced. It goes without saying that a broader context is needed to make the history of penal practices intelligible. But it is also necessary to reflect on the broader context in which it is placed. Can one say that it is a matter of society, social processes, a question of economic determinations? Yes, maybe. But being too easy, such an analysis runs the risk of being sterile or of universalizing the analysis along the lines of Kirchheimer (why punish through imprisonment? Response: capitalist slavery).[9] First of all, it seems to me that it would be interesting to place these penal practices back at the center of a first circle of intelligibility consisting of techniques of government: government understood in the larger sense as a means of forming, transforming, and directing the conduct of individuals. One might then recognize, perhaps, three broad types of technologies: techniques for producing objects; techniques of communication, through which individuals communicate between themselves; and techniques of government, through which individuals act on each other's conducts in order to attain certain ends or objectives.[10]

These three techniques are never independent of one another: there is no production without forms of communication and without domination and conduct of conduct; there are no pure techniques of communication; there are no techniques of government that do not put into play a system of communication, usually for producing something. The economic, semiotic, and strategic are perpetually tied together. But in order to render a practice and its transformation intelligible, these three sets of technologies are not equally efficacious, or in any case do not have the same immediacy. And, to avoid all imprudence, it seems to me that penal practice is best understood, in its organization and transformations, if we start by placing it back within the context of technologies of government. For example, it seemed to me that the ensemble constituted by the penitentiary system and by penal practice could be clarified if it were related to the disciplinary techniques and procedures that developed in European societies from the seventeenth to the nineteenth centuries. In the same manner, it seems to me that this development of avowal within penal practice could be related to procedures found elsewhere — in religious practices, in medical practices, for example — and that tend to tie the individual to the enunciation of his truth.

To begin with this problem: governing through truth.

I would like to place the analysis of the development of penal avowal back in the broader history of what could be called "technologies of the subject." I mean the techniques through which the individual is brought, either by himself or with the help or the direction of another, to transform himself and to modify his relationship to himself. In short, the analyses that I will begin have as their object the study of avowal in penal practice, insofar as they integrate regimes of veridiction and technologies of the subject.

[NOTES]

1. On François Leuret (1797–1851), see Michel Foucault, *Histoire de la folie à l'âge classique* (Paris: Gallimard, 1972), pp. 540–41, where the head doctor of Bicêtre and author of the work entitled *Du traitement moral de la folie*, published in 1840 in Paris, was associated with the "use of the famous 'moral treatments' which made confinement the primary means of submission and repression (Guislan and Leuret)"; in English see Michel Foucault, *History of Madness* (London: Routledge, 2006), p. 522; as well as Michel Foucault, *Le pouvoir psychiatrique: Cours au Collège de France, 1973–1974*, ed. Jacques Lagrange (Paris: Gallimard/Seuil, 2003), especially pp. 108–9 (see also the notes of Lagrange, p. 19 n. 13 and pp. 38–39 n. 22); English edition, Michel Foucault, *Psychiatric Power: Lectures at the Collège de France, 1973–*

1974, English series ed. Arnold Davidson, trans. Graham Burchell (New York: Palgrave, 2006), pp. 107–8, pp. 17–18 n. 13, and p. 37 n. 22.

2. On the therapeutic function of avowal that Leuret pursued among those he treated, cf. in particular the lecture of December 19, 1973 (Foucault, *Psychiatric Power*) where Foucault presents and comments a cure from François Leuret, *Du traitement moral de la folie* (Paris, J.-B. Baillière, 1840).

> In general, I think that what is at stake for Leuret here is making the patient accessible to all the imperative uses of language: [. . .] It is not a matter of turning the false into truth in a dialectic peculiar to language or discussion. In this game of orders and commands, it is simply a matter of putting the subject back in contact with language inasmuch as it is the carrier of imperatives; it is the imperative use of language that refers back to and is organized by a whole system of power. [. . .] The language one reteaches to the patient is not the language through which he will be able to rediscover the truth; the language he is forced to relearn is a language in which the reality of an order, of a discipline, of a power imposed on him, must appear (*Psychiatric Power*, pp. 150–51).

Avowal is one of those "supplements of power added to reality by the asylum" that allows the doctor "to get a grip on madness and reduce it, and therefore, to direct and govern it"; one of the instruments whose function is to render "reality medically intensified" (ibid., pp. 165–66). It proceeds with a distinction between truth and perceptions: its role is to bind the patient to his own history, but to his own history as it was established "from the outside through the system of family, employment, civil status and medical observation" and not according to how he perceives it (ibid., p. 159). The truth that Leuret wants the patient to pronounce as a result of these showers is not that of madness "speaking in its own name but the truth of madness agreeing to first person recognition of itself in a particular administrative and medical reality constituted by asylum power." It is at the moment when those who are experiencing the cure recognize "a biographical reality" that has been established that "the operation of truth" is completed (ibid., pp. 160–61).

The scene that opposes Leuret to "Monsieur A." is also recounted in the first of two conferences given by Foucault at Dartmouth in November 1980 under the headings "Subjectivity and Truth" and "Christianity and Confession" (Michel Foucault, "About the Beginning of the Hermeneutics of the Self: Two Lectures at Dartmouth," ed. Mark Blasius, *Political Theory* 21, no. 2, May 1993, p. 200).

3. Law of 30 June 1838 Concerning the Insane (*Loi sur les aliénés*). For an English translation of the 1838 law, see Robert Castel, *The Regulation of Madness: The Origins of Incarceration in France*, trans. W. D. Hall, Berkeley, University of California Press, 1988, appendix A, pp. 243–53. For discussion of the 1838 law, see the lectures of December 5, 1973 (in Foucault, *Psychiatric Power*) and February 12, 1975 (in Foucault, *Abnormal: Lectures at the Collège de France, 1974–1975*), as well as Robert Castel, "Les médecins et les juges," *in* Michel Foucault, *Moi, Pierre Rivière, ayant égorgé ma mère, ma sœur et mon frère: Un cas de parricide au XIXe siècle* (Paris: Gallimard, 1994), pp. 379–99, and generally, Castel, *The Regulation of Madness*, pp. 14–190.

4. On a rereading, with a different pen, Foucault crossed out the sentence "But what does this cost consist of?" The question of the cost of avowal introduces the question of risk inherent in *parrhēsia* and the courage of truth, developed in Foucault's last two series of lectures at the Collège de France. See Michel Foucault, *The Government of Self and Others: Lectures at the Collège de France, 1982–1983*, English series ed. Arnold Davidson, trans. Graham Burchell (New York: Palgrave, 2011); Michel Foucault, *The Courage of Truth: The Government of Self and*

Others II. Lectures at the Collège de France, 1984, English series ed. Arnold Davidson, trans. Graham Bruchell (New York: Palgrave, 2011).

5. This distinction introduces the point that Foucault uses to open the first lecture of his last course: the distinction between the analysis of epistemological structures and *alethurgical* forms (cf. Foucault, *The Courage of Truth*, pp. 4–5).

6. This question cuts across the last three Collège de France lecture series (cf. Michel Foucault, *Hermeneutics of the Subject: Lectures at the Collège de France, 1981–1982*, English series ed. Arnold I. Davidson, trans. Graham Bruchell [New York: Palgrave, 2005]; Foucault, *The Government of Self and Others*; Foucault, *The Courage of Truth*).

7. "Truth-telling" is capitalized in the original manuscript (*Dire vrai*).

8. This dialogue also opens Michel Foucault's 1978 essay in the *Journal of Law and Psychiatry* titled "About the Concept of the 'Dangerous Individual' in Nineteenth-Century Legal Psychiatry," reproduced in Michel Foucault, *Essential Works of Foucault, 1954–1984: Power*, Volume 3, series ed. Paul Rabinow, ed. James D. Faubion, trans. Robert Hurley and others (New York: The New Press, 2000), pp. 176–200.

9. Foucault is making reference to what he referred to in *Discipline and Punish* as "Rusche and Kirchheimer's great work" (trans. Alan Sheridan, New York, Vintage Books, 1979, p. 24), namely Georg Rusche and Otto Kirchheimer, *Punishment and Social Structure* (New York: Columbia University Press, 1939).

10. This point is developed in "Subjectivity and Truth" (Foucault, "About the Beginning of the Hermeneutics of the Self: Two Lectures at Dartmouth," p. 203).

FIRST LECTURE

April 22, 1981

A political and institutional ethnology of truthful speech. • Truth-telling and speaking justice. • Scope of the study. • *Veridiction* and *jurisdiction* in Homer's *Iliad*. • The competition between Menelaus and Antilochus. • The object of Antilochus's avowal. •
Justice and *agōn; agōn* and truth. • The chariot race and the challenge of the oath,
two liturgies of truth, two games designed to represent justly the truth of their respective
strengths. • A ritual of commemoration. • *Veridiction* and *jurisdiction* in Hesiod's *Works
and Days*. • *Dikazein* and *krinein*. • The oath of the accusers and the co-jurors in *dikazein*: a game of two parties, the criteria being the social status of the adversaries. •
The oath of the judge in *krinein*: a game of three parties, the criteria being *dikaion*. •
The social weight of adversaries and "the reality of things": *dikaion* and *alēthes*.

[. . .]* The series of lectures I am be-
ginning today—or that I started last time by way of a general introduc-

---

* The first sentence of the lecture is inaudible except for the following words and clarifica-
tions:

. . . that is, something slightly austere and rather boring that will probably take the form
of a kind of *explication de texte*. So I am slightly uncomfortable speaking in front of such a
large audience because, as you know, spatial effects are important for the type of speech
one gives and there are some slightly meticulous things that are difficult to say standing
up with microphones, a spotlight, and a ceremonial audience. I am not exactly sure how

tion—I would have liked to give this series an epigraph in the form of a text that I found in Georges Dumézil's work, *Servius et la fortune*. The text is as follows: "Looking back into the deepest reaches of our species' behavior, 'truthful speech' [*la parole vraie*] has been a force few could resist. From the earliest moments, truth was one of man's most formidable verbal weapons, most prolific sources of power, and most solid institutional foundations."[1]

This text seems to me to be a succinct and excellent introduction—not only succinct, but excellent—to what may be understood, in somewhat solemn terms, as a political and institutional ethnology of truth-telling [*le dire vrai*] or truthful speech [*la parole vraie*]. What I mean is the following: it is, of course, certainly possible, it is certainly legitimate, and certainly desirable to study truth-telling, to study the assertions from the point of view of the formal or empirical conditions that allow one to say whether they are true or false. But I think that one can also study truth-telling from something of an ethnological perspective, I mean truth-telling as a social practice—to study it as a weapon in relationships between individuals, to study it as a means of modifying relations of power among those who speak, and finally as an element within an institutional structure.

In sum, it would mean studying truth-telling, or I would say veridiction, within human relationships, inter-human relations, relations of power, and institutional mechanisms. To be more precise, my project here, in these lectures, is to study the relationships between what Georges Dumézil called "truthful speech," the relationships between veridiction and that other form of speech one might call "speech of justice" [*parole de justice*], which consists in short of saying what is just and what must be done for justice to be established or restored. Truthful speech [*parole de vérité*]* and just speech [*parole de justice*], veridiction and jurisdiction[†] [*juridiction*]: I

---

we should proceed; perhaps at some point I will change the organization and we will try to speak in a slightly less casual way, or at least *I* will try to speak in a less casual way.

* Translator's note: Foucault shifts here from *parole vraie* to *parole de vérité*. However, both are presented as synonyms of *véridiction*. In this case, it would appear that the shift is primarily a means of establishing a structural parallel between *parole de vérité* and *parole de justice*, just as he is trying to establish a parallel between the terms *véridiction* and *juridiction*. I have chosen to respect this parallel, although it would appear that the meaning has not changed.

† Translator's note: Foucault is using the word *juridiction* in an original way to mean literally "just speech." He is therefore playing off of the juxtaposition of *véridiction*, a word that

think that these are two fundamental forms of the act of speaking whose relationships have been without a doubt among the most complex and enigmatic problems that human beings and human societies have confronted. How can one tell truth and speak justice at the same time? How can truthful speech be a foundation for just speech? How and to what extent does just speech, or jurisdiction, need veridiction? This, I believe, is one of the great problems that has spanned our entire history.

It is within this framework, then, that I would like to proceed: the relationship between jurisdiction and veridiction. But of course I would like to limit this very general field, and I will do so in four ways. First, my analysis of jurisdiction and veridiction will be strictly historical. This is not to suggest, naturally, that the general and formal problems of the relationships between jurisdiction and veridiction are unimportant or uninteresting. It is undeniable that the relationships between truth-telling [*dire vrai*] and speaking justice [*dire juste*] deserve to be studied in their own right. But I will limit myself to a historical and cultural problem. I would like to try to understand how the act of truth-telling and the act of speaking justice, how the act of veridiction and the act of jurisdiction have been linked at different moments in our history and in different forms of the judicial institution.

Second, to this first limitation I would like to add a second. That is, I will limit my inquiry to the problem of penality. Of course, problems of jurisdiction and veridiction would also merit examination in relation to civil law, for example. This is obvious. But I will settle for considering the problem of penality only, both for the sake of ease and because, it seems to me, the correlations between judicial institutions and other social practices appear more clearly in this context. I will speak then on the problem of jurisdiction and veridiction precisely with regard to the question of "wrong-doing" in judicial institutions.

As for the third limitation, I will apply this question of the relationships between jurisdiction and veridiction solely to the problem of avowal. Once again, this is not to say that avowal is the only way to link jurisdiction and

---

does not exist in common usage, and the word *juridiction*, which has a common usage but which he is using in an uncommon way. The use of the term is important because it contains the two parts "*juri*" (referring to law) and "*diction*" (referring to speech). I have therefore decided to translate the term as "jurisdiction," in spite of Foucault's using it against common usage, in order to parallel his juxtaposition of an invented term ("veridiction") with a more common word used in an uncommon way ("jurisdiction").

veridiction. One could also explore the relationships between veridiction and jurisdiction through the problems of testimony or of the inquiry, for example. I have chosen avowal for the reasons I suggested the last time that we met:[2] namely, because I believe avowal to be a very particular, complex, and difficult procedure within our penal system and it seems to me that the question of avowal poses a series of larger problems regarding law more generally. Moreover, avowal can be found outside of the law within moral and religious practices, so it is no doubt interesting to explore the interferences between each of these practices of avowal.

Lastly, the fourth restriction—and then I will come to the subject of today's lecture—is that I would have liked to trace this history of avowal, as a form of linkage and relationship between veridiction and jurisdiction in penal practices, from its origins to the present. Obviously, I cannot exhaustively cover such a vast period in six lectures. So, I will focus on three moments that seem important to me, three realms, and will try to shed light upon each, knowing full well that I am not a jurist, that I am not even a legal historian.

I will examine three realms, then. First, the realm of the Greeks, or prelaw Greece as we say,* the domain of Greek law, because it seems to me that during this period there emerged an archaic form of the relationship between the true and the just—between what the Greeks called *alēthes* and *dikaion*—that was very different from our own.[3] Furthermore, it seems to me that through the agonistic structure of prelaw Greece, as well as the practice of oaths and the slow emergence of judicial power, one can see how the relationship between veridiction and jurisdiction was organized and how the problem of avowal appeared in this context with particular intensity. I will dedicate two lectures, then, to this realm of the Greeks: today's lecture will address the problem of competition, truth, and justice—*agōn, alēthes, dikaion*—and the next lecture will focus, of course, on Oedipus and the knowledge of the tyrant. The following two lectures

---

* Editor's note: The term "prelaw Greece" corresponds to what Foucault refers to as *prédroit grec*. It was used in an earlier period by French anthropologist-classicists, such as Louis Gernet. See, e.g., Louis Gernet, "Law and Prelaw in Ancient Greece," pp. 143–215, in Louis Gernet, *The Anthropology of Ancient Greece*, trans. John Hamilton and Blaise Nagy (Baltimore: Johns Hopkins University Press, 1981). We tend now to refer to this period as "early Greek law" when discussing the sorts of practices, laws, codes, etc., that existed in archaic Greece (which Homer represents both in his depictions and in being a representative of his own time); however, we have retained the term "prelaw Greece" here to capture Foucault's reference to Gernet.

will address the medieval and Christian realm: I will try to show you how medieval law opened up a space for conceptualizing the subject that initially emerged out of the Christian pastoral tradition, and how medieval law attached a certain practice of inquiry, which had been tied to the development of ecclesiastical and royal power, to this conception of the subject formed within the Christian pastoral. Those two following lectures, then, will explore the problem of avowal, confession, and inquiry. Finally, the last two lectures will focus primarily on the problems of avowal, examination, and expertise in the early modern and modern periods.

The first lecture, then, will focus on Greek law—to be exact, prelaw Greece—and how the earliest works in prelaw Greece tie together the problem of competition, truth, and justice—or, more precisely, the competition, the true, and the just. There exists a text, the first great text that attests to the existence and practice of something resembling judicial avowal. This text can be found in Homer.* One might say that this is the first emergence, the first appearance of a kind of judicial avowal or an equivalent to judicial avowal in a text by Homer. The extremely complex and elaborate scene, from verses 257 to 650 in book 23, presents a vast interplay between relations of force, manifestations of truth, and the settlement of a litigation.[4] This text, book 23, belongs to the narrative regarding the games held by Achilles to honor the memory of Patroclus. In these games, as the first trial of these games organized by Achilles, there is a chariot race. A certain number of competitors participate in this chariot race. In the order of their station, prerogative, and status, the competitors are—and as you will see, these questions are of the utmost importance—Diomedes, son of Tydeus; Eumelus, son of Admetus; Menelaus; Antilochus, son of Nestor; and lastly, someone who, as you will see, is of little importance, named Meriones.[5]

Among these competitors, Antilochus is in fourth position. And yet he is painted in a special light from the beginning. Antilochus is the son of Nestor and at the moment when he stands, after the other three, to demonstrate his intention to participate in the race—after Achilles has announced that there is going to be a chariot race and that those who would

---

* Translator's note: As noted in the Editor's Preface, p. 7, we have chosen to translate Foucault's own translations of the Greek and Latin texts, rather than reproduce published English translations, because they more accurately capture his thought in these lectures. References to published English translations are provided in the endnotes.

like to participate should stand, Antilochus stands—and at this point, his father, the wise Nestor, approaches him and says: "You know full well that your horses are slower than the others and, as a result, things will not go well for you in the race that is going to start. But," Nestor adds, "even if your horses are slow, there are ways, there are ideas, there are things you can do to ensure that strength does not always lead to victory. For example, a woodcutter, when he is clever, can easily accomplish more work than another who is stronger. Similarly, a charioteer does not simply need strength and vigor. He also needs to be resourceful. So, in the same way, even if your horses are slower than the others, you may be able to win if you are resourceful, if you learn something. And, I am going to teach you this thing that you don't yet know."[6]

At this point, Nestor explains how to turn around a post—what would seem a relatively simple technique, that is, of course, for those familiar with chariot racing. For in the race there's a back and forth, and all the chariots must turn around a post at one end. So Nestor teaches Antilochus that he must lean when he comes to the post.* As he leans to the inside, he must hold on to his horse and then push the horse to the exterior, and brush the post without touching it to avoid destroying his chariot. This is how he may correct, modify, or reverse the relations of force given at the outset.

So the race begins at this point, and it takes place. But the race is fraught with constant irregularities and these irregularities come first from the gods. The strongest competitor, Diomedes, starts in the lead, and he would have stayed in the lead the entire time if his enemy Apollo had not trapped him by making his whip fall out of his hands and preventing him from being able to drive his horses. When Athena sees Apollo sabotage her protégé Diomedes, she attacks his own protégé Eumelus by throwing him directly to the ground, injuring him and lightly damaging his chariot. Meanwhile, Athena returns the whip to Diomedes, who may then continue the race. So the race is completely sabotaged by the gods. But on the other side, there is also a human ruse, more precisely Antilochus's human ruse. Interestingly enough, though, Antilochus does not apply the wise Nestor's method. Antilochus does something else that is

---

* Foucault poses a question at this point: "He must lean towards the interior. Yes, I think it is the interior, or—I don't remember. No—he must lean to the outside, no? In any case, he must lean." The audience laughs.

going to be the object of contention, and which will necessarily lead to the establishment of a judicial procedure that must be examined closely.

What is it that Antilochus does that will bring about all of the problems that follow? Well, he does the following: Antilochus was behind Menelaus, because Menelaus was stronger than he, and therefore advancing faster. Antilochus leans on his own horses and says to them: "You had better hurry and run faster, for you should know that if you do not win a prize, Nestor, my father will have you sacrificed at the end of the race."[7] No sooner had the horses heard this than they leapt forward alongside those of Menelaus. And the two chariots are exactly even. Excuse me for so much detail, but you will see that it is important. So the two chariots are exactly even, but they are even at precisely the moment when the track narrows and only one chariot can pass at a time. And at that very moment Menelaus says, yelling at Antilochus: "Be careful, we are not both going to be able to pass at once. Let me go ahead and you will catch up if you can."[8] And Antilochus responds: "Not a chance. I am going to hold my chariot steady."[9] So he holds his chariot steady in such a way that there was going to be an accident until Menelaus slows down his chariot to avoid the accident, and lets Antilochus take the lead. And the race continues then to the end without incident. Diomedes, who recovered the lead thanks to Athena, wins the race. Antilochus, who did not let Menelaus pass, comes in second, and Menelaus takes third. Meriones, who has a minor role, comes in fourth. And poor Eumelus, who was thrown to the ground by Athena, injured, and with a broken chariot, stumbles in laboriously last.

At this point the prizes may be distributed. Of course the prize goes to Diomedes without any problem—or, more precisely, Diomedes seizes the prize, as is his right. And then, at that very moment, Achilles intervenes and states: "Okay, Diomedes, you won, you take the prize, but the second prize, I am going to give it to Eumelus, who was beaten by Athena and arrived last, but merits second place because he is very strong, even the best—*ho aristos*. As such, he deserves the second prize."[10]

Against this attribution of the second prize to Eumelus, Antilochus replies indignantly, "But I came in second! Eumelus may have been tossed aside by Athena, but that is a problem between him and the gods. It was up to him to pray to the gods and be on good terms with them. If he had, he would have taken his proper place. But he didn't, and therefore I should have the second prize. Achilles, if you like him enough to give him something, and if indeed he is worthy because he is a good charioteer, you should give him a supplemental prize, but not the second."[11] Achilles considers this response perfectly just and legitimate, and agrees to give Eumelus a supplemental prize, a cuirass, granting the second prize to Antilochus who had in fact come in second.

It is at this point that Menelaus rises and in turn dissents, addressing Antilochus in these terms: "Antilochus, you who were so wise until now, what have you done? You have tarnished my valor. You have wronged my horses by throwing yours, who were far inferior—*hoi toi polu kheirones ēsan*—ahead."[12] And on these grounds Menelaus claims the prize, the second prize. But he does not want it said that the second prize was won through violence to Antilochus, that he imposed his victory through treachery: he wants the truth of his victory to be recognized without violence and in truth. He proposes then that the chiefs, the guides of the Argives, decide who, between him and Antilochus, should have the second prize. He makes this proposition and then he immediately reconsiders, stating: "No, I will render the judgment myself—*egōn autos dikasō*. I will judge."[13] The French translation, or the one I have before me, reads: "*Ma sentence sera droite*"[14]—sentence [*sentence*], *dikē*; just [*droite*] *itheia*. But obviously *dikē* cannot be translated as "sentence," because it is clear that Menelaus cannot deliver a sentence. In fact, he proposes a mode of settlement. The *dikē* that he proposes is not justice. It is not a just sentence, but rather the just settlement of the dispute, of the conflict that opposes him to Antilochus.

How is it to take place, and what is this just settlement of the conflict between him and Antilochus? He proposes to Antilochus that he place himself in the ritual position of the oath, standing in front of his horses, holding the whip in his right hand, with the end of the whip touching his horses' foreheads. In this position he is to swear that he, Antilochus, did not voluntarily thwart Menelaus's chariot through trickery.[15] Such is the *dikē*, the settlement Menelaus proposes to Antilochus.

To this, Antilochus does not respond "I avow" or even "I refuse to swear." He simply says: "Yes, Menelaus, you are older and you are better—*proteros kai areiōn*.[16] Me, I am younger, and youth is subject to error. So I will give you the prize that I had nevertheless won. Take this second prize"—it is a mare—"and even if you want more than the prize given by Achilles, I am ready to give it to you. I am ready to give it to you because I do not want you, Menelaus, to put an end to your love for me. I do not want your heart to turn away from me, nor do I want to be guilty in the eyes of the gods."[17]

Upon which Menelaus responds magnanimously—he says to him: "Now that you have renounced taking the oath and have thereby recognized, I will renounce the disputed prize. I will let you have it, Antilochus, because you are usually wise and I know very well that if you committed such an act, it is because you were victim of your youthfulness; and because you fought against the Trojans for me, Menelaus. You, your father, and your brother all fought for me, and for that reason I will renounce my prize. But, from now on, I advise you not to trick someone better or stronger than yourself."[18] Consequently, following the additional prize given to Eumelus, the second prize goes to Antilochus. Menelaus receives the third prize, and the fourth goes to Meriones. We shall see what comes of the fifth prize, because it clarifies a part of this story.

Excuse me for having been so long and meticulous in telling this story, which perhaps many of you are familiar with already. In fact, the scene is very complex and I think that its meaning and structure deserve examination. The first question one may rightly ask is whether or not it is legitimate to insert this scene, to cite it, to evoke it in a history of judicial practices. Is this truly a judicial scene that we are dealing with? Is it anything more than the story of a competition between two athletes who were fighting in the course of the games? Is it not just a scene from the games? Is the true judicial scene not to be found in another passage from Homer, the famous passage of book 18 in which Homer describes Achilles's shield—a judicial scene where two people fight over the settlement of a blood prize, surrounded by others who have taken an oath, standing amidst a crowd in front of judges who are to deliver their sentence?[19] Perhaps this is the true judicial scene, and not the one I have just described, which is, after all, a scuffle between two athletes who coveted the same prize.

No, I believe this is indeed a judicial scene. It is a judicial scene because, first, all the decisions made by Achilles—to give the additional prize to Eumelus and accept Menelaus's challenge—all of these decisions were taken under the council of warriors who were around there and to whom it was asked if things could and should have happened in this way. Each time Achilles sought to modify the results of the race, he asked for these warriors' opinion.[20] Furthermore, the vocabulary used in this Homeric text and the gestures designated by its vocabulary are clearly juridical. When we see what each competitor does when he takes his prize or claims his prize, we find the same gestures that appear in later documents and are characteristic of those used to mark the appropriation of something.[21] Behind this scene and the gestures used by the different competitors to claim their prizes is the question of the juridical status of the prizes that are being given in this way. Who do they belong to? Do they belong to the person who bestows them until the moment they are attributed to the winner? Or should they be considered *res nullius*, waiting in the middle to be taken upon victory? What is the legal title, what legitimacy does victory grant over these prizes? There is in fact a series of precise and complex juridical questions that run throughout this scene by Homer and that can be found throughout the actions that are performed and the words that are employed.[22]

Above all, the proof that this is not merely an athletic competition but is indeed a judicial scene can be seen in the pledge proposed by Menelaus, which takes on a ritual form, a very precise juridical-religious form. Antilochus must stand up, whip in hand, and the whip must touch the head of the horses. Moreover, when he explains to Antilochus the oath's formula and tells him that he must "do this and that," at that moment, Menelaus is very clear that he is giving his *dikē*—that is, the form he has chosen for a judicial settlement—and, as well, that all of these forms, all of these rituals, are, as he says, in conformity with *themis*—in other words, with the rules that allow for the settlement of a dispute.[23] We are in the world of *dikē* and *themis*, the world of rules, the world of liquidating a conflict.

But if it is true that it is indeed a question of judicial procedure, one must also remember—and I think this is an important aspect of this entire story—that the judicial procedure is nonetheless in direct continuity with the competition, with the athletic rivalry, with the *agōn*. There is in fact no heterogeneity between the judicial scene and the *agōn*, or between the judicial scene and the competition. From the athletic combat to the judicial scene you have a kind of extension, you have a continuum, which does not at all prevent it from being a judicial scene, but which means that it is entirely set up as a confrontation, an athletic confrontation, a confrontation between two warriors, a confrontation between two heroes—but a confrontation nonetheless. The proof is that there is no judge in this story. There is no judge. Of course there is an audience; there are people who give their opinion and approval. But what do they approve? They approve the very regularity of the procedure, not the sentence. The warriors agree that this is the proper course of action. But there is no judge to say: "This is how things should be decided and the prize should go to this person."

It is the competitors themselves who confronted one another in the race and then in the judicial settlement. They confront each other in the race itself, they then confront one another over the conditions of the race's unfolding, and finally they confront one another over the conditions under which they may settle the debate and the conflict that arose between them. The oath itself took on exactly the same form as the struggle, because it is a question of Menelaus's challenging Antilochus. What Menelaus is really saying to Antilochus is: "Will you have the stomach to take an oath in Zeus's name and assert that you did not cheat? Are you capable of this?" And it is in this competition, in this confrontation, in this challenge that Antilochus, who took up the challenge of the race, renounces the challenge of the oath. It is here that he loses, just as one loses a combat when one is not up to the challenge put forward by one's adversary.

It is clear then that we are dealing with a scene that is typically and precisely judicial and, at the same time, that has entirely the texture of a conflict, an *agōn*. And I will quote for you, in this respect, a passage by Gernet on this altercation between Menelaus and Antilochus, from a very interesting and important work, *Droit et Société en Grèce*, which explains: "The law that begins to appear in the scene between Menelaus and Antilochus, the law that begins to appear in this scene does not appear to be a specialized or professional technique. The law itself emanates from the life of the games. There is continuity between the agonistic customs and the judicial customs. The question of competence is settled by itself; the *agōn*, the combat, the milieu that is preestablished for reaching a decision through competition, is also a milieu favorable to reaching a decision by means of a sentence."[24] The first point to keep in mind in analyzing this scene is therefore the continuity between the *agōn* and the judicial, between the confrontation through competition and the judicial confrontation. They have the same texture.

The second problem, the second point that must be emphasized, is the problem of truth and of the interplay of truth. Let's take this very question of the struggle, the whole question of the *agōn*, that is, of the race and the confrontation between different participants. The athletic form of struggle, the *agōn*, is the context within which the judicial procedure appears, but what happens in this struggle? Or, one might even wonder, what is the point of this race? Because in the end, the race that we see unfolding in the games, this race is fundamentally different from those that we know or from what we might expect. That is to say, the race does not consist of taking competitors who have an equal chance at the outset so that in the end, after the various adventures in the race, a winner emerges who must be as unpredictable as possible for the race to have been fair. Let's say that for us, a fair race is a race where everyone's chances are equal from the beginning, so that the winner is as unpredictable as possible. The adventures within the race then produce a winner out of this original equality.

One could say that the race, such as it is organized by Achilles, as it unfolds in this Homeric text, is precisely the opposite. When Achilles calls for a chariot race, the heroes stand one after the other. And what do we see when they rise? First, there is Eumelus, who is said to be the strongest, and then there is Diomedes, who is said to be extremely strong; next is Menelaus with his fast horses, followed by Antilochus whose horses are slower; and finally there is Meriones, about whom almost nothing is said. The very adjectives attached to their names reveal from the outset their respective strengths and the vigor of their teams. They are not at all considered equal from the beginning. To the contrary, they stand one by one according to their strength, in descending order from the one who must win to the one who has no chance of winning. The presentation of the heroes thus indicates their true strength. And then after the enumeration of the heroes comes the list of gifts that corresponds exactly to the places and to the competitors who were just enumerated: the first will be given a slave, the second a mare, the third a cauldron, the fourth two gold talents, and the fifth a vase with two handles.[25] Fundamentally, what is being presented is the strength of each hero and the value of the rewards in an order that corresponds to the truth. Such is the truth of each hero's respective strength, such is the value, brilliance, wealth, and beauty of each gift; all that remains is the pairing. That is to say, there is no reason to hold the race. We already know everything. But we already know everything because the race has an entirely different function than bringing forth an unpredictable winner out of a field of equals.

The order is already predetermined, so what is the function of the race, exactly? The function of the race is nothing more than to develop, in one sense, and dramatize an order of truth that is given from the beginning. And if the race is so dramatic, it is precisely because there are people who interfere. How do they interfere? By making it such that the truth does not come to light. This is what happens when Apollo on the one side and Athena on the other intervene by taking the whip from one and throwing the other to the ground. They prevent the race from fulfilling its true function, which is to be the visible ceremony of a truth that is already visible. The adventures of the race and the gods' interventions, as well as Antilochus's actions, mask the truth, hide it, and prevent it from being what it should be—that is, very simply, the liturgical unfolding of a truth already known. And the debate over the rewards is about how to restore the truth of the respective strengths that was given from the start when the competitors and the rewards were introduced—and which the race masked when it should have manifested or confirmed it.

The race should have, as its function, to manifest a truth that is already recognized. The race has, as its function, to solemnly reveal, in a combat that is at the same time a ceremony, the heroes' different strengths. The race's real function is to put them in the order of their true value. Consequently, far from being a test in which equal individuals can distinguish themselves so that an unpredictable winner emerges, the race is nothing more than a liturgy of truth. Or, if you will, to forge a term—or not exactly to forge a term, because one finds it already in the vocabulary of late Greek—one might employ the word *alethurgy*. That is, it is a ritual procedure for bringing forth *alēthes*: that which is true. And in the case of this race, understood as an alethurgy—a liturgy of truth—all of the various adventures will appear to be tricks, ploys, and ruses. From this point of view it is easier to understand what was so perverse in Antilochus's behavior vis-à-vis Menelaus, even though it seemed so normal to us.

And it is here precisely that I would like to return to the problem of the contestation between Menelaus and Antilochus. For there are a number of elements to be noted with regard to this very dispute and what happened between them. First, there are two elements that consistently reappear regarding Antilochus. Antilochus, the one who did this thing that is going to be contested, is constantly referred to, throughout the scene, as "the wise Antilochus." At each moment, it is said, "Antilochus, you who are so wise, in spite of your youth," "Antilochus, you who are so thoughtful."[26] Antilochus was wise, he was well-informed, thoughtful, at once because of who he is and because he is the son of Nestor, and therefore benefits from his advice, et cetera. Second, what also resurfaces on multiple occasions is that as wise as he is, he was duped. He was duped by what? By something, and this something is his youth. He says as much himself when he finally concedes: "My youth overcame my reason."[27] This does not prevent him from being wise, but there was a conflict within Antilochus, a struggle, a joust between his youth and his reason—and youth carried over reason, at least for a moment.

Now, what was the consequence of the fact that he, the wise Antilochus, was clouded and conquered by his youth, at least for an instant? What did he do in this famous race that provoked such worry and solicited such a complex judicial proceeding? Did he break a rule? Obviously not. In fact, as you will recall, Antilochus had caught up with Menelaus, and simply refused to yield to Menelaus at the point at which one of the two had to slow his horses down to allow the other to pass. He simply refused to cede the passage—and he refused to cede the passage to Menelaus, Menelaus who was the stronger of the two. This was the irregularity. It was not the fact that there was a rule forbidding one from passing under such conditions. The irregularity, or the point of contention, lay in the fact that Menelaus was the stronger of the two and that the one who was weaker hindered him and prevented the stronger from appearing as such. So at the end of the race, he was second in front of Menelaus who was third (though Homer adds—or rather the Homeric text reads—that if the race had lasted longer, Menelaus would have caught up with Antilochus once again, and Antilochus would have been defeated).[28] You see clearly that the point of difficulty, the point of contention is not that Antilochus violated a law, but that he prevented the truth from being manifested by not yielding to his better. He did not make room for what was true—that is, that Menelaus was the stronger of the two. He did not break a rule of the race; he upset the race insofar as it was to be a liturgy of truth.

How, then, is truth to be restored? It is to be restored through the oath. And here I must introduce a small element that I did not yet mention: that is, when the rules of the race are explained at the beginning of the text, it is stated that an *istōr*, or witness, named Phoenix,[29] would be sent to inspect the famous post around which they turn. And yet, during the debate between Antilochus and Menelaus, do they call upon this witness, the one who saw the event and was in a position to say "Yes, such and such a thing happened?" Absolutely not; there is never any question of Phoenix nor the *istōr* throughout the debate, and it will never be brought up again. The public is also present, but it only intervenes when it is a question of deciding the validity of the procedures. The public does not intervene at all in the establishment of the facts, nor in the justice of the sentence. So how is the truth restored? It is restored through the particular episode of the oath, or rather the proposition to take an oath in the ritual position. Antilochus must swear that he did not hinder Menelaus's horses, either voluntarily or by ruse. The word used here is worth noting: *kerdos*,[30] which does not exactly mean ruse, but rather may be used in a positive or negative sense to mean profit or seeking advantage. In this instance it has a negative meaning. In other words, an act that strikes us as completely normal and would even seem to be the very essence of any race—that each individual tries to profit and gain the advantage—becomes negative. Here it connotes a devious, mean, or perverse ruse, because in this race no one should try to gain the upper hand. The race must unfold in such a way that the truth—that is, the true relation and differences in strength— manifests itself, as in a ceremony and as in a liturgy.

The oath enters at this point and is presented as a judicial procedure, inasmuch as, from that moment on, from the moment the oath is demanded, there are only two possible outcomes. Either Antilochus takes the oath, and in that case Menelaus is forced to concede. But this would mean that the conflict between Antilochus and Menelaus would be transferred from the human to the divine realm. It would be in some way Zeus that Antilochus would be forced to confront, the very Zeus who makes the earth tremble and who Antilochus would have had to confront if he took the oath proposed by Menelaus. The challenge to take the oath transfers the *agōn* from the race to the dispute between the two partners and from the dispute to a settlement by oath. If the oath were taken, the *agōn* would remain a dispute, but would be transferred from the clash between Menelaus and Antilochus to the clash between Antilochus and Zeus. And Antilochus does not want to take this risk: the transfer of the agonistic structure from man to the gods, that is precisely what Antilochus is going to run up against.[31]

And this is indeed what happens. It is thus the second hypothesis that is confirmed: Antilochus refuses to take the oath. But it remains to be seen how this renunciation happens. Can it be said that this is truly an avowal by our standards? If by avowal we mean a defined and ritualized act through which, in the course of a dispute, the accused recognizes the validity of the accusations against him and the victory of his accuser, then of course we can say that Antilochus avowed. It is indeed an avowal. But this avowal does not consist of saying, "I committed this fault." It does not, for two reasons. First, because he does not say it and there is not the famous verbal act, "I did it. I admit it. I committed such and such an act"—this does not exist within such a procedure. Second, you can see that in truth it is not really a question of fault. In fact, the avowal consists of saying, "You were stronger; you were first; you were ahead of me (*proteros kai areiōn*—you were first; you were stronger)."[32] This does not at all mean that Menelaus was ahead, that Menelaus's chariot was ahead of Antilochus's. It means that according to the order, in a sense, of their true strength, according to the order of their true status, according to the order of the brilliance of each hero, indeed, Menelaus was the *proteros*, he was the first. The role of the race was to ritualize this situation and this relationship; and what Antilochus did—and is now renouncing—was to try to extinguish, suffocate, weaken Menelaus's brilliance. This would have meant casting a shadow upon him—doing him wrong, as Menelaus says[33]—and, as a result, surpassing him in this order of reality, which was also the order of brilliance and the order of glory. The quasi-avowal does not consist, then, of admitting a fault before a judicial body that demands to know what actually happened. Antilochus's quasi-avowal consists, in renouncing the struggle, in refusing to take up the new form of *agōn* proposed by the challenge of the oath, in declaring himself beaten in the new episode of the struggle. The avowal consists of allowing the truth to manifest itself—a truth that he had obstructed by his attitude during the race. The avowal consists of restoring, within the agonistic structure, the forms in which the truth of their strengths was supposed to ritually appear.

Now, let's add, to conclude this episode of the dispute between Menelaus and Antilochus—of the chariot race—a few words which confirm, I believe, that the function of this quasi-avowal was a voluntary restoration of the truth of their strengths within the ritual of the competition. These are the following. It should not be forgotten that the chariot race takes place as part of the ritual in honor of Patroclus's funeral. That is, these games were designed to immortalize or preserve the memory of Patroclus that the living might forget. And just as there were great animal sacrifices to create a vast bloody hecatomb to feed the already faded shadow of Patroclus, the games were designed as well to perpetuate his memory as long as possible among men. The games were destined to that purpose. In a general sense, they served as a memorial rite through which the radiance of the heroes' exploits was kept alive as long as possible.

And so, you may recall that within this somewhat curious story whose structure is at once very simple and very complex, there were five competitors, five rewards. There were the gods who prevented the truth from manifesting itself and Antilochus, who also prevented the truth from being manifested. Finally, Eumelus received an additional prize, such that there were five competitors, one of whom received an additional lot, and four others who received four of the rewards. There is then a fifth lot, which remains. What should be done with this lot? Well, Achilles takes it. He takes it and to whom does he carry it? He carries it to Nestor, the father of Antilochus. Why does he carry it to Nestor? Because Nestor is a wise man and of good counsel? Because he had given Antilochus a formula that was far more reasonable and less perverse than the one Antilochus himself used? Nothing in the text would indicate as much. In fact, what the text says in explanation of Achilles's act is the following: if Achilles takes the last of the rewards and gives it to Nestor, it is because Nestor is too old to compete. When he was young, Nestor was also a great athlete and a winning competitor. And when Nestor sees Achilles approach to give him the gift, this is precisely how Nestor interprets the act. He says: "I thank you for giving me this gift, for, indeed, I too shined among heroes—*meteprepon hēpōessin*. My heart is full of joy now that I see that you remember my goodness and have not forgotten to pay me the homage I deserve."[34]

It is clear that throughout this story of the race, of the dispute, and of the gifts, what is at stake is at once the manifestation of truth and the memory of great achievements. What is at issue is struggle and memory, competition and celebration as rituals of truth, as alethurgy, as manifestation of the truth in the full light of day. In this immense ceremony of memory, in this immense ceremony where the truth must be made manifest in the competition of the chariot race and must survive in the memory of men, in this great game of truth, Antilochus's avowal is nothing more than the renunciation of what, for a brief instant and by fraud, veiled the truth and the true brilliance of the heroes. Antilochus's avowal is a renunciation of that which could have prevented the truth of the strengths, of the exploits, of the victories from crowning the combats and the competitions and from being perpetuated in the indefinite celebrations of memory.

By placing this strictly judicial, properly judicial scene back in its general context, a certain number of important elements appear regarding what was no doubt the first scene of judicial avowal that we know of within Western culture. In this scene there is one and only one individual— Antilochus—who is at once the accused and the bearer of truth, the one who must also unveil the truth and has the power to unveil it, and all this within the structure of the *agōn*. The idea that there is an accused, that this accused bears the truth, that it is up to him to unveil it because he knows it and has the power to unveil it, as you know this very same structure can also be found in *Oedipus*.[35] Oedipus is also the accused. He too holds the truth. And he too must unveil it. He too, as king, has the power to reap the consequences by unveiling it. So there is the same structure between the avowal of Antilochus and the avowal of Oedipus or the same type of superimposition, but with one small difference: in the case of Antilochus, everything is situated within a framework that is the structure of the combat, the structure of the *agōn*, the structure of the joust between two warriors within a civilization, or at least within a social group of warriors. On the contrary, for Oedipus—and this is what I will explain next time— this same superimposition, namely that an individual bears a truth that will devastate him and that consequently he must reveal by himself, this manifestation and the procedures of manifestation will not unfold within this form of the *agōn*, in the form of the joust, the confrontation between heroes or between warriors. Rather, it is within a far more complex judicial and political structure. Here we will see a whole mottled effect, if you will, of diverse institutions—religious, aristocratic, tyrannical—that become the structures through which the accused emerges as the one who will have to tell the truth. Oedipus's path from the status of the accused to the one who speaks the truth, who avows what he is accused of, is infinitely longer than this immediate and hieratic figure who, in the course of the competition, having first prevented the truth from unveiling itself, then hesitates to confront Jupiter himself and the anger of Jupiter or Zeus, preferring to let the truth unfold according to its own liturgy. The unity of the act, the unique scene in which Menelaus challenges Antilochus with the oath and then he, Antilochus, cedes—we are going to see this scene fractured through a whole series of structures, institutions, and diverse political and judicial practices, when the accused is no longer a hero or a warrior but is rather a king or a tyrant, when the accused holds political power, which is completely different from the brilliance, prestige, and presence of a warrior hero from the Homeric era. For this, the appearance of a judicial body will be necessary: a judicial body who will tell the truth through procedures that are far more complex than the oath.

This concludes the first part of my lecture for this evening. However, I now see that our time has passed quickly, which is my fault because I lingered too long, due to the material conditions such as the fact that one speaks more slowly while standing, et cetera. So what I would like to propose to you, if you are not too tired, is that I field a few questions and then, if you have another ten or fifteen minutes to spare, I will move on to certain shifts that took place in the history of judicial avowal in Greece between the time of Antilochus and Oedipus.*

::::

[. . .]† What I wanted to evoke was the appearance in post-Homeric Greek law, in a period stretching from the seventh to the sixth centuries, of two forms of judicial settlement in which the oath played two important but different roles. One finds traces of these two modes of judicial settlement in Hesiod, verses 35–39 of *Works and Days*. There, Hesiod addresses Perseus, with whom he has a problem and is in difficulty, and says to him: "Let us settle our quarrel here—*diakrinōmetha neikos*—using one of these righteous judgments that, delivered in Zeus's name, are the best of all. You have already taken and pillaged enough from the goods of others, feeding the glory of our bribe-mongering lords who love to judge according to such justice—*basilēas dōrophagous, hoi tēnde dikēn ethelousi dikassai*."[36] There are then two words. The word *dikassai* or *dikazein* in classical Greek and the verb *diakrinōmetha*, whose classical and active form is *krinein*, to judge.[37]

It seems to me that there are two different forms of justice here. Hesiod's text simply indicates and opposes the second-rate justice of the kings, which is *dikazein*, and good justice, which he proposes to Perseus to settle their dispute. What is second-rate justice? It is the justice of kings, local chiefs, chiefs of aristocratic families, who are susceptible to gifts and corruption, and as a result render second-rate justice—which makes it possible to pillage the goods of others. To this second-rate justice, Hesiod opposes another type of justice, for which he uses a different word which is neither *dikazein* nor *dikassai*, but *diakrinōmetha* (*krinein*; well, it has *krinein* as its root). And the expression itself, or at least the term itself, would indeed seem to indicate that it is a procedure that would be pursued by common accord, by a preliminary accord between those who have decided

---

* The recording of the lecture is interrupted here while Foucault is in the process of saying: "Do you have. . . ." The break results from a change of the audiovisual tape that produced a permanent gap that cannot be filled by means of the original typescript deposited at the IMEC. The missing words do not seem to have been essential to the subject of the lecture. The recording begins again with a sentence on the lectures' format.

† The lecture resumes with a sentence of which only the final words are audible: ". . . work in common and the solemnity of this context renders things a little more difficult."

to settle their differences together in this way. It would seem as well, according to the text, that such a judgment must be made before an authority that delivers its sentence in the name of Zeus. Here Zeus is not
simply playing the role he played in Menelaus's oath, for example, when a
false oath subjected one to his anger and his vengeance. Here, through the
intermediary of an authority who speaks on his behalf, Zeus becomes the
guarantor of a proper sentence, as opposed to the second-rate sentences
of the kings.

Hesiod's text seems to suggest the existence of these two different judicial practices, but it is difficult to say much more. By contrast, Gortyn's[38]
legislation—which is among the oldest of ancient Greece, situated just
after Hesiod but before classical Greece—gives us some sense of what
these judicial forms, the *dikazein* and *krinein*, were: the *dikazein*, which was
characterized as taking place in the case of second-rate justice, and the *krinein*, which was used, to the contrary, in what Hesiod calls good justice.[39]

What happened with *dikazein*? With *dikazein*, the accusers also took an
oath as they did in the dispute between Menelaus and Antilochus. That is,
they exposed themselves to the vengeance of the gods against perjurers.
But there was more to this *dikazein*, there was something else that could
not be found in the confrontation between Menelaus and Antilochus, for
the accusers in this form of judicial procedure were accompanied by partisans. They were accompanied by people who swore alongside them but
who did not swear that they were witnesses or beholders of the truth.
They swore the same oath as those within the dispute. That is, they committed themselves to the individual they supported. In reality, they were
not truth-bearing witnesses who had come to establish what truly happened in order to separate out the accusers and adversaries. They were
co-jurors who were necessarily on one side or the other. And by serving
as co-jurors with each one of the accusers, they were also exposed to the
potential vengeance of the gods against all perjurers.[40]

What was the point of this oath, or of this joint oath by the partisans
on behalf of each of the two parties? Essentially, it would seem that they
manifested the social importance of each of the individuals who took the
oath.[41] And of course, the more co-jurors there were, the greater the manifestation of their social power, and the more they demonstrated that there
were people who were ready to risk commitment as well, to expose themselves to the gods' wrath if the oath was not a true oath.[42] This is why I
made reference earlier to a similar scene in book 18 of Homer. There is a

representation of two accusers on Achilles's shield, surrounded by people who look like co-jurors confronting each other, group against group.[43] In this practice of the shared oath we are still to some extent in the realm of the oath; we are still in confrontation, up to a certain point, in the same competition that we saw earlier between Menelaus and Antilochus, with one exception: it is now groups that confront one another in the form of the juror and his co-jurors. What is the role of the sentence in this practice? It has the role of proclaiming who will prevail as between the two adversaries; but it does so, on the one hand, by verifying the regularity of procedures, by verifying that the rules were indeed observed correctly, and on the other hand by proclaiming who is on the right side of the law and who won in the confrontation, as if it were a question of the outcome of relations of force. This is how the sentence had a role to play, at bottom, in recording the results of the confrontation. In the law of Gortyn it was explicit, for example, that in a conflict over property, the side that gathered nine witnesses won automatically.[44] One was victorious as soon as one had nine witnesses in one's favor. There is still then an agonistic structure. It is still a question of confrontation, of a relationship of force, which decides the outcome of the dispute, but with the small difference that it is the social groups confronting each other, and with the other small difference that, as opposed to the confrontation between Menelaus and Antilochus, there is a body that brings an end to the confrontation, proclaiming at once that the confrontation took place as it should have and that this one was victorious over the other. That is the *dikazein*. That is the *dikazein* that Hesiod does not appreciate apparently—in which he sees a whole series of possible irregularities coming from the kings, the chiefs of justice, and heads of families who are responsible for establishing or restoring the peace between two parties. Such is *dikazein*.

Next to this, Gortyn's law proposes a different type of judgment that was used, at least originally, before rules had been preestablished for settling disputes. The great difference in this other form of jurisdiction was that the judge himself took an oath.[45] So three oaths were taken: one by each of the two parties, and a third by the judge. Of course, legal historians have discussed this oath's meaning extensively.[46] Some, such as Dareste,[47] believed that the oath meant that the judge simply promised to obey the law.[48] In response, one may note that *krinein* was precisely the form of justice that was put into play when no explicit law existed. As a result, it is unclear why one would take an oath to obey the law when there was no law for cases submitted to this form of justice. Other historians have suggested that it was a kind of assertoric oath through which the judge stated: "In my opinion, this is the truth, this is what happened."[49] This is not a satisfying answer either, because in many cases—the case of inheritance, for example—it is not at all clear how an assertoric oath could be useful. This is why the legal historian Gernet suggests that it was an oath through which the judge exposed himself personally, taking the risk and tying his destiny to the value of his own sentence.[50] And he makes the connection between this judge's oath and what we find much later in the oath of *The Delphic Amphictyony*, for example, or with regard to the disputes over the property and territories of Apollo, when the judges took an oath at the beginning of the trial before passing judgment. The text of this oath reads: "Called upon to give a verdict on the goods and territories of Apollo, I will judge this case as much as possible according to the truth, without preference or hatred. I will not give a false decision in any way. If I maintain my oath, may I gain prosperity. If I violate it, may Themis, Pythian Apollo, Lēthē, Artemis, Hestia, and the eternal fire make me perish in misery and refuse me all salvation."[51]

I think that in this oath—in the existence of this procedure with the judge's oath—there are fundamental differences with the previous procedures.[52] The fact that the judge takes an oath and opens himself to the vengeance of the gods if he does not judge properly gives new meaning to the oath of the parties. Now when the two adversaries take an oath, they do not do so along the lines of an agonistic challenge such as "I open myself up to the vengeance of the gods by taking this oath. Do you expose yourself as well?" The oath of the two adversaries in such a procedure is no longer the instrument that allows them to settle the dispute. It is not the standard form within which the confrontation is going to manifest itself. It is simply an introductory, instantiating act. It is a means through which each of the two adversaries can demonstrate his position and formally and ritually solicit the judge's arbitration. As for the judge, as soon as he takes such an oath, he is no longer the one who guarantees proper procedures, or notes or measures the relative strength of each adversary. He becomes a third party who designates the victor, who decides how to settle the dispute, what reparations are due. As a result, the role of the sentence is no longer to determine the victor, who followed or broke the rules, or who, according to his own oath and that of his co-jurors, has more status or power. The role of the sentence and the role of the judge is to determine what is just in the case of the two opponents—that is, the *dikaion*.[53]

In the procedure presented in book 23 of Homer, it was never a question of *dikaion*—indeed, the word *dikaion* did not even exist in Homer's work. One does not ask of the sentence that it be just in its contents. One asks that it conform to Themis; that is, the whole set of rules and procedures that allow for a dispute to be settled. But once there was a judicial mechanism, external to the law and the rules of Themis, in which the judge decides the sentence between two adversaries who present their arguments, the sentence could depend on nothing but a domain of justice to be thought through, reflected upon by the judge, and accepted by those who were being judged and by the population in general—that is, all those who participated in one way or another in this judgment. That was *dikaion*.

The emergence of the term *dikaion*, the just element as the regulating principle in sentencing, corresponds to the appearance of a judge who by means of an oath affirmed his autonomy vis-à-vis the two parties. Here, the judicial proceeding no longer took the form of an *agōn* or confrontation between two parties. As long as the settlement took place within the form of the *agōn*—of the struggle that culminated in the oath—the judge could be nothing more than the guarantor or the witness that all procedures and proper form had been respected. This was what happened in the *dikazein*. Once there was a domain in which justice intervened as an autonomous body, judging the sentence's very contents and not simply the regularity of the forms, and once justice had to take sides between the two parties, then the judge had to make reference to something like *dikaion*. As a result, the agonistic structure was loosened. No longer were there simply two parties confronting one another with, at most, a guarantee of procedural regularity. There was a tripartite structure, with a judge and two parties. This scene then refers to a new domain, a realm inconceivable to Homer, that of *dikaion*.

It is clear—but here we are touching on historical problems that I can only point to—that on the one hand, the emergence of an autonomous judicial structure that affirmed its independence and, up to a certain point, its sovereignty, and on the other hand, the rise of the domain of *dikaion*, was tied to the appearance of, or at least a whole set of problems generated by, a rural economy.[54] The problem of debt, the problem of the distribution of property—a whole set of economic, commercial, and agricultural problems—could not, in the eyes of Hesiod, be resolved with the old aristocratic *dikazein*, in which two partners opposed one another by taking oaths before someone who only ensured proper form and who, in fact, served the interests of one or the other. What Hesiod called for, what he asked for, what he was reaching for when he invited Perseus to join him in something like a *diakrinein* or a mutual *diakrinesthai*, was precisely this recourse to arbitration, an arbitration agreed upon by each party and which was to be established according to *dikaion*.[55]

It seems to me that we have two different processes here that I simply want to flag. They are bound to the emergence of new economic and social problems, and to the entire crisis of the seventh and sixth centuries in Greece that gave birth to the classical age. In the middle of this crisis we see two processes: on the one hand, there was the emergence of an autonomous judicial body which placed itself above the *agonists*, above the competitors, and, on the other hand, the singling out of a region of *dikaion* where it was no longer simply a question of respecting the rules of Themis, where it was no longer simply a question of respecting good procedure, but of establishing what was in itself just. And why was it just? Because that was the reality of things: it was the *dikaion* and *alēthes*.[56] The truth no longer emerged out of or manifested itself in the protagonists' oath. The truth was manifested in the formulation of the *dikaion*, of what was just. And it was precisely at this moment that Greek poetry and philosophy emerged, and that each took up the task of telling both the *dikaion* and the *alēthes*—the *dikaion* and the *alēthes* that were inscribed in the very order of the world. I believe that this marks the introduction of an unprecedented juridical and philosophical world, as well as a very different world of knowledge. For the first time, it seems to me, there was a direct link between this *dikaion* and this *alēthes*, between the just and the true, which would become the problem, one could argue the constant problem, of the Western world.

OK. These are just a few general indications.*

---

* The audience applauds.

[NOTES]

1. Georges Dumézil, *Servius et la fortune: Essai sur la fonction sociale de louange et de blâme et sur les éléments indoeuropéens du cens romain* (Paris: Gallimard, 1943), pp. 243–44. The original French quotation, which Foucault slightly modifies, reads: "Aussi haut qu'on remonte dans les comportements de notre espèce, la 'parole vrai' est au contraire une force à laquelle peu de forces résistent . . . la Vérité est très tôt apparue aux hommes comme une des armes verbales les plus efficaces, un des germes de puissance les plus prolifiques, une des plus solides fondements pour leurs institutions." Foucault also makes reference to this passage in his lecture at the Collège de France on February 3, 1971. See Michel Foucault, *Leçons sur la volonté de savoir: Cours au Collège de France, 1970–1971*, ed. Daniel Defert (Paris: Gallimard/Seuil, 2011), p. 82.

2. Foucault, "Inaugural Lecture," this volume.

3. As Daniel Defert suggests in his edition of Foucault's *Leçons sur la volonté de savoir* (p. 78 n. 4), an important text that would have guided Foucault's interpretation of prelaw Greece is Louis Gernet's "Droit et prédroit en Grèce ancienne" in *L'Année sociologique*, 3e série (1948–1949), Paris, 1951, p. 21–119, which was reedited in Louis Gernet, *Anthropologie de la Grèce antique*, pp. 175–260 (Paris: Maspero, 1968) and in Louis Gernet, *Droit et Institutions en Grèce antique*, pp. 7–119 (Paris: Flammarion, 1982). This text can be found translated into English as "Law and Prelaw in Ancient Greece," pp. 143–215, in Louis Gernet, *The Anthropology of Ancient Greece*, trans. John Hamilton and Blaise Nagy (Baltimore: Johns Hopkins University Press, 1981). Another important text was Gernet's *Droit et société dans la Grèce Ancienne* (Paris: Recueil Sirey, 1955), referred to in these notes.

4. Homère, *Iliade*, chant XXIII, verses 257–650, ed. and trans. Paul Mazon, tome IV (Paris: Les Belles Lettres, 1938), pp. 108–23; English edition, Homer, *The Iliad*, book 23, trans. Richmond Lattimore (Chicago: University of Chicago Press, 1961), pp. 457–67. Foucault presented a sketch of this analysis in his lecture at the Pontifical Catholic University of Rio de Janeiro in May 1973 entitled "Truth and Juridical Forms," in Michel Foucault, *Power*, ed. James D. Faubion, pp. 1–89 (New York: The New Press, 2000) at pp. 17–18 ["La vérité et les formes juridiques" in *Dits et Ecrits*, tome II (1970–75), no. 139, Paris: Gallimard, 1994, pp. 555–56]; as well as in his *Leçons sur la volonté de savoir*, pp. 72 et seq. In the Rio de Janeiro conference, Foucault characterizes this episode in the *Iliad* as "a sort of testing game, a challenge hurled by one adversary at another" (p. 18).

5. Homère, *Iliade*, chant XXIII, ed. Mazon, verses 287–305, pp. 109–10, and verses 351–52, p. 112; Lattimore, book 23, pp. 458 and 459.

6. Ibid., Mazon, verses 306–50, pp. 110–12; Lattimore, p. 461.

7. Ibid., Mazon, verses 403–16, p. 114; Lattimore, p. 461.

8. Ibid., Mazon, verses 426–28, p. 115; Lattimore, p. 461.

9. Foucault adds this dialogue. See ibid., Mazon, verses 429–430, p. 115; Lattimore, p. 461.

10. Ibid., Mazon, verses 536–38, p. 119; Lattimore, p. 464.

11. Ibid., Mazon, verses 543–54, pp. 119–20; Lattimore, pp. 464–65.

12. Ibid., Mazon, verses 570–75, p. 120; Lattimore, p. 465.

13. Ibid., Mazon, verse 577–80, p. 120; Lattimore, p. 465.

14. Ibid., Mazon, verse 580, p. 120; Lattimore, p. 465.

15. Ibid., Mazon, verses 580–85, pp. 120–21; Lattimore, pp. 465–66.

16. Ibid., Mazon, verse 587–88, p. 121; Lattimore, p. 466.

17. Ibid., Mazon, verses 587–95, p. 121; Lattimore, p. 466.

18. Ibid., Mazon, verses 602–11, pp. 121–22; Lattimore, p. 466.

19. Homère, *Iliade*, chant XVIII, ed. and trans. Paul Mazon, verses 468–617, tome III (Paris: Les Belles Lettres, 1938), pp. 185–91; English edition, Homer, *The Iliad*, book 18, trans. Richmond Lattimore (Chicago: University of Chicago Press, 1961), pp. 387–91 (the descrip-

tion of Achilles's shield). *Cf.* Louis Gernet, *Droit et société dans la Grèce ancienne* (Paris: Recueil Sirey, 1955), p. 62 ("The oldest testimony of a judicial settlement is in Homer [*Iliade*, XVIII, verse 497 et. seq.]. It is the famous 'judicial scene' of Achilles' shield where we see two adversaries: one claims to have paid the price of blood and the other claims that he did not"). Foucault discusses this scene in his *Leçons sur la volonté de savoir*, p. 76–8.

20. Homère, *Iliade*, chant XXIII, ed. Mazon, verses 534–39, p. 119; Lattimore, book 23, p. 389. Gernet, *Droit et société*, p. 16. (In the chapter "Jeux et Droit, Remarques sur le XXIII chant de l'Iliade," Gernet elaborates on "this virtual law of the group" that takes place at precisely the moment when, he explains, "Achilles offers the second prize to Eumelus and a portion of the spectators ratify his decision."

21. Cf. Gernet, *Droit et société*, pp. 11–14.

22. Cf. ibid., pp. 9, 11–12, and 13–14. Foucault refers here to the chapter "Jeux et Droit," where Gernet develops his thesis on the use of a juridical vocabulary in Virgil and Homer to describe the games, the status of prizes, and the competition for prizes. Gernet argues, for example, "The prizes are deliberately and by definition *res nullius* . . . The prizes, according to Achilles (273) 'await' the competitors. They are left to those who will conquer them." Ibid., p. 13.

23. Homère, *Iliade*, chant XXIII, ed. Mazon, verses 580–85, pp. 120–21; Lattimore, book 23, pp. 465–66.

24. Gernet, *Droit et société*, pp. 17–18.

25. Homère, *Iliade*, chant XXIII, ed. Mazon, verses 262–70, p. 108; Lattimore, book 23, p. 457. The enumeration actually happens before the heroes rise.

26. See ibid., Mazon, verse 305, p. 110, and verse 570, p. 120; Lattimore, pp. 458 and 465.

27. Ibid., Mazon, verses 590–92, p. 121; Lattimore, p. 466.

28. Ibid., Mazon, verses 523–27, p. 118; Lattimore, p. 464.

29. Ibid., Mazon, verses 359–61, p. 112; Lattimore, pp. 459–60. The word *istōr* does not appear in book 23 of *The Iliad*. For a detailed discussion of the term and its significance and functions, *see* Daniel Defert's comments in his edition of Foucault's *Leçons sur la volonté de savoir*, p. 79, n. 12. Defert refers the reader to two texts that would have guided Foucault's interpretation: J. Gaudemet, *Les institutions de l'Antiquité* (Paris: Sirey, 1967), p. 140; and Marcel Detienne, *Les maîtres de vérité dans la Grèce archaïque* (Paris: Maspero, 1967, reedited in 1981), p. 101. On the figure of the *istōr*, see also *infra*, p. 89, n. 86.

30. Ibid., Mazon, verses 581–85, p. 121; Lattimore, p. 466.

31. On this point see Gernet, "Law and Prelaw in Ancient Greece," in Louis Gernet, *The Anthropology of Ancient Greece*, pp. 189–90:

What is the import of all this? If Antilochus refuses to take the oath, then Menelaus wins; if he takes the oath, then the chariot stays in his possession. This does not appear to be the equivalent of proof from which law could emanate. Following an archaic concept, what we would call the "administration of proof" is addressed not to a judge who has to essay it, but to an adversary whom the proof is designed to "conquer." Negatively, what defines prelaw in particular is that there is no possibility of an objective truth that would support a verdict. In this case, there is no place for a verdict, and the adversaries simply decide between themselves. Their testimony constitutes the verdict.

Proof can be various. In prelaw, one can say that it is always of the "ordeal" variety— that is, of a sort that allows settlement or ratification by sending one or both parties to another world, where their destinies are played out. In Greece in general there is abundant evidence of this practice in mythology. We do *not* see it as often as Glotz would have liked for the purpose of resolving conflict before the rule of law. But the mode of thought that governs it is the same one that requires the oath as a self-styled means of proof, and it is the same one that survives later, outside the law, in the ritual oaths that are, in fact, trials by ordeal.

32. Ibid., Mazon, verse 588, p. 121; Lattimore, p. 466.

33. Ibid., Mazon, verses 570–74, p. 120; Lattimore, p. 465.

34. Ibid., Mazon, verses 645–50, p. 123; Lattimore, p. 467. On this point, see Marcel Detienne, *Les maîtres de vérité dans la Grèce*, pp. 86–87 and, generally, pp. 82–87. The continuity between war and games—a continuity that is reflected in the similarity of institutional mechanisms such as sharing the spoils and awarding of prizes in games—allows us to understand better why Nestor is honored and why Menelaus reproaches Antilochus, who like his father and brother had fought for him, for not having respected him during the chariot race.

35. Sophocle, *Œdipe Roi*, trans. Paul Mazon (Paris: Les Belles Lettres, 2007); English edition, *Œdipus the King*, ed. David Grene and Richmond Lattimore (Chicago: University of Chicago Press, 1991).

36. Hésiode, *Les Travaux et les jours*, verses 35–39, in *Théogonie, Les Travaux et les Jours, le Bouclier*, trans. Paul Mazon (Paris: Belles Lettres, 1928), p. 87; English edition, Hesiod, *Works and Days*, trans. Richmond Lattimore, in *Hesiod* (Ann Arbor: University of Michigan Press, 1959), p. 23.

37. On this point, cf. Foucault, *Leçons sur la volonté de savoir*, p. 85 et seq.

38. See *Loi de Gortyne* in *Recueil des inscriptions juridiques grecques*, trans. and ed., with commentary, by Rodolphe Dareste, Bernard Haussoulier, and Théodore Reinach (Paris: Ernest Leroux, 1891–94), pp. 355–493; *The Law Code of Gortyn*, trans. and ed. Ronald F. Willetts (Berlin: de Gruyter, 1967). Gortyn's law was discovered in 1884 in the Greco-Roman ruins of Gortyn in Crete by Federico Halbherr. Dating from the fifth century BCE, this compilation of Greek family law is among the oldest and most complete of all ancient juridical texts. The text is written in the Dorian dialect and engraved in stone. Divided into seven chapters, it primarily treats inheritance, marriage, adultery, divorce, adoption, sexual crimes, damages caused by animals, the fate of escaped slaves, servant freedmen, and the administration of justice. The text is part of a larger set of legal texts to which it makes reference on a number of occasions. For more information on the law code of Gortyn, see Gernet, *Droit et société*, pp. 51–59, and Michael Gagarin, *Writing Greek Law* (New York: Cambridge University Press, 2008), chapters 6–7, pp. 122–75.

39. Cf. Gernet, *Droit et société*, p. 63–64: In the law of Gortyn, "if the judge is forced to pronounce by his own authority, and not through an application of the rules of proof, it is understood as *krinein* and not *dikazein*. This form of judgment is always accompanied by an oath on the part of the judge." See also Louis Gernet, "Appendice III. La désignation du jugement: *Dikazein et krinein*," in Louis Gernet, *Recherches sur le développement de la pensée juridique et morale en Grèce: Étude sémantique* (Paris: Ernest Leroux, 1917, reedited Paris, Albin Michel 2001), pp. 445–48.

40. Cf. Gernet, *Droit et société*, pp. 98–100.

41. For a parallel in feudal law and a discussion of the system of proof in its relationship to the social importance of the accused in the eleventh century, see Foucault, "Truth and Juridical Forms," p. 37.

42. Cf. Gernet, *Droit et société*, p. 99 ("We know that in ancient times [witnesses] could introduce themselves as co-jurors. It is so obviously not an objective truth to be discovered by a juridical organism nor a force that is demonstrated and asserted that this early procedure consists of enumerating those who support the case either in favor of or against it").

43. Homère, *Iliade*, chant XVIII, ed. Mazon, verses 468–617, pp. 185–191; Lattimore, book 18, pp. 387–91.

44. Cf. Gustave Glotz, *La solidarité de la famille dans le droit criminel en Grèce* (Paris: Albert

Fontemoing, 1904), p. 297: "Among the reciprocal duties of neighbors was protection from illegal seizure. But in this case, the one who asked did not choose the men: in Gortyn the nine closest property owners were called upon." See also Gertrude Smith, *The Administration of Justice from Hesiod to Solon* (Chicago: University of Chicago Libraries, 1924), p. 67, n. 2 ("The force of the sentence is that after each side has taken its oath that side wins on the majority swear. The nine neighbors evidently take an oath but the content is wholly omitted and the circumstances under which it is taken are very obscure"); and Michael Gagarin, *Writing Greek Law*, p. 140, which reproduces the original text and the English translation in the appendix. Glotz builds his analysis on the *Recueil des inscriptions juridiques grecques* edited by Dareste, Haussoulier, and Reinach ([1891–94], p. 432–34), where it is explained that in this period, a fixed number of witnesses was required: "The co-jurors, whose technical name is provided by a fragment of Gortyn and Lyttos, must be distinguished from the sworn witnesses who were mentioned earlier even though the two institutions were very similar. The difference is that the sworn witnesses testify about something that they know personally whereas the co-jurors necessarily support the cause of their client, who is usually a relative, because in general they are convinced of his loyalty" (*Recueil*, p. 434). Louis Gernet explains in his *Droit et société dans la Grèce ancienne* (Paris: Institut de droit romain, 1955), p. 99 n. 5: "We know that a minimum number of oaths must be taken from the cases of co-jurors that have been passed on to us. In an inscription of Gortyn, a property suit in the case of a seizure of real estate, there even seems to be the inscription . . . that the party who produces the most co-jurors among the different neighbors of the property will win the case. This is a reading that would seem to have been abandoned, but it would seem that in such a case we are very close the principle of the majority." See also Federico Halbherr, "Cretan Expedition III. Epigraphical Researches in Gortyna," *American Journal of Archeology* 1, no. 3 (May–June 1897, pp. 159–238), pp. 192–93 ("Disputes in these cases shall be referred to as the *neotas*, and of the *neotas* the seven who are elected as *agoranomoi* shall give judgment under oath. And judgment shall be rendered in favor of the party for which the majority shall have taken oath [that is to say, the judgment shall be given by the majority of votes] and this college of seven, having exacted the fine of the party which has lost the suit, shall give half to the party who has won the suit and half to the city"); Gernet, *Droit et société*, p. 99 n. 6 ("Sur la conception formaliste du témoignage à Gortyne [exigence d'un nombre fixe de témoins]" ["On the formalist conception of the testimony in Gortyn (the necessity of a fixed number of witnesses)"]); Glotz, *La solidarité de la famille dans le droit criminel en Grèce*, p. 296 ("The second system, that of a defined number of co-jurors, seems to have been used in Kymè . . . , Chaleion and Gortyn").

45. Cf. Gernet, *Droit et société*, p. 63 (in the law of Gortyn, "this form of judgment [*krinein*] is always accompanied by the judge's oath").

46. Foucault is building on the discussion in Gernet, *Droit et société*, p. 64 and n. 5 ("But first of all, what is the nature of the judge's oath? This is still being discussed. Some argue that it is a promissory oath and others suggest it is an assertoric oath"). Gernet distances himself from this debate, which he considers to be overintellectualized.

47. Rodolphe Dareste de la Chavanne (1824–1911), member of the Institut de France and *conseiller* at the Cour de Cassation was a paleographer, archivist, and historian of ancient law. He was the editor with Bernard Haussoulier and Théodore Reinach of the *Recueil des inscriptions juridiques* (1891–94) as well as the author of multiple works including *Études d'histoire du droit* (Paris: L. Larose et Forcel, 1889) and *Nouvelles études d'histoire du droit* (Paris: L. Larose, 1902).

48. Cf. Gernet, *Droit et société*, p. 64 n. 5 ("By this oath, the judge commits to making a decision according to truth and justice. It is a conception that emerged first among the moderns and it is that of the authors of the *Inscriptions juridiques* [I, 435, n. 2 "in one sense, the judge . . . gives a verdict as a juror"]). The principal editor of the *Inscriptions juridiques* was Dareste.

49. Gernet, *Droit et société*, p. 64 n. 5. According to Gernet, the theory of the assertoric oath—the oath as a guarantor of the truth of a given fact—was developed by Kurt Latte in his work *Heiliges Recht, Untersuchungen zur Geschichte der sakralen Rechtsformen in Griechenland* (Tübingen: JCB Mohr [P. Siebeck], 1920), p. 41.

50. Gernet, *Droit et société*, p. 64, n. 5 ("An oath is essentially a procedure in which the individual makes a commitment"); ibid., p. 65 ("The ritual of the oath binds the person who swears").

51. An oath of the same type, found on the site of the temple of Apollo Delios dating from the second or first century BCE: "Les stratèges feront prêter serment aux juges appelés à juger. . . . Le serment sera celui-ci: 'Je jure par Jupiter, par Apollon Lycien, et par la Terre, que je jugerai, dans l'instance liée entre les parties par leurs serments, selon ce qui me paraîtra le plus juste. Je ne jugerai pas d'après un témoin, si ce témoin ne me paraît pas dire la vérité. Je n'ai reçu aucun présent au sujet de ce procès, ni moi-même, ni un autre pour moi, homme ou femme, ni par quelque détour que ce soit. Puissé-je prospérer si je tiens mon serment, mais malheur à moi si je me parjure" ("The strategists will make the judges swear an oath . . . and the oath will be: 'I swear by Jupiter, by Apollo Lycien, and the Earth, that I will judge, in the occasion created by the parties through their oath, according to what seems to me the most just. I will not judge according to a witness if I think that this witness is not telling the truth. I have received nothing with regard to this trial, neither myself nor someone in my name, man or woman, nor by any other means. May I be empowered if I hold my oath, but may I be struck with evil if I perjure'"). *Recueil des inscriptions juridiques*, p. 158.

52. Cf. Foucault, *Leçons sur la volonté de savoir*, pp. 97–98.

53. Ibid., p. 98 et seq.

54. On this point, cf. Marcel Detienne, *Crise agraire et attitude religieuse chez Hésiode* (Brussels: Collection Latomus 68, 1963).

55. On the question of whether arbitration represents "the oldest form of judicial settlement," see Gernet, *Droit et société*, p. 62, and the chapter "Institution des arbitres publics à Athènes," pp. 103–19.

56. Cf. Foucault, *Leçons sur la volonté de savoir*, p. 103 et seq.

SECOND LECTURE

April 28, 1981

I owe you two types of apologies. The
first is a traditional apology that I should repeat (but will avoid doing so)
at the beginning of each lecture, namely that I am neither a jurist nor a
legal historian; so I hope you will not expect of me an unwarranted level
of technical expertise. What interests me in these reflections on law are,
of course, the philosophical questions posed by a number of juridical practices or techniques. I am also interested in the cultural context within
which judicial practices developed and were organized within the penal
system, either in relation to the problem of the prison or the problem of
avowal, for example. Thus, I will try to analyze the various themes that I
would like to explore by going back and forth between juridical and extra-
juridical references.

The second apology is that today I am going to offer what may be the millionth reflection on Sophocles's *Oedipus Rex*.[1] For this I can offer but one excuse: that this reflection will not be focused on that extraordinary, monstrous, and unique thing that Oedipus did, but, to the contrary, on the very regular way (I was even going to say ordinary way) in which this thing was brought to light by Oedipus and for Oedipus. In other words, what I would like to present—in a somewhat haphazard way, as a kind of textual commentary and nothing more, so that we might discuss afterwards—are a few reflections on how Oedipus's wrong-doing and truth-telling are tied together in Sophocles's play. In other words, it is not so much Oedipus and his interdiction or malediction that I would like to study,[2] but rather his veridiction.[3]

I will try to explore this question of veridiction in different forms of either judicial practices or cultural experiences. Oedipus—I mean *Oedipus Rex*, the play by Sophocles—is, as you know, a foundational representation of law. Naturally, in saying this I am repeating a platitude and a truism. Everyone knows that in Greek tragedy, the theme of representing law—of the foundational representation of law—is essential. Whether it be Aeschylus through *Prometheus* or *Oresteia*, or Sophocles with *Antigone* and *Electra*, the problem of the confrontation of rights, the confrontation between the law of the family and the law of the city, the problem of the foundation of the law, the original institution of the tribunal, or the question of vengeance—all of this constitutes a theme which, if not universal, is at least constant throughout Greek tragedy.

Moreover, it seems to me that, generally speaking, in most societies we would refer to as Indo-European, or at least from the theater of Greece to that of the sixteenth and seventeenth centuries, this question of the representation of law in theater was a constant. After all, the central problem in Shakespeare—or in the political plays among Shakespeare's works—it seems to me, is the question of the foundation of sovereign right: How [. . .] can a sovereign succeed in legitimately exercising power that he seized through war, revolt, civil war, crime, or violating oaths? It seems to me as well that classical French theater—I am thinking especially of Corneille, of course—touches on and represents these problems of public law. It also seems to me that the question of law and of representing the foundation of law through theater was essential for Schiller as well. It could be interesting, I think, to study the entire history of theater in our societies from the perspective of this question of the representation of law. One has the impression—or at least, it seems to me this is something that would merit further study—that from the time of Greek theater up to at least the end of the eighteenth century, one of the functions, although certainly not the sole function, of theater in European societies was to be the place or a stage for debating the problem of the law. This was unlike the novel, but not, perhaps, unlike the epic or the American Western, which, after all, also presents a problem of law, of the confrontation of rights, of the confrontation of law and vengeance, of the right of conquest. It seems to me that there is an entire side to the institutions of representation—of the representative arts—in European societies that are organized around this question of the foundation of law and whose significance and meaning is to manifest, in one way or another, the fundamental problems of law. But let's leave that question under the heading of possible areas for further study.[4]

In any case, *Oedipus Rex* is clearly a representation of law since it involves a crime, a crime in the double sense of an infraction of fundamental law and a religious sullying[5]—two aspects that are inseparable in ancient Greek thought and culture. It is equally a question of discovering who is responsible for the crime and, finally, a question of how to punish the criminal—a problem that remains unresolved in the play. Let's say in very schematic terms, for example, that in the case of *Electra* or *Antigone*, the problem was that of knowing how to make room for the law of the family within the law of the city, how they should confront one another, and how they should be coordinated. In the case of *Oedipus*, a more straightforward juridical problem is posed: the question of discovering the identity of the unknown murderer. The question of what procedure to employ in order to uncover the unknown murderer was a well-known question not only in classical Greek law, but also in classical Greek philosophy. For example, while book 9 of Plato's *Laws*, section 874a, does not evoke Oedipus explicitly, it discusses precisely his general situation.[6] Plato writes of a clear case of assassination, where the murderer remains unknown in spite of the investigators' best efforts. We have, then, a very simple juridical situation which is far less complex than the case of *Electra* or *Antigone*: a crime has been committed and the perpetrator, whose name and identity remain unknown, must be found. That being said, from the very start and throughout the play, the text contains a series of technical and precise juridical terms which were completely comprehensible for a Greek audience and which reveal that the play unfolds in the form of a trial. It is not, of course, a total and exhaustive representation of a trial, yet there is a perfectly clear judicial paradigm organized around the question of how to discover the guilty party whose crime has been established, but whose identity remains unknown.

By way of orientation, I will indicate a few of the elements of this general paradigm. For example, take the very beginning of the text, when Oedipus sends Creon to ask the oracle of Delphi why Thebes has been afflicted with the plague. Creon returns with the response, and Oedipus asks him: "Now, of what murder is Apollo informing us?"[7] The Greek text uses the verb *mē-nuein*, which the French translation[8] renders by suggesting that Apollo indicates the crime as the cause of the plague. In fact, the verb *mēnuein* is a technical term that designates a precise form of judicial process.[9] In classical Greek law, there were two ways of denouncing a crime: either before the council, the *boulē*, or before the assembly. One procedure, the *exangelesia*, could only be heard if the denouncer was a citizen. When the denouncer was not a citizen and could not present his denunciation in that form, he followed a different procedure called *mēnusis*—to which this denunciation corresponded. For indeed, Apollo was not a Theban, so he does not have to follow the procedure of *exangelia* as if he were a citizen. He introduces a *mēnusis*—which is the technical term employed here. So this is a case of a noncitizen who denounces a crime committed on the city's territory.[10] What is interesting is that Apollo's *mēnusis*, his denunciation, takes two forms: it takes the form of the plague, the plague that was sent in response to an impurity, as a consequence of the impurity provoked by the crime; and this denunciation, it is also the oracle that was delivered and that Creon brought back. The procedure—the judicial procedure, named by the text—is perceived as embedded within both divine action (Apollo's vengeance) and the religious ritual of prophecy (the oracle).

Oedipus responds to this *mēnusis*, to this denunciation by Apollo, as would a chief justice: "Because there has been a denunciation, I am going to start over"—I am citing the French translation—"I am going to start everything from the beginning."[11] This corresponds exactly to the procedure, which is also well defined juridically, that must follow the denunciation of the crime once it has been accepted either by the council or the assembly. Investigators, the *zētētai*,[12] are designated and charged with investigating the affair from the beginning to determine the truth of the denunciation. In order to mark the judicial character of the procedure that he has set in motion, first Oedipus promises a reward to anyone who discloses information; then he curses those who hide what they know; and third, he absolves those who would testify against interest.[13]

Naturally, through the extraordinary density and complexity of the text and the echoes that resonate throughout the play, we know well that the curse on those who hide their knowledge and the absolution of those who would testify against themselves, all of this is going to take on a dramatic meaning—or rather a tragic sense—that we know so well. But it is also important to recognize that these are not simply dramatic effects within the larger economy of the play. Oedipus's famous curse on the unknown criminal that ricochets back onto him is also a well-documented judicial procedure in classical Athenian law. For example, in the famous sacrilege trial of 415 (415 was a few years after *Oedipus*, if indeed the play was staged in 420), in this famous sacrilege trial recounted by Thucydides[14] and then Plutarch,[15] there are accounts of this type of procedure, in which a reward was promised to those who could provide information, just as impunity was ensured for those who would testify against interest. Oedipus's famous curse against the unknown criminal, who turns out to be himself, directly echoes, even in its very terms, a religious and judicial practice that was common during the period and to which Plato attests. In book 9 of the *Laws* it is written, precisely in the case of the unknown murderer: "If someone is found dead and the murderer is unknown and remains undiscovered by investigation, proclamations against the murderer must be made"—which Oedipus does—"and the herald must proclaim in the public market that the murderer, whoever he is, must not set foot in any sacred place in his own country or that of the victim."[16] Oedipus says exactly this. In such a case, "if he does this and it is discovered, may he be put to death and thrown outside the frontiers without burial."[17] This too is precisely what is discussed at the end of Sophocles's play.

So the very instruments of the inquiry are put in place. And once again this inquiry unfolds in a very recognizable juridical form. First there is Tiresias—Tiresias the seer, as you know—who comes, and comes entirely as a witness. The text states as much: "He came,"[18] *eiselēluthas*—*eiserchomai* means "to appear before" in the technical juridical sense of the term. "I have come," Tiresias says, "because you have called me," *kaleis*[19]—here again a juridical term. And Tiresias is going to act like a reluctant witness[20] who is under threat, while Oedipus finally puts an end to his testimony by dismissing him with another ritual saying, *aphes*—"be gone."[21] After Tiresias leaves, the chorus discusses his testimony just as a jury would discuss a witness's testimony. Creon follows Tiresias, but not as a witness. To the contrary, he comes to complain before the chorus, before the jury, that he has been the victim of Oedipus's slanderous accusations. To which Oedipus replies with another accusation. The specific term used in his accusation, *kakotechnia*,[22] is a juridical term which generally means a "deceitful maneuver" or may mean, in more specific circumstances, "subornation of a witness"—and indeed this is precisely what Oedipus accuses Creon of doing. He accuses him of having suborned the oracle as witness and having falsified the oracle's meaning. At least this is Oedipus's complaint against Creon. And finally the last scene, which leads to the revelation of the truth and to which we will return for a closer reading, is clearly a judicial scene of testimony and investigation—of interrogation, of extortion of an avowal under threat of torture, and ultimately avowal. Thus, the general framework of the play is a procedural one that is easily recognizable. Once again, it does not reproduce a trial exactly, but rather a judicial paradigm that would have been perfectly comprehensible and recognizable to a Greek audience and spectators.

So, after this slightly belabored and technical introduction, it is time to home in on the central question that I would like to pose: What exactly is being represented on this stage, in this judicial scene?

Since Aristotle, everyone knows—that is, those who are familiar with Aristotle know—that Greek tragedy traditionally rests on two elements: the peripety that reverses the good fortune of the characters and transforms happiness into misery or luck into misfortune;[23] and on the other hand, the other great technique is recognition, in which the real identity of some hitherto unknown or misknown person is revealed. Indeed, most Greek tragedies rely on these two mechanisms and, in general, the *peripeteia*[24]—that is, the reversal of the situation—allows one to recognize the truth of each. *Oedipus Rex* has the peculiarity of being among the very rare, if not the only, Greek tragedies in which the *peripeteia*—that is, the transformation of events or of the fortune of the characters—does not reveal the truth. It is the revelation of truth, the *anagnōrisis*,[25] the recognition of the character's real identity, that constitutes the peripety that leads to Oedipus's fall and turns this envied man, with what appeared a most desirable fate, into a man doomed to abomination and endless misfortune. It is thus a play built entirely on the mechanism of recognition, of *anagnōrisis*.

In fact—and here is where I would like to situate my own analysis with regard to the more common ones—it seems to me that there are two *anagnōrises*, two moments of recognition in *Oedipus Rex*. On the one hand, there is the axis stretching from Oedipus's own ignorance or lack of awareness of himself to his obligation to recognize who he is. This is the axis of individual recognition, the axis of Oedipus as the subject of an action he does not remember—or rather, for which he had neither the keys to, nor the possibility of, understanding the significance—but that is revealed at the end of the play as one that he not only committed, but committed as the son of the one he killed and the son of the one he married. So there is this individual *anagnōrisis*, the emergence of truth in the subject. And then there is another axis, and this is the one that I would prefer to focus on: the axis of establishing the truth not in the eyes of Oedipus but in the eyes of the chorus, a character that I believe to be absolutely central, as it is in all Greek plays. For if indeed Oedipus is searching for the truth, he is doing so precisely so that the chorus can recognize it—the chorus, that is, the citizens, the people in assembly, or what is constituted as the judicial body with the responsibility for discovering, establishing, and validating the truth.[26] How does Oedipus's truth establish itself in the eyes of the chorus? This is the axis I would like to study: the establishment of truth in valid and legitimate juridical terms.

There is indeed one thing that is striking in the play: that is, while it is true that until the end Oedipus is the one who does not recognize himself for who he is, nevertheless we must recognize that the truth, the truth of what he is, is known not only to the spectators before the beginning of the play—but what's more, the entire play is punctuated with elements reminding them that they know this truth. And the fact is, this truth is produced explicitly at least three times in the course of the play.

This truth that is so difficult to know and that Oedipus refuses to recognize, this truth is told entirely, completely, and exhaustively for the first time by two characters—for it is always two characters, coupled together, who produce this truth through their complementary dialogue.[27] The first couple that produces this truth is Apollo and Tiresias. Apollo indicates why there is the plague, and Tiresias states who is guilty. This is the first manifestation of truth, the first production of truth, the first veridiction, which, for a number of reasons that we will need to study, does not work, does not stick, is not accepted, is neither validated nor legitimated. Then there is a second production of truth, which is once again the work of two complementary characters, Jocasta and Oedipus. They recount their memories, providing all the necessary information to recognize Oedipus as his mother's husband and his father's assassin. This second veridiction, this second alethurgy, once again remains suspended and is not accepted; it is not validated, it remains surrounded by an element of uncertainty. It is only the third time, with the third alethurgy, when a new couple appears, that the truth is finally, not produced, because this had already happened, but this time accepted and validated, and can finally produce the judicial and dramatic effects that we expect of it. And this third couple that speaks the truth, this third couple of veridiction, this third wave of alethurgy, is presented by the messenger from Corinth and a slave, the shepherd of Cithaeron; together, once again combining the elements of their knowledge, they produce the truth. There is, then, Apollo and Tiresias on the level of the gods, Oedipus and Jocasta on the level of the kings and chiefs, and the messenger and the shepherd on the level of the slaves and servants. And it is the slaves and servants who produce the veridiction that the kings and the gods were unable to produce or, in any case, were unable to produce in such a way that they could be recognized as valid by the juridical institution. Three manifestations of truth, three alethurgies, three types of veridiction—this is precisely what I would like to study.[28] How did each of these veridictions unfold? How did each of these alethurgies unfold? And why is it the third that, in some way, worked? Why is it the third that effectively produced the truth?

So, turning to the first alethurgy, the first couple: the god and the seer. You will recall what has happened. The plague is raging in Thebes, and Oedipus has sent Creon to consult Apollo. Creon has returned from the oracle, and what has the oracle said? First, the plague will be vanquished through purification. "And why is purification necessary? Purification of what?" Oedipus asks. "Purification of a murder." But what murder then requires purification? The oracle's response, brought by Creon, is: "It is the murder of Laius." But who committed this murder? "Someone who is in this very country, who is in Thebes."[29] Such is the oracle's response, and not a word more is said because—as it is stated in the text—the god only says exactly what he sees fit to say.[30] We could say that we have, in one sense, half the story with this response from the oracle, because it is simply a denunciation by the god of a murder that was committed and whose victim is known to us. We know that it was this murder and this victim that brought on the plague. What remains is the other half, which in one sense must be discovered—namely, the half which is the assassin's identity. We know the victim; now we must learn who the assassin is.

Tiresias, who was also called as a witness by Oedipus, appears at this moment. Tiresias is in one sense Apollo's double, the god's double. He is his other side: blind, while of course the god sees all. And he is the one who is capable of interpreting what the god said and completing it with a complementary discourse, of saying who is the true assassin. Tiresias is interrogated in the juridically acceptable form of a reluctant witness. And since he refuses to tell the truth he knows, we see Oedipus's threats and how he reacts to the witness's refusal to say what he knows. Oedipus first blames him for the harm that has been inflicted upon his fellow citizens by his refusal to tell the truth[31]—that is his first reproach. The second reproach is graver still: "You have insulted the city and as a result not only have you wronged your fellow citizens, but the life and very existence of your city may be compromised by your attitude."[32] And finally, third, Oedipus reverses this refusal as he turns towards Tiresias, who refuses to speak, and makes an accusation against him: he suspects him of having committed the crime because he does not want to speak, or because he is speaking in a way that prevents proper understanding of what he is saying and whom he is accusing.[33] So when the seer is faced with Oedipus's accusation, he says everything. He tells all. He says: "Who committed the crime? It is Oedipus."[34] He even goes further and adds in the course of the discussion: "Not only did you assassinate Laius, but you also married your mother—Jocasta was your mother."[35]

So the truth has been spoken—the entire truth has been spoken, and in one sense the play could end here. Or rather, the problem arises of knowing why this truth, told in this way and by no small authority (after all, it comes from the oracle and a seer, and the text has insisted that they are never mistaken and always speak the truth), why this truth may very well be said under those conditions, and yet cannot be received. Of course it is not received by Oedipus; and we may well imagine that Oedipus's conduct is justified, since he would be accused, indeed he is the one accused by both the oracle's and the seer's responses. But what is more interesting, and what I would like to focus on, is the following: it is that the choragus and the chorus itself refuse the oracle's verdict. Or, in any case, they explicitly refuse to accept Tiresias's divination. For example, when Tiresias and Oedipus confront one another during the interrogation and Oedipus refutes Tiresias's accusations, the choragus says: "Anger has gotten the best of both of you, Oedipus and Tiresias."³⁶ And once Tiresias retreats, the chorus says: "I cannot believe what Tiresias has said. I can neither believe it nor refute it. What can I say? I do not know."³⁷ That is to say that the choragus and the chorus refuse to take sides between the two. Why do they refuse to accept the words of such sacred authorities? I believe that if we look at the way these words are presented in the play, we can understand why they are unacceptable for the choragus and the chorus.

First, the word of the god and the word of the seer are words that are only pronounced if the god and the seer desire it. This is emphasized on a number of occasions: no one can force the god to speak if he does not want to do so. And when Oedipus presses Tiresias, the seer, to speak, he responds: "But you do not command me, only the god does. I am the servant of Loxias and thus I will speak if I want to."³⁸ The refusal to speak, legitimated by the fact that the god is the god, and by the fact that the seer is the god's servant, is entirely typical. He refuses the politico-judicial authority that could and will, as we shall see at the end of the play, legitimately extract an avowal, testimony, or declaration. Within the judicial order, one is obliged to speak. And if one has the right to say during the interrogation, "I refuse to speak because I am not forced to obey you," then at that moment the judicial machine cannot work. So first, this word is only spoken if it wants to be spoken.

Second, it is a word that has a curious or strange relationship to the truth, or that is not in any case the relationship that an ordinary witness would have with the truth. Tiresias says as much: "The force of truth resides in me."³⁹ And the chorus responds to the prophecy of the god by saying: "It is shining and brilliant, the word gushes forth from snowy Parnassas."⁴⁰ That is, we are dealing with a word that has authority in itself, that decides for itself to speak or not, and that carries the truth by natural right. It holds the truth in itself: truth dwells within it, or it dwells within the truth. There is a bond of belonging between the word of the god, the word of the seer, and the truth. It is for this reason that they use the verb *phēmi*—I pronounce, I affirm.⁴¹ When it is used in the strictest, emphatic sense, *phēmi* means: "When I speak, I affirm that what I say is true." The affirmation, and the fact that I affirm it, is sufficient to constitute the law, the assurance, and the guarantee of this truth.

Third, the third aspect of this word is that it justifies itself through a seeing, but a peculiar form of seeing, naturally. First, of course, because as far as the god Apollo is concerned, he sees everything—there is, in fact, no difference between what Apollo sees and what he wants: he wants what he sees and he sees what he wants. It is sufficient that he see it for it to become effectively, sooner or later, truth and reality. On the other hand, the seer also has a peculiar relationship to what is said and what is seen—first of all because he is blind (and Oedipus does not miss the opportunity to remind him: "You are a blind man whose ears are as closed as his eyes. You live in darkness").[42] And at the same time, the seer, who sees even though he is blind, sees the future as he does the present and the past (so the seer says to Oedipus: "You do not see what misery you find yourself in at this moment. You cannot anticipate the flood of disaster that is going to ravage you and your children").[43] Which is to say, everything that humans cannot see (because it lies in the future and has not yet happened), the seer sees in an atemporality that is characteristic of his relationship to the truth.[44]

It is entirely understandable why Oedipus does not recognize himself in this word—in such a prophetic, oracular, or divine word. He cannot recognize himself in these accusatory words. And he says as much to the seer: "You speak nothing but foolishness.[45] You speak in vain."[46] The words are empty. Nor can the chorus recognize such words, or rather, it cannot recognize the validity of its own words. What I would like to emphasize, then, is that throughout this play there is a perpetual correlation between Oedipus's recognition of who he is and the chorus's recognition of the juridical validity of the truth. Oedipus will only be able to recognize himself once the chorus has recognized the validity of what is said. Oedipus cannot recognize himself in the words of the seer and the oracle of the god, and neither can the chorus recognize their validity. I believe that the chorus that is sung at this moment, after Tiresias's departure, is important because it shows the chorus's function throughout the play: the chorus is the body that tests, accepts, or refuses, and establishes the truth told. And no sooner has Tiresias left than the chorus begins its chant.

This chorus is very interesting and merits close study. There are two parts to the chorus. The first part is dedicated to the oracle and oracles in general. The chorus says the following: "Yes, the oracles tell the truth. When the oracle pronounces its word, we can be sure that what it says has happened, is happening, is going to happen. The arrow has been released, and the one who is targeted had better hurry and run quickly because the arrow is already behind him and will get to him no matter what. He runs and he should run, but he is condemned nonetheless. The arrow was released out of the flames and lightning."[47] We are in a world which is of course a world of fate, which is a world of brilliance and of light, which is therefore the world of the truth and the world of the inevitable.

And yet—this is where the second part of the chorus begins—the chorus says: "Yes, but this does not apply in my case." It isn't said exactly like that; it reads, "The arrow has been released amidst the flames and the lightning—but as for myself, my opinion drifts in the wind. I can neither believe nor deny what Tiresias has said. I see nothing, neither in front nor behind me."[48] In counterpoint and in opposition to the world of fate, atemporality, pure light, and the brilliance of the lightning that manifests the truth and guarantees destiny, the chorus asserts its right not to believe, not to know—its right to remain in the dark and only see precisely what is presented. Nothing beyond, in the realm of the future (or rather, for the Greeks, in the realm of the future, which is situated behind oneself), and nothing in the past (or what is in front of oneself).[49] It only has access to the imminent, and the chorus makes this explicit in stating: "Zeus and Apollo are clairvoyant, they are learned in the destiny of mortals, but humans? Humans?"[50] And the chorus then poses the question of Tiresias, the seer. It states: "Can the seer tell the truth?" Well, it says, "Can one truly claim that, among men, a seer possesses gifts superior to mine?"[51] And obviously, the very fact that it asks the question implies a negative response: "The seer does not have talents superior to my own," it says, "and if it is true that there are some men who know more than others, then they still must provide proof."[52]

I believe we have two important elements here. First, no one has talents superior to the chorus—that is, in the order of truth of this moment, there is no body that is superior to that of the just or of the assembly, to the power that, in the form of the tribunal, decides what is true and what is not, who is guilty and who is not. Consequently, this judicial body is superior. Second, this judicial body must function through proof, and in this context the chorus continues to speak of Oedipus, stating that he has provided proof. He has given proof of his wisdom and of his love for Thebes (of course, this is a reference to the Sphinx and to Oedipus's victory over the Sphinx). Since he has provided proof, only proof may count against him: "Before having seen," idioimi, says the text, "justification of the god's spoken words, I cannot approve them."[53] Idoimi, phanera:[54] this entire series of words suggests that we are in the order of seeing, but no longer a seeing that is of divine light, that both brings things forth and seals one's destiny. It is no longer the divine sight that cuts through time and is atemporal. What the chorus demands, and what prevents it from accepting what was so clearly spoken in the oracular veridiction, what it wants are visible elements, proof, a demonstration. The truth of seeing, seeing for oneself, seeing that constitutes proof—this is what the jury demands. This is what the chorus and the choragus seek. And this is why the first veridiction—in spite of the fact that everything was said—is refused, is sidelined.

Thus begins—I will skip a certain number of elements, in particular the episode with Creon that we may return to in the discussion later—thus begins the second alethurgy, the second wave of veridiction. This alethurgy takes place not on the level of the god and the seer, but on that of the kings, between Jocasta and Oedipus. Following Tiresias and Creon's departure, Jocasta is the first to intervene, and she picks up precisely where the chorus ended: that is to say the problem of prophetic and divine veridiction. Jocasta affirms, "If the god wants to reveal things, he can do so perfectly well and he knows perfectly well how to do so himself."[55] As for the seer, she says, "You'll see," addressing Oedipus, "that no human creature has ever possessed the art (techne) of predicting."[56]

I will return in a few moments to this problem of techne, but I think that Jocasta's first intervention situates the problem or the question well. Can there be a techne of prediction? And if there is not a techne of prediction, can there be another technique to produce the truth? On the basis of this refusal of divine and divinatory veridiction, Jocasta says: "That the seers do not possess the art of predicting, of that I am going," Jocasta says to Oedipus, "to give you the proof."[57]

"I am going to give you the proof of this." This scene of the proof, of the demonstration that the art of prediction is unfounded, this demonstration unfolds throughout the scene by means of an intervention by Jocasta, of a dialogue with Oedipus, and finally of a monologue or account by Oedipus. There are three elements, then: Jocasta, the dialogue between Jocasta and Oedipus, and Oedipus's monologue-account.

The initial element (that of Jocasta) and the terminal one (Oedipus's monologue): these two elements correspond to one another—they are absolutely symmetrical. In her first intervention, Jocasta demonstrates that predictions do not tell the truth by explaining to Oedipus what she did to prevent her own son from killing Laius in spite of them. At the end of the scene, in continuity with the demonstration that the seers do not tell the truth, Oedipus explains how, in spite of the prediction that he was to kill Polybius—in spite of the prediction that he was going to murder his father—he succeeded in not killing the one whom he believed to be his father, namely Polybius. We have here, with these two elements, initial and final, the deployment of human processes through which, first, one escapes the seers' predictions, and second, one may thereby show that the predictions of the seers do not tell the truth.

In between these two elements is a long dialogue between Oedipus and Jocasta that unfolds, once again, in the form of questions and answers, like in testimony. Oedipus interrogates Jocasta and asks her a number of questions. He interrogates her like a witness. Based on what? Based on what she has learned about the death of Laius: what she was told, public rumors, her memories, Laius's physical bearing, the number of people who accompanied him, and whether anyone survived or not. In short, it is an entire inquiry based on what Jocasta may have known or learned. And naturally, the truth is uncovered and is practically told through this game of questions and answers. It is almost told and yet it is not accepted—neither by Oedipus nor by Jocasta, who refuse to hear truly what they are saying. They are not going to draw the final conclusions that would allow them to identify and recognize themselves in the episodes that they themselves have just told. So they escape.

How do they escape? Well, first they escape because an element is missing in this story they tell; or rather there is an ambiguous element in their story, which is the number of people who killed Laius. The reported testimonies, the public rumors, and all the information that Jocasta could gather suggest that Laius was killed by several persons. Yet Oedipus, himself, who fears and is almost certain that the person he killed was Laius, knows full well that he was alone when he killed him. So this element provides a degree of uncertainty through which they may escape this hint of this truth that they are in the process of discovering. And then, they also escape the truth they have discovered by convincing themselves that one can escape destiny and that human technique allows one to pass through the web spun by the gods. Laius could not have been killed by his son, since he took all the precautions necessary to prevent it from happening.

The truth is told, then, but it remains unacknowledged by Oedipus. It is a truth in which Oedipus does not yet recognize himself, even if he is the one who formulated it. At this point the chorus intervenes for a second time. This intervention is also of capital importance because it is both very similar—very symmetrical to the one I evoked earlier, after the first wave of veridiction—it is at once similar and symmetrical and at the same time much less clear. First of all, this intervention is a reverse image of the first. In the first, you'll remember, the chorus began by affirming the omnipotence of the gods. It made reference to the arrow of the gods that always hits its target. But in the face of this, because it could see neither into the future nor into the past, it had asked for solid proof. In the chorus that follows the discussion between Oedipus and Jocasta, things, the unfolding of the text itself, is reversed. First, the chorus opens strangely with a curse against tyranny and excess, against the arrogance of tyrants who believe they are at the height of their fortune and then fall to the deepest depths.[58] After this curse against tyranny, they speak once again of this famous question of oracles—oracles about which it was stated in the first chorus that while their declarations were true, of course, something else was necessary. Here in this second chorus, the question of the oracles comes at the end, and what is proclaimed is the necessity of respecting them. They were insufficient in the first chorus, but now they must be respected absolutely; and cursed be those who refuse to accept the lesson of these oracles, who refuse to accept what is said by the oracles.[59]

There is then something slightly enigmatic that we must try to explain. Why on the one hand do Jocasta and Oedipus speak the truth, but remain incapable of recognizing themselves in it? And how is it possible, on the other hand, that the chorus, without of course saying that it recognizes the truth of what has been said, nevertheless ceases to take Oedipus's side directly? The chorus has an ambiguous and strange attitude when it criticizes tyranny and celebrates the oracles. As in the previous situation, where it was a question of asking ourselves what was exactly this divine veridiction (what was its form, and why was it unacceptable from the point of view of justice), I believe that here too we have to examine Oedipus's veridiction. How did he speak the truth and what did he know? In other words, instead of investigating Oedipus's ignorance, as we usually do, I would like to take a quick look at what he knew and how he knew it, because he knew quite a bit. Oedipus is full of knowledge.[60]

In the course of Oedipus and Tiresias's discussion, there is a remarkable passage: it is when Tiresias pits an accusation against Oedipus that the latter believes (and truly believes) to be false. Oedipus exclaims abruptly: "*O ploute kai tyranni technē technēs*—what jealousy you incite."[61] "*O ploute tyranni technē technēs*," oh wealth, oh tyranny—power, sovereignty, "crown,"[62] in Mazon's translation—and "*technē technēs*," supreme art. By evoking the three elements of wealth, tyranny, and supreme art, Oedipus naturally is attributing them to himself. If Tiresias is envious of him, it is because Oedipus has wealth, power, and *technē technēs*.

That power be accompanied by these two attributes seems important to me. The coupling of wealth and the exercise of power, of wealth and sovereignty, of wealth and tyranny (with all the ambiguity this last word implies), this coupling is classic and commonplace: one exercises power because one is rich, or one becomes rich because one exercises power—in any case, the joining of these two things poses no problem. On the other hand, what is this *technē technēs*, this supreme art or supreme knowledge, which constitutes the third element in the trilogy and symmetrically joins tyranny and wealth? It is rather remarkable, I think, because in the ancient texts, while power and wealth are always associated, power is never associated with the notion of *technē*. Power is never associated with the idea of technical knowledge or a particular art. On the other hand, it is a theme that is, as you know, absolutely capital and important in philosophical and political discussions of the fifth and fourth centuries. The entire discussion among the Sophists, Socrates, and Plato turns around this question: can the exercise of political power be considered a *technē*, a technique that can be learned, that can be taught, that can ensure that the political man exercise power just as it ensures an architect the ability to construct a house? This expression of *technē technēs* is important precisely because later on it becomes the traditional expression for designating government—government not only in the global general sense of a political art, but also, as you know, in the sense of the government of individuals by one another, the government of souls. The expression *technē technēs* will be used all the way up through the Christian pastoral to designate the manner—and therefore the art, the technique—that allows for the government of souls and for their guidance toward salvation.

Let's return to Oedipus's notion of *technē*. What is Oedipus's *technē*, and why is he able to evoke *technē technēs* in speaking of himself and his power? I believe that here Oedipus should be compared to two other characters who are specifically lacking in *technē* even though they exercise power.

First, with Creon—Creon who is of course his brother-in-law, the brother of Jocasta, and whom Oedipus sent to Delphi to consult the oracle. Creon returns and reports what the oracle says, and Oedipus accuses him of having falsified the oracle's response. Oedipus then accuses him of being one of Tiresias's accomplices and of trying to seize his power. Creon responds to this accusation by saying: "But you know very well that

I could not be jealous of you, nor do I have the desire to take your place and exercise power in your stead, because I have a good life."[63] This line of reasoning takes the form of a defense and is typically Sophist: in order to dismiss an accusation, one shows how implausible it would be (such a technique can be found in Antiphon, for example) to do that of which one is accused.[64] Thus, "It is completely implausible that I would want to take your place because I have a good life." And what is this good life that Creon describes? Well, he says, it is "the life of a king." It is "the life of a king in which I am given gifts, I am solicited, one seeks my favor, and I am surrounded spontaneously by honors. And all of this, thanks to my birth. As a result, I have no worries. The people give me gifts and you, Oedipus, shower me with kindness."[65] In other words, Creon's own description of himself is that of someone who lives like a king without being a king, or rather, without himself governing. He has *archē*, the highest rank. He has *dynasteia*—in other words, power. And he does not have *tyrannis*, he does not have tyranny—that is, he does not individually and personally exercise power.[66] Everything comes to him from his status. Everything comes to him from his prerogatives. Everything comes to him from this precedence. Therefore, he does not need *technē*; he does not need art, knowledge, or savoir-faire to have his place or benefit from it. This is why he will be able to use a very important word in speaking about himself; he will say that he is *sōphrōn*,[67] that he is wise, that he is thoughtful, that he is tempered. As he does not exercise power and does not need *technē*, the virtue that he is going to practice is good measure. This will allow him to avoid being either arrogant or excessive with regard to others while all the same exercising his precedence and prerogatives. The fundamental virtue of these aristocratic prerogatives is to be *sōphrōn*. And thus, there is no *technē*.

As for Tiresias, can we say that he too has a *technē* like Oedipus? The word *technē*, in Sophocles's text, is mentioned three times with regard to Tiresias, but each time in an entirely ironic sense. Oedipus uses the term *technē* twice with regard to Tiresias.[68] First, when Oedipus says to him, "But, at the moment when the Sphinx was ravaging the Theban lands, were you already exercising your *technē*?" This is a way of saying, "If you, Tiresias, you had *technē*, what were you doing with it and why did you not apply it at the moment when the Sphinx was destroying Thebes? You did not have *technē* then, did you?" In the same way, a little later, Oedipus tells him: "But with all of your *technē*, or your so-called *technē*, something that could be considered a technique, you were incapable of solving the enigma." And finally, Jocasta uses the term *technē* a third time with regard to Tiresias when she says, in the passage that I brought up earlier, "No mortal has ever possessed the *mantikē technē*, the art of divination."[69] That is, the seer does not have *technē* and the idea of a *mantikē technē*, a divine art, cannot be sustained.*

: : :

The gods [*inaudible*] are certain; men simply have *tekmērion*—they have the sign, they have the trace, they have the mark.[70] The word *tekmērion* can also be found in Aristotle to mean proof—it is what allows for demonstration. In the text of *Oedipus Rex*, it seems to me that *tekmērion* is used above all to designate a knowledge trajectory; it allows one to go from what one doesn't know to what one does know (and to constitute oneself as a subject who knows, even though one is ignorant) through a number of trajectories that stretch from the present to the past, the past to the

---

* There is a break here due to the tape change. The change is responsible for a lacuna that can be filled from the original typescript, deposited at the IMEC, of an audio recording that has since been lost. In the following paragraph we reproduce the entirety of the extract from the original typescript with a few small spelling corrections:

> In fact, what characterizes Tiresias's practice is not the possession of *technē*. If Tiresias tells the truth, it is because there is a natural link between what he says and the truth. The truth dwells in his words—"I have the truth within me and you know it," Tiresias says. And this possibility of truth-telling without having recourse to *technē* allows Tiresias. . . When he speaks of what he does, he uses the word *phronein*; he thinks, he reflects, he turns inward on himself. It is within himself that, hearing the words of the god, he grasps the truth and tells it. There are then three elements, if you will: first there is the power of Creon, which is aristocratic and is exercised through the law and by the law of precedence—it is a power that implies *sōphronēma* as a virtue. There is the power of Creon, which is a power to know the truth and tell it, but which does not require any particular technique because there is a shared nature between the truth and what he says. There is the power of Tiresias, who took part in an activity and demonstrated his strength and virtue as a man through reflection on himself and through the original profundity of his thought. What does Oedipus do in relation to all this? What does Oedipus's *technē* consist of? For he has *technē* while the others do not. It consists of his ability to discover (*euriskein*). Those who speak of Oedipus make reference to this capacity for discovery. This is what characterizes his *technē*. The city called upon him so that he might relieve them (verse 27) and he announced his solution to all the people (verse 68). He accused the Thebans of not taking on the task of finding the murderer that he was going to discover (verse 258). He tries to discover the murderer himself (verse 340). He believes he has discovered the plot spun by Creon (verse 546) and then Tiresias tells him as well, does the knowledge of men . . . The gods are certain [. . .] (typescript, lecture of April 28, 1981, pp. 14–15).

present, from presence to absence, or from absence to presence.[71] From
the present to the past: Oedipus explains that it is necessary to uncover
every moment of what happened the famous day that Laius was killed, on
the basis of what we have now before our very eyes—on the basis of witnesses who still exist, for example. Inversely, *tekmērion* is also what allows
us to return from the past to the present: this is what Jocasta would like
to do, and what she criticizes Oedipus for not doing. Starting from what
has happened—that is, from the fact that up to now it has been possible
to escape the predictions of the seers and the oracles of the gods—it must
be assumed that this possibility still remains open now, and that we are
not subject to predictions because we have been able to escape them thus
far. *Tekmērion* allows for the passage from presence to absence—that is,
by hearing the witnesses who are actually present, to try to uncover what
escaped and continues to escape understanding. It is a question of going
from the absence of those who merely heard or know that someone saw
something, to presence or witnesses who actually saw, heard, and were
there.

I believe that Oedipus's *technē* is this art of discovery that uses signs,
traces, and marks, that allows us to go from what we don't know to what
we do know by piecing together material elements that lead from one to
the other with high probability. And this art of discovery, Oedipus's art,
what does it shed light on? Certainly not the decrees of the gods, because
these are known to people like Tiresias in whom the power of truth dwells.
Certainly not the laws, those laws that the chorus says were born on Olympus and that no mortal could bring forth. Rather, Oedipus's *technē* allows
for the discovery of what he calls—he who calls himself son of *tychē*[72]—
it is what allows for the discovery of the meeting, of the event, of what
happens: the intersection between what happens to men—or the under-
takings of men, the agitations of men—and the gods' decrees. It is an
art of discovering, through clues, the events. To be more exact, we have
here an art, *technē*, which is attached—and Sophocles's text explains
this clearly—to two other *technai* of the same type: medicine, which is
mentioned twice, and the art of navigation, which is mentioned once.
Sophocles's text associates Oedipus's *technē* to these two other arts. This
trilogy—the art of governing, the art of healing, the art of navigation—
this trilogy, you know well, would remain absolutely essential to political thought up to the seventeenth and eighteenth centuries in the West.
During Sophocles's times, this classic trilogy made an analogy between

the political leader and the doctor and the pilot, demonstrating that there was a type of knowledge that was proper to the exercise of political power, and that this knowledge could not be reduced or summarized, nor could it really be based on what was said prophetically by the seers or by the gods. A knowledge that was proper to the exercise of political power — that knowledge had the technical form of a discovery of truth through material elements that are interrogated for their meaning or for their referents by means of a technique that was proper to the exercise of this knowledge.

This was of course an entirely novel idea at the time, an idea that was debated and in which one could recognize the idea that Oedipus was the man of *technē technēs*. For a Greek audience of the period, this was a perfectly contemporary discussion that was being articulated here and evoked in this way: philosophers and sophists discussed the very possibility of this new science of government, this new science that Oedipus laid claim to in connection with the exercise of political power or, more precisely, in connection with the exact form of the exercise of political power that was tyranny. Tyranny, of course, with the ambiguous meaning that it had in this period: tyranny which meant both the exercise of personal power by someone with the status of a hero and a privileged relationship with the gods that allowed him to give laws to the city; but tyranny as well — and this was the obverse side of the tyrant — as the man of excess or abuse who used his power beyond rule or measure. This in effect is what happens to Oedipus's *technē*: through his *technē*, Oedipus unleashes a series of investigations that ultimately uncover the truth by using the interplay of all the signs and signposts, all the *tekmēria*, that can be found. At the same time, though, with this same *technē* Oedipus believed he could escape the gods' decrees, and it is in this excess that he meets his doom. It is all very well that the *technē* of political power be sufficiently precise, sufficiently informed, sufficiently rational to discover the truth of things; but that one attempt to oppose the god's decrees with this *technē*, this is something that is inextricably linked to the very abuse of tyrannical power. This is how one may understand the chorus that brings the second alethurgy, the second veridiction, to a close when Oedipus and Jocasta, following the god and the seer, tell the same truth again.

The chorus may now be understood. First, the celebration of the laws, the *nomoi*, which, according to the chorus, all words and acts must obey: these *nomoi* are born on Olympus and no mortal gave birth to them. Second, in this chorus, the denunciation of the immoderation of the tyrant, who has his ups and downs and who, precisely, tries to escape what was fixed by the gods and by the laws in the exercise of his power; and a curse on those who display their pride, look only for wealth, and violate that which must not be violated. And lastly, the final point of the chorus, the elegy of the oracles that must be respected: with these tyrannical, violent, and excessive characters, who consider null and void and pretend to abolish the oracles brought to the old Laius, Apollo is deprived of all honor and, as a result, all respect for the gods disappears. The enigmatic chorus may be understood if its functions are placed in the context of the concluding scene between Oedipus and Tiresias. In that first chorus, it was a question of saying why the truth of the oracle was unsatisfactory. In the second chorus, now, after the second veridiction, it is a question of challenging Oedipus's knowledge or, rather, of picking up on the only part that conforms to *nomos* and, instead of condemning, of putting a malediction on that part of the *technē* that served to nourish the excesses of his tyrannical power.

Thus, the last alethurgy, the last production of truth, the last veridiction may begin. It is presented as being neither that of the gods (which was challenged for the reasons I mentioned) nor that of the kings (which was useful and fecund, but also had its excesses and its dark side). The veridiction that will be recognized is that of the servants. There are then two characters: the messenger from Corinth who comes to announce that Polybius is dead, and the shepherd of Cithaeron who Oedipus, with his *technē* and in search of *tekmēria*, went to find in the depths of his woods. These two characters, the messenger who arrives spontaneously and the shepherd who is summoned, are brought face to face. And at this point, of course, the truth appears through this confrontation. The chorus, for that matter, announces it in advance. Assuming in a paradoxical, almost ironic way the position of the prophet, it says: "If I am a good prophet, if the light reveals the truth to me, yes, by Olympus" — this is an explicit reference, at the moment when the truth is going to appear in the very mouths of the servants, to the oracle of the gods and the authority of the divine word — "yes, by Olympus, as early as tomorrow, you will see that the Cithaeron has become one of Oedipus's compatriots and the truth of Oedipus's birth will be known."[73]

How does this last alethurgy unfold? Well, it unfolds — entirely and exhaustively — like a true judicial interrogatoire that follows all the procedural rules.

First, there is the interrogation of identity. When the shepherd of Cithaeron arrives, Oedipus, in his role as chief justice, poses the question:
"Is this shepherd who has been brought to us truly the one who the messenger from Corinth once knew and who gave him the famous child who
was to be Oedipus?" So Oedipus asks the question, and he gives a first
element of response. He says: "I do not know him. I cannot even know if
he is the same. But I recognize the servants that brought him and those
servants are mine."[74] At this moment the choragus completes the point,
saying: "I recognize the shepherd. He is indeed the one who was in the service of Laius."[75] And the Corinthian, the messenger from Corinth, brings
the third element of recognition. Indeed, he says: "This man who I now see
before me is indeed the one of whom I spoke[76] and who in time past gave
me, handed me the child in question."[77]

After this interrogation of identity, the shepherd is questioned about
what he did and what happened. The shepherd, naturally, resists sharing
as much of his knowledge as possible. First, he refuses because he committed the fault of not killing Oedipus as Laius and Jocasta had asked of
him, and then because he knows full well that what he is going to say will
set off a catastrophe. But while the god could say at the beginning of the
play, "I only speak when I wish to do so," or in any case this is what was said
of the god, the god only speaks when he wants to; and while Tiresias could
say, "I do not obey you, because I am not your servant. I am the servant of
Loxias"; here, the shepherd will be obliged to speak. He is reminded that
he must speak. And since he is still reluctant, he is threatened with torture: "Bind his hands,"[78] says Oedipus, "I will make you speak or you will
be killed."[79] The threat of death punctuates the entire interrogation—this
was clearly stated in classical Athenian law: that is, to obtain an avowal,
torturing a slave was acceptable on the sole condition that it be authorized
by his master.[80] Now this was precisely the case here: Oedipus himself, as
the one who has power, who exercises power over the servant, threatens
him with execution, and consequently the servant is going to be forced to
tell the truth, to tell this truth, the truth of what he did. He is going to be
obliged to avow. And the interrogation, in effect, unfolds around a precise
point: what the witness himself did. It is no longer a question of prophetic
words. It is no longer this great vision that cuts through time. It is not this
light that comes from a released arrow. It is a question of what the witness
himself might have done. "Do you remember that I told you this?"[81] says

the servant of Corinth. "Who gave you the child? What was your intention in doing this or that?"[82] And the servant's response is grammatically very distinct. Each time the servant responds: "Yes, I myself found this child in the Valley of Cithaeron. Yes, I was keeping a herd. Yes, it was I who released your two feet."[83] "Yes, I am the one to whom Jocasta handed you."[84] "It is I who did not kill him—*autos*."[85]

I believe that we have here the very blueprint—and the introduction onto the stage—of this procedure of avowal, which is also characterized in the play by the acceptance of the chorus as being that which, as opposed to the other forms of veridiction, effectively produces an incontestable truth. For the truth to be juridically acceptable, it is not necessary that the gods speak. For the truth to be accepted, it is not necessary that it be produced by kings—because, if indeed they use the wise method of *tekmēria*, of signs, they may also use it to escape the destiny of the gods. With the slave, we have truthful speech [*une parole de vérité*], a truthful speech that does not even necessitate a consideration of the more or less probable signs that allow one to pull what one wants to know from what one doesn't know. This is a speech that is entirely true because the one who speaks may say: "Yes, I did that. Yes, I am the one, *autos*. I saw it. I heard it. I gave it. I did it."[86] And with this word, despite the fact that it emanates from the mouth of a slave who is threatened with execution, Oedipus's truth will appear. The chorus recognizes and accepts this truth. It alone ensures justice. And once this truth is effectively recognized, or rather, the very moment this truth is recognized by the chorus and by everyone—and by the spectators—at that moment, Oedipus recognizes himself. He recognizes himself as the one who did it all.

While all the elements of truth that he had already spoken, while all the predictions around him already told him, and had already told him on multiple occasions what had happened, Oedipus could only recognize himself when faced with an avowal—an avowal that, you will note, did not come from himself. Oedipus does not avow. What would he avow, in any case? Oedipus does not avow. The avowal comes from the slave. And it is when the slave produces this avowal, by means of this procedure, that Oedipus is able to say—recognizing himself and inhabiting in some sense this character that was designated by the slave's avowal—Oedipus is able to say: "In this way, all will be true in the end! I reveal myself to be the son of the one of whom I should not have been born. I reveal myself to be the husband of the one I should not have married. I reveal myself to be the murderer of the one I should not have killed."[87] In turn, Oedipus is finally able to say "I" about all his crimes.

Please excuse this somewhat long and, in any case, very partial reading of Sophocles's play. Do not think for a moment that I wanted to present anything like a global or exhaustive interpretation of *Oedipus Rex*. Nor should you think I wanted to present you with a chapter on the legal history of the emergence and establishment of avowal in Greek penal procedure. I simply wanted to show you how this procedure of avowal that was, if not recent at the moment when Sophocles wrote *Oedipus Rex*, at least a part of the judicial apparatus, part of a judicial practice that classical Athens was both proud of and celebrated but also questioned—it seems to me that it is interesting to see how avowal introduced itself with such solemnity into something as culturally and politically important as this ritual representation of law that the city of Athens gave itself.

I would like to underscore as well that Oedipus's realization advances exactly in step with the chorus's validation—or rather, what is discovered in himself, which is where most of the commentaries and analyses will end, this discovery of the self by Oedipus is fundamentally nothing more than the obverse side of the legitimate production of truth that is juridically acceptable and that is effectively accepted by the chorus. This legitimate truth is the one that is produced neither in the form of a prophecy nor in the form of a deduction through clues, but in the form of the interrogation of witnesses, the interrogation of oracular witnesses who are ultimately forced to avow what they have seen themselves, said themselves, done themselves.

Finally, what I wanted to emphasize is that, as you see, Oedipus, because he is a man of *technē*, finds himself placed between the prophetic word and the testimony of avowal. In one sense, we have Oedipus, with his *technē* and his tyranny as well, to thank for this procedure of searching out witnesses. He is the one who challenged the prophetic and oracular form of veridiction. He is the one who also wanted the interrogation of witnesses. He is the one who sent someone in search of the shepherd of Cithaeron. In this sense—and this is the good aspect of the tyrant—at this point he is still the savior of the city; he is still the one who righted the city; he is still the good pilot. And it is even thanks to this, thanks to this truth that is produced, that the city will possibly be saved. But—and this is the other side, that of tyrannical immoderation—in wanting to use the *technē* against the decrees of the gods in order to escape them, he simply tightens destiny's grip to the point of sealing the condemnation that had been spun for him.

In this sense, Oedipus was necessary for the truth to appear. He was necessary for the creation of this well-regulated form of the judicial machine that is capable of producing the truth. But he was eliminated, as a kind of "excess," now, by the very judicial machine he brought forth. And from the perspective of the foundation of law, the lesson of the tragedy is that the veridiction obtained by the correct procedure—while it did not take the same path as the word of the gods, even though one cannot dispense with it because the gods had spoken—this indispensable veridiction could do nothing but confirm, if properly done, the prophetic word of the gods. Oedipus's drama was his desire to escape the prophetic word of the gods precisely by establishing a procedure of veridiction. Once veridiction was obtained through the correct procedure—once the judicial machine functioned so well that it could extricate the most essential truth from the lips of the most unessential character (the slave)—at that moment, the truth that appeared through this purely human procedure in conformity with *nomos* and the law, this procedure only confirmed the prophetic words of the gods. This veridiction, thus developed and regulated in this way, does not obey the tyrant's excess: rather, it conforms with *nomos*, with the law, the law that comes from Olympus. And it is this law and fidelity to *nomos* that allows the truth-telling of the slave who saw to guarantee for the chorus the truth-telling of a seer who was blind. The public square that stages the judicial institutions assures, guarantees, and confirms what has been said through the flash of divine prophecy.

So this is how *Oedipus Rex* may serve not, once again, as a direct testimony of Athenian judicial procedure, nor as a direct testimony of its true history, but rather as the first dramatic representation of this relatively new judicial practice (relatively new at the time) that made avowal and all other regular procedures of avowal an essential piece of the judicial system.

Well, I have been a little long, so if you have any questions . . . .*

---

* One question is asked. It is inaudible. The recording ends.

[NOTES]

1. Foucault also analyzed *Oedipus Rex* in the following contexts: in 1971 in *Leçons sur la volonté de savoir: Cours au Collège de France. 1970–1971*, ed. Daniel Defert (Paris: Gallimard/Seuil, 2011), pp. 177–92; in March 1972 in a lecture given at SUNY Buffalo ("Le savoir d'Oedipe"), published in *Leçons sur la volonté de savoir*, pp. 223–53; in 1973 in "Truth and Juridical Forms," in Michel Foucault, *Power*, ed. James D. Faubion, pp. 1–89 (New York: The New Press, 2000), pp. 18–33; and in 1980 in *Du gouvernement des vivants: Cours au Collège de France, 1979–1980*, ed. Michel Senellart (Paris: Gallimard/Seuil, 2012), especially lectures of January 9, 16, 23, and 30, 1980. The theme of truth as the product of the confrontation of two half-truths was taken up again in the context of a comparison between *Oedipus Rex* and *Ion* in 1983. See Michel Foucault, *Le gouvernement de soi et des autres: Cours au Collège de France, 1982–1983*, ed. Frédéric Gros (Paris: Gallimard/Seuil, 2008), lectures of January 19 and 26, 1983, pp. 71–136; English edition, Michel Foucault, *The Government of Self and Others: Lectures at the College de France, 1982–1983*, English series ed. Arnold I. Davidson, trans. Graham Burchell, pp. 75–147. This comparison also takes up the themes of the necessary succession of moments of veridiction, a necessity that is carried over from the assumption of truth by the subject in *Wrong-Doing, Truth-Telling* to the right to speak in *Le gouvernement de soi et des autres* (French edition, p. 140; English edition, p. 152).

2. This is possibly a reference to the interpretation of the tragedy proposed by Sigmund Freud in *The Interpretation of Dreams* (1899). Foucault had contested Freud's reading as early as 1971 in his *Leçons sur la volonté de savoir*, where he referred to "Freud's error," as well as to that "of cultural theorists regarding Freud's error"—an allusion, according to Daniel Defert (in Foucault, *Leçons sur la volonté de savoir*, p. 193 n. 18), to Bronislaw Malinowski's book *La sexualité et sa répression dans les sociétés primitives* (Paris: Payot, 1939). For a similar reading see Jean-Pierre Vernant, "'Œdipe' sans complexe," *Raison présente* 4 (1967), pp. 3–20 (re-edited in Jean-Pierre Vernant and Pierre Vidal-Naquet, *Œdipe et ses Mythes* [Brussels: Édition Complexe, 2006], pp. 1–22); see also Bernard Knox, *Oedipus at Thebes* (New Haven: Yale University Press, 1957), pp. 4–5.

3. On this point see Louis Gernet, "Le temps dans les formes archaïques du droit," *Journal de Psychologie* 53 (July–September 1956), pp. 379–406; English translation, "The Concept of Time in the Earliest Forms of Law," pp. 216–39, in Louis Gernet, *The Anthropology of Ancient Greece* (Baltimore: Johns Hopkins University Press, 1968); see also Marcel Detienne, *Les maîtres de vérité dans la Grèce archaïque* (Paris: Librairie François Maspero, 1967), p. 130 n. 101.

4. Foucault mentioned this theatrical question on multiple occasions. On February 25, 1976, he offered a series of remarks on Greek tragedy as "tragedy of law," and on Shakespearean tragedies as "rituals of re-memorization of problems of public law," which he extended to the tragedies of Corneille and Racine. See Michel Foucault, *"Il faut défendre la société": Cours au Collège de France 1975–1976*, eds. Mauro Bertani and Alessandro Fontana (Paris: Gallimard/Seuil, 1997), pp. 155–57; English edition, Michel Foucault, *Society Must Be Defended: Lectures at the College de France, 1975–1976*, English series ed. Arnold I. Davidson, trans. David Macey (London: Penguin, 2004), pp. 174–75. On March 15, 1978, Foucault offered a series of remarks on the "theatrical practices of the reason of state." Here he evoked the appearance in the classical age of a "political theater with the functioning of theater as its opposite, in the literary sense of the term, as the privileged site of political representation and particularly the representation of the coup d'état." He observed that Shakespearean theater as well as the theater of Corneille and Racine offered "many representations of *coups d'état*." Michel Foucault, *Sécurité, territoire, population: Cours au Collège de France 1977–1978*, ed. Michel Senellart (Paris: Gallimard/Seuil, 2004), p. 271; English edition, Michel Foucault,

Security, Territory, Population: Lectures at the College de France 1977–1978, English series ed. Arnold I. Davidson, trans. Graham Burchell (New York: Picador, 2007), p. 265.

5. On this point, cf. Foucault, *Leçons sur la volonté de savoir*, pp. 161–93 (lectures of March 10 and 17, 1971). On the question of religious sullying, it is possible that one of the sources Foucault consulted was Louis Moulinier, *Le pur et l'impur dans la pensée et la sensibilité des Grecs jusqu'à la fin du IVe siècle avant J.-C.* (Paris: Klincksieck, 1952), a text which is discussed by Jean-Pierre Vernant in "Le pur et l'impur," *L'Année sociologique*, 1953–54, Paris, pp. 331–52 (reproduced in Vernant, *Mythe & société en Grèce ancienne*, Paris, François Maspero, 1974, rééd. 1982, pp. 121–40).

6. See Platon, *Œuvres complètes. Les Lois. Livres VII–X*, trans. and ed. Auguste Diès (Paris: Les Belles Lettres, 2003); English edition, *The Laws of Plato*, trans. and ed. Thomas L. Pangle (New York: Basic Books, 1980). Two excerpts from book 9 of *The Laws* are applicable to Oedipus's situation. The first establishes the punishments that must be applied when someone kills his father or mother (book 9, 869 a–c, Diès, pp. 121–22; Pangle trans., pp. 263–64). The second, which Foucault presents in detail later in the same lecture, establishes the procedures to be employed when the murderer is unknown (book 9, 874 a–b, Diès, pp. 128–29; Pangle trans., p. 269).

7. Sophocle, *Œdipe Roi*, verse 102, trans. P. Mazon (Paris: Les Belles Lettres, 2007), pp. 10–11; English edition, *Oedipus the King*, ed. David Grene and Richmond Lattimore (Chicago: University of Chicago Press, 1942), p. 15 ("Who is this man whose fate the God pronounces?). Note that the Greek word used here is *tychē* (fate); on the various significations of *tychē* in the text of Sophocles's tragedy, see Knox, *Oedipus at Thebes*, pp. 176–81.

8. Daniel Defert (in Foucault, *Leçons sur la volonté de savoir*, p. 192 n. 1) gives as the edition of reference *Œdipe-Roi*, in Sophocle, *Œuvres*, tome 1, ed. and trans. P. Masquenay (Paris: Les Belles Lettres, 1922). At Louvain-la-Neuve in 1981, Foucault also uses the translation by Paul Mazon without specifying the exact edition, which could therefore refer to either *Œdipe Roi*, in Sophocle, *Œuvres*, tome 2, ed. A. Dain and trans. Paul Mazon (Paris: Les Belles Lettres, 1972), or *Œdipe Roi*, in Sophocle, *Tragédies complètes*, trans. Paul Mazon (Paris: Gallimard, coll. "Folio," 1973). The references to the French text we will henceforth use will be to Sophocle, *Œdipe Roi*, trans. Paul Mazon (Paris: Les Belles Lettres, 2007).

9. On the notions of *mēnuein* and *mēnusis*, see Knox, *Oedipus at Thebes*, p. 80, on which, it would appear, Foucault rests his analysis here and in the following three paragraphs.

10. Ibid., p. 81.

11. Sophocle, *Œdipe Roi*, verse 132; Mazon pp. 12–13; Grene and Lattimore, p. 16 ("I will bring this to light again").

12. Cf. Knox, *Oedipus at Thebes*, pp. 80–81.

13. Sophocle, *Œdipe Roi*, verses 224–75; Mazon pp. 18–23; Grene and Lattimore, pp. 19–21; cf. Knox, *Oedipus at Thebes*, pp. 81–82; Detienne, *Les maîtres de vérité dans la Grèce archaïque*, pp. 48–59.

14. Thucydide, *La guerre du Péloponnèse*, book 6, sections 27–29 and 60–61, trans. Louis Bodin and Jacqueline de Romilly (Paris: Les Belles Lettres, 1955), pp. 21–22 and 44–46; English edition, Thucydides, *The Peloponnesian War*, ed. Martin Hammond and Peter John Rhodes (Oxford: Oxford University Press, 2009), pp. 322–23 and 339–40. Cf. Knox, *Oedipus at Thebes*, p. 82.

15. Plutarque, *Les vies des hommes illustres: Vie d'Alcibiade*, sections 18–23, trans. Dominique Ricard (Paris: Lefèvre, 1838), pp. 488–92; English edition, Plutarch, *Lives, Volume IV: Alcibiades and Coriolanus; Lysander and Sulla*, trans. Bernadotte Perrin (Cambridge, MA: Loeb Classical Library, 1916), chapters 18–23, pp. 47–67; cf. Knox, *Oedipus at Thebes*, p. 82.

16. Platon, *Œuvres complètes: Les Lois, livre IX*, 874a–b, ed. Diès, p. 128; trans. Pangle, p. 269.

17. Ibid., 874b, Diès, pp. 128–29; Pangle, p. 269.

18. Sophocle, *Œdipe Roi*, verse 319; Mazon, pp. 26–27; Grene and Lattimore, p. 23 ("What is this? How sad you are now you have come!"); cf. Knox, *Oedipus at Thebes*, at 84 and p. 226 n. 134.

19. Sophocle, *Œdipe Roi*, verse 432, Mazon, pp. 34–35; Grene and Lattimore, p. 29.

20. Cf. Knox, *Oedipus at Thebes*, p. 83: "But when Oedipus's appeal to the prophet is followed by Tiresias's disturbing regrets that he has come, we find ourselves suddenly in a familiar ambience, the examination of a reluctant witness."

21. Oedipus dismisses Tiresias by asking him to leave (see verse 431; Mazon, p. 34–35; Grene and Lattimore, p. 29: *apostrapheis apei*), but he does not use the term *aphes*, which indeed means "be gone." Foucault is probably citing Sophocles's text from memory. According to Knox, *Oedipus at Thebes*, p. 84, *aphes* is the technical term, in ancient Greek penal procedure, for release, acquittal, or dismissal.

22. Sophocle, *Œdipe Roi*, verse 642–43; Mazon, pp. 50–51; Grene and Lattimore, p. 38; cf. Knox, *Oedipus at Thebes*, at p. 90 and 229 (discussing Plato, *The Laws*, book 11, 936d).

23. According to Aristotle, histories are simple or complex depending upon whether the actions they imitate are simple or complex. An action that is "as one continuous whole, I call simple, when the change in the hero's fortunes takes place without Peripety or Discovery"; while a complex action is where the reversal takes place "when it involves one or the other, or both." Aristote, *Poétique*, X, trans. M. Magnien (Paris: Le Livre de Poche, 2008), p. 100; English edition, Aristotle, *Poetics*, in *The Basic Works of Aristotle*, ed. Richard McKeon (New York: Random House, 1941), p. 1465.

24. *Peripeteia*, a reversal. Aristotle cites Oedipus as an example: "Here the opposite state of things is produced by the Messenger, who, coming to gladden Oedipus and to remove his fears as to his mother, reveals the secret of his birth." Ibid., XI, ed. Magnien, p. 101; ed. McKeon, p. 1465.

25. Recognition or discovery (*anagnōrisis*), the other element of complex action, is the "change from ignorance to knowledge, and thus to either love or hate, in the personages marked for good or evil fortune." Ibid., XI, ed. Magnien, p. 101; ed. McKeon, p. 1465. Aristotle uses Oedipus twice as an illustration of tragic beauty. In chapter 11 he writes: "The finest form of Discovery is one attended by Peripeties, like that which goes with the Discovery in *Oedipus*." Ibid., XI, ed. Magnien, p. 101; ed. McKeon, p. 1465. In chapter 16 Aristotle writes: "The best of all Discoveries, however, is that arising from the incidents themselves, when the great surprise comes about through a probable incident, like that in the *Oedipus* of Sophocles." He then makes a distinction between four different forms of recognition (by distinctive signs, imagined by the poet, brought about by memory, and based on a deduction). Ibid., XVI, ed. Magnien, pp. 109–10; ed. McKeon, pp. 1471–72. Cf. Jean-Pierre Vernant, "Ambiguïté et renversement: Sur la structure énigmatique d'"Oedipe-Roi,'" in *Échanges et Communications: Mélanges offerts à Claude Lévi-Strauss à l'occasion de son soixantième anniversaire* (Paris: Mouton, 1970) vol. 2, pp. 1253–73; republished in Jean-Pierre Vernant and Pierre Vidal-Naquet, *Mythe et tragédie en Grèce ancienne* (Paris: La Découverte, 1972), vol. 1, pp. 99–131. Foucault refers to this study in his lecture of January 16, 1980, at the Collège de France in *Du gouvernement des vivants*; and Foucault, "Le savoir d'Œdipe," in Foucault, *Leçons sur la volonté de savoir*, p. 225.

26. This is possibly a reference to Marcel Detienne, *Les maîtres de vérité dans la Grèce archaïque*, p. 102.

27. The idea of truth being produced by two persons, in a couple, who speak in complementarity—what Foucault refers to in "Le savoir d'Œdipe" as the "law of halves" (p. 226)—refers both to the thematic of proof (Foucault, "Le savoir d'Œdipe," p. 229; *Leçons sur la volonté de savoir*, p. 191), and to what Marcel Detienne called the "secularization of speech" in

Les maîtres de vérité dans la Grèce archaïque, p. 81; see also Detienne, ibid., pp. 100–101, and Louis Gernet, "Le temps dans les formes archaïques du droit," 1982 edition, pp. 129–37.

28. In 1971, 1972, and 1973, Foucault analyzes Sophocles's tragedy not in terms of a succession of alethurgies, but instead as the clash of different types of knowledge [*savoirs*]. See lecture of March 17, 1971, and "Le savoir d'Œdipe," in Foucault, *Leçons sur la volonté de savoir*, pp. 189–92 and 225–51. The differentiation of types of knowledge, as Daniel Defert notes, was theorized by Foucault in his *Archaeology of Knowledge* (1969). The theorization of the different forms of alethurgy will be further developed and completed in *Le courage de la vérité: Cours au Collège de France, 1984*, ed. Frédéric Gros (Paris: Gallimard/Seuil, 2009), especially in the lecture of February 1, 1984; English edition, Michel Foucault, *The Courage of Truth: The Government of Self and Others II: Lectures at the Collège de France, 1983–1984*, English series ed. Arnold I. Davidson, trans. Graham Burchell (New York: Palgrave, 2011).

29.

> Creon: King Phoebus in plain words commanded us to drive out a pollution from our land, pollution grown ingrained within the land; drive it out, said the God, not cherish it, till it's past cure.
> Oedipus: What is the rite of purification? How shall it be done?
> Creon: By banishing a man, or expiation of blood by blood, since it is murder guilt which holds our city in this destroying storm.
> Oedipus: Who is this man whose fate the God pronounces?
> Creon: My Lord, before you piloted the state we had a king called Laius.
> Oedipus: I know of him by hearsay. I have not seen him.
> Creon: The God commanded clearly: let some one punish with force this dead man's murderers.
> Oedipus: Where are they in the world? Where would a trace of this old crime be found? It would be hard to guess where.
> Creon: The clue is in this land; that which is sought is found; the unheeded thing escapes. . . .

Sophocles, *Œdipus the King*, verses 96–111; Grene and Lattimore, pp. 14–15; Mazon, pp. 8–11.

30.

> Choir: . . . but since Phoebus set the quest it is his part to tell who the man is.
> Oedipus: Right; but to put compulsion on the Gods against their will—no man can do that.

Ibid., verses 278–81; Grene and Lattimore, p. 21; Mazon, pp. 22–23.

31. Ibid., verses 322–23; Mazon, pp. 26–27; Grene and Lattimore, p. 23.

32. Ibid., verses 330–31; Mazon, pp. 26–27; Grene and Lattimore, p. 24.

33. Ibid., verses 345–49; Mazon, pp. 28–29; Grene and Lattimore, p. 25. The enigmatic character of prophetic veridiction will become, in *The Courage of Truth*, one of the traits by means of which Foucault will distinguish this form of truth-telling from *parrhēsia*.

34. Ibid., verses 352 and 362; Mazon, pp. 28–29; Grene and Lattimore, pp. 25–26.

35. Ibid., verses 366–67; Mazon, pp. 28–29; Grene and Lattimore, p. 26; also ibid., verses 445–61; Mazon, pp. 34–37; Grene and Lattimore, p. 30.

36. Ibid., verses 404–05; Mazon, pp. 32–33; Grene and Lattimore, p. 28.

37. Ibid., verses 485–86; Mazon, pp. 38–39; Grene and Lattimore, p. 31.

38. Ibid., verses 408–10; Mazon, pp. 32–33; Grene and Lattimore, p. 28.

39. Ibid., verse 356; Mazon, pp. 28–29; Grene and Lattimore, p. 25.

40. Ibid., verses 473–75; Mazon, pp. 36–37; Grene and Lattimore, p. 31.

41. See, e.g., ibid., verse 362; Mazon, pp. 28–29; Grene and Lattimore, p. 26 ("I say you are the murderer of the king whose murderer you seek").

42. Ibid., verses 370–71 and 374; Mazon, pp. 30–31; Grene and Lattimore, p. 26.

43. Ibid., verse 413 and 424–25; Mazon, pp. 32–33; Grene and Lattimore, p. 28.

44. According to Jean-Pierre Vernant ("Figuration de l'invisible et catégorie psychologique du double: Le colossos," presentation at the conference on "Le signe et les systèmes de signes," Royaumont, April 12–15, 1962, in Vernant, *Mythe et pensée chez les Grecs, II* [Paris: Maspero, 1974], p. 75 n. 32), the seer, like the colossus, "belongs at the same time to the world of the living and to that of the dead. It's this ambiguity that is conveyed by the image of the 'blind person who can see.'" Cf. Marcel Detienne, *Les maîtres de vérité dans la Grèce archaïque*, p. 47.

45. Sophocle, *Œdipe Roi*, verse 433; Mazon, pp. 34–35; Grene and Lattimore, p. 29.

46. Ibid., verse 365; Mazon, pp. 28–29; Grene and Lattimore, p. 26.

47.

Who is the man proclaimed by Delphi's prophetic rock as the bloody handed murderer, the doer of deeds that none dare name? . . . For the child of Zeus leaps in arms upon him with fire and the lightning bolt, and terribly close on his heels are the Fates that never miss. [*Antistrophe*] Lately from snowy Parnassus clearly the voice flashed forth, bidding each Theban track him down, the unknown murderer. In the savage forests he lurks and in the caverns like the mountain bull. He is sad and lonely, and lonely his feet that carry him far from the navel of earth; but its prophecies, ever living, flutter around his head.

Ibid., verses 463–82, Grene and Lattimore, pp. 30–31; Mazon, pp. 36–39.

48.

The augur has spread confusion, terrible confusion; I do not approve what was said nor can I deny it. I do not know what to say; I am in a flutter of foreboding; I never heard in the present nor past of a quarrel between the sons of Labdacus and Polybus, that I might bring as proof in attacking the popular fame of Oedipus, seeking to take vengeance for undiscovered death in the line of Labdacus. [*Antistrophe*] Truly Zeus and Apollo are wise and in human things all knowing; but amongst men there is no distinct judgment, between the prophet and me—which of us is right. One man may pass another in wisdom but I would never agree with those that find fault with the king till I should see the word proved beyond doubt.

Ibid., verses 483–506; Grene and Lattimore, pp. 31–32; Mazon, pp. 38–39.

49. In his March 24, 1982, lecture in *The Hermeneutics of the Subject*, pp. 445–48 of the French edition and pp. 464–67 of the English translation, Foucault explains why, for the Greeks, one's back was turned to the future, so that one had the past in front of oneself and the future behind. This is helpful background to this intriguing passage. Thanks to Daniel Nichanian for this useful reference.

50. Sophocle, *Œdipe Roi*, verses 497–99; Mazon, pp. 38–39; Grene and Lattimore, pp. 31.

51. Ibid., verses 499–500; Mazon, pp. 38–39; Grene and Lattimore, p. 31.

52. Ibid., verses 502–6; Mazon, pp. 38–39; Grene and Lattimore, pp. 31–32.

53. Ibid., verses 504–6; Mazon, pp. 38–39; Grene and Lattimore, p. 32 (". . . but I would never agree with those that find fault with the king till I should see the word proved right beyond doubt").

54. Ibid., verse 508; Mazon, pp. 40–41; Grene and Lattimore, p. 32.

55. Ibid., verses 724–25; Mazon, pp. 56–57; Grene and Lattimore, p. 42.

56. Ibid., verses 708–9; Mazon, pp. 54–55; Grene and Lattimore, p. 41.

57. Ibid., verse 710; Mazon, pp. 54–55; Grene and Lattimore, p. 41.

58.

Insolence breeds the tyrant, insolence if it is glutted with a surfeit, unseasonable, unprofitable, climbs to the roof-top and plunges sheer down to the ruin that must be, and there its feet are no service. But I pray that the God may never abolish the eager ambition that profits the state. For I shall never cease to hold the God as our protector. [*Strophe*] If a man walks with haughtiness of hand or word and gives no heed to Justice and the shrines of Gods despises—may an evil doom smite him for his ill-starred pride of heart!—if he reaps gains without justice and will not hold from impiety and his fingers itch for untouchable things. When such things are done, what man shall contrive to shield his soul from the shafts of the God? When such deeds are held in honour, why should I honour the Gods in the dance?

Ibid., verses 872–96; Grene and Lattimore, p. 48; Mazon, pp. 66–67.

59. Ibid., verses 906–10; Mazon, pp. 68–69; Grene and Lattimore, p. 49 ("The oracles concerning Laius are old and dim and men regard them not. Apollo is nowhere clear in honour; God's service perishes").

60. Foucault had already privileged the knowledge of Oedipus, rather than his lack of knowledge or unconscious, in "Le savoir d'Œdipe" (Foucault, *Leçons sur la volonté de savoir*, pp. 234, 245, and 250–251). These themes concerning the will to know and Oedipus's knowledge are also developed by Vernant in his essay "Ambiguïté et renversement. Sur la structure énigmatique d'"Œdipe-Roi,'" and by Knox in *Oedipus at Thebes* (see especially the index entries for "Oedipus" at pp. 276–77, including "and the scientific spirit," "intellectual progress," "as investigator," "as questioner," "as revealer," "as teacher," "as discoverer," "as physician," and "as mathematician").

61. Sophocle, *Œdipe Roi*, verses 380–82; Mazon, p. 30; Grene and Lattimore, p. 27.

62. Ibid., verses 380–81; Mazon, p. 31; Grene and Lattimore, p. 27 ("Wealth, sovereignty and skill outmatching skill for the contrivance of an envied life! Great store of jealousy fill your treasury chests . . .").

63. Ibid., verses 583–86; Mazon, pp. 46–47; Grene and Lattimore, p. 36 ("Not if you will reflect on it as I do. Consider, first, if you think anyone would choose to rule and fear rather than rule and sleep untroubled by a fear if power were equal in both cases").

64. The reference here is either to Antiphon the Sophist, mentioned by Xenophon, or his contemporary, Antiphon the logographer, mentioned by Thucydides. The latter Antiphon was born around 480, and started out by devoting himself to the oratorical arts and writing defense pleas and speeches before playing a leading role in the oligarchic revolution of the Four Hundred; brought to justice after the fall of the oligarchs, he was sentenced to death and executed in 411 for having contributed to the overthrow of Athenian democracy. See Antiphon, *L'apologie d'Antiphon; ou, Logos peri metastaseos: D'après des fragments inédits sur papyrus d'Égypte*, ed. Jules Nicole (Geneva-Basel: Librairie Georg, 1907), at pp. 12–14. The question of knowing whether Antiphon the sophist and Antiphon the logographer were the same person is discussed by, among others, Louis Gernet in his introduction to Antiphon, *Discours*, followed by *Fragments d'Antiphon le Sophiste*, ed. and trans. Louis Gernet (Paris: Les Belles Lettres, 1923), a work that Foucault probably knew, and later by Gerard Pendrick in his introduction to Antiphon, *Antiphon the Sophist: The Fragments*, ed. and trans. Gerard J. Pendrick (Cambridge: Cambridge University Press, 2002).

65. Sophocle, *Œdipe Roi*, verses 587–600; Mazon, pp. 46–47; Grene and Lattimore, p. 36

("I, at least, I was not born with such a frantic yearning to be a king—but to do what kings do. . . . As it stands now, the prizes are all mine—and without fear. But if I were the king myself, I must do much that went against the grain. . . . Now every man's my pleasure; every man greets me; now those who are your suitors fawn on me,—success for them depends upon my favour. Why should I let all this go to win that? My mind would not be traitor if it's wise . . .").

66. Foucault is possibly making reference to the following verses in which three concepts are mentioned: *archē*, *dynasteia*, and *tyrannis*. "Comment pourrais-je donc trouver le trône [*turannis*] préférable à un pouvoir [*arkhes*], à une autorité [*dunasteias*] qui ne m'apportent aucun souci?" Ibid., verses 592–93; Mazon, pp. 46–47; Grene and Lattimore, p. 36 ("How should despotic rule seem sweeter to me than painless power and an assured authority?").

67. "Je ne suis pas né avec le désir d'être roi [*turannos einai*], mais bien avec celui de vivre comme un roi (*turanna dran*)." Ibid., verses 587–89; Mazon, pp. 46–47; Grene and Lattimore, p. 36 ("I, at least, I was not born with such a frantic yearning to be a king—but to do what kings do. And so it is with every one who has learned wisdom and self-control").

68. The word *technē* appears in the dialogue between Oedipus and Tiresias in verses 357 and 389. The first time it is mentioned is in the following line: ibid., verse 357, pp. 28–29; Grene and Lattimore, p. 25 ("And who has taught you truth? Not your profession surely!"). The word appears for a second time in the passage where Oedipus, after having deplored the jealousies generated by his wealth, power, and *technē technēs*, calls upon Tiresias, who is blind to his art. Ibid., verses 389–92; Mazon, pp. 30–31; Grene and Lattimore, p. 27.

69. Ibid., verses 708–9; Mazon, pp. 54–55; Grene and Lattimore, p. 41.

70. According to Knox (*Oedipus at Thebes*, pp. 122–23), this refers to a sentence of Alcmaeon of Croton, philosopher and medical theorist of the fifth century BCE, who used the verb *tekmairesthai* in a scientific sense, "to describe human knowledge as distinguished from that of the gods: 'The gods have certainty, for men there is inference.'" Ibid. at p. 123; see also ibid. at p. 239 n. 55.

71. The word *tekmērion* does not appear in the text of *Oedipus Rex*. However, the form *tekmairetai*, which is built from the same radical, is mentioned once by Jocasta. Sophocle, *Œdipe Roi*, verses 914–15; Mazon, pp. 68–69; Grene and Lattimore, p. 49; cf. Knox, *Oedipus at Thebes*, p. 123.

72. Sophocle, *Œdipe Roi*, verses 1080–1081; Mazon, pp. 82–83; Grene and Lattimore, p. 58 ("But I account myself a child of Fortune, beneficent Fortune, and I shall not be dishonoured"). On this identification, see Vernant, "Ambiguïté et renversement: Sur la structure énigmatique d"Œdipe-Roi.'" Note that Foucault had already cited this verse in "Le savoir d'Œdipe," where he referred to it to characterize tyrannical power (p. 236) and knowledge (p. 243), and in both cases associated it with Oedipus's pride.

73. Sophocle, *Œdipe Roi*, verses 1087–1107; Mazon, pp. 82–83; Grene and Lattimore, pp. 58–59.

74. Ibid., verses 1110–16; Mazon, pp. 84–85; Grene and Lattimore, p. 59 ("If some one like myself who never met him may make a guess,—I think this is the herdsman, whom we were seeking. His old age is consonant with the other. And besides, the men who bring him I recognize as my own servants. You perhaps may better me in knowledge since you've seen the man before").

75. Ibid., verses 1117–18; Mazon, pp. 84–85; Grene and Lattimore, p. 59.

76. Ibid., verse 1120; Mazon, pp. 84–85; Grene and Lattimore, p. 59.

77. Ibid., verses 1142–43; Mazon, pp. 86–87; Grene and Lattimore, p. 60 (The messenger from Corinth asks: "Do you remember giving me a child to bring up as my foster child?").

78. Ibid., verse 1154; Mazon, pp. 86–87; Grene and Lattimore, p. 61.

79. Ibid., verse 1158; pp. 86–87; Grene and Lattimore, p. 61.

80. On this point, see Louis Gernet, *Droit et société dans la Grèce ancienne* (Paris: Recueil

Sirey, 1955), p. 153, where he writes that "torture of slaves was commonly practiced in murder cases and there are many examples." Similarly, "the consent of the master" is necessary to ensure the appearance of the slave as witness because as "owner, he has the right of opposition." However, the text explains that "the faculty of witnessing excludes the use of torture. And yet, the torture of slaves was commonly practiced in murder cases and we have multiple examples [. . . .] The law declared that a slave's testimony was acceptable. As a result, it was not forbidden to use another means of evidence. In other words, the slave would only testify if the adversary consented. The adversary could insist that the slave be tortured." See the chapter "Aspects du droit athénien de l'esclavage," pp. 151–72; Knox, *Oedipus at Thebes*, pp. 97–98.

81. Sophocle, *Œdipe Roi*, verses 1132–40; Mazon, pp. 86–87; Grene and Lattimore, p. 60 (The messenger from Corinth says: "That is no wonder, master. But I'll make him remember what he does not know. For I know, that he well knows the country of Cithaeron, how he with two flocks, I with one kept company for three years—each year half a year—from spring till autumn time and then when winter came I drove my flocks to our fold home again and he to Laius' steadings. Well—am I right or not in what I said we did?").

82. The question is posed by Oedipus to the shepherd. Ibid., verses 1163–74; Mazon, pp. 88–89; Grene and Lattimore, pp. 62–63.

83. These elements are given by the messenger from Corinth:

Oedipus: Was I a child you bought or found when I was given to him?
Messenger: On Cithaeron's slopes in the twisting thickets you were found.
Oedipus: And why were you a traveller in those parts?
Messenger: I was in charge of mountain flocks. . . .
Oedipus: What ailed me when you took me in your arms?
Messenger: In that your ankles should be witnesses.
Oedipus: Why do you speak of that old pain?
Messenger: I loosed you; the tendons of your feet were pierced and fettered.

Ibid., verses 1025–28 and 1031–34; Grene and Lattimore, pp. 54–55; Mazon, pp. 76–79.

84. Ibid., verse 1174; Mazon, pp. 88–89; Grene and Lattimore, p. 63.

85. Ibid., verse 1179; Mazon, pp. 88–89; Grene and Lattimore, p. 63.

86. Foucault, in his *Leçons sur la volonté de savoir*, p. 179, portrays the shepherd of Cithaeron not as an avowing subject but rather as a witness, an *istōr*; and the same is true as well in "Le savoir d'Œdipe," p. 248. On the notion of the *istōr*, see "First Lecture," this volume, n. 29; see also Detienne, *Les maîtres de vérité dans la Grèce archaïque*, at p. 101; Gernet, *Droit et institutions en Grèce antique*, pp. 152–53; and Foucault, *Leçons sur la volonté de savoir*, pp. 77–78.

87. Sophocle, *Œdipe Roi*, verses 1182–85; Mazon, pp. 90–91; Grene and Lattimore, p. 63.

THIRD LECTURE

April 29, 1981

Hermeneutics of the text and hermeneutics of the self in early Christianity. • Veridiction of the self in pagan antiquity. • The Pythagorean examination of conscience: purification of self and mnemotechnics. • The Stoic examination of conscience: the government of the self and the remembering of codes. • The Stoic *expositio animae*: medicine of passions and degrees of liberty. • Penance in early Christianity. • The problem of reintegration. • Penance as a status that manifests a particular state. • The meanings of *exomologēsis*. • A life in the form of avowal, an avowal in the form of life. • A ritual of supplication. • Beyond the medical or judicial, the model of the martyr. • Veridiction of the self and mortification of the self. • From the public manifestation of the self as sinner to the verbalization of the self: temptation and illusion.

Following this prehistory of avowal borrowed from the Greeks, I would now like to move on to the history of avowal, of this avowal that has been so important for morality, law, religion, literature, institutions and, in short, all of Western culture. I think that this avowal, this avowal that interests us and whose form has penetrated into, if not dominated, so many of our practices and institutions, this avowal through which we are called upon to recognize ourselves—I believe that this avowal hardly existed before Christianity.

We are of course accustomed to characterizing Christianity as a religion that binds the individual to and through obligations of truth. However, generally speaking, when we think of the obligations of truth that Christianity imposes on individuals, we envision the truth of a dogma, we envision the truth of the text, we envision the truth of the tradition, or we envision the truth of a teaching which is guaranteed and authenticated, as you know well, by an institutional authority. But I think that Christianity also contains and has always contained another kind of obligation to truth that is situated in an entirely different dimension. It has played a role in the history of our culture and of our institutions, as well as the history of our subjectivity, that has been just as important as the obligations to what we might refer to as the faith.

Indeed, it seems to me that one of the most fundamental traits of Christianity is that it ties the individual to the obligation to search within himself for the truth of what he is. Christianity has bound the individual to the obligation to search for a certain secret deep within himself and in spite of everything that might hide this truth—a certain secret that, when brought into the light of day and manifested, must play a decisive role in his path towards salvation. Thus there is an obligation to search for the truth of oneself. There is an obligation to interpret this truth through all obstacles in order to take a decisive move or step toward one's salvation. And finally, third, there is an obligation not only to discover the truth, but to manifest it—to manifest it not only to oneself through a certain number of acts or actions such as examining one's conscience, but also the obligation to manifest this truth to others, or at least to one other, through a certain number of rituals, processes, and procedures that are, as you know, partially, but only partially, located in the sacrament of penance.

The obligation to look for the truth of oneself, to decipher it as a condition of salvation, and to make it manifest to someone else—it seems to me that this is a very different kind of obligation of truth from the one that ties the individual to a dogma, text, or teaching. And it seems to me that one of the great historical problems of Christianity was precisely to know what link could be established between one or the other of these obligations. How can the obligation to believe be tied to the obligation to discover the truth within oneself? How can the truth of faith be tied to the truth of the self? How could a textual hermeneutics and a hermeneutics of one's conscience be mutually articulated? It seems to me that this problem has spanned all of Christianity. In any case, it was precisely this problem that exploded in the fifteenth and sixteenth centuries and gave birth to the Reformation—the Reformation in general or, rather, the Reformations—Protestantism being the great enterprise through which Western culture, European culture, or Western Christianity tried to resolve this problem or to pose anew the link between the obligation to believe in the truth and the obligation to discover within oneself something that is a truth, which would be at once the truth of the text and truth of oneself. This was the great challenge taken up by Protestantism.

But this is obviously not what I would like to emphasize today, nor of course, a fortiori, to study. On the contrary, I would like to examine the specificity and singularity of this type of obligation to truth which is not the obligation to be committed to faith, but rather the obligation to a hermeneutics of the self. It seems to me that this obligation was of great importance in the history of Western religions—an event no doubt in the history of the traditional religions of the Mediterranean basin, which was equally fundamental in the history of subjectivity. If it is true that Christianity has often been credited with the curious invention of sin—a theme, an idea that can be easily criticized, I think, since it was no doubt unnecessary to wait for Christianity to discover sin—what is far more important for the historical definition of Christianity, for the very historicity of Christianity, is the fact that it never developed independently of these great techniques that it discovered, or at least fostered—these great techniques that were supposed to assure what I would call, referring to an expression I used earlier, the veridiction of oneself. The obligation to tell truth about oneself.

I would like to study this obligation in Christianity—at least in the early Christianity that we could say ended and culminated in Saint Augustine. In this evening's lecture I would like to quickly project spotlights on three areas. First, I will pass quickly over the problem of veridiction of oneself [*véridiction de soi-même*] in ancient civilization, primarily within philosophical practice before Christianity. This will serve as a reference map in sketching out the background, that will help to better situate, I hope, the specificity, particularity, and importance of veridiction of the self [*véridiction de soi*] in Christianity.* Then, in the second part, I will try to show

---

* Editor's note: We have chosen to use the term "veridiction of the self," rather than "veridiction of self," to translate the French term that Foucault uses, "*véridiction de soi.*" There are, to be sure, good reasons to use the neologism "of self," and there is an increasing tendency in Foucault scholarship to drop the particle "the" from "of the self," especially when discussing the later lectures. It can serve, possibly, to distinguish Foucault's use of "*de soi*" from his use of "*du soi*"—as, for instance, in "*vérité de soi*" (p. 110) versus "*vérité du soi*" (p. 167), or "*mortification de soi*" (p. 110) versus "*mortification du soi*" (p. 137). It could also be a way to distin-

you what veridiction of the self consisted of in canonical penance up to the fifth century. And then, in a third part, I will try to study veridiction of the self, not in canonical penance, but in monastic life and practices of the fourth and fifth centuries.

The first part, then, is veridiction of the self in pagan antiquity. This obligation to tell the truth about oneself, naturally, was not invented by Christianity. It was far from inexistent in ancient culture. Quite simply, to give you a few indications, you must first remember that the obligation to tell the truth—or at least, the incitement to tell the truth—existed in religious practices.

[On the one hand,] it could be found in the religious practices of the common people. For example, inscriptions have been found in numerous temples, at sites such as Epidaurus or Knidos, which show individuals, after having committed a fault, trying to seek the pardon of the god who has been offended by recognizing their fault—and recognizing it publicly.[1] For example, in the temple of Knidos a stele was recovered on which the party at fault recognizes that he is guilty of stealing and announces it publicly.[2] Other inscriptions have been found, for example, on which a vic-

---

guish between the formation of the self and situations where something is done to an already constituted self. These issues raise deep philosophical and linguistic challenges. In this edition we have chosen to remain more faithful to English linguistic usage, and, in this, we have been guided by the fact that Foucault himself, in the lectures that he wrote and delivered in English, used the term "of the self" and avoided the neologism "of self." See "Technologies of the Self," in *Ethics: Subjectivity and Truth*, ed. Paul Rabinow, pp. 223–51; and "About the Beginning of the Hermeneutics of the Self: Two Lectures at Dartmouth," ed. Mark Blasius, *Political Theory* 21(2), pp. 200–223 (the latter were also delivered in English at Berkeley and the audio files are available online). There are other compelling reasons to use "of the self." First, Foucault himself was not entirely consistent in his own use of "*de soi*" versus "*du soi*" in French, even when using the same substantive predicate. This is evident in these Louvain lectures, where Foucault varied his usage based on a possible play on words, alternating between "*hermeneutique de/du soi*" or "*vérité de/du soi*" depending on the parallel he wanted to draw; see also *infra* p. 144 (discussing techniques of the self, Foucault alternates between *de* and *du*, saying "*les techniques de, techniques du soi, technologies de soi*.") Second, the linguistic constraints in English are different from those of the French language. The term "of self" in English is a neologism, whereas in French "*de soi*" and "*du soi*" are both proper usage. Third, there are, naturally, profound philosophical questions about the ontological status of the self, its formation, its temporality, its constitutiveness, etc. These are deep philosophical matters that cannot be resolved by eliminating the particle "the" before "self." We prefer not to pretend to decide these important questions with a sleight of the translator's hand. Finally, there is a long philosophical tradition in the English language that addresses "the self" and which is in conversation with Foucault's work. Naturally, by using the term "the self," we do not intend to resolve these philosophical puzzles; instead, we take guidance from Foucault's spoken word in English and merely privilege a long history of English usage.

tim of theft asks through the inscription that the thief return the stolen clothes, and he asks that the clothes be returned and that the thief recognize his fault so that he may be pardoned.[3]

On the other hand, outside these religious practices [. . .] of the common people, procedures of avowal and confession of a fault were common in the Eastern religions that became increasingly important during the Roman Empire. Take, for example, Juvenal's famous sixth satire, where he explains that in the religion of Isis, when a woman has sexual relations with her husband on a day when she should have practiced sexual abstinence, she seeks out the priest of Isis, avows that she had sexual relations with her husband during a forbidden period and—thanks to the gift of a fattened goose—she is pardoned for the fault she committed through this gift and by this avowal.[4]

So there existed—I won't insist any further—a certain number of religious practices for avowing faults in order to be pardoned within common religious practices. But what I am far more interested in are practices of veridiction, discovery, and manifestation of the truth of oneself in philosophical practice and in the different philosophical currents, because they can be found throughout a number of transformations in monastic practice during the fourth and fifth centuries. And these practices of veridiction took on, I believe, two major forms: first, the form of examining one's conscience, and second, the form of exposing one's soul or *expositio animae* to someone such as a friend, a guide, or a director of conscience, et cetera.

First, there is the examination of conscience.[5] There is very early evidence of examining one's conscience in the practice and philosophical life of ancient Greece. The practice, as you know well, had its origins in Pythagoras—or at least the Pythagorean current. A number of Pythagorean verses were regularly recounted by a whole series of authors such as Plutarch, Arrian, Diogenes Laërtius, Porphyry, and Hierocles.[6] And these Pythagorean verses, which were cited throughout antiquity, were the following: "Do not allow sweet sleep to slide under your eyelids before you have examined each one of your daily actions. What have I done wrong? What have I done? What have I omitted that I should have done?"[7] And certain authors like Hierocles and Porphyry add two verses to these, which they also attributed to Pythagorean antiquity: "Begin with your first actions and follow them all. Then, if you find that you have committed a misdeed, upbraid yourself, but if you have acted correctly, rejoice."[8] It is generally accepted that these last verses by Hierocles and Porphyry are inauthentic.⁹ And indeed, their sonority is so clearly and so typically Stoic that there is little chance they belong to the ancient tradition of Pythagoras. Nonetheless, these ancient verses of the Pythagorean tradition are important because they attest to a well-established practice.

What is interesting in this call to examine one's conscience is, first of all, that it takes place in the evening—and you know full well, if you received a proper Christian education, that examining one's conscience is an evening activity. You are in this sense Pythagoreans. And the examination of one's conscience has been vesperal since the Pythagoreans for a very precise reason which is tied to Pythagoras's very doctrine: that is, in sleeping, we receive dreams; it is through the intermediary of these dreams that we are brought into contact with the spiritual or ideal world and, consequently, one must purify oneself before possibly coming into contact with this other world through the intermediary of sleep and dormancy. Just as one purifies one's body before coming into contact with a religious place or performing a rite, in the same way, purifying one's soul is necessary before coming into contact with the other world through dreams. And examining one's conscience is a purifying practice.[10]

It seems to me, on the other hand, that the Pythagorean examination had another meaning and value as well. Indeed, in one of the numerous texts that make reference to these verses in Pythagoras, and which can be found in Cicero's *De senectute*, Cicero says that the Pythagoreans recommend the examination of one's conscience in the evening—and, as a result, the memorization of what was done during the day—this is [. . .] *"memoriae exercendae gratia,"* in order to exercise one's memory.[11] Here again, you are no doubt familiar with the importance of memory practices among Pythagoreans,[12] for they [. . .] have been credited with the invention of mnemotechnics; in any case, the spiritual value of memory and the exercise of memory were fundamental for the Pythagoreans. Going over one's day, remembering everything that one has done, for good or for ill, has then both the value of purification in preparation for the other world with which we are going to enter into contact, and then the value of exercising the fundamental faculty of memory. It is a method of mnemotechnics.

I will skip the long history of these practices of direction of conscience in the different philosophical schools, which, I should add, is hardly known and difficult to study for lack of documents. Instead, I would like to go di-

rectly to what we might refer to as one of the last great forms of examining conscience in antiquity before Christianity: the Stoic examination
of the conscience, which is described precisely in the third book, section
36 of *De ira* by Seneca.[13] I would like to read the following passage to you:
"What is more beautiful," Seneca writes, "than this custom of investigating one's day? What blessed sleep is it that follows this review of one's actions. So calm, profound, and free is one's rest when the soul has received
its portion of praise and criticism and, subject to its own control and its
own censor, it secretly conducts a review of its own behavior. I exert this
authority over myself and every day I call upon myself, I summon myself
when the light has faded and my wife is finally quiet. I examine myself and
take stock of my acts and words. I hide nothing. I overlook nothing. Why,
indeed, would I fear anything among my errors when I can say to myself:
'Make sure not to do it again. I forgive you today. In such a discussion, you
spoke too aggressively: you did not correct the one who you were criticizing; you offended him.'"[14]

This examination of conscience poses a certain number of problems or,
at least, merits a few remarks. Of course, it is first of all paradoxical to see
Stoics like Seneca—even if Seneca is referring explicitly in these practices
to a habit of Sextius, which can also be found in Marcus Aurelius, to which
Epictetus also makes reference[15]—there is something paradoxical in seeing all of these Stoics accord such importance to a practice like examining
one's conscience, if the function of the examination of conscience was to
measure the importance of faults relative to one another and if the function of the examination of conscience was to measure in some sense the
gravity of the sin. Since, for Stoics, all faults are equal one to the other (it
is sufficient to have committed one infraction, regardless of its gravity; as
long as it is an infraction, there is no order of magnitude once one has committed a fault). So the text must be referring to something other than the
search for the degree of guilt.

What does the text say? To begin with, as in the case of the Pythagoreans, it appears that here as well, the examination is directly tied to sleep.
The examination of conscience appears to be a preparation for sleep. But
it does not seem that a Pythagorean purifying intention could be attributed to this Stoic practice. It seems to me that if the quality of one's sleep
is important and if the quality of sleep depends in part on this exercise of
the examination of conscience, it is because the quality of sleep reveals the

state of the soul, its tranquility, and the mastery one has maintained over all of one's desires and all of one's appetites. Good sleep reveals a tranquil soul that has mastered itself. These then are the preparations for sleeping.

Moreover, what is also noteworthy in this text, I believe, is the vocabulary that is used, a vocabulary that you see is not at all the medical vocabulary of the illnesses of the soul and of their symptoms. At least at first glance, it is a vocabulary that appears primarily judicial. One finds expressions that are manifestly juridical expressions: "*cognoscere de moribus suis*," "*causam meam dico*"—I plead my cause, I know such and such a thing.[16] It would seem then that the subject in this examination of conscience is, in regard to himself, at once the judge and the accused or, if you will, that in this examination he divides himself in two. On the one hand he accuses himself or judges himself, and on the other hand he is the one who is judged. In one sense, the examination organizes a judicial scene where the subject should play both roles at once.

But upon closer examination you will notice that, in spite of the two or three references to judicial practice, the vocabulary rings differently. In fact, the vocabulary is far more administrative than judicial. It is the vocabulary associated with the management of a possession, it is the vocabulary of the management of a territory, it is the vocabulary of government and administration. For example, in this text Seneca says that he is "*speculator sui*"—the *speculator*. He is the one who oversees the correction of an operation, who oversees that things have been done correctly.[17] It is also said: "*totum diem mecum scrutor*"—that he examines for himself the entire day that has passed.[18] And he also says that he repeats these practices with regard to the things that he could have said or done—"*remetiri*."[19] He is not, then, so much a judge of himself as an administrator; an administrator who, once the work is done or the year of management ends, makes an accounting, takes stock, and sees if everything has been done correctly. And when we see what the faults were for which Seneca reproaches himself at the end of the examination of his conscience—you'll remember that at the end of his examination of conscience he remembers having spoken too aggressively in a discussion with someone, or not to have properly corrected someone he criticized because instead of criticizing in a way that would have edified him, he merely offended him—these different faults that he discovers in his examination of conscience are nonetheless of a curious nature. Because, can we truly speak of faults here? In fact, he says it himself, they are errors; he made a mistake, rather than having committed something like a sin or a fault. And why did he commit these errors? Because he did not sufficiently bear in mind the ends that should guide the sage. When, for example, a sage has a relationship with another, he must see to the good of the other. He should have acted in such a way that his criticisms would have done the other some good, but they did not. He did not attain the end he should have set for himself; and according to this measure—in relation to this inability or this error in his calculation that prevented him from achieving the proper result—there is something that the examination of one's conscience had to reveal and note. He did not appropriately apply the rules of conduct that could be deduced from the general principles that must regulate the conduct of individuals.

Here, consequently, the examination of conscience takes the form of memorizing acts committed during the day—but the primary aim of this memorization is to reactivate the fundamental principles that must regulate the conduct of individuals, and the examination must also permit to better adapt one's conduct to these fundamental principles. Here again, it is an undertaking of memorization, a form of mnemotechnics. But, in contrast to the [Pythagoreans], for the Stoics one is not simply cultivating the art of memory.* One cultivates this art of memory, or rather one performs an act of memory in order to remember and reactualize, to better inculcate in one's thought and in one's conduct, the rules and codes that must govern in general one's behavior in life.

As you can see, this examination of conscience cannot, under any circumstances, be considered a search to discover a truth hidden deep within the subject himself. It is not a question of discovering a truth that has been hidden deep within the self, but of remembering and memorizing a truth that one may have forgotten, or a truth that may be forgotten the next day. It is a question of memory, then, that does not go in search of something forgotten deep within oneself, but that addresses a code of conduct that must be constantly remembered for fear that one day it will be forgotten. And what the subject forgets is not himself, it is not his nature, it is not his origin, it is not such and such a fault. It is what he should have done, it is the set of rules of conduct. Remembering the errors committed during the day serves to measure the distance between what was done and what should have been done.

The subject practicing such self-examination is not the site of some

---

* Foucault said "Stoics."

more or less obscure processes that must be decoded and brought to light. In this case, the subject is nothing more, essentially, than the intersection between rules of conduct that must be remembered and the point of departure for future actions that should conform to this code. The subject is situated at precisely the point of intersection between the code and actions; and the act of examining one's conscience is situated exactly there. Did indeed one's actions conform to this code? And, in taking this measure, one reactivates the code for future actions. Past actions, updating one's memory, and future actions: such is the functioning of Seneca's examination of conscience. It is by no means a hermeneutics of the self, nor the decoding of a secret that is sealed deep within oneself. There is no subjectivity in Seneca's examination of conscience.

There is a second text by Seneca which refers to a different practice, and which I would like to evoke here as well for its importance in ancient philosophy and for its future importance in Christianity and in monastic life: it is the problem of avowing to another and of the relationship to a director of conscience. This other text is found at the very beginning of Seneca's grand treatise *De tranquillitate animi*.[20] You know what this treatise is about. Seneca, in a more or less fictional way—but this is of little importance—opens his treatise on the tranquility of the soul with a request from his friend Serenus who has asked him for a consultation. The treatise *De tranquillitate animi* is the response to this request for a consultation.

So Serenus, Seneca's young friend, asks him for counsel. And here the request takes the precise form of a medical consultation on the state of Serenus's soul, addressed to Seneca—I refer you here, for example, to Galen's famous text on the passions of the soul, where Galen speaks of medical consultations that are given by doctors, not for problems of the body but of the soul.[21] This is how Serenus addresses Seneca. "Why," says Serenus in this letter that is no doubt fictional but which Seneca attributes to him, "why wouldn't I avow the truth—*verum*—to you as one does to a doctor? I do not feel sick exactly, and at the same time I do not feel that I am entirely in good health."[22] And Serenus develops this point, stating, "Indeed, neither completely ill nor in perfectly good health, it is as if I were in a state of malaise, as if I were on a boat that doesn't move forward and is tossed about."[23] In short, he is seasick and he fears that he will remain at sea in this boat that is not moving forward, looking out toward solid ground—[the] solid ground, [that is,] the Stoic virtues towards which he would like to go, where he would like to land, whose solidity he is aiming for, but which remain inaccessible to him. So in order to escape this state of instability and at the same time of immobility, where he is at once agitated and standing still and incapable of landing on the solid ground of Stoic life, in this state of unstable immobility he decides "*verum fateri*," to avow the truth to Seneca.

What is this *verum*? What is this truth that Serenus tells Seneca when he approaches him as one would a doctor, explaining the state of his soul? What is this *expositio animae*, this genre or practice that was so important in philosophical life—and in individual lives, for that matter—and for the whole of a prominent social class in the Roman Empire? What is this relationship to a director of conscience? Is this *verum* that is given, that is, manifested in the *expositio animae*, are they faults, are they secret thoughts, are they shameful desires? No, not at all. In fact, when we look at the *expositio animae* that Serenus presents to Seneca so that he may perform his medical operation, the text appears to be an accumulation of frankly relatively unimportant details. Serenus explains, for example, that he uses the dishes he inherited from his father, that he loses his temper easily, and that he gets carried away when giving public speeches. In fact, underneath the apparent disorder of these seemingly anecdotal notations, it is easy to recognize, evidently, the three great domains that correspond to the three great modes of life traditionally found in Greco-Roman philosophy: the domain of wealth, the domain of political life, and the domain of glory. Acquiring wealth, participating in the affairs of the city, and gaining esteem or being honored by public opinion are a freeman's three great possible activities. These are the three great moral questions posed by philosophy: Should one search for wealth? Should one retreat or not from the affairs of the city? Is it worth searching for the esteem of others and immortal glory? Unlike the examination of conscience that we spoke of earlier, you'll notice that the framework of Serenus's exposé is not exactly defined by the real events of his past life. It is absolutely not determined by his biography. Nor does it make reference to a theory of the soul or of its elements. It is purely a traditional classification of the different types of activities that can be performed and of the ends that can be pursued. Serenus thus exposes his attitude, and ultimately his soul, in each one of these domains.

But what of his soul does he expose? And here there is a word that recurs practically throughout the text and seems to me to be an important thread with regard to each of the domains and their different aspects: the word "*placet*," "*mi placet*"—this pleases me, this does not please me. It is the guiding thread of his analysis. For example, in his relationships with others, he says: "It pleases me to do favors for my friends."[24] Or, with regard to riches and luxury, he says: "It pleases me to eat simple food and only to have the furniture I inherited. But, on the other hand," he says, "the spectacle of luxury pleases me."[25] Or "I take pleasure in inflating my speeches in the hopes that they will be retained for posterity."[26]

You see that by thus exposing what pleases him, Serenus is not at all looking to reveal those profound desires that Christians will consider to be some of the manifestations of a deep concupiscence that is always present but hidden. By enumerating what pleases him and what doesn't, he is simply indicating as precisely as possible the things to which he is attached and those from which he has already detached himself. "What pleases me is simple food, and what does not please me is to stuff myself like a pig; but the spectacle of luxury pleases me nonetheless, and I am content to be well received when I am invited by someone else."[27] Thus the equilibrium, or rather the spotting, of what pleases him and does not please him is not at all an index of the presence in him of a hidden desire or concupiscence. It is simply an indicator of liberty. It is an indicator of liberty that allows him to say: "This is what I can do without, and this is what I am still unable to give up."

This *verum* that he proposes to tell himself and that he proposes to tell Seneca, as if he were a doctor, is the test, in terms of pleasure, of the ties binding him to things he does not master. It is not at all the revelation of a hidden nature: it is, in fact, this *expositio animae*, what one might call an inventory of dependencies, quite literally—almost in the accounting sense—a statement of his liberty. Including, as with any accounting statement, the positive elements (all of the simple things that please him and that consequently demonstrate to what extent he has already detached himself), and all of the negative elements (all of the pleasures that still tie him to the things he cannot master).

One must therefore understand Serenus's avowal as the enactment [*la mise en œuvre*] of a corpus of moral rules that he knows well. He is responding, as it were, to an everyday questionnaire that has been accepted by everyone. If we wanted to make this questionnaire explicit, it would be something like this: "With regard to money, where are you on the scale of liberties? Where are you on the scale of your emancipation [*affranchissement*]? With regard to public life, with regard to your political worries, with regard to your career concerns, where are you exactly in terms of your liberty? What importance do you place on the opinions of others?" Serenus shows that he knows full well the response a sage would give to these questions. I will spare you Seneca's response, because what interests me mostly in this passage is Serenus's *expositio animae*—but Seneca's response is at exactly that level (because Seneca must respond as a doctor since he has been asked for a consultation). Seneca's response does not consist of diagnosing a secret malady that would explain Serenus's malaise. His response is pitched exactly in the register of this type of scale or statement of liberty and dependencies. Seneca simply satisfies himself with saying: "Do not believe that you are ill and have not yet been cured. You are simply a formerly sick person who doesn't fully realize he has been cured. As far as the state of your liberties is concerned, for the most part you have detached yourself from what bound you in an exaggerated fashion. So, as far as that goes, you are cured. But there are still a certain number of small ties that hold you back, and you must liberate yourself from them."[28] In sum, Seneca simply indicates to Serenus his place on the trajectory that leads to the solid ground of Stoic virtues. Seneca provides a precise accounting of the situation.

You see that we have here a perfectly systematic and perfectly coherent type of veridiction of the self that, moreover, corresponded to an extensive and common practice in late antiquity. You can already imagine how far this was from the type of veridiction that was to develop in Christianity. Here the test of veridiction took place essentially in terms of a code of conduct and the degree of liberty, while veridiction of the self in Christian penance would evidently take on an entirely different aspect and form.*

:::

Veridiction in Christianity: I would like to approach the question from two perspectives.† To begin with, I would like to speak of veridiction in Chris-

---

* Foucault interrupts his lecture and poses a question to the audience: "So, then, I would like to ask you a question, if you will, on method. Since in general I speak far longer than I would like, both because I am perhaps like Serenus—I get carried away—and also because there are so many of you, something I congratulate myself and thank you for, but which does not facilitate speaking quickly. So, then, would you like us to stop for five minutes and discuss, for example, what I have just said? Or shall I move on for another half-hour or forty-five minutes to a discussion of Christian veridiction? You are for a break or you are . . . no? Who would like to stop? Raise your hands. I fear that I am not going to stop; I'm sorry. OK."

† Foucault stops once again and addresses the audience: "Excuse me. This is somewhat dis-

tian penance. Delivering my lectures here at a Catholic university, I will not offend you therefore by reminding you what you already know so well: that the contemporary Catholic practice, with [. . .] an annual obligation, at the very least, to perform the sacrament of penance in a ritual including the avowal of sins, was invented relatively recently, dating more or less from the twelfth century. Penance was not a sacrament; it did not require avowal, nor was it obligatory for all Christians. I will skip over the very long debate on the origins of penance and its status in early Christianity. It is in *The Shepherd of Hermas* that we have what is considered one of the first accounts of the existence of penance, and the problem that penance raised there, in short, was the following.[29] The problem of penance in early Christianity was this: Once one was baptized, one should no longer sin; if one sinned, then one was to be rejected by the ecclesiastical community; was there nevertheless a recourse that allowed an individual to be reintegrated even though his sin should have excluded him, or in spite of the fact that he had excluded himself from the community through sin? In other words, penance introduced the problem of a second baptism. Could one be baptized a second time? Or could one be reintegrated by something other than a second baptism? Such was the general framework, if you will, within which the problem was posed in the second century.

Let's leave this problem of origins behind. I would simply like to remind you that penance did not take on the forms that we know until after the twelfth century; and from the end of the second century to the Middle Ages [. . .] penance was nonrenewable. It was performed once in one's life and only once; this is because if it was already quite a good deal to have committed a grave sin after baptism and not be excluded from the community, such a practice obviously could not be renewed indefinitely. There was, then, only a single penance.

Second, this penance was sometimes the consequence and followed a grave and established sin—for example, the sin of adultery, or when one had renounced Christianity (this is the famous problem of the *lapsi*).[30] But penance could also [intervene]—and quite often it did—simply when the individual considered that he had committed enough sins or in any case

---

continuous, slightly formal; these are just points of reference. This is not a history, a continuous and close history of evolutions, transformations, overlaps. This is, if you will, more along the lines of prompts for future research or indications of possible work than a complete and exhaustive analysis."

that his Christian life had been sufficiently bad to desire a global change, to repent all sins and prepare, once and for all, a penance before death that would ensure his salvation.

Third, you must remember that this penance did not involve a particular procedure. It did not consist of performing such and such activities, such as, for example, fasting, almsgiving, or prayers. Penance was a status. It was a status that embraced all aspects of one's existence. In truth, one did not perform penance. Rather, one *became* a penitent—and becoming a penitent meant living differently from others. Naturally, this meant having a particular, spatially determined place in the community. It involved a certain mode of nourishment, through fasting. It also involved, of course, abstinence from all sexual relations. There was the impossibility of becoming a priest, even after penance. For penance was a status that one solicited from an authority, from a bishop. Once the status of penance was accorded, once one had performed one's penance, and lived under this status for a long enough time—there was the problem of knowing whether or not there was a predetermined duration or if it ended upon the bishop's or even the community's behest, but let's leave all these institutional problems aside—in any event, what is important is that one returned to the Church and the community after penance with a second ceremony, that of reconciliation. Imposing penance; the unfolding, then, of the status of a penitent for months, years, or sometimes even until death; and then reconciliation through a ceremony that could even take place, for that matter, on the individual's deathbed.

So, in all this, what was the place of veridiction in this solicited and imposed status of penance that affected every aspect of one's existence and ended in a particular ceremony? Did one have to tell truth? How was one supposed to tell truth? How was one to manifest the truth? And what truth was one supposed to manifest?

Well, the place of veridiction was no doubt very important in the practice and the institution of early penance. The immediate proof is that the very practice of penance—the ensemble of conducts, behaviors, and acts that characterized the penitential status—was often described in the literature of the period with one word: a word found in Greek texts, but also in Latin texts, in its Greek form, as if the Latins could not provide an adequate translation. And this term, it is that of *exomologēsis—exomologēsis, exomologein. Homologein* means giving one's accord, coming to agreement. *Exomologein* means to recognize something. Recognize something, give one's accord: this is a common term in classical Greek. Moreover, it is a term that has the precise meaning of avowal within juridical vocabulary (in the text of *Oedipus Rex* that I cited yesterday, when the slave is forced to recognize that he was the one who gave Oedipus, alive, to the shepherd of Corinth against Laius's orders, he says *"exomologēo"*—I recognize, yes, I avow).[31] This is the term used for avowal.

In Christian literature, the word *exomologēsis* actually designates a certain number of things. First, it designates the act of faith: when one recognizes the truth of a teaching that has been received, it is *exomologein*. The term may also designate the act through which one recognizes oneself as a sinner before God. And in a text—you know, this very old text, in the *Didachē*, the first collection of texts that provides information on community practices in early Christian churches—there is a famous passage that explains that when one prays collectively, it is necessary to *"exomologein hamartēmata,"* that is, it is necessary to recognize one's sins.[32] One obviously tendentious interpretation of this text, which was imposed for centuries, suggested that avowal of one's sins was practiced from early Christianity onward, one avowed one's sins collectively in front of everyone during collective prayer—and this gave birth to the legend of the public confession of sins. In fact, this passage from the *Didachē* means only one thing: one must recognize oneself as a sinner before God in the course of a prayer that is, itself, a collective prayer. But there is no avowal, nor is there any verbal formulation, nor is there a verbal enunciation of sins designated in the text of the *Didachē*. By contrast, when it is a question of penitential practice itself—that is, of accepting, imposing the actual status of penance, its unfolding, and reconciliation—the term *exomologēsis* is also regularly employed, and here it has a very precise meaning. At the risk of being somewhat schematic, one could present the text in the following terms.

First, when penance was solicited or imposed, an exposition of one's faults was necessary. Why and how was it necessary? Well, if the penitent solicited the priest or the bishop—let's assume that during this period there was no difference—when the one who wanted to be a penitent asked to receive penance, he addressed the bishop and expressed his reasons for wanting this status. And apparently, even though we do not have precise indications, there must necessarily have been a sort of verbal enunciation of faults committed. It would appear that this is the practice that Saint Cyprian refers to when he speaks of *expositio causae*: the exposition of the cause, an absolutely juridical term which shows that this first phase of penance, or rather that the initial steps that led to a penitential status, were indeed conceptualized in juridical terms.[33] But it should be noted that this *expositio*, this confidence that one expressed to the bishop to solicit penitential status, on the one hand did not belong to the ritual of penance itself—[it] was simply its preparation—and on the other hand was evidently a private practice. Not necessarily secret, but nevertheless it took place one-on-one and, once again, outside the ritual of penance itself. And, for that matter, it does not seem that the word *exomologēsis* was used to designate this exposition of the fault that would lead to the imposition of the status of penitent.

By contrast, the word *exomologēsis* was used explicitly for two other things. First, if we begin at the end of the procedure, at the very moment of reconciliation—during the moment of reconciliation, that is, at the moment of the ceremony that often took place on Good Friday.* A number of texts attest to the existence of this particular episode. For example, with regard to penance, Saint Cyprian often refers to the following three things: *paenitentiam agere, exomologesim facere, impositio manus.*[34] That is, one does one's penance—it is the status of being a penitent that is maintained until the moment of reconciliation. There is, then, *exomologesim facere*, doing this *exomologēsis*; and then *impositio manus*, the rite through which one is actually reconciled. So *exomologēsis* takes place between the penitential status and the laying on of hands. What does it consist of? In fact, Saint Cyprian does not say, but we have precise information in earlier and later texts.

Among the earlier texts, it can be found in Tertullian. It can be found more precisely in Tertullian's *De pudicitia*, which, you know far better than I, was written at the time when Tertullian was a Montanist—which may evidently raise some degree of skepticism as to whether the text was a real description of the rites of penance.[35] However, it is important to examine carefully what was at stake when Tertullian addressed the rites of penance in this *De pudicitia*. He did not condemn the practice of penance. On the contrary, he was absolutely favorable to it. What he did not want, and what he criticized, was that one could put an end to one's status as penitent and be reconciled. It was on the matter of reconciliation and not on the matter

---

* At this point Foucault says: "No, that took place, excuse me, well here, yes, I'm sorry, the day of the celebration of the Crucifixion or of the Resurrection, well, yes, Friday."

of penance that he was in conflict with other religious authorities—or, if you will, with the religious authority.

In *De pudicitia* he describes two things. On the one hand, in chapter 3, section 5, he evokes the penitent at the door of the Church. This is the only form of penance that Tertullian accepts. It is the one, he says, that was sent solely by God. And the penitent who observes this rite prefers to blush before the Church than stay in communion with it: "She remains standing at the door and serves as an example to others through the example of her humiliation. She calls upon her brothers' tears to save her."[36] It would seem that this is a description of the penitential status before reconciliation. But on the other hand, in chapter 13, section 7 of the same text, Tertullian evokes what he is against, which is the rite of reconciliation, because he does not want those who are doing penance to be reconciled. And here he breaks out in a rage against the rite, no doubt in perhaps a somewhat emphatic and exaggerated tone; but listen to what he wrote nonetheless. He addresses himself to the priest who plays the role of a shepherd bringing back the lost sheep: "You bring the penance of a fornicator into the Church to soothe the indignation of the Christian assembly. You take the guilty party by the hand, hidden under his hair shirt, covered in ashes, mournful and dejected. You force him to prostrate himself publicly before the widows and priests, to implore the assistance of our brothers, to kiss the ground before each of them, and to roll humbly at their feet."[37] It is probable that Tertullian's text, which is critical of this practice, is nevertheless describing a real practice. And if, in the theatricality of Tertullian's text, we can hear a note of indignation against such practices, it seems that we have here a certain number of precise gestures that characterize the *exomologēsis* of the one who is to be reconciled—a hair shirt, taking him by the hand, being covered in ashes, prostration, kissing the steps of one's brethren, and rolling humbly at their feet.

Moreover, later texts confirm that it is undoubtedly in this way that *exomologēsis* did indeed take place (the manifestation of truth in penance, the recognition of the truth in penance), as illustrated, for example, when Saint Jerome evoked Fabiola's penance. Fabiola in effect was divorced from her husband and had remarried before the death of her first husband, which was considered wrong. She thus performed her penance, and in letter [77], Saint Jerome describes her penance in the following terms: "Before the eyes of all Rome, during the days preceding Easter, she stood among the ranks of the penitents, the bishop, the priests, and the weeping populace crying with her, her hair disheveled, deathly pale, her hands soiled, her head sullied with ashes, and she humbly bowed, with her chest bare and that face that had seduced her second husband. She laid bare to all her wound, and on her pale body, Rome contemplated her scars with tears."[38] We have here a ritual, a great ritual of supplication that, it must not be forgotten, was similar in many respects to the rituals of supplication found in Greek tragedy and which were effectively enacted in Greek society—the Roman version was no doubt slightly different. In short, one has here a ritual that has a deep tradition; it is a ritual of supplication, but one that had a well-defined place in penitential procedure. And this ritual, you see, specifically called *exomologēsis*, did not include an avowal of sins, but a spectacular manifestation of the fact that one had sinned, of one's awareness of being a sinner, of remorse for being so, and of the will to be a sinner no longer and be reintegrated.

But outside of this very precise episode that was called *exomologēsis*, the term *exomologēsia*—the term for recognition that was not generally translated into Latin, but occasionally translated as confession—this word *exomologēsia* also referred more broadly to the entire unfolding of penance itself. It is nonetheless important and central that the word *exomologēsia* ultimately meant to be a penitent, to lead the life of a penitent, and that the life of the penitent was called recognition, confession, avowal. In Irenaeus's *Adversus haereses*, book 1, chapter 13, section 5, it is said, for example, that someone returned to the Church after having left it and that he spent all the rest of his life in *exomologēsia*.[39] In Tertullian's *De paenitentia*, chapter 12, it is said of a king of Babylon that he performed *exomologēsia* for seven years.[40] It is well understood that the word *exomologēsia* here does not refer, of course, to this very peculiar ritual that took place in the church at the moment of reconciliation. Rather, it is the penance itself that is called in its entirety *exomologēsia*.

In what way could the life of the penitent be at once an *exomologēsia*, at the same time an avowal, and simultaneously a recognition? Tertullian says of this penitential practice that it should not unfold simply *in conscientia*, in one's conscience, that it should be *actus*, an act that must be understood almost in the theatrical sense of the word.[41] It must be a clear manifestation through *actus*, it must also be a *disciplina*, says Tertullian—an entire mode or rule of life that is connected to *habitus* and *victus*, the manner of holding and the manner of nourishing, feeding oneself.[42] In the *De paenitentia*, chapter 9, Tertullian makes explicit what this life of penance should be: one must lay beneath the sack and the ashes, wrap one's body in dark rags, give up one's soul to sadness, use rough treatments to correct one's faulty members. Normally, the penitent nourishes his prayers by fasting. He whines, he cries, he bellows day and night toward the lord God. He rolls at the priests' feet. He kneels before those who are dear to God. He implores his brothers to be intercessors in favor of his pardon.[43] And this is what constitutes at once penance and *exomologē-sia*. And in later texts there are references to the same types of practices. In a letter written by a cleric of the Roman Church to Cyprian, he says of the apostates: "It is time for them to perform penance (*paenitentiam agere*), to show (*probare*) the pain they feel, to express (*ostendere*) their shame, to demonstrate (*monstrare*) their humility and exhibit their modesty (*modestiam exhibere*)."[44] Penance cannot exist without the activity that consists of exhibiting, showing, expressing, and manifesting. Cyprian in the *De lapsis* says: "Join your tears to ours, add your sorrow to our sorrow."[45] Ambrose in *De paenitentia*, book 1, chapter 5, section 24 says: "*Confitentur gemitibus, confitentur fletibus, confitentur liberis, non coactis vocibus*" — "they confess through their groaning, they confess with their tears, they confess by speaking—*vocibus, liberis non coactis*—freely, without being under constraint."[46] And in the *Paraenesis* [. . .]*

---

* There is a break here, corresponding to a change in the audiovisual tape. The resulting lacuna can be filled using the original typescript deposited at the IMEC. The original typescript material reads as follows (typescript, lecture of April 29, 1981, pp. 16–17):

In Pacian's *Paraenesis*,[47] penance is defined as something that should take place not in a nominal fashion but prior to the ashes, the sack, the fast, the affliction, and the participation of a great number in prayer. What may be retained from all this information is the following: penance cannot be dissociated from what is called *exomologēsia*, which either is the crowning moment in the penitent's life leading to the final reconciliation or may be understood as a spectacular, theatrical form of the life of penance. One cannot be a penitent without practicing *exomologēsia*, which is at the same time a practice of veridiction that is integral to the penitential process itself. But this veridiction never takes the form of a verbal enunciation of faults. Of course there can be cries, lamentations, and recognition of the fault that has been committed. One can even proclaim that one is a sinner and that one has committed sins. But there is nothing that resembles an examination of one's conscience, a thoughtful and analyzed expression of the fault. It is an expressive, theatrical truth: a spectacle in which one doesn't tell of the sins one has committed, but where one shows that one is a sinner. It seems to me that Tertullian found the best translation of this word *exomologēsia* that the Romans had such a difficult time translating. He used the word *publicatio sui*, to publish oneself: to render public the fact that one is a sinner and open up to the public one's status as sinner, to appear before the public with the status of sinner.

: : :

[To what model does the practice of *exomologēsia* refer? One finds] medical and judicial arguments. One often finds the following, for example: when one visits a doctor, one must show him one's wounds to be healed. Similarly, if one wants to be healed of one's sins, one must show one's wounds to the healer, to the *Christus medicus*, the one who heals and leads us to salvation. One can also find arguments of a judicial type, such as: When an accused seeks the judge's pardon, he knows full well that if he avows and humbly recognizes his fault, he will appease the judge. Likewise, recognize our sins before God and perhaps we will appease him. Or, for example, one also finds the following argument: When the devil rises up to accuse us on judgment day, if we have not spoken first, God will be more severe. However, if we have already spoken before the devil's accusation through our penance, if we have shown ourselves to be penitents in the eyes of God, the devil will be forced into silence on that terrible day.

But, to tell the truth, both this medical and judicial explanation of the practice of *exomologēsia* and the necessity of veridiction do not seem to me to be the fundamental reasons. The true model to which this practice of *exomologēsia* refers, [this] great spectacular manifestation of oneself as sinner, the true model is neither the illness nor the wound and the doctor, nor crime and judgment. The true model, as I am sure you suspect, is the martyr. That is, in practicing penance, the one who has committed a sin does what only can be done by those who have confronted the persecutions of the pagans for the glory and honor of God and as his witness.

The entire organization of penance revolved around the great question of the *lapsi*, those who did not want to confront martyrdom in order to save themselves. And the penance that was organized in part (only in part, but partially nonetheless) to respond to this question: "How can the *lapsi* be reintegrated?"—that penance was a means of substituting for the real martyrdom that one did not want to confront a kind of little martyrdom, a miniature martyrdom, imposed upon oneself to live up to those who did become martyrs. Penance was mortification, mortification in the strictest sense. Meaning, first of all, that one showed oneself to be a sinner who belonged to the domain of the dead. In sackcloth and ashes, one showed that, in effect, in the truth of oneself as a sinner, one belonged to the world of the dead and had not chosen the world of life, even if it meant death to this world. By subjecting oneself to this mortification, one showed that, even if one had sinned, and through sin one had chosen the world of life which was also the world of death, one was now ready to choose the other world, and for this one was ready to confront death. One killed within oneself the world of death that one had refused to leave through the act of sin. One showed oneself as one was: dead through sin, ready to die so as never to sin again.

Veridiction and mortification are intimately linked in this practice of penance. If the practice of penance implies *exomologēsia*, it is because through penance one must be dead to this world and, second, one must publicly attest before the eyes of this world that one is ready to sacrifice oneself in this world in order to arrive in the other world. That is, there is here a veridiction of oneself, a ritual act through which one shows the truth of oneself. But in relationship to what, and as a function of what, in connection with what? With mortification of oneself, that is, with the sacrifice of oneself. One produces the truth of the self only insofar as one is capable of sacrificing oneself. The sacrifice of the self for the truth of the self, or the truth of the self for the sacrifice of the self: that is the heart of the rite of penitential *exomologēsia*. You see clearly that we have here something that is fundamentally different from veridiction as it is found in the Stoic practices of Seneca that I spoke about, [but it is also far from] the practice of veridiction, or the examination of oneself, that can be found in many other forms of Christian practice.

In any case, it seems to me that the connection between veridiction and mortification is absolutely essential in this first ritual of Christian penance. So what I would have liked to do, but I think it is too late now, is to explore another form of veridiction from the fourth and fifth centuries: a form that developed within monastic institutions and also ties together, in a certain way, veridiction and mortification, but through entirely different practices and entirely different rituals. Whereas here, in the veridiction that I have just described, in the penitential *exomologēsia*, you see that the entire production of truth is accomplished in a sort of great staging of life, the body, and gestures, with the verbal aspect playing only a minor role. To the contrary, in the monastic practices that began to develop in the fourth and fifth centuries, self-mortification was still tied to veridiction, but through the intermediary of a new and fundamental medium that had a certain importance in the history of Western culture and subjectivity—that is, language. It was through a continuous verbalization of oneself that the monk was to generate, himself, the link between veridiction and mortification. Let's say that the penitent established this link between veridiction and mortification in his body. The monk, on the other hand, while he also established it in his body because to a certain degree he was a penitent as well, also established it through the continuous and permanent exercise of language.

[*This lecture was followed by a discussion with the audience that is reproduced here in its entirety.*]

Foucault: So this is what I will explore either this evening or next time, because time has passed quickly. Would you like to ask a few questions? OK, yes?

Questioner: Could the custom that seems to have existed in the Middle Ages, but after the fifth century, in which older people retired to the monastery after an active family life be considered an attenuated form of penance?

Foucault: Yes, of course. This vast ritual of penance that I spoke of through the texts of Tertullian did not vanish just like that, you know. Its importance and scope declined for a number of reasons—the appearance of a fixed penance after the seventh and eighth centuries, which I will speak of next time; the organization of a sacramental penance after the twelfth and thirteenth centuries—but the practice remained; that is, the acquisition of the status of a penitent with a particular and spectacular lifestyle continued. It continued to exist primarily in two forms, or one might even say three forms. The monastic life is one way of choosing the status of penitent, it is a modality of the life of a penitent. Second, there are those who at the end of their lives retired and led the life of penance before dying, a practice that conformed to a practice attested to in the fifth century. The religious authority did not look highly, for that matter, upon people waiting for the moment when they were too weak to begin their penance, but it was at once a way of ensuring one's salvation with the greatest certainty while performing penance for as short a time as possible. That's obvious. And then the third thing concerns, of course, the fraternities of penitents that imposed a relatively peculiar mode of existence, but with recurrent obligations during yearly festivals and under certain conditions. So, if you will, it hardly disappears, it does not disappear at all.

Questioner: How did this dramatic penance, at certain moments [*inaudible*] break away from the obligation of veridiction that already existed in pagan antiquity? You practically suggested that the problem of the obligation to be true with regard to oneself already existed in pagan antiquity.

Foucault: Yes, but in an entirely different form.

Questioner: So Christianity took up this form of veridiction but it was different?

Foucault: No, it is the form of veridiction that can be found in the philosophical schools with the examination of conscience, relationship to a director, consultation with another. An equivalent can be found for this, or at least that which was the continuation of the philosophical existence in Christianity. The continuation of the philosophical existence in Christianity, as you know, is the monastic life. The true philosophical life was defined—especially in the original monasticism, that is, in Oriental monasticism—as the true philosophical life. So it is entirely normal—and this is what I will explain next time—that one finds this practice. The practice of penance that is attested to in the first Christian centuries had nothing to do with this philosophical practice. It was entirely different. In reality, it was a rite of supplication. If it was the continuation of something, it was the continuation of the great rites of supplication found in Greek civilization.

Questioner: If someone else is interested, I would like to know what exactly was the relationship of the sackcloth and ashes to death?

Foucault: Well, I think that the sackcloth was in fact a sack made of goat's wool and this sack of goat wool—and here I do not have the exact references in mind, but even before, independently even of Christianity and outside of Christianity, in many societies of the eastern Mediterranean, the sack, the clothing made of goat's wool, was a sign of renunciation and of entry into the world of death. As for the ashes, I think that the symbolism is obvious enough.

Questioner: Yes but the fact of being dead in the sackcloth and ashes, you seem to be saying that one is thereby accepting death, when this mortification would seem to represent instead the will to return to life through mortification and not the externalization of . . .

Foucault: I must have expressed myself poorly. But there is, if you will, an inversion. This is what constitutes the richness and intensity of this practice of veridiction. He who sins is the one who, instead of choosing what is called in the *Didachē*, in the tradition of the Judeo-Christian communities, the path of life, rather than choosing the path of life, the one who sins has chosen the path of death. He is therefore dead to the only true life, that is, the Christian life or the life of God. He is therefore on the side of the dead. To bear the sackcloth and ashes, in effect, is to demonstrate that one is in truth someone who has chosen the path of death. What can one do once one has chosen the path of death to turn onto the path of life and choose life? Well, one must die to the path of death, renounce it, in order to enter into the true spiritual life that implies death to this life. So, if you will, it is this inversion between the manifestation of the fact that one is truly dead as a result of one's sin and the will to die to this world of sin in order to live another life, this is what is manifested and what absolutely ties the rite of veridiction to this notion that I did not speak of because I did not have the time, but that you see is central: *metanoia*. Metanoia is when one converts and one chooses the true world in the place of the world of death, or true life instead of death.

Questioner: Here, has the role of public opinion completely disappeared?

Foucault: Oh no, it has not disappeared at all, since it is precisely in front of everyone that this is done. And at the moment of reconciliation, reconciliation—you will remember from the description that Tertullian gave, or that Saint Jerome gave in relation to Fabiola—it takes place in the church; the penitent who pleaded before the church door is taken by the hand and crosses the entire church moaning, crying, begging his brothers to admit him back into their community. And so, if you will, the participation of the others is manifested in this way. Furthermore, I think that in the text of Saint Jerome (or perhaps somewhere else), it is stated that the audience cries as well with the one who has asked for reintegration. So, if you will, there is a rite of participation.

Questioner: And is there no longer a necessity of recognition of the truth through public opinion, just as there was the necessity of recognition by the chorus?

Foucault: Indeed it is no longer at all a juridical form of validation that says: "This is indeed the way things happened." It is sufficient that it be the subject himself who says "I am a sinner" for it to become truth. There is no need for a system of proof. I mean a system of proof is unnecessary, in fact there are thousands of signs that in a certain number of cases . . . and in particular the famous and diabolical affair of the *lapsi* during the period of Saint Cyprian made it such that, for example, before reconciling someone, one sought out information, one asked people if indeed they had effectively repented. One asked for letters. There were requests for information. So if you will, there was a whole effort of inquiry, but which was not integrated into the ritual. The ritual, and this is what interests me here, was not so much, if you will, the system of verification that the Church or the ecclesiastical authority could elicit; what interests me is how the subject himself was called upon to manifest himself in his truth. The reason why I have gone on so long about this is that it is interesting to see how in Seneca, for example, and in the rules of a Stoic life, the obligation to—or rather the recommendation that one exposes one's own soul to someone else, the recommendation to examine oneself—we begin to see that this is fundamentally a problem of reactualization, of reactivating codes and of determining where one is exactly in the philosophical progression towards liberty. They do not speak about themselves, and the only word that seems to refer to one's subjectivity that is employed by Serenus or by Seneca, namely *placet*—here is something that pleases me, here is something that displeases me—does not at all reveal one's subjectivity, but rather the type of action, the degree of liberty. With the rite of Christian penance, what is very interesting is to see, then, the complete lack of verbal elaboration or, if you will, the lack of the precise analytical tasks that could be found among the Stoics. Rather there is something very massive, or a little coarse, if you will, very theatrical, but in which what is shown, what must be shown, is the truth of the subject himself. What he truly is. And his truth, his truth at the intersection or at the point of inflection of *metanoia*, of conversion, right where one is at once dead and one wants to resuscitate another life. And it is his subjectivity, his subjectivity of living death, of a dead man who has chosen life—this is what must be grasped. So, what I would like to try to show you next time, with regard to monastic life, is that the monks, to a certain extent, take up this form again. They, too, seek to express their subjectivity, but through an extraordinarily complex and extraordinarily analytical verbal grid that is going to open up, to the field of analysis and also to the relationship of self to self, a domain that was absolutely unknown in antiquity.

Questioner: [. . .] there is a rapport that could be established as well with the Christian notion of guilt. One feels very heavily the weight of guilt. Can this guilt only appear because there is anthropo . . .

Foucault: Yes, yes, or at least I see . . .

Questioner: . . . anthropologization . . .

Foucault: I can't say it either.

Questioner: . . . anthropologization of the subject, whereas there is no anthropologization of the subject in the examination of the Stoic conscience?

Foucault: I would not say "anthropologization," I would say there is practically no subjectification.

Questioner: On the Stoic side, but not on the Christian side . . .

Foucault: Well, on the Christian side, you see a subjectification, in one sense. That is, once again, it is indeed the truth of the subject that . . .

Questioner: . . . and culpabilization at the same time . . .

Foucault: So the problem of culpabilization, yes, of course, obviously. But I, what I did here if you will—and I am pleased that we are having this discussion because, fundamentally, my aim was to put some documents on the table and propose a few elements of discussion on which we could work a little bit afterwards—if I told you this, it is because there are two things that should be emphasized. First, what is important within Christianity seems to me to be far more this relationship of the individual to his truth than the problem of sin. Because, after all, God knows if the Pythagoreans, God knows if the Stoics didn't keep rattling on about this, about sinning, about sins—about the notion of *hamartēma*, for example, about the notion of fault. So we always say that Christianity gave meaning to the notion of sin; but what does this mean, the meaning of sin? Here once again, the Stoics, the Pythagoreans had an extremely demanding and complicated code of conduct; one needed to pay attention at every moment not to commit a fault. What seems to me to have been the essence of Christianity and to have made a break in the history of Western subjectivity is the technique, the relationship of truth, and all the techniques put forward and perfected to draw out the truth of oneself with regard to sin. But it is, rather, the truth of oneself with regard to sin that seems more important to me than the meaning of sin. And the second thing that I wanted to emphasize, which is why I have been taking some time to explain this to you, is that it is impossible to trace a straight line directly between Socrates's *gnōthi seauton* and what I have been speaking to you about. That is, the Christian requirements of self-knowledge do not derive from the *gnōthi seauton*. To go further yet, I would say, the Stoic practices of the examination of conscience or of *expositio animae* are also completely different from *gnōthi seauton*. *Gnōthi seauton* is a philosophical act through which one establishes a certain mode of relation with *the* truth in general. It is not a means of establishing a relationship to one's own truth. For Socrates and Plato, one must know oneself well in order to know mathematics. In any case, it is in order to know the eternal truths that one must know oneself. Whereas among Stoics and the Epicureans, while one finds something similar, the techniques of knowing oneself are different and take on an entirely different object than [that] of being a condition for knowledge in general. And this is even more the case in Christianity. And it is this specificity of techniques of self-knowledge, which cannot be reduced to *gnōthi seauton*, that I wanted to underscore.

So I would like to pose a purely practical question, since I am behind with regard to the program that I had set out for myself. Next time, I wanted to focus on medieval law, or at least to discuss a little medieval law. Would you still like for me to speak about monastic practices of the examination of the self? Yes? That is not a problem? In the end, this will deviate from the frame that I had given myself and that was supposed to be oriented towards legal historians. Does that seem . . . that is not a problem for you? May I? Very good. Thank you.

[NOTES]

1. On the inscriptions at Knidos, see Wolfgang Blümel, *Die Inschriften von Knidos* (Bonn: R. Habelt, 1992); Angelos Chaniotis, "Under the Watchful Eyes of the Gods: Divine Justice in Hellenistic and Roman Asia Minor," pp. 1–43 in Stephen Colvin, ed., *The Greco-Roman East: Politics, Culture, Society*, (New York: Cambridge University Press, Yale Classical Studies Vol. 31, 2004), pp. 3–10; H. S. Versnel, "Beyond Cursing: The Appeal to Justice in Judicial Prayers," in Christopher A. Faraone and Dirk Obbink, eds., *Magika Hiera: Ancient Greek Magic and Religion* (Oxford: Oxford University Press, 1991), pp. 60–106; and Henk S. Versnel, "Peprêmenos: The Cnidian Curse Tablets and Ordeal by Fire," in Robin Hägg, ed., *Ancient Greek Cult Practice from the Epigraphical Evidence: Proceedings of the Second International Seminar on Ancient Greek Cult* (Stockholm: Astroms, 1994), pp. 145–54. On the inscriptions of Epidaurus, see *Recueil des inscriptions juridiques grecques*, ed. and trans. Rodolphe Dareste de La Chavanne, Bernard Haussoulier, and Théodore Reinach, (Paris: Ernest Leroux, 1891–94), pp. 494–99 (inscriptions on a tablet in Epidaurus "revealed the names of debtors to the god of Epidaurus"). More generally, see Walter Burkert, "Causalité religieuse: La faute, les signes, les rites," in *Mètis: Anthropologie des mondes grecs anciens*, Vol. 9 (1994), no. 1, p. 34 ("One could add multiple inscriptions from sanctuaries throughout Asia Minor referred to as penitent inscriptions, *Bussinschriften*, which indicate that the one who dedicated the inscription fell ill, recognized his offence, became penitent and was cured: he offered the tablet then to witness the god's grace"); and Walter Burkert, *Creation of the Sacred* (Cambridge, MA: Harvard University Press, 1996).

2. See Chaniotis, "Under the Watchful Eyes of the Gods: Divine Justice in Hellenistic and Roman Asia Minor," pp. 3–6 (discussion, examples, and bibliographical references to studies of inscriptions that contained avowals and confessions).

3. See ibid., pp. 6–10 (discussion, examples, and bibliographical references to studies of inscriptions that contained maledictions against wrongdoers).

4. Juvénal, satire VI, verses 526–41, in *Satires*, trans. Olivier Sers, ed. Pierre de Labriolle and François Villeneuve (Paris: Les Belles Lettres, 2002), pp. 122–23; English edition, Juve-

nal, *The Satires*, trans. Niall Rudd, introduction and notes by William Barr (New York: Oxford University Press, 1991), pp. 55–56:

> ... she will make her way to sweltering Meroe, beyond the border of Egypt, in order to fetch some water that she may sprinkle in Isis' temple .... He intercedes whenever a woman has failed to refrain from sex with her husband on days which ought to be honoured as holy, when a heavy penalty is due to be paid for polluting the mattress, and when Isis' silver serpent is seen to nod its head. Anubis' tears ensure, along with his ritual murmurs, that Osiris will not refuse to forgive the sin—provided, of course, he is bribed with a big fat goose and a little cake ...

See also Juvénal, *La fureur de voir: Onze satires*, trans. Oliviers Sers (Paris: Les Belles Lettres, 1999), p. 80. Foucault discussed the cult of the Egyptian goddess Isis in his discussion of the care of the self during the second hour of his lecture on January 20, 1982, in *Hermeneutics of the Subject: Lectures at the Collège de France, 1981–1982*, English series ed. Arnold I. Davidson, trans. Graham Burchell (New York: Picador, 2005), p. 114. Frédéric Gros provides useful information and references on Isis; see ibid., pp. 122–23 n. 13.

5. Foucault analyzed the Pythagorean examination of conscience in other courses as well. In *Hermeneutics of the Subject*, in the course of March 24, 1982, during the second hour Foucault interprets the Pythagorean examination of conscience as enabling "a purification of thought before sleep," and as not "intended to reactualize something like remorse." Ibid., p. 480; see also the course of January 27, 1982, second hour, ibid., pp. 163–64 (drawing together the examination of the conscience, the direction of conscience and *parrhēsia*), and the first hour of the course on January 13, 1982, ibid., p. 50 (discussion of the examination of one's conscience as a technology of the self). Frédéric Gros also makes reference to the Collège de France lecture of March 12, 1980 (*Du gouvernement des vivants*), where "Foucault attempted an archaeology of the Christian coupling of the verbalization of faults and the exploration of oneself, taking great care to indicate an irreducible discontinuity between the Pythagorean-Stoic examination and the Christian examination at the three levels of their field of exercise, instruments, and objectives." Ibid., p. 488, n. 9. See also notes 7 and 8 by Gros, ibid., p. 62, for useful information on the thought and organization of the first groups of Pythagoreans.

6. Peter Cornelis van der Horst, in his edition of the *Golden Verses* of Pythagoras, comments in detail and follows the ulterior articulations of this Pythagorean examination of conscience in the works of Horace, Seneca, Arrian, Porphyry, Plutarch, Diogenes Laërtius, Cicero, and others. See Pythagore, *Les vers d'or pythagoriciens*, ed. P. C. van der Horst (Leiden: Brill, 1932), pp. 22–25. Foucault explores these developments of the examination of conscience in the thought of Epictetus, Marcus Aurelius, Plato, Porphyry, and Seneca in his lecture of March 24, 1982, during the second hour, in *The Hermeneutics of the Subject*, pp. 480–86; see also the notes by Gros, pp. 488–89 n. 13–26.

7. Pythagore, *Les vers d'or pythagoriciens*, verses 40–42, ed. P.C. van der Horst, p. 2 (ancient Greek); Pythagore, *Les vers d'or*, trans. Mario Meunier (Paris: L'Artisan du livre, 1925), p. 28 (French translation); English edition, Hierocles, *Commentary of Hierocles on the Golden Verses of Pythagoras*, trans. Nicholas Rowe (London: Theosophical Publishing House, 1971), p. 86.

8. Hiéroclès, *Commentaire sur les vers d'or des Pythagoriciens*, verses 42–44, trans. M. Meunier (Paris: L'Artisan du livre, 1925), pp. 28 and 218–28; Pythagore, *Les vers d'or pythagoriciens*, verses 42–44, ed. P. C. van der Horst, p. 2 (ancient Greek); English edition, trans. Rowe, p. 86. Apparently, in his *Life of Pythagore* Porphyry does not add these last two verses. See *Vie*

de Pythagore, section 40, lines 18–20, in *Vie de Pythagore, Lettre à Marcella*, trans. Édouard des Places (Paris: Les Belles Lettres, 1982), p. 54; English edition, *The Pythagorean Sourcebook and Library: An Anthology of Ancient Writings which Relate to Pythagoras and Pythagorean Philosophy*, ed. David R. Fideler, trans. Kenneth Sylvan Guthrie (Grand Rapids, MI: Phanes Press, 1987), at section 40, p. 131. Porphyry does, however, add the duplicated form of the examination of conscience in the morning, see section 40, lines 20–23, p. 54. For an analysis of the double form of examination in the Pythagorean tradition, see the commentary by van der Horst, p. 23; as well as Foucault, *Hermeneutics of the Subject*, lecture of March 24, 1982, p. 481.

9. See the commentary by van der Horst in Pythagore, *Les vers d'or pythagoriciens*, ed. van der Horst, pp. 23–24 (for an analysis of the question of whether or not verses 42–44 date from a later period).

10. Cf. *Hermeneutics of the Subject*, lecture of March 24, 1982, second hour, pp. 480–81.

11. Cicéron, *Caton l'ancien (De la vieillesse)*, chapter 11, section 38, trans. Pierre Wuilleumier (Paris: Les Belles Lettres, 1961), p. 105 ("[. . .] ius augurium, pontificium, ciuile tracto, multumque etiam Graecis litteris utor, pythagoreorumque more, exercendae memoriae gratia [to exercise one's memory], quid quoque die dixerim, audierim, egerim, commemoro uesperi"); English edition, Cicero, *On the Art of Growing Old*, trans. Herbert Newell Couch (Providence: Brown University Press, 1959) pp. 43–44 ("I devote a great deal of attention to Greek literature, and, in order to keep my memory alert, I follow the custom of the Pythagoreans and each evening call back to mind whatever I have said, heard, or accomplished in the course of the day").

12. See commentary by van der Horst in Pythagore, *Les vers d'or pythagoriciens*, p. 24 ("the passage from Cicero *de Senectute* XI 38 is remarkable for the addition of *memoriae exercendae gratia* [to exercise one's memory]. . . . It would seem that mnemotechnics played an important role in these evening meditations").

13. Sénèque, *Dialogues*, vol. 1, *De ira*, book 3, section 36, trans. Abel Bourgery (Paris: Les Belles Lettres, 1951), pp. 102–3; English edition, Seneca, *On Anger*, section 36 in *Moral Essays*, vol. 1, trans. John W. Basore (London and New York: Heinemann and Putnam's Loeb Classical Library, 1928), pp. 338–41. Foucault also analyzes this text in *Le Souci de soi*, pp. 77–78; English edition, Foucault, *The Care of the Self* (New York: Vintage, 1988), pp. 60–61; *Hermeneutics of the Subject*, lecture of March 24, 1982, second hour, pp. 481–84; *Du gouvernement des vivants*, lecture of March 12, 1980 (for a summary, see *Hermeneutics of the Subject*, p. 489 n. 17, analysis by Frédéric Gros).

14. Sénèque, *De ira*, livre 3, section 36, 2–4, p. 103; English edition, Seneca, *On Anger*, trans. Basore, book 3, section 36, 2–4, pp. 340–41:

> See that you never do that again; I will pardon you this time. In that dispute, you spoke too offensively; after this don't have encounters with ignorant people; those who have never learned do not want to learn. You reproved that man more frankly than you ought, and consequently you have not so much mended him as offended him. In the future, consider not only the truth of what you say, but also whether the man to whom you are speaking can endure the truth. A good man accepts reproof gladly; the worse a man is the more bitterly he resents it.

15. Marc Aurèle, *Pensées*, V, 1, trans. Amédée I. Trannoy (Paris: Les Belles Lettres, 1925), p. 41; English edition; Marcus Aurelius, *The Meditations of Marcus Aurelius Antoninus*, 2 vols., trans. Arthur S. L. Farquharson (Oxford: Clarendon Press, 1989), p. 34; Épictète, *Entretiens*, III, 10, 1, trans. Joseph Souilhé (Paris: Les Belles Lettres), 1963, p. 38; English edition, Epictetus, *The Discourses as Reported by Arrian*, 2 vols., trans. William A. Oldfather (Cambridge, MA: Harvard University Press, 2000), book 3, chapter 10, section 1, pp. 70–71. Cf. Foucault, *Her-

meneutics of the Subject, lecture of February 3, 1982, second hour, pp. 187–202, and March 24, 1982, second hour, pp. 477–89.

16. Sénèque, *De ira*, livre 3, section 36, 2, p. 103; ibid., section 36, 3, p. 103; English edition, Seneca, *On Anger*, trans. Basore, book 3, section 36, 2, pp. 340–41 ("And how delightful the sleep that follows this self-examination—how tranquil it is, how deep and untroubled, when the soul has either praised or admonished itself, and when this secret examiner and critic of self has given report of its own character!"); ibid., section 36, 3, pp. 340–41 ("I avail myself of this privilege, and every day I plead my cause before the bar of self").

17. Sénèque, *De ira*, livre 3, section 36, 2, p. 103 ("et speculator sui censorque secretus"); English edition, Seneca, *On Anger*, trans. Basore, book 3, section 36, 2, p. 341 (". . . and . . . this secret examiner and critic of self . . .").

18. The Latin text reads, "totum diem meum scrutor" ("I examine my entire day"). English edition, Seneca, *On Anger*, trans. Basore, book 3, section 36, 3, pp. 340–41.

19. Ibid.; English edition, Seneca, *On Anger*, trans. Basore, book 3, section 36, 3, pp. 340–41 ("When the light has been removed from sight, and my wife, long aware of my habit, has become silent, I scan the whole of my day and retrace all my deeds and words").

20. Sénèque, *Dialogues*, vol. 4, *De la tranquillité de l'âme (De tranquillitate animi)*, trans. René Waltz (Paris: Les Belles Lettres, 1950), pp. 71–106; English edition, Seneca, *On Tranquillity of Mind* in *Moral Essays*, vol. 2, trans. John W. Basore (Cambridge: Loeb Classical Library, 1979), pp. 202–85.

21. Galien, *Traité des passions de l'âme et de ses erreurs*, chapters 2 and 3, trans. Robert Van der Elst (Paris: Delagrave, 1914), pp. 71–76; English edition, Galen, *On the Passions and Errors of the Soul*, trans. Paul W. Harkins (Columbus: Ohio State University Press, 1963) pp. 29–36. Cf. Foucault, *The Hermeneutics of the Subject*, lecture of March 10, 1982, second hour, pp. 396–400; note by Frédéric Gros, ibid., p. 269 n. 21; Foucault, *Le souci de soi*, pp. 75–81; English edition, Foucault, *The Care of the Self*, pp. 58–64.

22. Sénèque, *De la tranquillité de l'âme*, section 1, 2, p. 71; English edition, Seneca, *On Tranquility of Mind*, trans. Basore, book 9, section 1, 2, pp. 202–03: "Nevertheless the state in which I find myself most of all—for why should I not admit the truth to you as to a physician?—is that I have neither been honestly set free from the things that I hated and feared, nor, on the other hand, am I in bondage to them; while the condition in which I am placed is not the worst, yet I am complaining and fretful—I am neither sick nor well."

23. Sénèque, *De la tranquillité de l'âme*, section 1, 17, pp. 74–75; English edition, Seneca, *On Tranquility of Mind*, trans. Basore, book 9, section 1, 17, pp. 210–13 ("I know that these mental disturbances of mine are not dangerous and give no promise of a storm; to express what I complain of in apt metaphor, I am distressed, not by a tempest, but by sea-sickness. Do you, then, take from me this trouble, whatever it be, and rush to the rescue of one who is struggling in full sight of land").

24. Sénèque, *De la tranquillité de l'âme*, section 1, 10, p. 73 ("Placet uim praeceptorum sequi et in mediam ire rem publicam; placet honores fascesque non scilicet purpura aut uirgis abductum capessere, sed ut amicis propinquisque et omnibus ciuibus, omnibus deinde mortalibus paratior utiliorque sim"; English edition, Seneca, *On Tranquility of Mind*, trans. Basore, book 9, section 1, 10, pp. 206–7 (a more literal translation, in accordance with Foucault's argument, would read: "It pleases me to obey the commands of my teachers and plunge into the midst of public life; it pleases me to try to gain office and the consulship, attracted of course, not by the purple or by the lictor's rods, but by the desire to be more serviceable and useful to my friends and relatives and all my countrymen and then to all mankind").

25. Sénèque, *De la tranquillité de l'âme*, section 1, 7–8. pp. 72–73 ("[I.7] placet minister incultus et rudis uernula, argentum graue rustici patris sine ullo nomine artificis, et mensa non uarietate macularum conspicua nec per multas dominorum elegantium successiones ciuitati

nota . . . [I.8] Cum bene ista placuerunt, praestringit animum apparatus alicuius paedagogii, diligentius quam in tralatu uestita et auro culta mancipia et agmen seruorum nitentium . . ."); English edition, Seneca, On Tranquility of Mind, trans. Basore, book 9, section 1, 7–8, pp. 204–7 ("[I, 7] . . . the servant that I like is a young home-born slave without training or skill; the silver is my country-bred father's heavy plate bearing no stamp of the maker's name, and the table is not notable for the variety of its markings or known to the town from the many fashionable owners through whose hands it has passed. . . . [I, 8] Then, after all these things have had my full approval, my mind is dazzled by the magnificence of some training-school for pages, by the sight of slaves bedecked with gold and more carefully arrayed than the leaders of a public procession, and a whole regiment of glittering attendants . . .").

26. Sénèque, De la tranquillité de l'âme, section 1, 15, p. 74 ("Rursus, ubi se animus cogitationum magnitudine leuauit, ambitiosus in uerba est altiusque ut spirare, ita eloqui gestit, et ad dignitatem rerum exit oratio. Oblitus tum legis pressiorisque iudicii, sublimius feror et ore iam non meo"); English edition, Seneca, On Tranquility of Mind, trans. Basore, book 9, section 1, 14, pp. 210–11 ("Then again, when my mind has been uplifted by the greatness of its thoughts, it becomes ambitious of words, and with higher aspirations it desires higher expression, and language issues forth to match the dignity of the theme; forgetful then of my rule and of my more restrained judgment, I am swept to loftier heights by an utterance that is no longer my own").

27. Ibid., section 1, 6–8, pp. 204–7.

28. Sénèque, De la tranquillité de l'âme, section 2, 1–2, p. 75; English edition, Seneca, On Tranquility of Mind, trans. Basore, book 9, section 2, 1–2, pp. 212–13:

> [II, 1] In truth, Serenus, I have for a long time been silently asking myself to what I should liken such a condition of mind, and I can find nothing that so closely approaches it as the state of those who, after being released from a long and serious illness, are sometimes touched with fits of fever and slight disorders, and, freed from the last traces of them, are nevertheless disquieted with mistrust, and, though now quite well, stretch out their wrist to a physician and complain unjustly of any trace of heat in their body. It is not, Serenus, that these are not quite well in body, but that they are not quite used to being well; just as even a tranquil sea will show some ripple, particularly when it has just subsided after a storm. [II, 2] What you need, therefore, is not any of those harsher measures which we have already left behind, the necessity of opposing yourself at this point, of being angry with yourself at that, of sternly urging yourself on at another, but that which comes last— confidence in yourself and the belief that you are on the right path, and have not been led astray by the many cross-tracks of those who are roaming in every direction, some of whom are wandering very near the path itself.

29. Hermas, Le Pasteur, trans. Robert Joly (Paris: Les Éditions du Cerf, 1997); English edition, The Shepherd of Hermas, in The Apostolic Fathers, Vol. II: Epistle of Barnabas. Papias and Quadratus. Epistle to Diognetus. The Shepherd of Hermas, ed. and trans. Bart D. Ehrman (Cambridge, MA: Harvard University Press, 2003).

30. Cf. Foucault, Sécurité, territoire, population: Cours au Collège de France, 1977–1978, lectures of February 22, 1978, pp. 172–74, 189 n. 16, and 190–91 n. 27; English edition, Foucault, Security, Territory, Population: Lectures at the College de France 1977–1978, pp. 169–70, 187 n. 16, and 188 n. 27. As Michel Senellart points out in the last note (n. 27), on the question of the lapsi, see the introduction of Chanoine Bayard to the Correspondance de saint Cyprien (Paris: Les Belles Lettres, 1925), pp. xviii–xxiii.

31. Sophocle, Œdipe Roi, verses 1155–85, trans. Paul Mazon (Paris: Les Belles Lettres,

2007), pp. 86–91. English edition, *Oedipus the King*, ed. David Grene and Richmond Lattimore (Chicago: University of Chicago Press, 1991), pp. 61–63.

32. *La doctrine des douze apôtres: Didachê*, chapter 4, section 14, lines 27–30, trans. W. Rordorf and A. Tuilier (Paris: Les Editions du Cerf, 1998), p. 165 ("In the assembly, you will confess your faults and you will not go to pray with a guilty conscience. That is the way of life"); English edition, *Didachê*, in *The Apostolic Fathers, vol. I*, ed. Jeffrey Henderson (Cambridge, MA: Harvard University Press, 2003), pp. 316–17.

33. Saint Cyprien, *Correspondance*, vol. 2, letter LV, section VI.1, trans. Chanoine Bayard (Paris: Les Belles Lettres, 1925), p. 134 ("ut ad communicationem temere prosilirent, sed traheretur diu paenitentia et rogaretur dolenter paterna clementia, et examinarentur causae et uoluntates et necessitates singulorum, secundum quod libello continetur quem ad te peruenisse confido, ubi singula placitorum capita conscripta sunt"); English edition, Saint Cyprian, *The Letters of St. Cyprian of Carthage, Volume III*, letter 55, section 6.1, trans. Graeme W. Clarke (New York: Newman Press 1984), p. 36 ("Rather they should undergo prolonged penitence, and with grief and tears beg for indulgence from the Father; their various cases should be scrutinized individually, along with their personal attitudes and the special pressures under which they may have acted. ¶ All this is contained in the document which I am sure must have reached you; in it there are listed, in summary form, the various resolutions we passed").

34. See Saint Cyprien, *Correspondance*, vol. 1, letter 15, section I.2, trans. Chanoine Bayard (Paris: Les Belles Lettres, 1925), p. 43 ("ante actam paenitentiam, ante exomologesim grauissimi adque extremi delicti factam, ante manum ab episcopo et clero in paenitentiam inpositam . . ."); English edition, Saint Cyprian, *The Letters of St. Cyprian of Carthage, Volume I*, letter 15, section 1.2, trans. G. W. Clarke (New York: Newman Press 1984), pp. 90–91 ("before penance has been done, before confession of the most serious and grievous of sins has been made, before there has been the imposition of hands by the bishop and clergy in token of reconciliation . . ."). Bayard describes this passage in the margin as "the process of penitential discipline"; ibid., p. 43 n. 1.

35. Tertullien, *La Pudicité (De pudicitia)*, trans. Charles Munier (Paris: Les Éditions du Cerf, 1993); English edition, Tertullian, *Treatises on Penance: On Penitence and on Purity*, trans. and annot. William P. Le Saint (Westminster, MD: Newman Press, 1959).

36. Tertullien, *La Pudicité*, trans. Munier, chapter 3, section 5, pp. 160–61; English edition, Tertullian, *Treatises on Penance*, trans. Le Saint, pp. 60–61.

37. Tertullien, *La Pudicité*, trans. Munier, chapter 13, section 7, pp. 208–9; English edition, Tertullian, *Treatises on Penance*, trans. Le Saint, p. 87.

38. See Saint Jérôme, *Lettres*, vol. 4, letter 77, sections 4 and 5, trans. Jérôme Labourt (Paris: Les Belles Lettres, 1954), pp. 43–45; English edition, Frederick A. Wright, *Select Letters of St. Jerome* (Cambridge, MA: Harvard University Press, 1975), p. 317 ("One the eve of Passover, in the presence of all Rome, she took her stand among the other penitents in the church of that Lateranus who perished formerly by Caesar's sword. There before bishop, presbyters, and weeping populace she exposed to view her disheveled hair, wan face, soiled hands, and dust-stained neck") and p. 321 ("She laid her wound to all, and Rome beheld with tears the scar upon her livid body. She uncovered her limbs, bared her head, and closed her mouth").

39. Irénée de Lyon, *Contre les hérésies*, book 1, chapter 13, section 5, trans. Adelin Rousseau and Louis Doutreleau, vol. 2 (Paris: Éditions du cerf, 1979), pp. 200–201; English edition, St. Irenaeus of Lyons, *Against the Heresies, Book I*, chapter 13, section 5 (New York: Paulist Press, 1992), pp. 57–58 ("When, however, with much effort the brothers converted her, she spent the whole time doing penance amid weeping and lamentation over the defilement she had suffered through this magician," ibid. at p. 58).

40. Tertullien, *La Pénitence (De paenitentia)*, chapter 12, section 7, trans. Munier (Paris:

Les Éditions du Cerf, 1984), pp. 188–91; English edition, Tertullian, *Treatises on Penance*, trans. Le Saint, p. 36 (". . . performing his exomologēsis for seven squalid years, his nails growing wild like the talons of an eagle, his hair unkempt like the shaggy mane of a lion. Oh the blessedness of this harsh treatment! One whom men shunned with horror, God received!").

41. Tertullien, *La Pénitence*, trans. Munier, chapter 9, section 1, pp. 180–81; English edition, Tertullian, *Treatises on Penance*, trans. Le Saint, p. 31 ("Since this second and last penitence is so serious a matter, it must be tested in a way which is proportionately laborious. Therefore it must not be performed solely within one's conscience, but it must also be shown forth in some external act").

42. Tertullien, *La Pénitence*, trans. Munier, chapter 9, section 3, pp. 180–81; English edition, Tertullian, *Treatises on Penance*, trans. Le Saint, p. 31 ("Exomologēsis, then, is a discipline which leads a man to prostrate and humble himself. It prescribes a way of life which, even in the matter of food and clothing, appeals to pity").

43. Tertullien, *La Pénitence*, trans. Munier, chapter 9, section 4, pp. 180–81; English edition, Tertullian, *Treatises on Penance*, trans. Le Saint, pp. 31–32.

44. This is an excerpt from a letter of the priests and deacons of Rome to Cyprian on the question of the reintegration of apostates. The Latin text can be found in the *Patrologie Latine*, vol. 4, col. 306: "Tempus est igitur ut agant delicti poenitentiam, ut probent lapsus sui dolorem, ut ostendant verecundiam, ut monstrent humilitatem, ut exhibeant modestiam, ut de submissione provocent in se Dei clementiam, et de honore debito in Dei sacerdotem eliciant in se divinam misericordiam." We thank Bernard Coulie for this reference.

45. Saint Cyprien, *Liber de lapsis*, PL 4, col. 463–94/*De ceux qui ont failli*, section 16, trans. Denys Gorce, in *Textes* (Namur: Éd. du Soleil levant, 1958), p. 97. It can also be found online at www.abbaye-saint-benoit.ch/saints/cyprien/tombes.htm. Cyprian, *De lapsis*, section 32, p. 49, in *De lapsis* and *De ecclesiae catholicae unitate*, trans. Maurice Bévenot (Oxford: Oxford University Press, 1971), p. 49 ("Join your tears to ours, add your sorrow to our sorrow").

46. Ambroise de Milan, *La Pénitence (De paenitentia)*, book 1, chapter 5, section 24, lines 53–55, trans. Roger Gryson (Paris: Éditions du Cerf, 1971), p. 72 ("Negarunt sermone, sed confitentur gemitibus, confitentur heiulatibus, confitentur fletibus, confitentur liberis, non coactis vocibus"; [they confess their faith by their groaning, they confess it by their lamentations, they confess it with their tears, they confess it by speaking freely, without being under constraint]); English translation, Ambrose, *Concerning Repentance*, book 1, chapter 5, section 24, available online at http://www.newadvent.org/fathers/34061.htm.

47 The typescript deposited at the IMEC reads "Paranèse de Patien." The word "Paranèse" should read "Parénèse," a literary genre (consolation, exhortation) that was common among ecclesiastical authors authors of the first centuries. Foucault refers to the same text in *Du gouvernement des vivants*. According to Michel Senellart, this reference is to a text by Saint Pacian, the bishop of Barcelona in the fourth century, titled *Paraenesis sive exhortatorius libellus ad poenitentiam*, PL 13, col. 1082d; a French translation appeared under the title "Exhortation à la pénitence" in *Le Pécheur et la pénitence dans l'Église ancienne*, C. Vogel, ed. and trans. (Paris: Les Éditions du Cerf, coll. "Chrétiens de tous les temps," 1966; rééd. Paris, Les Éditions du Cerf, coll. "Traditions chrétiennes," 1982), pp. 88–101.

FOURTH LECTURE

May 6, 1981

Practice of veridiction in monastic institutions of the fourth and fifth centuries: the *Apophtheg-mata patrum* and the writings of Cassian. • Monasticism: between the life of penance and philosophical existence. • Characteristics of the direction of conscience in ancient culture. • Characteristics of the direction of conscience in monasticism: an obedience that is continuous, formal, and self-referential; humility, patience, and submission; the inversion of the relationship to verbalization. • Characteristics of the examination of conscience in monasticism: from action to thought. • Mobility of thought and illusion. • *Discrimen* and *discretio*: avowal and the origin of thought. • Veridiction of the self, hermeneutics of thought, and the rights-bearing subject.

In my previous lecture I briefly touched on the forms of avowal that can be found in early Christianity, very precisely—or, more precisely—in rituals of penance. And it seemed to me that this avowal found in the rituals of penance of the first centuries of Christianity, this avowal was fundamentally different from what we call, strictly speaking, confession—that *confessio oris*, that verbal avowal of sins that would be institutionalized and become part of the sacrament of penance, but much later, not before the eleventh or twelfth centuries. This avowal that was tied to rituals of penance in the first centuries of Christianity, it seemed to me, should be understood as a kind of manifestation, a manifestation of the self, an expressive and symbolic manifestation of the self, with two characteristics: first, it did not have as an objective, purpose, or end the discovery of a truth hidden deep within oneself; and second, it did not use verbal expression as its principal instrument. And I believe it is with monastic practice that we see emerge—only later, in the fourth and fifth centuries—a new practice which, it seems to me, was of fundamental importance in the history of what we might call the relationships between subjectivity and truth in the West. In other words, it was not within canonical penance but within monastic practices located in particular institutions—albeit institutions that were of great cultural and social importance well into the heart of the Middle Ages—it is within these monastic institutions and these monastic practices that one finds the great change that will introduce us to the central and major problems of avowal in Western cultures.

Regarding monastic institutions, I would like quickly to recall two elements of fourth- and fifth-century monasticism that should never be forgotten.

First, monasticism had an ambiguous relationship to asceticism. It is absolutely true that the great development and proliferation of monastic institutions in the fourth century was part of a broader ascetic movement which, for multiple reasons, spread throughout and stirred the Christian world from the middle or the end of the third century to the beginning of the fifth century. Monasticism was integral to this ascetic movement, but it must be remembered that monastic institutions were also a way of organizing, regulating, slowing down, and restricting this ascetic movement of which they were a part. They took the movement up and gave it an institutional body to prevent behavioral and doctrinal excesses, zeal, and discrepancies that might have emerged in a competitive individual asceticism. It was a question, then, of struggling against these divergences, these individual excesses, as well as fighting, of course, against the Gnostic and Manichean influences that were manifesting themselves in many aspects of the ascetic movement. So, it was an asceticism, but it was an asceticism that was becoming institutionalized. And the cenobitic institution—or the *cenobite*, the life in common, the organization of a communitarian monasticism with a strong hierarchical structure—clearly shows that robust power structures, and not merely an ascetic aspiration, prevailed at the heart of monasticism.

The second thing that must be remembered with regard to this monasticism is that it was located at the crossroads of the two institutions or practices that I mentioned last time. It was located at the crossroads of penance, on the one hand, and of the practices and the techniques of philo- sophical existence on the other.

Indeed, [on the one hand] monasticism took on the form of a life of penance. The monk's life is a *vita paenitentiae* (a life of penance); that is to say it is a life of mortification designed to ensure that the individual was dead to this world and being born into the true life. And it is within this life of penance that we will find again many of the elements of the rituals of penance that I discussed last time, such as fasting, the prohibition of sexual relations, and the special clothing. To some extent, all of this would transpose into organized monastic life a certain number of important ele- ments that already existed within the penitential status that I discussed with you last time.

On the other hand, these penitential practices intersected with a whole series of other practices that came directly from philosophy. This intersec- tion of the life of penance with the philosophical life was in all likelihood one of the essential aspects of the monastic institution. The monastery, or monastic life, was considered the true philosophical life. The organization of monasteries—and here a discussion of Antioch would be in order, but I'll spare you the details—the organization of the monastery was done in part in reference to the organization of philosophical schools. And the monastery was called—but also defined itself as, and claimed to be—a philosophical school because monastic life, like the philosophical life, was designed to provide access to truth. To live like a philosopher or to live like a monk, to lead the true philosophical life in a monastery, meant giving oneself the possibility of accessing truth, and of acceding to truth through self-mastery and knowledge of the self.

So with monasticism, if we consider monasticism's ambiguous position within the broader movement of asceticism, when we think of its place at the intersection of rituals of penance and the philosophical life, then it seems to me that we can see a certain number of absolutely fundamental elements that root monasticism deeply in the tradition of the culture of antiquity.

First, there was the idea that access to truth was impossible without paying for such access through a specific mode of existence: not all types of existence led to truth, and those who sought the truth needed to pursue a particular way of life. This idea of ancient philosophy, or rather, charac- teristic of ancient philosophy—it is not "of" ancient philosophy, because

it can be found elsewhere as well, but it is characteristic of ancient philosophy—you can find this idea here: the monk would be entitled to have
access to truth.

Second, this access to truth required self-purification, a purification
that took on two forms that were paired and intimately tied to one another: namely, renunciation and mortification. To live a life akin to death
that, precisely because it was like death in this world, ensured access to the
other life—and, on the other hand, tied to this renunciation and mortification, knowledge of the self. Monasticism considered that this purification by mortification and knowledge of the self—precisely because of the
situation in which monasticism found itself and the institutionalization of
individual asceticism—could only be achieved through a certain relationship. This relationship was not only to oneself—not merely a relation of
knowledge to oneself or a relationship of asceticism and self-mortification
in relation to oneself—but equally and at the same time a relationship to
the other, a relationship to the master.

It seems to me that this set of fundamental characteristics can explain
the development, within monastic practice, of what I would like to explore
more closely today: that is, the practices of veridiction of oneself, or how,
in monasticism, truth-telling about oneself became an absolutely fundamental element, an essential element of this life, and how it was ultimately
injected into, grafted upon, and deeply implanted in Western culture in an
entirely new form. From this point on, this practice of avowal, this tre-
mendously complex technology of veridiction of oneself, developed with
considerable success. So this evening I would like briefly to study veridiction of oneself, telling truth about oneself within monastic institutions.

I will study these practices through a number of well-known texts.[1] The
first are the famous *Apophthegmata patrum*,[2] that is, those collected stories
consisting of anecdotes, of *exempla*—of examples, of little scenes with
symbolic and educative value that circulated in different monasteries, or
from one monastery to another, and which contained a lesson. A lesson on
how to live, on the good way to live within a monastery, based on a certain
number of anecdotes and examples.

Second, and above all, I will draw on Cassian's writings. As you know,
Cassian was a Christian from Illyria who, following a stay in Rome, was
drawn to the monastic movement that was already well developed and
largely institutionalized in Syria and Egypt. Like a number of Western
Christians, he went to visit these monasteries in Syria and lower Egypt.

He stayed for some time, living the life of the monks, frequenting the most famous among them, and eventually returning to the West. There, at the request of the bishop of Aix, I believe, he wrote two texts. One was entitled *Cenobitic Institutions*,[3] where he explained the institutionalization of monasticism in lower Egypt and Syria and the rules of life that were imposed essentially upon novices; in his *Institutions*, we have a schema for the organization of a possible monastery—and it was indeed with the intention of establishing, of organizing a monastic institution that Cassian wrote the text. And another much longer text is the *Conferences*,[4] where he recounted a certain number of important conversations with the most famous and most pious monks of the communities of Syria and Egypt. Cassian, at heart, is the one who introduced the practice and the theory of monastic life into the West. He was the principal agent in the transfer, in the translation of [Oriental] into [Western] monasticism.[5]* Of course there were others such as Saint Jerome, but Cassian's texts undoubtedly provide the most detailed account of monastic practices at the end of the fourth and the beginning of the fifth century. Thus, Cassian played an absolutely determinative role in the organization of Western monasticism. Later, Saint Benedict developed a considerable number of his ideas and principles. But one fact led to the relative erasure of Cassian's name within the spiritual tradition of Christianity—erased in name, even if his ideas were crystallized into institutions: Cassian, like many of the monks of lower Egypt, was steeped in the Origenian tradition. The condemnation of Origenism sometime after or before—I don't remember—Cassian's death[6] meant that his name was erased even though, once again, the tradition that he carried and imported into the West fundamentally shaped the birth and development of monasticism in western Europe. So I will build my analysis around these texts.

The first thing concerning [this] duty, this obligation, this practice of veridiction of the self in monastic institutions that seems fundamental to me is the following: in monastic practices such as they were described in the *Apophthegmata patrum* or the works of Cassian, the obligation to tell truth about oneself was always inscribed within a relationship to another, a relationship to another that was considered indispensable, foundational, and that was at the same time a relationship of obedience, a relationship of submission. I believe that this inscription of the duty to tell

* Foucault said "in the translation of Western into Oriental monasticism."

truth about oneself within a relationship of obedience to another was something both fundamental and new. You might argue that it was not that new since, after all, all of pagan antiquity—as we say—was familiar with this type of singular and important relationship between the disciple and the master, or the director and the directed. But I believe that the difference between the disciple-master relationship in pagan antiquity and the disciple-director, or directed-director relationship in monasticism and monastic institutions was precisely that in antiquity a relationship of obedience did not exist, and it was invented—or perhaps imported—by Christianity.[7]

Let me explain. In antiquity, naturally, there was this common idea that one who did not know an art and wanted to begin life, access wisdom, and learn philosophy needed a director—a director who would guide him, take him by the hand, and help him along the path. It was perfectly acceptable that this director be a guide and have authority. The Epicureans, for example, had a very strict and hierarchical organization in which those who guided, who were directors for the youngest among them, those who were less advanced in their philosophical path, carried the name of *hēgemones*: they were the ones who guided.

In antiquity, this direction could take on many forms. It could take on specific forms depending on the circumstances—for example, when one was in a difficult moment and it was necessary to ask someone who was more advanced along the path of wisdom, or more master of himself, or more familiar with the techniques of the self that I discussed earlier, to help in this difficult moment: a time of mourning, the death of a spouse, of parents, or of children, a reversal of fortune, an exile. These were circumstances in which people in antiquity—of course they were of a certain social milieu, affluence, and culture—could seek someone to help them overcome a difficult moment. This was the art of consolation, an art with its own specialists. For example, a Sophist named Antiphon[8] had a consolation office in Athens where one could pay for help to get through these difficult times. Someone like Crantor,[9] for example, wrote treatises of consolation that were recopied and that one either purchased or offered as a gift to a friend in just such trying times. These were examples of momentary or provisional guidance, evidently, as opposed to a more continuous guidance found in the philosophical schools. The latter took on an individual at a rather young age, although not necessarily, and then guided him for a certain number of years until he finally had acquired the wisdom that would allow him to apply the rules of living he had learned.* This is what the philosophical schools did, but it was also what a number of individuals would do outside the institution of the schools. When Seneca, for example, wrote the treatise *On Tranquility of Mind* for Serenus,[10] he was at bottom taking an individual under his wing: he was proposing to Serenus rules for a moral life and effectively overseeing the way in which Serenus would progress. The long correspondence between Seneca and Lucilius[11] was of this type: it offered guidance outside of a strictly philosophical institution, but guidance by the one who was more advanced. This is found as well in medical practice, where the doctor was not only treating illness but also giving a life regimen. And this life regimen was not simply a question of a regimen of medications, but of how to live to stay in good health, to be in good health, to take greatest advantage of one's life. It was doctors— doctors who followed the individual and also watched to ensure that he had indeed internalized and learned the rules—who provided these rules and regimens for living.

This leads us precisely to a certain number of characteristics in the ancient practice of direction that opposed it very clearly to the directed-director relationship found in monasticism. Indeed, in this ancient direction, of which I gave you a few examples, it is very clear that the entire operation was directed toward an end—toward an end that was understood at once as the goal of the operation and the end point—at which point it would stop. One was guided, for example, until one recovered one's health and could oversee one's own health. One was guided during the entire period in which one needed consolation. One was guided until one became *sophos*, until one became wise. The first characteristic, then, was that there was an objective, a precise goal; and, as a result, guidance was provisional.

Second, guidance in antiquity obeyed a principle of competence: the guide knew more than the one who asked to be guided. Of course, we have at least one famous example that was precisely the reverse: the example of Socrates. Socrates guided by pretending that he did not know, and that those who he guided through questioning knew far more than he. But after all, this was nothing more than a mirror reversal of a certain type of relationship. It was a question of leading the individual to the point where

---

* Foucault said, but seemed to correct himself: "until he attained the rule, acquired the wisdom that would allow him to apply the rules . . ."

he would know—or, in any case, where he would discover that he already knew. And there was at least one thing that Socrates knew and the other did not: that is, the other knew without knowing that he knew. To this extent, with this final turn, you see that we always find again this same principle of superior competence, of more knowledge in the one who guides than the one who is guided.[12]

The third characteristic of ancient direction is that it consisted essentially in learning a code, a rule of conduct, a way of life that was often extremely detailed, and that was to serve as a permanent code of behavior for the rest of one's life.

And then finally there is one last point that summarizes all the others: once the code was finally learned—once the regulation of behavior had been well internalized, thanks to the greater competence of the one who guided because he was the one who knew—the formerly unknowing individual, the individual who had been guided, finally could do without his master; and he could do without a master because he had become master of himself. That is, the operation of guidance consisted essentially of a substitution of mastery: one accepted the mastery of the other in order to ensure mastery over oneself and by oneself. And when Seneca, for example, examined his conscience as I described last time, he had become master of himself and could, as sovereign master of himself—of the self—judge his own actions, examine them, say what was good and what was not. He was literally master of himself—that is to say, he no longer needed a master; he was his own master.

To give you a very schematic example of this type of apprenticeship, of this type of mastery, I would simply like to refer to a medical text by Athenaeus, the first-century doctor whose texts were cited by Oribasius. In volume 3 of the Daremberg translation,[13] page 161, you have a description of a rule of medical life and the manner—very schematically summarized, of course—that one had to put oneself under the guidance of a doctor in order to be able to become master of one's own life, master in some sense of one's own health. Athenaeus wrote: "After the age of fourteen, it is useful, or rather necessary, for everyone to understand, among the subjects taught, not only the other sciences, but also medicine, and to listen to the precepts of this art."[14] Note the word *listen*; we will return to it. You see in any case that it is a question of apprenticeship of a science, the apprenticeship of a body of knowledge [*connaissances*]—but by knowledge, one must have in mind what the Greeks designated with the word *gnōmē*:

it was both an understanding [*une connaissance*], but at the same time a precept; it was at once a truth and a rule. It was thus a question of learning medicine as an indissociable corpus of competences [*connaissances*] and of precepts, of knowledge [*savoir*] and of rules. One needed to listen to the precepts of this art to become for ourselves accomplished counselors regarding the things useful to one's own health. The objective, as you see, was to become one's own accomplished counselor, to become master of oneself and ultimately one's own guide. "For," Athenaeus continued, "there is almost no moment of the night or day when we do not need a doctor, whether we are walking or sitting, performing unction or taking a bath, eating or drinking, sleeping or awake. In a word, whatever we may do in the course of our lives and amidst all of our diverse occupations and all that is tied to them, we need counsel."[15] That is to say, the arts of conducting oneself and being conducted were characterized by the idea that one could not live, the *bios* or life could not be properly lived, [without]* a rule telling one what to do and not to do at each instant, from every angle, in each moment no matter what the activity was. One cannot live, the *bios* cannot be lived without a system of regulation, without an extremely strict codification that determines what one should do or should not do at each instant. One had a perpetual need for counsel, or, in this case, since this is what is being treated here, medical counsel. But, as Athenaeus wrote, "we need counsel throughout our lives. We need advice to live our lives usefully and without inconvenience. And yet it is tiring and impossible constantly to address oneself to a doctor about all of these details."[16] So things are clear, one needed to regulate one's life entirely through a permanent and strict code of conduct—and only medical knowledge held this code. So there was a need at every moment for a sort of medical director of life who would tell us what to do; one needed advice at each instant. And since this was obviously impossible, one needed to learn through a master who provided this knowledge [*savoir*] in the form at once of competences [*connaissances*] and precepts. And once these had been acquired, then one could become one's own counselor.

You see, then, the process or the general arc that guidance followed in the ancient practice of direction. Let's just say that the relationship to mastery, as it is described here, this relationship to mastery was modeled entirely on a form with which you are familiar: that of pedagogy, the dis-

* Foucault said "if."

ciple and the master, and the disciple who accepted the authority of the master for a given period in order to become, in turn, master, master of his talents, of his health, of his body—master of himself and eventually master of other disciples, if he so desired and was capable of doing so. It was, then, a question of achieving mastery.

It is, however, this pedagogical model of guiding individuals that, I think, broke down in monasticism, producing at that very moment the real, great rupture in the history of this famous ancient pedagogy or psychagogy. I think that monasticism broke the ancient form of the pedagogical relationship by introducing or inserting within it the decisive and perhaps fatal element of obedience, of *obedientia*. There was a *de-pedagogicalization* of this relationship of mastery that, I believe, made up one of the essential and characteristic traits of monastic practice.

What was the relationship of obedience, or this obligation of obedience that restructured and at the same time drastically shifted the entire relationship of ancient pedagogy? How did the relationship of obedience present itself?

To begin with, it took on the form of the following principle: one needed a director for any and every situation and all the time. There is a sentence that would be repeated for more than a millennium on spiritual direction. It is a sentence, or rather, it is a text that is borrowed from *Proverbs*, that reads: "He who has no director—he who is not directed," rather—"falls like a dead leaf."[17] Of course, this was true for beginners. It was true for novices—and in Cassian's *Institutions* there was an entire chapter dedicated to taking charge of novices by those who had to direct them. A director looked after novices as soon as they entered. First he looked after them for a few days, then a new director took care of them for longer in small groups of ten.[18] This was similar to the organizational model of certain philosophical schools. This normal process of looking after someone fit entirely within the tradition of the master-disciple relationship in ancient philosophical practice. But what I think was specific to the monastic institution was that even when one ceased to be a novice, one could not do without some form of direction.[19] Of course, there was no institution related to the form of direction that was specifically addressed to the advanced. While the novices had a designated director, this was not the case for the more advanced. But all of the collected narratives, whether the *Apophthegmata* or the *Conferences*, all of these texts concerning monastic life show clearly that one failed precisely when one believed oneself to be one's own master and to be able to continue without a master or anyone else, when one presumed and believed that one no longer needed another and could therefore direct oneself. Even the one who was furthest along on the path of saintliness could fall when he did not admit, or no longer admitted, the possibility or obligation of being directed, and chose to be master of himself. So there was no evidence or any account of direction instituted for everyone until the end of one's life, but there was clearly the principle that direction could not be provisional, that in any case, there was a fundamental, continuous, and permanent need for the direction of every soul. In fact, as you no doubt recognize, the essential issue in all of this was the idea of a state of perfection. There was no state of perfection for the Christian monk, in spite of what certain philosophers or schools of ancient philosophy might have said. There was no state of perfection, no matter what certain Gnostics or Dualists argued. This is what was affirmed and illustrated in the principle of *directability*, if you will, or in the principle that there should always be a potential relationship of direction throughout the individual's existence.

I will cite just one example of the recognition that one needs permanent direction: an anecdote from the *Apophthegmata* which was also recounted at least twice by Cassian.[20] It is the story of the monk Pinufius, who was of such saintliness that he attracted around him, as a consultant precisely, individuals who needed to be guided. His saintliness was so widely recognized that the monks of his monastery wanted to make him the superior. But each time he found himself in this situation, he went to hide in another convent where he introduced himself as a gardener, a cook, et cetera—the most modest positions. Quite simply, his saintliness shined through each time, and consequently he attracted once again new disciples who asked him to be their guide. And each time, he fled once again. So Pinufius exemplified the principle that one should never consider that one had attained a definitive state of mastery with regard to others, of course, but also with regards to oneself. One should never believe that one had achieved a state of mastery. As a result, one should always be in a situation of dependence and submission to the other—to another.

There was, then, a second characteristic. After the indefinite relationship of obedience or relationship of mastery to the other, there was the formal aspect of the relationship of obedience in monasticism. What I mean is this: you remember that in antiquity, following a master was the condition for the transmission of a certain knowledge, a certain capacity possessed by the master who was more competent than the disciple; and the master's knowledge, the master's competence was transmitted to the disciple thanks to the disciple's provisional submission or his listening to the master. The master's authority was built on his competence—technical competence or wisdom. In monasticism, on the contrary, obedience was a practice whose value depended neither on the one who was obeyed nor on the nature or the very quality of the order that one obeyed. Rather, the value of obedience was drawn from the mere fact that one obeyed. This is important. Of course one should try to put oneself under the control of the best possible guide. But who was the best possible guide in monastic practice? It was the one who was the least indulgent, the one who granted his disciple the least liberty or put him under the greatest degree of submission. But there is more. What made one advance on the path of saintliness, and thus on the path to life and to truth, was the pure fact that one obeyed no matter who the master or what his order. No matter who the master was: one finds in both the *Apophthegmata* and in Cassian a certain number of examples of disciples who advanced quickly on the road to saintliness because their master was a horrible master, an unjust master, a cantankerous master, a master who gave absurd orders—because, in the end, the master could be anyone.

There is a famous example. I do not remember anymore the person's name, but the example concerns a woman, a wealthy woman who had decided to renounce life and had accepted as the form of renunciation to become the servant of someone else. She came upon a mistress who was just towards her—not indulgent, but just. She therefore asked the bishop to find her an old and particularly unjust and cantankerous woman whose caprices she followed so well that she achieved salvation precisely due to the fact that the person she served was unjust.[21] There are also these famous stories of absurd orders that recur frequently in the *Apophthegmata* and in Cassian's writings. For instance, the story of Abbot John, who took the path of saintliness as the disciple of a monk who, one day, told him to plant a dried stick in the desert far from any well or spring. He told him to water it twice a day, promising him that the stick would blossom (this is an addition from a later version, but no matter). No need to tell you how the story ends: at the end of the year, the stick was still withered. The master criticized his disciple Abbot John for not having watered it sufficiently, and so he watered it for another year, and of course the tree finally blossomed.[22] There is also the story of Patermutus, who entered a convent with his young son. He was asked, to prove his obedience to the orders of his superiors, to drown his son in the river. And Patermutus goes to drown his son, but is, of course, stopped by the head of the convent.[23] Obviously, these two stories—of the dried stick that blossoms and of Patermutus sacrificing his son—recall the great scriptural figures that you know as well as I. But it was not simply because these scriptural figures were present here—Abbot John watering the withered stick, Patermutus sacrificing his son[24]—it was not simply because they were reproducing these scriptural figures that they were saints, or that they advanced along the path of saintliness. It was because, through these figures, they practiced a pure form of obedience that did not owe its value to the order itself, but simply to the fact that it was followed. The principle of obedience to *x* was a principle of obedience under any and all circumstances.

Caution is necessary here as well, because this idea was not completely foreign to the pedagogy of antiquity. In the *Apology of Socrates*, for example, you will find a clear distinction between *didaskalia* and *ōpheleia*. The master would not only teach—that is *didaskalia*, to pass his knowledge on to the disciple who did not possess it—but also had to be useful, that is to say to make the individual do a certain number of exercises that would allow him to advance on the path of virtue. These exercises were not, in fact, a transmission of knowledge or competence from one who was more accomplished to one who was less so. But nonetheless, it was always emphasized—and it was very characteristic to see—that in the *Apophthegmata patrum*, as well as in Cassian's writings, the master never taught the disciple anything. The master is never the one who, as the bearer of greater competence, taught or imparted in terms of knowledge or in terms of precepts what was to be done. He subjected the disciple to a number of tests, which were tests of obedience.

The third characteristic of this obedience—it was thus continuous, that was the first characteristic, it was continuous and indefinite; second, it was formal—so the third characteristic: I would say that it was self-referential. It was self-referential insofar as obedience in monastic institutions had one sole objective, only one goal. It was supposed to lead the disciple to what, exactly? To be obedient, to be in a permanent state of obedience. And this permanent state of obedience—which ultimately was not the limit, but rather the constant objective of the relationship of obedience to a master—this permanent state of obedience manifested itself in three virtues that, I believe, need to be properly characterized.

The state of obedience[25] that resulted from the challenge of continual obedience manifested itself in *humilitas*, humility, which consisted of always considering oneself last among all others. To be the last meant that all the others, no matter who they were, could give you orders, and that you should, under such conditions, obey those orders. It was a relationship of obedience to the other—the other defined not, once again, through his competence or his value, but the other defined as any other. One owed obedience to all others. That was *humilitas*.[26]

The second aspect was *patientia*. *Patientia* meant never resisting a given order. Saint Nilus wrote—an expression that would have the historic legacy that you know so well: "Not to differ from an inanimate body or an artist's raw materials, to be like a cadaver, to be like an inanimate body, to be like raw material in the hands of another, and never to resist."[27] The example, story, *exemplum* that illustrates this principle is the story of the copyist. Copying and recopying the sacred word was obviously, outside of the psalmody and participation in collective ceremonies, the highest, most saintly, and sacred activity: to copy, recopy the sacred word. And in this regard, the good copyist was the one who was able to set aside his quill at the very instant that his master called him and to obey what his master demanded of him, even if he was tracing the most saintly names or even God's name on his parchment or papyrus.[28] In other words, he does not resist. We have here the principle of the abolition of all autonomous will: the abolition of autonomous will in one's relationship to any other.

The third virtue, after *humilitas* in one's relationship to others, after *patientia* as the absence of autonomy, was the most interesting, paradoxical, and fundamental virtue: *subditio*. *Subditio* meant submission, to be subjugated, and was a very important concept.

It was very important because it was opposed—it must be opposed—to the idea of being subject to the law, for example, in ancient political, moral, and philosophical thought. Of course, antiquity was familiar with the principle of obedience, but what was one to obey? One had to obey the law. Here, in *subditio*, in submission, it was not a question of obeying the law as a code of obligations and interdictions. It was a question in fact of letting the principle of obedience penetrate one's entire behavior; one was not to do anything that was not commanded by someone else. An absolutely fundamental sentence in Saint Basil reads: "Any act"—any act—"that is done without an order or the permission of a superior is a sacrilege that will lead to death and not to profit, even if it appears to be good."[29]

One was not to do anything that was not in some way commanded by another. Saint Barsanuphius,[30] as reported in Cassian's *Conferences*,[31] said that youths should never leave their cells without the attendant knowing, and they should not even assume the superior's authorization to satisfy their natural urges. There was, then, there needed to be, a total renunciation of one's will such that nothing in one's behavior appeared, nothing could be done in the course of one's life, or entire existence, during the day or the night, that had not been ordered. I believe that at the very heart of the notion of *subditio* was the total penetration of one's entire existence and of all one's actions with the will of another, of others, of an *x*; and this is important because it was opposed to the idea of obedience to a law. The law is what obliges you to do or forbids you to do something; consequently, it implies that you are free to do the rest. So there was a radical opposition between monastic *subditio* and Greco-Roman submission to the law.

This is an important notion because, you see, it leads to the exact opposite of the self-mastery that was the objective of ancient pedagogy. In these monastic practices, one sought precisely the opposite; that is to say, one was never to be master of oneself, but rather one was to ensure that there was always within oneself someone who was the master and the master of everything. It was a question then of annulling oneself as a willful being, of renouncing oneself, of renouncing the will to be and being oneself, and renouncing being oneself in and through one's will. This was the important transition—or rather, the important coupling—between the theme of the mortification of the body, which characterized penance and which continued to characterize the penitential life of the monk [and the mortification of the self]. There was a shift away from the mortification of the body, or rather, there was the addition of mortification of the self to the mortification of the body:[32] one must destroy oneself as a self. And this coupling of mortification of the body and mortification of the self was at the very heart of the relationship of obedience.

Finally, the third reason why this relationship of obedience was fundamental in its singularity was that in order to reach this *subditio*, in order to ensure that one always had the will of another in the place of one's own, or of someone else who transformed all of one's voluntary acts into an act of submission—in order for this to be possible, there was obviously a requirement. One simple, obvious requirement: one needed to speak. One had to speak, one had to say everything that took place within oneself, everything one wanted to do, all of one's desires, everything one intended to do, everything that was going on within oneself, and all the movements of one's thoughts. And this—that *subditio* to another, the renunciation of the self took place through verbalization to another—this was clearly and simply explained in a text that was, I think, absolutely fundamental to Western history. In chapter 4 of Cassian's *Institutions*, you read the following: young monks must learn to conquer their will by obeying orders that are the most contrary to their inclinations. And in order to succeed in this task more easily, beginners are taught not to hide any of their thoughts through false shame—"*nullas cogitationes*," we will come back to this because it is very important—not to hide any of the thoughts that eat away at their hearts; but as soon as they are born, they must be revealed to the elder.[33]

Obviously, the principle of perpetual avowal was directly tied to this general principle of obedience.[34] Indefinite obedience, formal obedience, and obedience that must lead to a *state* of obedience—*humilitas, patientia, subditio*—all this necessarily required verbalization. And I think that we have here something fundamental in the history of Western culture: it is what one could call the inversion of the axis of verbalization in the relationship of mastery.

In antiquity, the one who spoke was obviously the master. The strongest evidence that the master was the one who spoke is that the disciple's obedience to his master was manifested in an act, in an activity, in an attitude that was designated by the Greek word *akouein*: he listens. To listen and obey is the same thing; they are bound together because commanding was tied to the activity of speech. The director spoke, while the directed listened. And once again, if Socrates serves as a counterexample, it is a sophisticated exception that proves the rule, since Socrates of course made his disciples speak. But why did he make the disciple speak? So that at a given moment the disciple finally, at the end of the day, discovered the truth in himself and could tell it. The moment he told the truth, he had arrived at a point where he could be master of himself—or, in any case, master of his knowledge.

So whereas in antiquity verbalization emanated from the master in the direction of the disciple who served as the listener, to the contrary, in the new relationship of obedience that developed in monastic institutions, the structure was completely reversed. To obey—at once because one obeyed and to obey, and in order to always remain in a state of obedience—one needed to speak. One had to speak about oneself. Veridiction was a process; veridiction of oneself—truth-telling about oneself—was an indispensable condition for subjection to a relationship of power with another. As a result, it was the other who listened, and it was the one who was subjugated who spoke. In this inversion, you can see all of the historical echoes that have radiated and rebounded throughout our culture ever since. I think that it marked a fundamental break.

The problem, then, is: How did this veridiction operate? How was it organized and how did it develop so that the relationship of obedience, the fundamental relationship to the other, could be formed through and by this veridiction?*

:::

So how was this veridiction done? Truth-telling about oneself in order to be able to obey and attain a state of obedience [. . .] obviously implied two things: first, self-examination, and second, telling it effectively, through a verbal act.

First, there was self-examination. There is one thing which is very characteristic: you will find almost no mention in early Christianity of the examination of conscience that, as I showed you last time, was a common practice in pagan antiquity and in a number of philosophical schools. In particular, the rituals of penance that I discussed earlier did not at all suggest that one should ask of the individual: "Gather yourself, think about your sins, try to remember, and then you will tell them to someone." Not at all—the ritual of penance did not take this form. One finds almost no reference to the examination of one's conscience, except a few cases that I will recount to you precisely because they allow us to situate properly the transformation that was to come and that could only emerge with monasticism.

In the works of Clement of Alexandria you can find the idea that it is important to know oneself: *auton gnōnai, auton heauton*. Why is it important to know oneself? asked Clement of Alexandria. Because when one knows oneself, one recognizes God within oneself, and one can begin to resemble God as soon as one recognizes the presence of God within oneself.[35] Here

---

* Foucault addresses the audience: "So perhaps you would like to take a quick break? Perhaps you have had enough? Let's stop for five minutes, and then begin again—or would you like to ask some questions? What would you prefer? Tell me . . . pardon. OK, let's stop for five minutes, because the rest may be rather long."

you have a version of the theme of recognition, of Platonic reminiscence: we are very far from the examination of conscience that we found in ancient philosophical texts, or that we will find in monasticism. There is also a text by Origen—it is in the second book of commentary on the *Song of Songs*.* In the text, Origen comments a passage of the *Song of Songs* where it is written: "If you do not know yourself, if you do not know the reasons for your beauty, you will go to the kids' stable."[36] And Origen commented that kids are animals that are both worrisome and errant, which is the image of sin: if we do not know ourselves, therefore, we will fall into sin. What is this knowledge? asked Origen. He commented, saying: "There are two modes of self-knowledge [. . .]: either knowing oneself in substance or knowing oneself through one's affects."[37] The first question, knowing oneself in substance (*ousia*): the problem was to know, to recognize, to know how to recognize if the soul was corporeal or not, whether it was simple or complex, created or not-created, if it was contained or not in the seed of one's parents, or if it was acquired afterwards. So you see, it was a fundamentally philosophical question on the nature of the soul—this is what Origen called knowing oneself. He also explained that there was another mode of knowing oneself, which was knowing one's affects, knowing oneself through one's affects: to know if they were good or bad, if the soul was distant from its goal or not, if it had done something wrong purposefully or not, if it knew how to master itself, if it could control its changes in mood. That is, as you see, Origen was making reference to a practice, to a type of knowledge of the self that corresponded exactly to what could be found among the Stoics. So in Clement of Alexandria, we find again [an] echo of the principle of Platonic reminiscence, [and] in Origen an obvious echo of the practices that could be found among the Stoics—that you will find in Seneca, for example.

On the other hand, when we examine later texts that pertain directly or indirectly to monastic practices, then we see that the question of the examination of conscience—of the scrutiny of the soul by itself—became a question that was both important and technical, and posed extraordinarily complex technical problems, or at least problems that were far more complex than those found in Origen or in Clement of Alexandria. The examination of conscience took on essentially two forms.

---

* Foucault adds: "For those of you who are interested, I will give you the exact reference if you like."

First, the use of the practice of vesperal examination, the examination of conscience that was to be done each evening and for which Pythagoras (or Pythagoreans) and Seneca (or, in any case, those like him) had provided the example, the formula. There is a description, or rather there are several descriptions of the vesperal examination in different texts of Chrysostom, who, as you know, alongside Saint Jerome, was one of the most impenitent chatterboxes ever produced by Christianity. So the good Chrysostom came back regularly to the examination of one's conscience. In a homily on Psalm 4, for example, you find this: "One must not fall asleep before reflecting upon what one has done. Ask," wrote Chrysostom, "for an account of your conscience with regard to your daily actions every evening and condemn your sinful thoughts."[38] You see how close the vesperal examination was to that of Seneca.[39] In the sixtieth homily on Genesis, it is written: "Be seated without witness at the tribunal of one's conscience."[40] You will find, then, in Chrysostom, the same image that you had in Seneca: one must be one's own judge, and one must every evening be seated in the tribunal as one's own judge and one's own accused. In another text by Chrysostom it is written: "If you expel your sins from your memory, God will remember them. If you retain them in your memory, God will forget them."[41] That is, the memory of God and the memory of man are inverse and complementary: if you forget, God remembers; if you remember, God forgets. The soul keeps one's sins within and dreams serve as witnesses. So, in fact, the text was extremely complicated and merits close study because, you see, there was this idea that when one remembered one's sins, God forgot them. But why did God forget? Because when one remembered one's sins, the soul no longer kept them within; and when it kept them within—that is, when the soul did not remember them, or it forgot them—they returned in dreams, and dreams are testimonials.* This is a very interesting idea as a mechanism, but you see that there was still a distinct echo of Pythagoras in such a text on the relationship between memory and dreams.[42] In Chrysostom, in the homily on Psalm 50, you also find the following with regard to the examination of conscience: "Do you not have a book where you write your daily accounts? You must have a book in your conscience—*eche biblion en tō suneidoti*.[43] You must have a

---

* Foucault addresses the audience: "That is, one must, if you will—for those of you who are interested in these questions, you can go directly to the texts. I will give you the exact reference."

book in your conscience and write your faults down in it. When you go to bed, before going to sleep, retrieve the book and read what is inside."[44] The idea, then, that one must . . . you see, has already begun to shift away from the Stoic practice. This idea that one needed to always have by one's side a little notebook, a little book of notes, where one took note of what happened as it took place, of one's acts, faults, and bad thoughts. Chrysostom wrote that one should note them, or act as if they were noted. Then, in the evening, one pretended to pull out this book of the day where the entire day was written, and one went over it again.

This theme that one must have a tablet next to oneself in order to note little by little everything that happens—this idea relates back, in fact, to a monastic practice that Athanasius described in his *Vita Antonisi*, in which he attributed the following precept to Saint Anthony: "Everyone shall maintain a daily register of what he does night and day. Everyone shall note it in writing."[45] Chrysostom presented this later as a kind of metaphor: "Act as if you had a book." In fact, it was presented by Athanasius and attributed to Saint Anthony as a real practice, an effective precept. "May each one write his actions and the movements of his soul"—that is, not only what one did, but the very movements of the soul—"that they be noted in writing, as if they needed to be made known to others. Let the written word play the role of our companions."[46]

So here, the text was fundamental. One needed to write. One had to write down everything one did, one needed to write all of the movements of the soul. And why did one need to write? Because once it was written, or engraved in letters, it was as if they were being shown to others. And the famous problem of the choice between anchoritic and cenobitic, between solitary life and community life, you see that this problem was evoked here. Saint Antoine Anchorite, as opposed to the monks such as his Pacomian or Basilian successors, said that once one had written, it was as if one had a companion, because the written letters were virtually readable, virtually read by someone else; and this relationship to the other was assured by noting everything that took place in the soul through the medium of writing.

I believe that this was the precise turning point in the technologies of the self* found in ancient pagan philosophy; at the cusp between these

---

* Foucault said: "les techniques de, techniques du soi, technologies de soi" (the techniques of, the techniques of the self, technologies of the self).

techniques and the new techniques [. . .] which were essentially characterized by the fact that the relationship to the other—and the submission
to the other—was fundamental, and characterized as well by the fact of
their exhaustiveness and continuity. One needed to tell all, to someone, all
the time—to x, who was the other or who was the principle of the other.
This is what can be found in these texts on the book and on writing: the
necessity of having a book giving an account of oneself, by one's side, for
the potential gaze of the other. These are the elements that appear in the
text of Saint Athanasius. These are the elements that were developed in
monastic life and described in detail by someone like Cassian. And how in
effect was the examination of the conscience to unfold or, more precisely,
of what did it consist in Cassian's *Institutions* and the *Conferences*? What
is its specificity?

The first question to pose is, fundamentally, what does the examination of conscience take as its object? Recall that in the case of Seneca, the
examination of conscience focused on actions taken, which were not so
much faults one thought one had committed, as points where one felt one
had acted inappropriately, fallen short of one's desired aims, or diverged
from one's principles. In any case, it was always a question of actions, actions that were judged and measured—the term can be found in Seneca—
in relation to the principles. It was the polarity between principles and
actions that was the raw material, the object, or the field upon which the
examination of conscience had to be applied. What must one become conscious of in the examination of conscience described by Cassian? What is
the object of one's conscience? The text is very clear: "*Nullas cogitationes
celari.* Hide no thoughts, no reflections."[47] In other words, the essential
point of this examination was no longer action and its adequacy or inadequacy with regard to a principle. It was the thought itself. "What was I
thinking? What am I thinking?"

What is the significance of this displacement from *actum* to *cogitatio*?
Is it an essential displacement? Obviously it does not mean that the problem of actions did not arise in monastic life. I suppose one could argue
that the question was not posed to the extent that, when an illegal act was
committed, the monk was sent away if the action was serious—or, in any
event, he was subject to a punishment, an extremely codified punishment,
by the way, if the action, if the misdeed, if the infraction was not so serious. But this was not the key question in the examination of conscience. In
the examination of conscience it was a question of *cogitatio*. And why was

cogitatio, thought, so important? Simply because the objective of monastic life was contemplation.[48] It was contemplation; that is to say, the monk's objective was to succeed in seeing [*voir*] God, or better, to succeed in looking toward [*regarder*] God, or even better yet, to succeed in keeping the mind's eye fixed on God—on God as the unique Being. In other words, all of one's contemplative thoughts were to be unified toward this object and by this object that thought attained and that was God; and through this unity, thought found its immobility. All these techniques of monastic life pointed toward contemplation as an exercise of unification and immobilization of thought in God.

You understand clearly that under these conditions, if the monk's objective was to unify and immobilize his thoughts by looking toward God, then the obstacle, the enemy, what needed to be defeated and thrown aside was the *cogitatio*, in the sense that Cassian used the term *co-agitatio*,[49] that is, in the sense of movement of thought. The chief obstacle for the one who sought to contemplate God was the myriad thoughts, the constant movement of thought produced by the mind. The internal agitation of one's thought was the major problem of the technique of a directed spirituality oriented toward contemplation. While the principal problem for the morality of the ancients was the agitation of the body and passions brought about by external events, the fundamental problem of monastic life was not the agitation of affects through external events, but the agitation of thought by internal movement. And this is what was analyzed at length in a chapter that—if you are interested in these things—you should absolutely and unconditionally read, and that is, I believe, absolutely fundamental to the history of technologies of the self in Western history, in Western culture: the eighth *Conference* of Cassian, which is dedicated to the mobility of thought.[50]

In this chapter, in this *Conference*, it is said that the mind [*l'esprit*] is [fundamentally in movement]. And it was, for that matter, typical that Cassian used the Greek word even though the text was in Latin. He used two Greek words that came from his master Evagrius. [. . .] He wrote that the mind was *aeikinētos* and *polykinētos*;[51] that is to say, the mind was always in movement, and that it makes these various movements in all directions: remaining idle was contrary to its nature. This idea that the mind was fundamentally in movement had certain consequences.

The first important consequence was that the very notion of *cogitatio*, which corresponded to the Greek *logismos*, took on a pejorative meaning.

The Greek term *logismos* referred to a thought process, a pattern of reasoning: it was a neutral, or rather positive, notion.[52] To the contrary, in the texts of spiritual Christianity the word *logismos* and the word *cogitatio*—which were, for that matter, mostly employed in the plural—were always pejorative terms: it was this agitation of thought, this tangential thought, this thought that was dispersed in all directions and prevented contemplation.[53]

The second characteristic of this thought, which required that it be watched over, was that it was not only agitated, thus preventing the contemplation of God, but it also misled itself. This is an equally important point. For the Stoics, the challenge in effect was to work on one's own thoughts. But why? To prevent the harboring of false opinions in one's mind. One needed to avoid being wrong about things—about the order of the world, about the universal laws that regulate nature. One needed to avoid being mistaken about what *physis* was; one needed to avoid being mistaken about *kathēkontai*. The challenge for Christian spirituality, on the other hand, was not to know whether one's thought was mistaken about things. Rather, the challenge was to know if thought was deluding itself or not. What did it mean to delude oneself? Well, the problem was very simple—once again, it was a technical problem. An idea entered the monk's mind. This idea, such as deciding to fast, appeared to be good; and because it was a good idea, it could be received by the mind. Indeed, the idea of fasting, if it were put into practice, could help direct one's mind toward God and was therefore part of the movement of convergence toward God. But what guarantee was there that the idea of fasting was not, in fact, an attempt to increase one's standing among one's fellow monks by showing one's ability to fast more than the others? What proof did one have that this idea of fasting would not ultimately weaken one's body to such an extent that one could not resist the temptation of gluttony? Consequently, this good idea of fasting could, in fact, be bad.[54] One needed to question the idea, then, not in terms of its truth with regard to things, but in terms of its internal quality; or rather, one needed to question the idea itself in order to determine whether something was hidden behind it.* This obviously marked a fundamental difference with Stoic examination.

And we arrive then at this other question: Why might thought fool

---

* The end of the sentence is practically inaudible. Foucault could be saying "hidden behind this good idea" or "hidden behind this quality."

itself? Because of our poor judgment? Yes, in one sense, but this was insufficient. The Stoics could satisfy themselves with this response, but when the monk saw rising up in him—from the very first moment, from the first inkling—an idea like that of fasting, he needed to ask himself where this thought came from because only this response could guarantee whether his thought was good or not; in other words, whether this thought came from God or from Satan. If it came from God, then it would be a good idea and there would be no illusion in this idea that presented itself: your thought would not delude itself. By contrast, if it came from Satan, it would be misleading.

Thus, you see that what characterized Christian examination, the examination of oneself, was that instead of focusing on acts, it focused on thought—on thought and the movement of thought. Through this examination, it was a question of knowing whether or not one's thought was deluding itself and [. . .], in order to decide whether or not there was illusion, of determining the very origin of the thought.

So you see clearly that when the objective of the examination of conscience was to examine one's thoughts to see their origins and the power of illusion contained within them, its form was fundamentally different from what one found in the Stoics or even in Chrysostom's vesperal examination. You understand clearly that under these conditions—if one had to examine thus the nature of one's thoughts, their origin and potential illusion—it was not a question of waiting until evening to remember and memorize the things one had done. It was an ever-present and permanent relationship: a sort of vertical relationship through which one examined [*surveille*] oneself and constantly examined one's own thought. Moreover, you see clearly that it could not be a question of verifying if such and such a thing conformed to a rule, as was the case with the Stoics. It was a question of discovering what was hidden deep within oneself—that is to say, from where did the thought come, what were its intrinsic qualities, and whether or not it carried an illusion. In short, it was not, as with the Stoics, a question of revealing the truth of things so that one could regulate one's behavior. It was a question of drawing out the elements of truth—or of illusion; in this case, truth was opposed to illusion and not to error—the element of truth or illusion within the thought itself.

I believe that this moment marked the birth of what we might call a hermeneutics of the self in the Western world. A hermeneutics of the self whose primary object—historically speaking, the object that first appeared in the practices of the hermeneutics of the self—was the *cogita-tio*, its *qualitas*, and its *origo*: thought, [its] quality, and its origin. And to understand what this examination consisted of and what form it should take, Cassian would refer on several occasions to three comparisons that, I think, were characteristic of this attitude of self-examination focused on one's thought, its quality, and its origin. There was the comparison to the miller: we should be our own miller; we should be the miller of our own thought—that is to say that just as the miller, when the grain arrives to be ground, verifies if the grain is good or not, if it is dry or humid, if it is rotten or healthy, in the same way we should be millers of our own thought. When the mill of our mind is in the process of turning from the very movement that is precisely the agitation of our mind, we must at each instant try to follow each grain to pick out the good and the bad thoughts.[55] Another metaphor is that of the centurion: the sergeant who, watching the men parade before him, immediately identifies those who are fit to be soldiers and those who are not, those who can do this or that and those who cannot, those who are in good health and those who are ill. We should be the centurion, the sergeant officer, the permanent inspector of our own thoughts.[56] And finally, the third metaphor—again, used on a number of occasions—is the metaphor of the moneychanger. The moneychanger is the one who verifies the coins when one brings him money. What does he do with them? He performs the *probatio*, the test. He tests them to determine three things. First, is the metal pure? Second, is the workshop that made the coins legitimate, legal, and do they carry a legitimate effigy? Third, has the weight been altered? Has usage or metallic corruption not unduly lightened the coin? We must constantly be the moneychangers of our own thought, of our thoughts.[57] With each idea that arises, at each moment of our cogitations, we must ask ourselves the question: Is this a good idea? Is its metal pure? What workshop does it come from? Does it come from the workshop of the demon or from the workshop of God? And is its weight accurate? Has it not been used or corrupted? That is, has it not been mixed with bad desire?

This constant activity that made us the miller of our thought, the centurion of our ideas, the moneychanger of what was perpetually taking place in our mind, this is what Christian spirituality called—in a word that was conserved for centuries—*discretio*,[58] discretion, or *discrimen*, the possibility of sorting through one's thoughts. This, fundamentally, is what the examination of conscience was to accomplish. You see that this was a far cry from the metaphor of the judge or the administrator who, with Seneca, measured his actions each evening to know if they conformed to the rule or not. This was an entirely different technique of the self; we enter into an entirely different system of the relationship to the self, and into an entirely different system of veridiction.

But you can see that this immediately posed a new problem, which was the following: If at each instant we could be misled about ourselves, if at each instant we could take a bad idea for a good one or vice versa, what guarantee was there that this *discretio*, this *discrimen*, this activity of discrimination among our own thoughts, would not itself be illusory? What ensured that there was not some malicious spirit within us that was constantly tricking us, such that at the moment we believed things were good, just when we believed they were true, in reality they were false because we were being constantly tricked? This little hypothesis—which may ring a bell for those among you who have studied philosophy[59]—this little hypothesis of the evil trickster within us, how would we master it?

Well, we would master it by means of a practice that was, precisely, the practice of avowal. This *discrimen*, this discrimination that was necessary for the examination of our own conscience, was to be achieved by speaking. We needed to examine ourselves at all times, but what was going to assure us that we did not trick ourselves in our examination, and that we separated the good from the bad grain, the bad soldier from the good soldier, the good coin from the bad coins, what would reassure us of this was to never stop talking—that is, if we said the things, if we said what happened in our mind as and when the thoughts appeared to our mind.

And why did avowal allow us to escape this paradox of the examination that could fool itself? Well, if avowal provided the means to escape this paradox, it was for two reasons: the first was secondary and the other was fundamental. The secondary reason was that by speaking with the director, he could provide counsel or advice, indicating the necessary prayers, recommended readings, and proper conduct. In the counsel of the director there was a point, an element or instrument of discrimination. But you must note that this part of the director's action, the director's counsel, was extraordinarily reduced if we consider Cassian's texts: [he] was very reserved on this issue and gave only the most schematic indications on, for example, the remedies of this medicine of the mind. The true reason why avowal made possible *discretio*, discrimination, was that avowal itself—the sole fact of speaking, speaking out loud, and speaking to someone else—

was in itself an operation of *discretio*. And if avowal was a process of *discretio*, it was in two ways and for two reasons.

First, if one's thoughts were honest, if their origin was pure, if they were good gold pieces, they would be easily avowed. If, to the contrary, they were born of evil, if the coins that presented themselves to our thought were of an impure gold or were corrupted, then they would have difficulty manifesting themselves. They would refuse to be said, and would tend to remain hidden. The shame of avowal was always a sign of the evil nature of what one avowed: "The devil" — I am quoting Cassian — "in all his slyness will not be able to deceive or cast down the young monk unless he tricks him, either by haughtiness or by embarrassment, into covering up his thoughts. The Elders affirm that it is a universal and diabolical sign for us to blush at the idea of manifesting [our thoughts] to our director."[60] And why were thoughts avowed so easily when they were good and with such difficulty when they were bad? Why did we blush and why did we hesitate? It was for the cosmo-theological reason that an evil thought, of course, came from Satan, and Satan, the angel of light, was condemned to darkness because of his pride: daylight was thus forbidden to him.*

: : :

[. . .] The link between the power of illusion and the self, to some extent, may draw Christianity closer to Buddhism — but with this important difference: In Buddhism it is the very principle of individuation that is at the heart of illusion, whereas in Christianity the principle of illusion is in one's attachment to oneself, in a certain mode of the relationship to oneself that is one of affirmation and preservation. Why? Because the relationship to oneself, when it takes on the form of attachment, is nothing more than the effect of the temptation by the other, the temptation by the other that is the work of the demon.

The third reason why all of this was, I think, so important is that the illusion one had about oneself, this illusion that Christianity placed within

---

* There is a gap here, resulting from a second change of the audiovisual tape. The original typescript at the IMEC reads as follows: "[He could only live] in the obscurity of one's conscience, amidst the mysteries of *conscientiae*. As a result, avowal pulled him out of the obscure labyrinth of thought and forced him to confront the most hostile of all elements, light. And if the devil was all-powerful in the shadows and the night of one's conscience, he was rendered impotent in the light of day and in light of the discourse" (typescript, May 6, 1981, lecture, p. 22).

the self and not within the body, was entirely different from the error that the Stoics chased. The Stoics wanted to make sure that they were not mistaken in their opinions about the world. But now it was a question of not being mistaken about oneself: this was the essential issue of this spirituality and of this technique.[61] We could say that the hermeneutics of the self is an invention of Christianity. What Christianity invented was absolutely not contempt for the body, nor, absolutely not, the meaning of sin. What Christianity invented—what it introduced, I believe, into ancient culture—was this principle of a veridiction of the self through a hermeneutics of thought. And I think that from this point of departure, an entire series of forms—of cultural, moral, religious, and philosophical forms— would become possible. I also think that Christianity, by introducing this principle of a veridiction of the self through the hermeneutics of thought, introduced a particular form of subject that the law, that juridical thought, that judicial practice has never been able to assimilate. This would become one of the great issues of Western culture: to know how to connect one to the other, how to join together, into one unique subject, the subject of spiritual veridiction as it was constituted through these monastic techniques and the subject of law which, for that matter, was implicated by the institutions. It is precisely this interplay between the subject of spiritual veridiction and the juridical subject on the problem of avowal—the penitential avowal and the judicial avowal—that I will develop in the next two lectures.*

[NOTES]

1. For background regarding the early Christian sources that Foucault consulted, see Philippe Chevallier, "Foucault et les sources patristiques," pp. 137–42, in Philippe Artières, Jean-François Bert, Frédéric Gros, and Judith Revel, eds., *Cahier de L'Herne 95: Michel Foucault* (Paris: L'Herne, 2011), as well as Philippe Chevallier, *Michel Foucault et le christianisme* (Lyon: ENS-éditions, 2011), pp. 188–93. In addition to the secondary sources mentioned by Philippe Chevallier, it may be worth adding, with regard to the direction of conscience, Irénée Hausherr, *Direction spirituelle en Orient autrefois* (Rome: Pont. Institutum Orientalium Studiorum, 1955); English edition, Irénée Hausherr, *Spiritual Direction in the Early Christian East*, trans. Anthony P. Gythiel (Kalamazoo, MI: Cistercian Publications, 1990). A number of passages cited by Foucault can be found in that text.

* Foucault ends by addressing the audience: "Excuse me for being so long. Do you have any questions, or would you like to leave immediately?"

2. *Les Apophtegmes des Pères: Collection systématique. 1. Chapitres I–IX; 2. Chapitres X–XVI,* ed. and trans. Jean-Claude Guy (Paris: Editions du Cerf, 1993, 2003). The *Apophthegmata patrum* are a collection of maxims, sayings, and wisdom stories attributed to the early Christian monks circa the fifth century CE. The different collections of sayings evolved organically over time, in different languages (Coptic, Greek, Latin, Armenian, Ethiopic, etc.), without a single official textual version even in late antiquity. As a result, it is difficult to designate an official English version, but most scholars rely on the English translations of Benedicta Ward. See Benedicta Ward, trans., *The Sayings of the Desert Fathers: The Alphabetical Collection,* Cistercian Studies 59 (Kalamazoo, MI: Cistercian Publications, 1984); Benedicta Ward, trans., *The Wisdom of the Desert Fathers: The Apophthegmata Patrum (The Anonymous Series)* (Oxford: S.L.G. Press, 1975); Benedicta Ward, trans., *The Desert Fathers: Sayings of the Early Christian Monks* (New York: Penguin Classic, 2003). To help place Foucault in relation to these texts and the scholarship available to him on the *Apophthegmata patrum* (much of which was done in French), a helpful resource is the discussion and listings in William Harmless, *Desert Christians: An Introduction to the Literature of Early Monasticism* (Oxford: Oxford University Press, 2004), pp. 183–86; see also Chevallier, *Michel Foucault et le christianisme.* Special thanks to Margaret Mitchell for guidance on these references.

3. Jean Cassien, *De institutis coenobiorum et de octo principalium vitiorum remediis / Institutions cénobitiques,* ed. and trans. Jean-Claude Guy (Paris: Editions du Cerf, 1965); English edition, John Cassian, *The Institutes,* trans. and annot. Boniface Ramsey (New York: Newman Press, 2000).

4. Jean Cassien, *Collationes sanctorum patrum / Conférences,* ed. and trans. Dom E. Pichéry (Paris: Editions du Cerf, ("Sources chrétiennes" nos. 42, 54, and 64), 1955, 1958, 1959); English edition, John Cassian, *The Conferences,* ed. and trans. Boniface Ramsey (New York: Paulist Press, 1997).

5. See Christian Badilita and Attila Jakab, eds., *Jean Cassien entre l'Orient et l'Occident* (Paris: Editions Beauchesne, 2003).

6. Origen was born in Alexandria ca. 185 and succeeded Clement at the head of the Alexandrian school of catechism. His works included, among others, the *Hexapla,* which contained six versions of the Old Testament in both Hebrew and Greek and constituted "the first attempt to establish a critical text." As a theologian and exegete, he was imprisoned and tortured during the persecution ordered by Decius and he died in Caesarea around 254. Read through the theories of his disciples, among whom was Evagrius Ponticus, he is classified as a heresiarch. In the fourth century his most influential critics were Saint Jerome, who admired the exegete and the theologian's cause, and Epiphanius of Salamis. In the sixth century, Origen was condemned by the synod assembled by Justinian in 543 and by the fifth ecumenical Council of Constantinople in 553. These condemnations came after the death of John Cassian in approximately 435. See Jean-Claude Polet, ed., *Patrimoine littéraire européen: I. Traditions juive et chrétienne* (Brusells: De Boeck Université, 1991), p. 249.

7. Cf. Michel Foucault, *Sécurité, Territoire, Population: Cours au Collège de France. 1977–1978,* ed. Michel Senellart (Paris: Gallimard/Seuil, 2004), p. 177 et seq.; English edition, Michel Foucault, *Security, Territory, Population: Lectures at the College de France 1977–1978,* English series ed. Arnold I. Davidson, trans. Graham Burchell (New York: Picador, 2007), p. 174 et. seq.

8. On Antiphon and the topic of consolation, see Antiphon, *Antiphon the Sophist: The Fragments,* ed. and trans. Gerard J. Pendrick (Cambridge: Cambridge University Press, 2002), pp. 44, 252, 396, and 469; and Plutarque, *Vie des dix orateurs,* "Antiphon," § 18 in Antiphon, *Discours suivis des Fragments d'Antiphon le Sophiste,* ed. and trans. Louis Gernet (Paris: Les Belles Lettres, 1923), p. 27 ("At the time he devoted himself to poetry, he established an art of healing grief, like that which doctors apply to diseases: in Corinth, near the agora, he arranged a room with a sign where he specialized in treating emotional pain through discourse;

he inquired into the causes of grief and comforted his patients. But, finding this business below him, he turned to rhetoric").

9. On Crantor (335–275), philosopher of the Academy, see Diogène Laërce, *Vie, doctrines et sentences des philosophes illustres*, book 4, trans. Robert Genaille (Paris: Garnier Frères, 1933), vol. 1, pp. 185–87. English edition, Diogenes Laertius, *Lives, Teachings and Sayings of Eminent Philosophers* (Cambridge, MA: Harvard University Press, 1931–38). According to C. E. Manning (*On Seneca's "Ad Marciam"* [Leiden: E. J. Brill, 1981], p. 12), who makes reference to Cicero among others (*Acad.*, II, 44, 135), the Romans held Crantor's *Peri penthous pros Hippoclea* in high esteem and saw in him the first practitioner of consolation as a specific literary genre. On this point, see also J. van Wageningen, "Bijdrage tot de kennis der 'Consolatio mortis' bij Grieken en Romeinen," *Verslagen en Mededeelingen der koninklijke Akademie van Wetenschappen* (Amsterdam: Afdeeling Letterkunde, 1998), pp. 175–98.

10. Sénèque, *De la tranquillité de l'âme*, trans. Colette Lazan, with an essay by Paul Veyne (Paris: Rivages poche / Petite bibliothèque, 1991); English translation, Seneca, *On Tranquility of Mind*, in *Moral Essays*, vol. 2, trans. John W. Basore (Cambridge: Loeb Classical Library, 1932).

11. Sénèque, *Lettres à Lucilius*, ed. François Préchac and trans. Henri Noblot (Paris: Les Belles Lettres, 1956); English edition, *The Epistles of Seneca*, 3 vols., trans. Richard M. Gummere (Cambridge, MA: Harvard University Press, 1989).

12. Foucault explored this theme in *Le courage de la vérité: Le Gouvernement de soi et des autres II. Cours au Collège de France, 1984*, ed. Frédéric Gros (Paris: Gallimard/Seuil, 2009); English edition, Michel Foucault, *The Courage of Truth: The Government of Self and Others II: Lectures at the College de France 1983–1984*, English series ed. Arnold I. Davidson, trans. Graham Burchell (New York: Palgrave Macmillan, 2011). There is, however, a fundamental shift in these later lectures: Socrates is still presented as claiming "to be someone who does not know" (ibid., English edition, p. 27), but he leads the individual not simply to the point where he discovers that he already knew, but to the point where he discovers that he knows nothing: "Where the teacher says: I know, listen to me, Socrates will say: I know nothing, and if I care for you, this is not so as to pass on to you the knowledge you lack, it is so that through understanding that you know nothing you will learn to take care of yourselves" (ibid., English edition, p. 89).

13. On Charles-Victor Daremberg, see P. Dumaître, "Charles-Victor Daremberg (1817–72), Médecin helléniste," *Clio medica* 20 (1985–86), no. 1/4, pp. 45–57.

14. Athénée, in Oribase, *Collection des médecins grecs et latins: Livres incertains*, ed. and trans. H. C. Bussemaker and C. Daremberg, III (Paris, Imprimerie impériale, 1858), p. 164. Books 1 and 4 of Oribasius's medical texts have been translated into English with extensive commentary by Mark Grant; see *Dieting for an Emperor: A Translation of Books 1 and 4 of Oribasius' Medical Compilations with an Introduction and Commentary*, ed., trans. and commented by Mark Grant (Leiden: Brill, 1997).

15. Ibid. This point on Athenaeus is also recounted by Foucault in *Histoire de la sexualité: Le souci de soi* (Paris: Gallimard, 2000), p. 123; English edition, Michel Foucault, *The History of Sexuality, Volume 3: The Care of the Self*, trans. Robert Hurley (New York: Vintage, 1988), p. 100.

16. Athénée, in Oribase, *Collection des médecins grecs et latins: Livres incertains*, p. 164.

17. Michel Senellart observes, in a note to *Sécurité, Territoire, Population*, p. 191 n. 29 (English edition, Foucault, *Security, Territory, Population*, p. 188 n. 29), that the sentence mentioned by Foucault can be found neither in Proverbs (which is given as the source in *Wrong-Doing, Truth-Telling*) nor in Psalms (which is given as the source in *Security, Territory, Population*). He notes that "the phrase probably derives from a combination of two passages": (1) Proverbs 11:14 ("Faute de direction, un peuple succombe"; "In the absence of direction, a people succumbs") and (2) Isaiah 64:6 ("Tous, nous nous flétrissons comme des feuilles mortes"; "We all fade like dead leaves"). If this hypothesis is correct, the source of the sec-

ond passage could be Psalms 1:1–3. However, in the context of the other quotations Foucault used in this lecture, it is equally possible that he used I. Hausherr, *Direction spirituelle en Orient autrefois* (Rome: Pont. Institutum Orientalium Studiorum, 1955), p. 169 (English edition, Hausherr, *Spiritual Direction*, p. 172), which cites Dorothée de Gaza ("Il est dit dans les Proverbes: ceux qui ne sont pas gouvernés tombent comme des feuilles; le salut est dans un abondant conseil") and which gives as its source "ceux qui ne sont pas gouvernés tombent comme des feuilles": Proverbs 11, 14, 70. The same phrase is mentioned in *The Hermeneutics of the Subject*, p. 398.

18. Cassien, *Institutions cénobitiques*, IV ("De la formation de ceux qui renoncent [au monde]"), section 7, p. 131; English edition, Cassian, *The Institutes*, trans. Ramsey, pp. 81–82:

> When, therefore, a person has been admitted, has been proven in the perseverance about which we have spoken, and has put aside his own garments and been clothed in the monastic habit, he is not permitted to join the community of the brothers immediately but is assigned to an elder who dwells not very far from the entrance of the monastery, who is responsible for travelers and strangers and is particularly devoted to welcoming them and to being hospitable to them. And when he has served for a full year there and has without any complaining waited upon travelers, having in this way been exposed to his first training in humility and patience and having been recognized for his long practice therein, and he is about to be admitted from this to the community of the brothers, he is given over to another elder who is responsible for ten younger men, who have been entrusted to him by the abba and whom he both teaches and rules, in accordance with what we read in Exodus was established by Moses.

19. Cf. Cassien, *Institutions cénobitiques*, IV ("De la formation de ceux qui renoncent [au monde]"), section 37, p. 177 et seq.; English edition, Cassian, *The Institutes*, trans. Ramsey, p. 99:

> For the wily serpent is ever at our heels — that is, he lies in wait for our end, and he seeks even to the close of our life to overthrow us. Therefore, to have started well and to have seized with full fervor upon the beginnings of renunciation will be of no profit if a fitting end does not in similar fashion crown these things and bring them to their conclusion, and if you have not held on to the humility and poverty of Christ, which you have now professed in his presence, until the last moment of your life, just as you seized upon it. In order to carry this out you must always be on the watch for his heads — that is, the beginnings of your thoughts — and bring them at once to your elder. For thus you will learn to crush his dangerous initiatives, if you are not ashamed to reveal any of them to your elder.

20. According to Jean-Claude Guy, the narrative on Pinufius presented in the *Cenobitic Institutions* is "reproduced almost word for word by Cassian himself, *Conférences*, XX, 1, 2–5." Cassien, *Institutions cénobitiques*, p. 165, n. 1.

21. Cassien, *Conférence de l'abbé Piamun*, "Des trois sortes de moines," *Conférences*, vol. 3 ("Sources chrétiennes" no. 64), XVIII, section 14, pp. 101–7; English edition, John Cassian, "Conference XVIII: The Conference of Abba Piamun: On the Three Kinds of Monks," section 14, pp. 646–48, in John Cassian, *John Cassian: The Conferences*, ed. and trans. Boniface Ramsey (New York: Paulist Press, 1997).

22. According to Jean-Claude Guy, there are multiple versions of this story, often narrated in the Western literature on obedience. The first, provided by Cassian in *Cenobitic Institutions*, presents Jean de Lycopolis, "one of the most celebrated figures of Egyptian monasticism of the fourth century," who was born ca. 305 and died in 395 (Cassien, *Institutions cénobitiques*,

p. 152, n. 2). The second, which is presented in the *Apophthegmata patrum*, attributes it to John Colobos of Scete, who was born ca. 339 and died in 409 (*Les Apophtegmes des Pères: Collection systématique. Chapitres I–IX*, trans. and annot. Jean-Claude Guy [Paris: Editions du Cerf, 1993], pp. 66–68); this second version adds the miracle of the stick that takes root and bears fruit. A later, more elaborate version is given in the Coptic panegyric of Jean Colobos by Zacharias, at the end of the seventh century (ibid., pp. 254–57). Foucault recounts the first version in *Sécurité, Territoire, Population*, p. 180; English edition, *Security, Territory, Population*, pp. 176–77. He refers to the second in *Wrong-Doing, Truth-Telling*. According to Jean-Claude Guy, it is probable that the version proposed in the *Apophthegmata patrum* came after that of Cassian (see Cassien, *Institutions cénobitiques*, pp. 156–57 n. 1; the passage in the English edition is at Cassian, *Institutes*, book 4, chapter 24, pp. 90–91).

23. Cassien, *Institutions cénobitiques*, pp. 160–63; English edition, Cassian, *The Institutes*, pp. 92–93. In the version of the episode recounted by Cassian, the brothers "were sent immediately to the side of the river" to draw out "the child who had just been thrown as if from his bosom," preventing "the final execution of the elder's orders that the father had already satisfied through his devotion." Jean-Claude Guy suggests that a similar narrative can be found "according to a different tradition that corresponds to a context of 'vie anachorétique,' in the collection of apothegms": *Alphabeticon*, sisoès 10 (*Patrologia Graeca* 65, 393 C), and *Systématique*, XIV, 8 (*Patrologia Latina* 73, 949 D). Foucault also recounts this as the test of Lucius, recounted in the *Histoire lausiaque*; according to Michel Senellart, it is not there (*Sécurité, Territoire, Population*, pp. 180 and 191 n. 33; English edition, *Security, Territory, Population*, pp. 176–77 and 189 n. 33).

24. Cassian explicitly relates the sacrifices of Patermutus and Abraham. See Jean Cassien, *Institutions cénobitiques*, pp. 162–63; English edition, Cassian, *The Institutes*, trans. Ramsey, section 28, p. 93: "The man's faith and devotion were so acceptable to God that they were immediately confirmed by divine testimony. For it was straightaway revealed to the elder that by this obedience he [Patermutus] had performed the deed of the patriarch Abraham. And when after a short space of time the same abba of the cenobium was departing this world for Christ, he preferred him to all the brothers and left him to the monastery as his successor and as abba."

25. On the importance of the notion of obedience, see Foucault, *Sécurité, Territoire, Population*, p. 180; English edition, *Security, Territory, Population*, p. 176–77. Senellart observes that Foucault had, in the manuscript of these lectures, circled the word "état" and made a note in the margins: "notion importante."

26. On *humilitas*, see Cassien, *Institutions cénobitiques*, IV ("De la formation de ceux qui renoncent [au monde]"), section 39, p. 181; English edition, Cassian, *The Institutes*, trans. Ramsey, pp. 99–100:

> Humility, in turn, is verified by the following indications: first, if a person has put to death in himself all his desires; second, if he conceals from his elder not only none of his deeds but also none of his thoughts; third, if he commits nothing to his own discretion but everything to his [elder's] judgment and listens eagerly and willingly to his admonitions; fourth, if in every respect he maintains a gracious obedience and a steadfast patience; fifth, if he neither brings injury on anyone else nor is saddened or sorrowful if anyone else inflicts it on him; sixth, if he does nothing and presumes nothing that neither the general rule nor the example of our forebears encourages; seventh, if he is satisfied with utter simplicity and, as being an unfit laborer, considers himself unworthy of everything that is offered him; eighth, if he does not declare with his lips alone that he is inferior to everyone else but believes it in the depths of his heart; ninth, if he holds his tongue and is not loudmouthed; tenth, if he is not ready and quick to laugh. . . .

27. Nilus [Evagrius Ponticus], *Logos Asceticos*, chap. 41, *Patrologia Graeca* 79, 769D–772A, cited in Hausherr, *Direction spirituelle en Orient autrefois*, p. 190; English edition, Hausherr, *Spiritual Direction*, p. 197.

28. Cassien, *Institutions cénobitiques*, IV ("De la formation de ceux qui renoncent [au monde]"), section 12, p. 137; English edition, Cassian, *The Institutes*, trans. Ramsey, pp. 83–84: "Thus the person who is busy writing does not dare to complete the letter that he has begun, but at the very moment when the sound of the knocking reaches his ears he jumps up with the utmost haste, not even dotting an *i* but abandoning the unfinished lines of the letter. He is not thinking in terms of abbreviating and saving his efforts so much as he is striving with all his energy and zeal to pursue the virtue of obedience . . ." According to Jean-Claude Guy, "The *Apophthegmata patrum* recount a particular example that corresponds exactly to this general practice: Marc, disciple of Silvain, 1." See also Hausherr, *Direction spirituelle en Orient autrefois*, p. 200; English edition, Hausherr, *Spiritual Direction*, p. 209, which makes reference to *Patrologia Graeca* 65, 273D–296A. Foucault uses the same example in *Sécurité, Territoire, Population*, p. 179; English edition, *Security, Territory, Population*, pp. 175–76.

29. Basile, *De renunt. saec.*, n. 4, *Patrologia Graeca* 31, 363B, cited in Hausherr, *Direction spirituelle en Orient autrefois*, pp. 190–91 ("Every act which is completed without an order or the permission of a superior is a sacrilege that leads to death and not to one's profit, even if it appears good"); English edition, Hausherr, *Spiritual Direction*, p. 198.

30. Saint Barsanuphius, who lived in the fifth and sixth centuries, was a hermit who dwelled near a monastery in the region of Gaza and corresponded with Jean de Gaza. Jean de Gaza, *Correspondance* (Paris: Editions du Cerf, ("Sources chrétiennes" nos. 426, 427, 450, 451, 468), 1997, 1998, 2000, 2000, 2002).

31. Cassien, *Institutions cénobitiques*, IV ("De la formation de ceux qui renoncent [au monde]"), section 10, pp. 134–35; English edition, Cassian, *The Institutes*, trans. Ramsey, p. 83.

32. Cf. Cassien, *Institutions cénobitiques*, IV ("De la formation de ceux qui renoncent [au monde]"), section 35, p. 175; English edition, Cassian, *The Institutes*, trans. Ramsey, pp. 97–98:

Our cross is the fear of the Lord. Just as someone who has been crucified, then, no longer has the ability to move or to turn his limbs in any direction by an act of his mind, neither must we exercise our desires and yearnings in accordance with what is easy for us and gives us pleasure at the moment but in accordance with the law of the Lord and where it constrains us. And just as he who is fixed to the gibbet of the cross no longer contemplates present realities or reflects on his own affections; is not distracted by worry or care for the morrow; is not stirred up by the desire for possessions; is not inflamed by pride or wrangling or envy; does not sorrow over present slights and no longer remembers those of the past; and, although he may still be breathing in his body, believes himself dead in every respect and directs on ahead the gaze of his heart to the place where he is sure that he will go; so also it behooves us who have been crucified by the fear of the Lord to have died to all these things, not only to have fleshly vices but to every earthly thing as well, and to have the eyes of our soul set upon the place where we must hope that we shall go at any moment. In this way we shall be able to put to death all our fleshly lusts and feelings.

For secondary sources see Hausherr, *Direction spirituelle en Orient autrefois*, pp. 160–67; English edition, Hausherr, *Spiritual Direction*, pp. 169–75.

33. Cassien, *Institutions cénobitiques*, IV ("De la formation de ceux qui renoncent [au monde]"), section 9, p. 133; English edition, Cassian, *The Institutes*, trans. Ramsey, pp. 82–83. On this point, Jean-Claude Guy refers to what he calls "*l'ouverture de conscience*." Hausherr,

Direction spirituelle en Orient autrefois, pp. 152–77; English edition, Hausherr, *Spiritual Direction*, pp. 155–84.

34. Cf. Hausherr, *Direction spirituelle en Orient autrefois*, pp. 171 and 200–201; English edition, Hausherr, *Spiritual Direction*, pp. 175 and 207–8.

35. Clément d'Alexandrie, *Le pédagogue, Livre III*, trans. Claude Mondésert and Chantel Matray, notes by H.-I. Marrou (Paris: Editions du Cerf, "Sources chrétiennes" no. 158, 1970), p. 13: "It would seem indeed that the greatest knowledge of all is knowledge of oneself; for he who knows himself will have knowledge of God and, with that knowledge, will be made in God's image"; English edition, Clement of Alexandria, *Christ the Educator*, trans. Simon P. Wood (New York: Fathers of the Church, 1954), p. 199.

36. There is no reference to kids in Origen's second homily on the *Song of Songs*. Foucault is probably making reference to the passage at I, 9 of Origène, *Homélies sur le Cantique des Cantiques*, introduction, trans., and notes Olivier Rousseau (Paris: Editions du Cerf, "Sources chrétiennes" no. 37bis, 2007), p. 99; English edition, Origen, *The Song of Songs: Commentary and Homilies*, trans. and annot. R. P. Lawson (Westminster, MD: Newman Press, 1957), p. 281: "If thou have not known thyself, O fair one among women, go forth in the steps of the flocks and feed—not the flocks of sheep, nor of lambs, but—thy goats. He will set the sheep on the right hand and the goats upon the left, assuredly' . . . 'In the steps of the flocks,' He says, 'Wilt thou find thyself at last, not among the sheep, but among the goats; and when thou dwellest with them thou canst not be with me—that is, with the Good Shepherd."

37. Origène, *Commentaire sur le Cantique des Cantiques*, I. *Livres I et II*, trans., intro., and notes by Luc Brésard and Henri Crouzel, with the collaboration of Marcel Borret (Paris: Editions du Cerf, "Sources chrétiennes" no. 375, 1991), pp. 359 (II, 5, 7) and 379 (II, 5, 21); English edition, Origen, *The Song of Songs*, trans. Lawson, p. 130: "It seems to me, then, that the soul ought to acquire self-knowledge of a twofold kind: she should know both what she is in herself, and how she is actuated; that is to say, she ought to know what she is like essentially, and what she is like according to her dispositions;" and ibid, p. 134: "For the soul, therefore, these things will include a certain self-perception, by which she ought to know how she is constituted in herself, whether her being is corporeal or incorporeal, and whether it is simple, or consists of two or three or several elements . . . ."

38. Jean Chrysostome, "Homélie sur le Psaume quatrième," *Œuvres complètes*, vol. 8, trans. Abbé Joly (Nancy: Bordes, 1867), p. 157; English edition, St. John Chrysostom, *Commentary on the Psalms*, vol. 1, trans. Robert Charles Hill (Brookline, MA: Holy Cross Orthodox Press, 1998), pp. 60–61:

> After dinner, he is saying, when you go to bed, when you are on the point of lying down, when no one is present and the silence is complete, with no disturbance and with profound peace, awaken the tribunal of your conscience, demand of it a settling of accounts, what evil designs you concocted during the day, hatching schemes, outwitting your neighbor, entertaining lethal desires. Bring these out into the open at that quiet time, apply your conscience to these unruly thoughts, tear them to shreds, do them justice, straighten the errant intention . . . Let this be your daily practice, and do not go to sleep, mortal creature, before giving thought to the day's transgressions; and next day you will be altogether more reluctant to attempt the same . . . [C]all your soul to account at evening time, pass sentence on your errant reasoning, suspend it as though from a gibbet, interrogate it, bid it never attempt the same again.

39. On the proximity of the conceptions of the examination of one's conscience in Seneca and Saint John Chrysostom, see Michel Foucault, "Technologies of the Self," in Luther H. Martin, Huck Gutman, and Patrick H. Hutton, eds., *Technologies of the Self: A Seminar with*

Michel Foucault (Amherst: University of Massachusetts Press, 1988), pp. 16–49; also reproduced in Michel Foucault, *Ethics: Subjectivity and Truth. Essential Works of Foucault, 1954–1984, Volume 1*, ed. Paul Rabinow (New York: New Press, 1998), pp. 223–51.

40. Saint John Chrysostom, "Homily 60," *Homilies on Genesis, 46–67*, trans. Robert C. Hill (Washington: Catholic University of America Press, 1992), pp. 184–85:

> . . . let us daily require an account of ourselves for words and glances and execute sentences on ourselves so as to be free from punishment there. . . . So let us take the initiative in passing sentence on ourselves with all goodwill, holding the court of conscience unbeknown to anyone; let us then examine our own thoughts, and determine a proper verdict so that through fear of imminent punishment our mind may forbear to be dragged down and instead may check its impulses, and by keeping in view that unsleeping eye may ward off the devil's advances.

41. Jean Chrysostome, Homélie 24, "De Peccato et confessione," *Patrologie grecque* 63, col. 741: "Oh nobility of the soul; the memory of sin was not forgotten, but even once it was forgiven it was engraved in his conscience like an image. And see what happens: if you keep the sin in your memory, God will not remember; if you forget, God will remember. Did you do something wrong? Remember it, so that the Lord may forget it. Did you do something good? Forget it so that the Lord may remind you of it." (We thank Bernard Coulie for the original translation.)

42. Cf. Jean-Pierre Vernant, "Aspects mythiques de la mémoire et du temps," *Journal de psychologie*, 1956, pp. 1–29, reprinted in Jean-Pierre Vernant, *Mythe et pensée chez les Grecs*, vol. 1 (Paris: François Maspero, 1974), pp. 80–107, especially pp. 94 et seq.; and Jean-Pierre Vernant, "Le fleuve 'amélès' et la 'mélétè thanatou,'" *Revue philosophique*, 1960, pp. 163–79, reprinted in ibid., pp. 108–23. The latter essay provides valuable discussion of the notions of *melētē, epimeleia, epimeleia mnēmēs, ameleia, amelētēsia,* and *amelētēsia mnēmēs,* and announces some of the themes that Foucault will develop in his lectures on the care of the self.

43. The complete sentence reads: "Eche biblion en tō suneidoti, kai graphē ta hamartēmata ta kathēmerina." We thank Emmanuel Francis and Vincent Francis.

44. Jean Chrysostome, seconde homélie sur le Psaume 50, "In Psalmum Homilia," *Patrologie grecque* 55, col. 581: "Do you not have a book in your home where you write your daily accounts? Keep a book in your conscience and write your daily sins within it." (We thank Bernard Coulie for the translation.)

45. Athanase d'Alexandrie, *Vie d'Antoine*, trans., intro., and notes by G. J. M. Bartelink (Paris: Editions du Cerf, 1994), section 55, p. 286, pp. 7–9; English edition, Athanasius, *The Life of Antony and the Letter to Marcellinus*, trans. and intro. Robert C. Gregg, pref. William A. Clebsch (New York: Paulist Press, 1980) section 55, pp. 72–73: "Now daily let each one recount to himself his actions of the day and night. . . . And may this remark serve as a precaution so that we might not sin: Let each one of us note and record our actions and the stirrings of our souls as though we were going to give an account to each other."

46. Athanase d'Alexandrie, *Vie d'Antoine*, section 25, pp. 286–87; English edition, Athanasius, *The Life of Antony and the Letter to Marcellinus*, section 55, p. 73:

> And you can be sure that, being particularly ashamed to have them made known, we would stop sinning and even meditating on something evil. For who wants to be seen sinning? Or who, after sinning, would not prefer to lie, wanting it to remain unknown? So then, just as we would not practice fornication if we were observing each other directly, so also we will doubtless keep ourselves from impure thoughts, ashamed to have them known, if we record our thoughts as if reporting them to each other. Let this record re-

place the eyes of our fellow ascetics, so that, blushing as much to write as to be seen, we might never be absorbed by evil things.

47. Cassien, *Institutions cénobitiques*, IV ("De la formation de ceux qui renoncent [au monde]"), section 9, p. 133; English edition, Cassian, *The Institutes*, trans. Ramsey, pp. 82–83.

48. Cassien, *Première conférence de l'abbé Nesteros*, "De la science spirituelle," *Conférences*, vol. 2 ("Sources chrétiennes" no. 54), XIV, section 13, pp. 199–201; English edition, Cassian, *Conferences*, trans. Ramsey, XIV, section 13, pp. 517–19.

49. On this point, cf. Foucault, "Les techniques de soi" in *Dits et Ecrits*, IV, no. 363 (Paris: Gallimard, 1994), p. 810; Foucault, "Technologies of the Self," Amherst Seminar, p. 46 ("There is an etymology of *logismoi* in Cassian, but I don't know if it's sound: *co-agitationes*."); p. 247 in Foucault, *Ethics*.

50. Cassien, *Première conférence de l'abbé Serenus*, "De la mobilité de l'âme et des esprits du mal," *Conférences*, vol. 1 ("Sources chrétiennes" no. 42), VII–VIII, section 4, pp. 416–85; English edition, Cassian, *Conferences*, trans. Ramsey, VII–VIII, pp. 241–322.

51. Cassien, *Conférences*, VII, section 4, pp. 428–29; English edition, Cassian, *Conferences*, trans. Ramsey, VII, section 4, para. 2, p. 249 (referring to the mind or the human spirit as "always changeable and as manifoldly changeable").

52. *Logismos* is derived from *legō*, originally meaning "to gather, to collect, to choose," like *logikos*, "in relation to the spoken word, reason and logic." It is translated as "calculation and reasoning" ("calcul, raisonnement") in *Dictionnaire étymologique de la langue grecque: Histoire des mots*, II (Paris: Editions Klincksieck, 1968), p. 626.

53. Similarly, see also the additional note by Laurence Brottier in Jean Chrysostome, *Sermons sur la Genèse*, intro., trans., and notes by Laurence Brottier (Paris: Editions du Cerf, ["Sources chrétiennes no. 433], 1998), p. 373. In the works of Saint John Chrysostom, for example, *logismoi* "can take on . . . the neutral meaning of *thoughts* . . . ; a positive meaning of reasoning [*raisonnements*] . . . , a characteristic of man in the stoic tradition, or more commonly a negative connotation . . . of Jewish origin transmitted by Origen . . . and given currency by Evagrius in the ascetic tradition where logismoi and demons are often interchangeable. . . . Thus, the logismoi that result from the passions . . . designate either the passions frequently represented by the image of a tumultuous sea . . . , or personal opinions, that are opposed to ecclesiastical faith, and particularly the system of heretics. . . ."

54. For this example, using John of Lycopolis, cf. Jean Cassien, *Première Conférence de l'abbé Moïse*, "Du but et de la fin du moine," *Conférences*, vol. 1 ("Sources chrétiennes" no. 42), section 21, pp. 141–43; English edition, Cassian, *Conferences*, trans. Ramsey, I. section 21, pp. 61–62.

55. Ibid.: French edition, pp. 129–31; English edition, p. 57. See also Foucault, *The Hermeneutics of the Subject*, p. 299; and Foucault, "Technologies of the Self," Amherst seminar, pp. 46–47.

56. Cassien, *Première conférence de l'abbé Serenus*, "De la mobilité de l'âme et des esprits du mal," VII, section 5, pp. 430–37; English edition, Cassian, *Conferences*, trans. Ramsey, VII, section 5, pp. 251–53. On the metaphor of the centurion, cf. Foucault, "Technologies of the Self," Amherst seminar, p. 46.

57. Cassien, *Première Conférence de l'abbé Moïse*, "Du but et de la fin du moine," *Conférences*, I, sections 20–22, pp. 135–45; English edition, Cassian, *Conferences*, trans. Ramsey, I, sections 20–22, pp. 59–63. See also *The Hermeneutics of the Subject*, p. 299; and Foucault, "Technologies of the Self," Amherst seminar, pp. 46–47. For a comparison of the meanings of the metaphor of the money changer in Epictetus and in Evagrius Ponticus and Cassian, see *The Hermeneutics of the Subject*, p. 503, and Foucault, "Technologies of the Self," pp. 38–39. No comparison is made here with the theme of the changing of the value of money among the

Cynics, which is developed in *Le courage de la vérité*, pp. 208–9 and 221–23; English edition, *The Courage of Truth*, pp. 226–27 and 239–42.

58. On the notion of *discretio*, see Cassien, *Première Conférence de l'abbé Moïse*, "Du but et de la fin du moine," *Conférences*, vol. 1 ("Sources chrétiennes" no. 42), I, section 20, p. 135; English edition, Cassian, *Conferences*, trans. Ramsey, I. section 20, pp. 59–61.

59. Foucault is making a direct reference to the philosophical concept of the "evil genius doubt" formulated by Descartes in his first meditation of his *Méditations sur la philosophie première* (1641) (*Meditations on First Philosophy*, ed. and trans. John Cottingham [Cambridge: Cambridge University Press, 1996]). For background on the notion of the evil genius, also known as the evil demon, see Oets Kolk Bouwsma, "Descartes' Evil Genius," *The Philosophical Review*, vol. 58, no. 2, pp. 141–51 (1949). The audience at Louvain may have heard echoes, in Foucault's discussion of the evil genius, of the Foucault-Derrida polemic over the relationship between evil genius doubt and madness in Descartes's *Meditations*. The polemic centered on Foucault's analysis of the *Meditations* in his prefatory comments to the second chapter of *Histoire de la folie à l'âge classique* (Paris: Plon, 1961); English edition, *History of Madness*, trans. Jonathan Murphy and Jean Khalfa (London: Routledge, 2006). See Jacques Derrida, "Cogito et histoire de la folie," in Jacques Derrida, *L'écriture et la différence* (Paris: Seuil, 1967); English translation by Alan Bass, "Cogito and the History of Madness," in *Writing and Difference* (London: Routledge, 1978); Michel Foucault, "Mon corps, ce papier, ce feu," Appendix II, in Foucault, *Histoire de la folie à l'âge classique*, 2nd edition (Paris: Gallimard, 1972); and Michel Foucault, "Réponse à Derrida," in Foucault, *Dits et Ecrits*, vol. 2, no. 104 (Paris: Gallimard, 1994). These texts are collected as appendices to the 2006 Routledge edition of *History of Madness*, pp. 550 et seq.

60. Cassien, *Institutions cénobitiques*, IV ("De la formation de ceux qui renoncent [au monde]"), section 9, p. 133; English edition, Cassian, *The Institutes*, trans. Ramsey, pp. 82–85: "Indeed, the devil in all his slyness will not be able to deceive or cast down a young man unless he inveigles him, either by haughtiness or by embarrassment, into covering up his thoughts. For they declare that it is an invariable and clear sign that a thought is from the devil if we are ashamed to disclose it to an elder."

61. On the question of controlling the representations of the examination and the guidance of conscience such as they were practiced among the Stoics and the Christians, see *The Hermeneutics of the Subject*, pp. 502–4. According to Foucault, for the Stoics it is a question of "testing the individual's independence in relation to the external world" because the representations are considered "the opportunity for recalling a number of true principles concerning death, illness, suffering, political life, etc.," and in this way "we can see if we are capable of reacting in accordance with such principles—if they have really become . . . that master's voice which is raised immediately the passions growl and which knows how to silence them." For the Christians, Foucault makes reference to Evagrius Ponticus and to Cassian, for whom it is a question of "prescribing a hermeneutic attitude towards oneself: deciphering possible concupiscence in apparently innocent thoughts, recognizing thoughts coming from God and those coming from the Tempter."

FIFTH LECTURE

May 13, 1981

[. . .]* In my previous lecture, I tried to
situate for you a practice that was, in my opinion, very unique, very important as well in the history of Western culture, that developed in monastic
institutions of the fourth and fifth centuries, and that Cassian analyzed
in detail in his *Cenobitic Institutions* and especially in his *Conferences* —the
practice that the Greeks commonly referred to as *exagoreusis*, which may
be translated, if you will, as permanent avowal of oneself. If I insisted on

---

* The recording begins with an incomplete sentence: "We stopped last time, you remember. . . ."

this practice of *exagoreusis*, it is because it seems to me that with it, avowal enters into the history of Western culture as an important and polyvalent dimension whose effects, results, and consequences can be found in a series of domains, religious, philosophical, juridical, et cetera.

What was this practice of *exagoreusis*, of the permanent avowal of oneself, and why was it important? First, it was important in its own right, it seems to me, through its form and through its internal mechanism, which is very curious and differed fundamentally, I believe, from anything one can find earlier, either in the philosophical practice of ancient morality or in the penitential rites of Christianity. In its form and internal mechanism, you will recall, *exagoreusis* — the permanent avowal of oneself — had nothing to do with actions. It focused on thoughts — on the representations, on the images, on the wishes, on the desires, on this kind of uninterrupted and always agitated flux that the Latin Fathers called the *cogitationes*, the *logismoi*, this constantly moving reality of thought that, at that precise moment, one was beginning to learn to mistrust as one would an internal and incessant danger.[1]

Second, this type of examination associated with *exagoreusis* did not unfold in the form of memory. I need not remind you of the importance of memorization in ancient culture and for a great part of Greek philosophy. The examination of oneself did not take the form of memorization, but rather the form of a permanent control, the form of a sort of vertical relationship of self to self that allowed one to watch over oneself and to see, to verify, to test everything that entered into one's conscience at a given moment. In other words, one was one's own censor. And you may recall that we had found this image of the censure that was, in Cassian's writings, so strikingly similar to what Freud, in another dimension, would describe later.

Third, in this method of permanent examination of oneself, in this censoring of thought's constant flux, it was absolutely not a question of measuring one's thoughts according to a criterion of truth. It was not a question of knowing if one's thoughts were true or false, if one's opinions were well-founded or not. Nor was it a question of measuring up one's thoughts to a moral law. It was a question — and it is this, I think, that is very important — of knowing if one's thoughts were not presenting themselves as something other than what they were — that is to say, if they were not bearing illusions. We are not in a world of error or fault: we are in the world of illusion or in the suspicion of illusion.[2]

The fourth characteristic of this *exagoreusis* was that in this work one performed on oneself, one did not determine one's guilt or innocence, nor did one determine if one was truly responsible for a given act, a given thought, or a given desire. It was a question of knowing where what was happening within oneself came from; if what was happening within me came from God, came from another, or came from the Other par excellence, that is to say Satan. And it was thus within the dimension of the internal other that the practice of *exagoreusis* was deployed.[3]

The fifth characteristic of this *exagoreusis* is that it was inseparable from a continuous practice of verbalization, since one could neither discriminate between thoughts nor test the illusions within to find their origin without the unceasing and constant practice that consisted of telling everything that came to mind as one thought it.

Finally, the sixth characteristic was that this search for a principle of illusion within and its potential roots in the insidious presence of another did not aim to establish total or perfect self-mastery, as had been the case for ancient wisdom. It was not even a question of liberating oneself from the other who was within in order to restore one's identity. Instead, in this *exagoreusis* it was a question of destroying and renouncing oneself; and this renunciation of the self played two roles or held two positions simultaneously [. . .]. On the one hand, to know myself well, to exert the necessary control over myself, I must renounce all autonomous will, all will that might be my own.[4] I must submit myself to another, and give as pledge of my submission to another the fact that I am telling him my every thought. Thanks to this, as a result and as a permanent effect of this constant work — of being entirely submissive to the will of another and having purified my heart of all the moving thoughts that trouble it — I may then open myself to God and have no other will than the will of God. And thus I will go from one renunciation of my will to another.[5] Or rather, there will be a global process of renouncing my will that will carry me from the world of Satan to that of God, from one kingdom to another, or from one law to another. So we have here, I think, a case, in which the very form itself is important.

It seems to me that this *exagoreusis* is also important for another reason. One could say that this *exagoreusis* was the opening or the beginning of what we might call the hermeneutics of oneself. This is what I explained, I believe, or at least tried to situate in the first lecture.[6] It seems to me that an absolutely fundamental aspect of Christianity is that it is a religion bearing two sets, two types, two modes of obligation of truth. On the one hand, there is an obligation to believe in a revealed truth or dogma; this is also the truth of the text. And on the other, in Christianity, [either] through the *exomologēsis* that I spoke of two weeks ago or the *exagoreusis* that I spoke of last week, and that I have just summarized, in all of this we see the appearance of an obligation of truth. This obligation does not take the form of believing in dogma, nor does it take the form of an act of faith. Rather, it is an obligation of truth that takes the form of the necessary exploration of oneself, of the necessary discovery of a truth within the self, of the fundamental obligation to tell this truth. Truth of the text, truth of the self. Truth of the text, truth of the soul. Hermeneutics of the text, hermeneutics of the self.

You may ask: Does one have the right to use the words "hermeneutics of the self" in speaking about the practices of *exomologēsis* and especially *exagoreusis*? I think that here we have an important problem that would merit further study at some point. I say "at some point" because unfortunately, with the time remaining, and the format of our talk, or rather monologue, it would be a little difficult to stop and discuss. So I am merely setting up markers or proposing areas that may interest you, and perhaps at some point you will pursue them or we could discuss them at another time.

But there is one essential point: between the obligation to believe and the obligation to discover oneself, there is an affiliation, there is a fundamental connection. Between the text and the self, Christianity created a profound link. In effect, if I may come to know myself—if I may little by little, through this constant censorship exercised on my thoughts, sort the good from the bad ideas and use the necessary discrimination—it is precisely because I have a stable, well-established relationship to the truth of dogma and the truth of the text. It is within the act of faith [. . .], in the relationship to revealed truth, that I may [effectively] do this work of deciphering or of revealing myself. But inversely, for me to be able to completely and fully adhere to the faith that is proposed to me or, better yet, to be able to effectively understand the teaching that is given to me or, even better still, to be able to understand the text of the Scripture down to the very letter, it must be the case that my heart is pure. I must have a pure heart; that is to say, I must have purified my thoughts and performed on myself the work of bringing them forth, bringing them to light, that is accomplished through *exagoreusis*. So these two relationships to truth condition each other: I must know my truth to adhere to the truth of the text, and it is the truth of the text that is going to guide me in the search I pursue among the secrets of my conscience. There is, then, a fundamental link between the reading of the text and the verbalization of the self. If I want to read and understand the text, I must put myself into words.

It seems to me that this link, in Christianity, between reading the text and verbalizing the self is fundamental. And yet, in spite of this connection, there are, I believe, two hermeneutic techniques that are entirely distinct. In other words, a different type of interpretation is going to be put into place, at least in early Christianity, for the hermeneutics of the text and the hermeneutics of the self. From the earliest centuries of Christianity, the hermeneutics of the text had recourse to techniques of interpretation that were perfectly elaborated and well known, in either the Jewish or the Hellenic tradition. The text was the object of numerous techniques of interpretation that were complex and well established. By contrast, the hermeneutics of the self—that is to say, the possibility of discovering something hidden deep within myself, the path that allowed me to discover not so much the unknown as the hidden, which is the definition of hermeneutics in general—I believe that this approach, with regard to the self, did not have the antecedents or the instruments available to a hermeneutics of the text either in Greek culture or in Judaic culture.

The hermeneutics of the text was already an established cultural practice. On the other hand, the hermeneutics of the self—if the thesis that I am trying to explain to you is correct, that is, if indeed the hermeneutics of the self was an invention that grew out of the asceticism and monasticism of the fourth and fifth centuries—did not have its own specific technique. Indeed, when one examines the regimens and procedures that Cassian described or, before him, Evagrius, or of which we have testimonies in the *Apophthegmata patrum*, one sees that there was not actually any interpretation, that the hermeneutics of the self took place entirely through the act of verbalization. It was simply a question of whether or not one could speak, it was simply the fact of speaking or not, or what happened in the act of speaking: Did I blush or not, did I hesitate or not, did the devil escape in my words or, to the contrary, did my words flow freely without any dramatic effect? This is what allowed for *discretio*, for *discrimen*: it is what allowed me to tell what was good or what was not good in my thought, where there was illusion, where there was not illusion, where there was the presence of the devil and where there was not the presence of the devil. In other words, it was the verbal act in itself that had interpretive value and nothing else. So, if you will, it was a relatively (to say the least) rudimentary technique that was located entirely within the act of speech; whereas for the text, on the contrary, there were far more developed techniques.

The third reason why I insisted on *exagoreusis*—there is first its internal structure, there is second [the] relationship between the hermeneutics of the self and the hermeneutics of the text that I consider important to Christianity—the third reason is that, finally, this duality between hermeneutics of the text and hermeneutics of the self was, I believe, of fundamental importance for the entire history of Christianity. It seems to me that between these two types of hermeneutics, there has always been—at least for a millennium and a half or two millennia—a tension, an interplay, an equilibrium, a disequilibrium that was the life and drama, or at least one part of the drama, of Christian culture. [. . .] In thus opposing the hermeneutics of the text and the hermeneutics of the self, I am not simply proposing that they represent two forms of thought, but rather two types of practices and two modes of experiences, two ways of living Christianity. And it seems to me that we could follow this opposition and this interplay throughout the history of Christianity.

We can see very clearly how throughout the Middle Ages—in spite of the prestige and the precedence of the hermeneutics of the text—the hermeneutics of the self gave rise to a whole series of spiritual experiences, of forms of mysticism that were often parallel, but also at times divergent or even in contradiction with the institutional structures of the text that had been authorized by the institution itself. And I think that what happened during the fifteenth and sixteenth centuries—that is to say during the Reformation, or the movements that accompanied, surrounded, and brought about the Reformation—during this period, we can clearly grasp or see the conflict that erupted between the hermeneutics of the self and the hermeneutics of the text. It seems to me that what we see during the Reformation was of course a refusal of the Church's authority in its institutional structure; this was the refusal to submit the hermeneutics that one practiced on the text to a dogmatic institutional authority; it was also a refusal to submit the hermeneutics of the self to the jurisdictional authority of the priest within an institution or a sacrament such as penance.

Freeing both the hermeneutics of the text and the hermeneutics of the self: that is what Protestantism achieved. But it did more than this, that is, free these two hermeneutic practices from the authority of the Church, from the authority of instruction, or from the authority of penance. Protestantism tried to adjust [them] to each other, to put them in communication, such that the truth one discovered within was the very truth of the faith, that is to say the very truth that was given in the text. In order to resolve this fundamental tension within Christianity, Protestantism tried to follow a path of internalization or doubling, of involution such that the truth of the text, I would find it within me; and what I would find within myself would be the truth of the text.

I would like to conclude these general reflections on the hermeneutics of the self in Western culture with one last consideration. It seems to me that all too often we forget that the hermeneutics of the self was not only central to the history of Christianity, but was also fundamental to the history of philosophy. What has been called and what we generally study under the heading of "the relationships between philosophy and religion" is generally focused on the relationships between, let's say, revealed truth or the truth of the text and the truth of reason. But it seems to me that in fact [. . .]—and this was clear throughout the Middle Ages—the question posed [by] philosophy has always been: What are the relationships between the truth of the text, the truth of reason, and the truth of the self? In any case, it seems to me that many aspects of seventeenth-century philosophy are clarified from such a point of view.

For instance, with regard to Descartes, or for that matter Empiricist philosophy, at bottom what occurred during the seventeenth century was that philosophy renounced, in a definitive way, the authority of the text as its essential reference. And when I say "the authority of the text," I am thinking not simply of the authority of the revealed text, but the authority of *all* text, of any text transmitted through the Western cultural tradition: none of them were thereafter authoritative enough to be able to impose their own truth. The philosophical approach would—this is evident in Descartes, it is evident as well with the English Empiricists—have to emanate solely from itself; that is to say, it would have to emanate solely from the philosopher himself. And as a result, at that very moment, the problem of the truth of the self was posed in the most striking terms: instead of posing the question of the relationships between the truth of reason and the truth of the text, the philosophical approach shifted the problem toward the question of the relationships between the truth of reason and the truth of the self.

Here we find again the famous danger that has haunted the entire matter of the hermeneutics of the self since the spirituality of Evagrius and of Cassian: Is there not something within me, a power [*une puissance*] that creates illusion, such that even when I think I know the truth I am fooling *myself*, not in the sense that I am wrong about things, about eternal truths, or about principles of reason, but to the extent that there is something, a power, which is misleading me? I may be misleading myself in thinking that I see the truth: you see that this is precisely the Cartesian problem, which could only be resolved, of course, through the exclusion of that famous power, the evil genius — the exclusion of which was not necessitated by some philosophical radicalism specific to Descartes, but was an absolute cultural necessity, inscribed in the very history of Western culture as of the fourth or fifth century, when the relationship of the self to the self was burdened and mortgaged by this danger of the illusion that had been discovered, brought forth, and incessantly denounced by Christian spirituality.

Am I not deluding myself about myself? It was the evidence of the *cogito* that allowed Descartes to dismiss this danger, which was posed, marked, and indicated by Christian spirituality. Let's just say that the empiricist solution, Locke's solution, was to find it not in evidence but rather in sensation — in sensation which by virtue of its immediate relation to exteriority would escape the dangers proper to the interiority of thought. As a result, we are going to have (and this is what characterized classical thought at least up to Kant, that is, that there was absolutely no danger that I was deluding myself): I could be mistaken, of course, but what was going to mislead me were either sensory errors, metaphysical errors, or errors in reasoning. This possibility of the illusion of myself to myself had been warded off, and was only reintroduced into Western philosophy after Kant's critique and to some extent either thanks to [or] through the breach Kant's critique opened up, when Schopenhauer rediscovered not only the possibility of, but also the fundamental connection between, individuality of the self and illusion.

It seems to me that this is where the problem of the unconscious — which Freud later found precisely where Schopenhauer had located it — was introduced and took root within Western thought. Freud was a Schopenhauerian, and one must always keep in mind that Schopenhauer and the questions he posed dominated nineteenth-century philosophy throughout Europe. Schematically speaking, one could say that what Freud did by taking up the question of the illusion of the self about the self, right where Schopenhauer had indicated its possibility on the basis of Kant's critique

. . . to resolve, to treat this question, he used the interpretive methods of the text that the Christian tradition—or in Freud's case, the Jewish tradition—had already refined for centuries. And this type of asymmetry that I pointed out to you with regard to *exagoreusis* and which proved to me that while the hermeneutics of the self was absolutely tied to the hermeneutics of the text, the hermeneutics of the text disposed of interpretive techniques that were unavailable to the hermeneutics of the self: with Freud—well, with Schopenhauer—the possibility, necessity, and inevitability of the illusion of the self about the self returned for the first time since Descartes. And with Freud we witness the development of a hermeneutics of the self that would have its own interpretive techniques.

So this is how we could, very broadly, not necessarily reinterpret the whole of Western philosophy, but by developing a few of these schemas, by following some of these leads, one might recross diagonally the history of Western thought or of Western philosophy (I would prefer to say the history of Western thought), recross it from the perspective of the impact of specific forms of spirituality that were put into place in Christianity during the fourth and fifth centuries. So that is a quick sketch of the conclusion I had hoped to present last time but did not have the time to develop, and that I wanted to indicate now in order to begin.

So, of course, it is not this history of avowal—of *exagoreusis*—in philosophy or in Western culture that I would like to continue with now. Rather, [I would like to] try to study the effects of this form of avowal and this principle of the veridiction of oneself, the effect of this obligation to tell the truth about oneself: to follow the effects within the juridical order. I will therefore study today the problem of the juridification of telling truth about oneself within the ecclesiastical tradition and institution, and then next time I will study some of the effects and problems of truth-telling about oneself in the juridical institution proper.

First, the juridification of avowal in the ecclesiastical institution.* In my lecture two weeks ago, I studied a form of veridiction of oneself—the one found in the rituals of penance that were put in place, developed, and used in Christian communities in general. Then, last week I studied *exagoreusis*—that is to say this very different practice that consisted of speaking

---

* Foucault addresses the audience: "Would you like . . . excuse me, my introduction was a bit long; conclusion-introduction. Would you like me to stop for a few minutes, to discuss, or would you like me to continue? Pardon? Continue? Yes? OK."

indefinitely about oneself and the movements of one's thought, a practice that developed exclusively, or was at least privileged, in monastic communities. So there was *exomologēsis* in penance and *exagoreusis* as an ascetic and spiritual practice in monastic communities. In reality, these two practices—*exomologēsis* of penance and spiritual *exagoreusis*—represented far more two poles between which there was a series of graduated forms, than two institutions or two practices that were perfectly distinct one from the other. However, it seems to me that during the first centuries—and this will be the first part of today's lecture—that is to say between the fourth and seventh centuries, one sees little by little a contamination between these two forms that is more and more noticeable, at the same time as an adaptation or adjustment of each [of them], within the Christian communities on the one hand and in the monastic communities [on the other]. An adaptation that indicates already a kind of shift towards juridical forms.

[1] Let's begin with the matter that I spoke to you about last time, that is to say *exagoreusis* in Christian communities. It is clear that this practice, which consisted once again of the obligation to tell one's every movement of thought to one's spiritual director, could only be a sort of ideal program and was perfectly unrealizable as such. When I say perfectly unrealizable, this does not mean that this rule was forgotten, or that the existence of this general principle did not have an impact or matrix effects on a certain number of other practices. In particular, the principle of opening one's heart—the principle of a spiritual direction necessary without fail for novices, but also for all monks—this principle would continue to be maintained and could be found in all monastic institutions of the Early Middle Ages and Middle Ages.

I will take two examples; one is well known and the other is less so. The well known example, of course, is the Benedictine Rule established in the West, which posed the principle—I will quote one wording of this Benedictine rule—that it is a great consolation in life to have *"cui aperias pectus tuum,"*[7] (someone to whom you open your heart); someone with whom *"arcana participes,"*[8] ([. . .] someone who must participate with you in the secrets of your conscience); and [. . .] someone in whom you must confide *"secreta cordis tui"*[9] (the secrets of your own heart). And another text—this one addressed to communities of women (it is the *Regula ad virgines*, which dates from the seventh century and is attributed to Saint Donatus)[10]— where it is said: "The sisters must zealously and continuously confess all of their thoughts and everything they have said, as well as all their useless acts or even all *commotio animi* (all movement of the soul); and this must be done *omnibus deibus, omnibus horis, omnibus momentis* (every day, every hour, every moment). Such that nothing is hidden from the spiritual mother, even *parva cogitata* (even one's little thoughts): even those must not be neglected or withheld from the confession."[11] So you see that the rule of *exogoreusis* was maintained, but as a kind of ideal point, a hearth that one must draw nearer to and that, in fact, in concrete terms, would take on a whole series of different forms, such as the regular examination of the conscience in the evening and the morning or at certain hours of the day, the confession of sins to one's spiritual director, long-standing relationships with a director, conversations [*des entretiens*].

But beyond this and the necessity of adjusting this impossible and untenable rule of complete *exagoreusis*, there was an entire series of other factors that brought, within the very monastic practices, monastic institutions, monastic communities,* [. . .] other practices that were increasingly shifting, increasingly drifting toward sorts of quasijuridical practices.

One must not forget, to start with, that the Pacomian monasteries of the Orient in Egypt had [. . .] a form, an objective, and a type of organization rather different from those of which Cassian could offer an account — far different, in any event, from those communities whose objective was essentially contemplative. The Pacomian monasteries were, first of all, monasteries of the poor. They were populated by Egyptian *fellahs*, for whom the spiritual exercises were evidently somewhat difficult to learn. They were people who had a problem to solve, that of life and survival: the problem of begging. How would one be able to live? Should one beg or should one work? And the Pacomian order precisely imposed work in place of begging, which became one of the fundamental choices in Christian monasticism until the reappearance of mendicant orders under Saint Francis. So they worked. And at the same time, with the large number of monks who were part of the community, well, naturally there was a necessity of a colonial or military type of organization, a military organization with the obligation to work, certain hours, groups of ten with superiors — in short, there was an entire administrative apparatus that was in the process of putting itself into place within monastic communities.

The Benedictine monasteries that we are familiar with in the West were

---

* Foucault corrects himself. It seems that he meant to say not "monastic practices," but "monastic institutions and communities."

marked by the same imprints as the Pacomian monasteries, up to a certain point, but with two more particular attributes. On the one hand, there
was the influence of Augustinianism, which is the true reason why Cassian
was a bit forgotten. Augustinianism, what does it mean? It meant that
one was going to be wary of everything that could be considered at the
time a remnant of Origenism, that is to say the idea that one could, by oneself and through a spiritual action performed upon oneself, ensure one's
own salvation and purify one's own heart. With Augustinianism—that is
to say with the idea that one could not be saved without God's grace—it is
evident that everything that could have been considered a spiritual exercise lost the greater part of its efficacy in assuring salvation. And as a result, in the monasteries infused with Augustinianism, the problem of the
purification of oneself, the problem of the sanctification of the self, the
voluntary progression through spiritual experiences toward perfection,
this would disappear in favor of work that would be imposed, organized,
and regulated.

And if we consider that, added on to this Augustinianism, there was a
very important economic and social role of Benedictine monasteries since
the very Early Middle Ages—well, since late antiquity and throughout all
the very Early Middle Ages—we see why, finally, the Benedictine monasteries began to function on a very different model than those on which
Cassian could provide insight. Work became a fundamental activity—of
course, with a spiritual value, since work reduced up to a certain point the
dispersion of thoughts that was one of the conditions for contemplation,
[and] work also imposed a necessary humility on the individual. But work
is also, of course, the instrument that provided the independence of the
liturgical function ensured by the monasteries; work was also responsible
for these communities' economic importance, which manifested itself and
exerted itself through this type of regulation; and through this, of course,
there was an entire type of discipline that imposed regulation, hierarchy,
surveillance, and of course the sanction of sins. And this is how we come
to, little by little—or rather quickly, actually—within monastic orders, beneath that general principle of constant avowal to another, an increasingly
strict codification concerning the sins not to be committed, the avowals to
be performed for one's sins, and the appropriate punishments.

Second, if we look at *exomologēsis*, the other form of the manifestation
of truth found in the rituals of penance, you will remember that these obligations of truth did not consist of avowing the perpetual movement of

thought, as in *exagoreusis*. Rather, it was a question of manifesting one's general state as sinner. When one had committed grave sins, when one felt the weight of the accumulation of all one's sins, or when one felt death nearing, one took on the status of penitent and tried to free oneself from the weight of one's sins by showing oneself to everyone in one's state as sinner.

The status of penance was evidently as difficult to manage and implement as the rule of perpetual avowal in ecclesiastical communities. [On the one hand], penitential status was in effect very onerous, since when the individual had become penitent, he was isolated from the rest of the community, with all the spiritual inconveniences—and all the social and economic inconveniences, for that matter—that were entailed. He was moreover banished from society; in any event, there were a certain number of things he could not do, such as, for example, marry or have sexual relations with his wife if he was married. . . . In short, the status of penitent invalidated the individual, and this status did not last just a few days or weeks. Rather, this great penitential dramaturgy unfolded over years. On the other hand, the fact that the penitential status was so onerous meant that often, instead of doing penance, of taking on the status of the penitent when one had committed a sin, precisely because it was a grave sin, people preferred waiting for the end of their lives when they felt they were really on their last legs to seek the status of the penitent—which was perceived in their eyes as guaranteeing salvation, and avoided their need to endure such a burdensome status for too long. The third inconvenience was the public character of the status of the penitent, which meant that if the public status of the penitent was natural or acceptable when the sin was itself scandalous and public, [by contrast] when the sin was secret, the public status of the penitent posed a number of problems vis-à-vis the community because it could turn into a scandal, if you will; penance itself became scandalous by revealing a sin that had not hitherto been known.

In short, this all brought about—and rather early, we have indications of this around the fourth and fifth centuries—a rather significant modification in the general economy of what could be referred to as the regime of penance in Christian communities. On the one hand, the habit emerged of distinguishing between public and private penance. This generated the principle that for public sins one performed public penance, while for secret sins penance was private (this private penance, of course, took place through avowal to the bishop or priest, who decided the appropriate type of satisfaction, such as fasting, for example, or sexual abstention, prayer, or occasionally pilgrimage—a certain number of penances, of satisfactions that would amount to the reaction, the response, or the sanction to the secret sin).* And, in connection with this, with this diffi-culty of managing the penitential status in general, there developed an ex-tension of the practices of spiritual direction that were somewhat similar to those found in monastic communities, but that would become a relay instrument, an intermediary form, an attenuated form of the practice in cases in which one could not ask the individual to take on the status of penitent. And this is how we find this definition, dating from the fourth century, in the Christian Orient: it is the text of Gregory of Nazianzus, in which he shows [. . .] how spiritual direction, an ascetic practice, a practice which had essentially been designed for monastic communities, was in the process of diffusing itself throughout Christian communities in general.

This text of Gregory of Nazianzus is very important because it was quoted consistently up to the seventeenth century whenever one made reference to the direction of conscience as a *technē technēs*, art of arts. This famous expression *technē technēs*, pronounced by Oedipus—well, which Sophocles put in Oedipus's mouth to designate political power, the *technē technēs*, this art of arts that allowed one to direct men and to conduct their conduct—this expression was now applied to spiritual direction. Gregory of Nazianzus wrote: "It seems to me that to guide man, that di-verse and changing animal, is a question of *technē technēs*, the art of arts, of *epistēmē epistēmēs*, the science of sciences. This may be understood by comparing the healing of souls to the curing of bodies; if, knowing how difficult is the first, one examines to what extent the second, our spiri-tual direction, is even more difficult, either because of the nature of the subject to be treated or by the force of the science to be employed, or by the aims it hopes to attain."[12] A long analogy follows between medicine and spiritual direction. And the paragraph ends with the following: "One must keep in mind all of the differences, the differences between men and women, young and old, rich and poor, those who are gay and those who are sad, those in good health and those who are sick, the leaders and the subordinates, the single and the married, those who live in the country-side and those who reside in the city, those who are simple and those who are clever. One must care for these souls with different methods and pro-

---

* Foucault corrects himself. It seems that he meant to say not "penances," but rather "sat-isfactions."

cesses, either through words or through example, either by the spur or by the rein, through praise or through reprimands, in public or in private."[13] This is what Gregory of Nazianzus said in his second discourse.

This text is very interesting because, as you can see, he was not addressing a monastic community. Rather, he transformed spiritual direction into a general pastoral function that any pastor, any priest, any bishop, anyone who in general had a responsibility with regard to a community, no matter what kind, should exercise. I think that with the development of the pastoral function inside Christian communities, one sees the ritual of *exomologēsis* lose some of its importance; it was modified, softened, and mitigated as spiritual direction began to penetrate.

So there was a double movement. In the monastic communities, the difficulty of applying the rule of constant avowal led to the penetration of other techniques—in particular, the technique of punishing the sin in an individual manner once it was committed. And inversely, there was an attenuation of *exomologēsis* in the nonmonastic communities: the obligation for those who had sinned to take on the status of penance was slowly substituted or doubled with another obligation of an adjusted penance, which was adapted according to the needs of spiritual direction; it was adjusted at once to the individual who had committed the sin and to the sin that had been committed. Broadly speaking, two grand foyers emerged. The first was the convent, the monastic community, both a spiritual and an economic foyer whose community structure had become increasingly strong and which finally received a strict regulated organization. There the practices of spiritual direction were inflected in the direction of a codification of behaviors and sanctions. The second foyer was the lay community under the direction of the bishop or the presbyters. This was simultaneously a pastoral and administrative foyer with a communitarian structure, but one that was far weaker than it was in the monasteries. There, the practice of penance was juridified in a different way, through a kind of contamination with judicial and administrative procedures.

There was therefore a co-penetration, a reciprocal contamination between these two forms. Up to a certain point, there was a tendency towards homogenization between them without the dimorphism between these two forms of life ever being undermined because, to the contrary, this separation was to remain one of the essential dimensions of Christianity—or, in any case, of Catholic Christianity. But two points merit mention here. On the one hand, in the monastic communities as well as

the churches, one could not be a part of the community without an obligation of truth, of truth about oneself, of truth of oneself which was tied to a
specific relationship of dependence on someone else. And second, in both
forms of communities, these obligations of truth [. . .] to formulate the
truth to someone else interpenetrate one another, and slowly this tended
toward an obligation to avow one's sins defined according to a code, with
sanctions that followed this same code.

[2] This movement, which lasted from the fourth to the sixth and
seventh centuries, would then be multiplied and intensified from the
seventh century onward, when there appeared [. . .] within Christian institutions what we could call the first great juridification of penance—that
is to say, fixed penance [*la pénitence tarifée*].

I suppose that many of you know what fixed penance is: it is a form of
penance that began to spread from the seventh century and was diffused
by Irish monks, who played a central role in the evangelization of western
Europe in portions of Gaul and Germany. Fixed penance was peculiar in
several ways. First of all, it was a penance that was exercised, that needed
to be practiced when *one* sin was committed: it responded to each sin point
by point; for each sin there corresponded a penance. Second, and consequently, the great originality of this penance was that it could be reiterated: while the great *exomologēsis*—that great penitential status that used
to be imposed on sinners—could only be done once (one became penitent
and remained so until death; or if one was reconciled, one could not take
on the status of penitent again; one could only be excluded from the community, excommunicated), to the contrary, in the case of fixed penance
one could or one should complete as many penances as one had committed
sins, for however many sins one committed. This was evidently and absolutely fundamental to the process of juridification, as it marked a great
departure from anything that had existed up to that point, either in the
form of *exomologēsis* or in the form of *exagoreusis*.

What were the origins of this fixed penance? It had two origins, clearly.
The first was in the monastic model I spoke of earlier. As the convents became firmly regulated communities with a precise or at least an important economic function, with permanent hierarchical structures, systems
of surveillance, and a permanent regulation of life, it is evident that it
became impossible to function without a certain number of sins being
defined along with the sanctions that corresponded to these sins. If this

model of monastic regulation diffused, it was for a very simple reason: when someone, a lay person, had committed a great sin and wanted to repent by taking on the status of penitent, where could he take on this status of penitent and lead a life of penance if not in the monastery? So when one decided to make up for a grave sin one went to the convent, and there, the monks proposed to those who wanted to do penance not that grand status of penitent, which in any case could only be granted by the bishop, but punishments like the regulating sanctions found in the monasteries. For example, there was fasting, genuflection, or not sleeping for a certain amount of time in order to sing the psalms. These were monastic types of punishment.

On the other hand, the other model that intervened and that also had an important influence on the history of this juridification was the model of Germanic law. It was the model of Germanic law, for we can see very well . . . in this idea that upon committing a sin, one must provide satisfaction that will enable the reparation for that sin, we find very clearly the principle of Germanic law that an offense could always be repaid by satisfying the one who had been wronged. And just as repayment equaled punishment and was therefore double-sided—one satisfied the party that had been wronged, and at the same time suffered punishment—in the same way, one responded to one's fault toward God with a penance that satisfied God and would be a punishment for the sinner. We find the same structure here.

We also find in the system of fixed penance another element of the Germanic model: there was a calculated proportionality established between the sin and the appropriate satisfaction to be made. You remember well that in the *exomologēsis* I spoke of previously, there was no proportionality: one had committed a fault or felt that one was a sinner, and therefore one needed to show in the most dramatic and intense way possible how much remorse one felt for one's own sin. And the more one added on, the more one rolled in the dust, the more one fasted with intensity, the more one cried and pleaded for others to participate through their prayers in one's salvation, the greater were one's chances of being saved—but one's chances of being saved were proportional to one's will to be saved, and not to the weight of one's sin. With fixed penance, by contrast, there was a codification like the one found in Germanic law. For example, when a cleric stole a head of cattle, the penitentials of the seventh and eighth cen-

turies provided for a penance of one year of bread and water; three years
of bread and water plus three years without wine or meat if the cleric had
killed without premeditation or hate.

The third characteristic that drew fixed penance closer to Germanic law
was that punishment itself could be bought back. It could be bought back,
for penance was of course extremely onerous and there was a system of
transaction. As in Germanic law, where one could compromise with the
person one had wronged by arguing, "No, that is really a bit too expensive,"
in the same way one could say to God or the monk who represented him
that one could not accomplish the particular penance, but that it could
be substituted with something else. There was even a code of substitution. For example, when one hesitated to do an entire year of penance
because it was too difficult—such as no wine nor meat, or only bread and
water, I believe, three days a week, or sexual abstinence—there was a substitute, an *area*, which was three days enclosed in a saint's tomb without
food, drink, or sleep while singing psalms throughout those three days.
Or, for example, instead of a special fast, one could recite one hundred
psalms while performing one hundred genuflections. Or again, one could
sing fifty-seven canticles three times. There was, then, an entire structure
of reparation that clearly introduces us to a system of juridical order.

Lastly, the fourth important aspect of this fixed penance that shows
well the process of juridification is that the penance—the satisfactions
imposed by the Church or by the ecclesiastical community—was inter-
twined with civil penalties; and often, one finds in the penitentials satisfactions that were manifestly both civil and religious. For example, in
the penitential of Saint Columbanus[14] one reads the following: "If a cleric
has assassinated someone, he will be exiled for ten years." Here we are in
the realm of penance, of satisfaction. Thus, "he will be exiled for ten years.
He will give the parents the lawful compensation that is due [to] the victim." The Church ensures that the lawful compensation is indeed [. . .] dis-
bursed, but [. . .] this requirement is part of the satisfaction. So, "will give
the parents the lawful compensation due [to] the victim. He will put himself in the service of the father and the mother."[15] Here again, this is taken
directly from Germanic law. Or again, "the lay person who has intention-
ally harmed someone will be required to give compensation for the harm.
If he does not have enough to pay, he will take care of the victim's affairs
until the victim is healed."[16] So you see that there was here an overlapping

of civil and canonical penalties, or civil and religious. In fact, one finds here a phenomenon that was already partially present in Saint Augustine or in the period of Saint Ambrose: namely, that the Church had taken on a non-negligible part of the jurisdictional functions that had previously been the privilege of civil authorities. And consequently, by becoming a jurisdictional power, the Church ensured or served as the link between the civil juridical structures and these forms of penance—which, at their origin, were so distinct, if we take the cases of *exomologēsia* and *exagoreusis* as I have described them to you.

You see, then, how this contamination took place. In a practice like fixed penance, evidently, the form of penance required procedures that were very different from those used either in *exomologēsia* or in *exagoreusis*: it was a question neither of a grand dramatic scene nor of telling one's every thought.

This is not to say that all of that had entirely disappeared. First, it is important to remember that the practices of public penance, the great *exomologēsia* that I described to you—those do not disappear in a certain number of serious cases with special status: the exclusion from certain liturgies, the external and violent demonstrations of humiliation and mortification. In some cases these forms of public penance remained in place up to the thirteenth, fourteenth, and even fifteenth centuries—there was also to be, for that matter, a hierarchy between solemn penance, public penance, and private penance. So, the practice of *exomologēsia* continued but was increasingly marginalized and reserved for a certain number of altogether particular cases. But [. . .] the very rituals of this private penance that became so juridified in form, these very rituals still contained certain elements of dramatic *exomologēsia*. This is how a penitential—of Saint Colombanus, I believe, but I am not sure—explained the following with regard to confession to a priest who imposed satisfaction: "At the moment the sinner avows his sins to the priest and the priest imposes the satisfaction he must complete, the penitent must be on his knees on the ground with his hands forward, with his face covered in tears; and at this moment, he must express his contrition. Then, when the priest imposes his penance, the satisfaction proper, at that moment he shall lay flat with his face to the ground moaning, sighing, and crying."[17] You have, then, elements of *exomologēsia* that remain within this juridified realm.

Nonetheless, in spite of the persistence of these ancient and traditional forms of dramatic penance, fixed penance did constitute a new practice that gave [. . .] .*

::::

[. . .] the difficulty of the very status of this penitential act, which only began to be reflected upon as of the tenth and eleventh centuries. Because, what did it mean and what was the effect of a penance like this? We are not yet at a time when penance is a sacrament: the penitent did nothing more when he asked for penance than anticipate, both through avowal

---

* There is a break here in the audiovisual recording, corresponding to a change in the tape. As a result there is a lacuna that can be partially filled through the original type-script deposited at the IMEC. The original typescript reads as follows (May 13, 1981, lecture, pp. 17–18):

Nonetheless [. . .] in spite of the persistence of these ancient and traditional forms of dramatic penance, fixed penance did constitute a new practice, which gave an important place to the manifestation of truth, a manifestation of truth that was only partially built on previous forms, a manifestation of truth that was verbal from this moment forward. It was verbal and needed to be verbal for the very system of fixed penance to function. First, it was necessary to have an analytic declaration of the fault by the one who committed it. This analytic declaration was rendered necessary because there was a code, which established a given penance or satisfaction for a given fault. It also determined modifications of the satisfaction according to any modifications of the circumstances of the fault. The penitent, the one who solicited the penance or the one upon whom it was imposed, exposed the circumstances of his act, his intentions, the regularity of his habits. He stated his status, the status of the victim if he had wronged someone (of course, the importance of the fault was not the same if one killed a slave or a free man, a poor or a rich man, etc.). There was the necessity of an anamnestic declaration.

Second, the necessity of a dialogue entered at this stage. An important element of this dialogue was that it operated as a form of interrogatoire because, at this point and in the context of a coded system, the one who committed the fault was not supposed to know the exact code. That is, he did not know what was going to make a difference in the definition of the fault, what would lead to the aggravation or the attenuation of the satisfaction according to such and such a circumstance. . . . Only the one who imposed the penance, only he knew this. So the one to whom we confess our faults and who imposed penance posed questions; he needed to interrogate. And the Romano-Germanic penitential states: "The one to whom one confesses one's faults must pay careful attention that the penitent does not hide any of his spiritual defects, that none of the sins to be eliminated in the penance remain hidden. The one to whom one confesses will place all of these things into the memory of the penitent through his insistence."

One does not yet find the word "confessor" in these texts, but it was not long before it appeared. In any case, the figure appeared. Not the figure who imposed penance because it was asked of him and because he has the authority; but the one to whom one spoke, the one to whom we avow, and the one who is able to respond to this avowal through a series of questions that allowed [. . .].

and through the satisfactions he made, the judgment and the condemnation that God could deliver. By condemning himself a little, by accepting himself and willingly performing this satisfaction, he thereby hoped to lighten the punishment that would necessarily be imposed during the last judgment.

In fact, this posed a series of theoretical difficulties, and throughout the texts we see two models that constantly overlap. On the level of practice, of the very organization of the procedure, it was a world or a practice where the judicial model was, if not all-powerful, at least extremely present. Codes, faults, sanctions: we are in a judicial model. But if it were a judgment—if it was veritably a judgment with a condemnation and a punishment fixed according to the fault—then God would find himself bound by the priest's decision to accord penance and impose a satisfaction. And by consequence, there would be no reason for the last judgment: human judgment would be substituted for God's judgment, which was obviously inadmissible. Hence, the constant references to a medical model within this clearly judicial practice. In reality, penance was a medicine. One was sick, and sin was an illness or sin was a wound. And just as one explained one's illness [to the] doctor, showed one's wounds, or undressed to show where one was suffering, in the same manner avowal here took on the form of a medical visit. One showed the priest one's wounds, and the priest suggested a medication; and one then accepted the medication in the hopes of being cured. It is striking that within a practice that was, in fact, completely juridified, the impossibility of understanding penance as a tribunal led to the reactivation of the theme of penance as medicine—a theme which was present in the texts of the third, fourth, or fifth centuries, and there drew its utility from the impossibility of thinking the juridical reality of actions that were nonetheless being done through juridical forms.

The second point that must be insisted upon is that from this point on the verbalization of the fault became essential. The verbalization of the fault took on the form that I explained earlier, organized by the existence of a code. The verbalization of the fault was also justified by the necessity, of course, that the one who imposed penance know the fault. This verbalization was justified a third time by reference to the medical model. Finally, you find in the texts of the fourth century [this] justification, [this] valorization of the verbal act: in avowing a fault, one made a sacrifice. Whereas verbalization in monastic *exagoreusis* was a true renunciation of the self, in this case verbalization appears as a sacrifice—a sacrifice that was in some sense partial, a beginning of satisfaction. The expression appears as of the tenth and eleventh centuries: the avowal itself was a beginning of satisfaction because it produced shame. One was ashamed of avowing one's act to someone else, and this sacrifice through verbalization was the beginning of the satisfaction. It was the beginning to such an extent that, in extreme cases or cases of emergency, in particular in the face of death and often in battle, the possibility of confessing to a layperson was perfectly admitted. We are not in a world of sacraments: the power of the one who imposed penance was in truth simply a form of knowledge; the person knew what penance needed to be performed in order to be pardoned for one's sins. So, it was good to find someone who knew—but whether he was a priest, whether he had a particular status, whether he had, as we say, the "power of the keys" was not yet an issue. And since the mere act of avowal was already a form of satisfaction, if need be and again if one found oneself in great danger, it was perfectly legitimate to confess one's fault to someone, anyone, even the first person one found. And the verbal sacrifice that was performed in this way through avowal would amount to satisfaction.

[3] There was then the third transformative moment that marked the true juridification of penance, which took place between the eleventh and the thirteenth centuries and by means, paradoxically, of the sacramentalization of penance. Oddly enough, it is from the moment that penance became a sacrament that it was totally and entirely juridified. There are both technical and more general historical reasons for this. I would like first to evoke rapidly the organizational schema of all this.

As you know, Canon XXI of the Fourth Lateran Council of 1215 required all Christians to confess at least once a year for Easter.[18] This was a general obligation, regardless of whether or not one knew that one had sinned: whether one was conscious or not of having sinned, one needed to confess—you see the stark contrast with fixed penance, which was designed to respond to a precise sin that one was conscious of having committed. Here, in any case, confession was obligatory (which evidently posed a certain number of problems): either because, as Alexander of Hales said,[19] one had committed venial sins,[20] (this was also Saint Bonaventure's thesis) or rather (and this was the thesis that was finally retained) because this rule of annual confession was of ecclesiastical institution. Confession was obligatory because one was part of the Church: one did not confess because one had committed a sin, but because to be Christian and to belong to the Church imparted the necessity of confession. This argument marked a fundamental shift.

Second, in the famous Canon XXI, this obligation to penance was associated with a vast institutional apparatus. First, it was grounded in a territorial apparatus because one confessed to one's own priest—that is to say the priest of one's parish—unless one had authorization, which created all of the conflicts that some of you know and that others of you can imagine. Second, it was also tied to a liturgical apparatus, because confession was made necessary within the liturgical cycle at Easter. It was also aligned with a punitive apparatus, because there were special sanctions either for the faithful who refused this duty or for the priests who were obliged to hear the confessions of their flock. And they, too, were to be punished if they shirked their duties or did not perform them properly. Finally, it was connected to a rather precise procedural apparatus, since the canon explains in broad outline how the confession must unfold—[. . .] we will return to this point in a moment.

It is equally significant that, at the same time as this universal obligation of penance was thus confirmed at the Fourth Lateran Council, the principle of penance as sacrament also emerged. The idea that penance was a sacrament did not surface at all before, approximately, the eleventh and twelfth centuries. The idea had already existed before the Lateran Council, of course: it had already been present in Lanfranc,[21] for example, whose *De celanda confessione*[22] places the sacrament of penance among the sacraments of the Church, next to faith, baptism, and the consecration of the body and blood. In the middle of the twelfth century, it was none other than Peter Lombard[23] who defined the famous *sacrum septenarium* in which penance was placed fourth after baptism, confirmation, and the Eucharist.

However, as you can imagine, in becoming a sacrament penance could no longer perform the role it had played in fixed penance: that is to say, an assurance that the sinner sought to secure on his future salvation. As a sacrament, penance was now a complex operation involving three figures: the sinner, the priest, and God. This operation unfolded at once in time and in eternity. The priest absolved; he was actually responsible for the absolution. And here we see a clear difference in the formulations: in the eleventh and twelfth centuries still, there were formulas of deprecative absolutions—that is, where the priest who was asked for penance asked God to absolve the penitent. As of the thirteenth century, the declarative formulation of absolution became regular: the priest would say "I absolve you," and once the priest said, "I absolve you," one was absolved. And at the same time that the sacramentalization of penance gave this real power of absolution to the priest, the priest was then free at that point to choose the satisfaction he considered most appropriate. And, as a result, the code that existed and that was in place for fixed penance—a given sin necessitated a precise satisfaction . . . here, now, the priest, through his power to absolve, could decide in complete liberty the penance, the satisfaction that he considered necessary and sufficient. I say "complete liberty"; this is too schematic. In fact there were limits and rules, but basically he was free to choose.

And yet, at the same time and by the very fact that penance became a sacrament—that is to say a real operation that effectively absolved the sinner of the sin he had committed—in a single stroke, we see penance, paradoxically, becoming completely juridified. That is to say, instead of the earlier situation of fixed penance as a juridical metaphor, where it was a kind of judgment and a manner of anticipating the true judgment at the end of time . . . well, instead of serving as an anticipation and being placed in this symbolic position, the act of penance—the penitential ritual—became in effect an act of a juridical nature: restructuring of the entire judicial system in which penance was caught up and by means of which it had been haphazardly contaminated. This restructuring was first achieved through the clear distinction between penitential and nonpenitential jurisdiction: a distinction between the tribunal, the *forum iustitiale* [on the one hand], with the power of jurisdiction and discipline that was tied to the ecclesiastical hierarchy and would have been transmitted to the apostle insofar as he was the prelate—it is there, before the *forum iustitiale*, that are decided the canonical punishments, interdiction, deposition, and infamy—and then, on the other hand, the *forum paenitentiale*, the penitential tribunal whose power was given to the apostle insofar as he was a priest, through the famous sentence that took on its full meaning and status at this point: "For if ye forgive men their trespasses, your heavenly Father will also forgive you."[24] And there, in this *forum paenitentiale* which the priest exercised because of his status and, through the power of the keys, at the same time as his ordination, there in this *forum paenitentiale*, the priest effectively absolved. He absolved. But to absolve, he still had to receive the special power given to him by the bishop alongside the power of the keys, which meant that his decision to absolve or not to absolve, in effect, took on the form of a sentence; and ultimately it had to rely on knowledge of both the law and the sins committed.

At this point, you see, there is a clear superimposition (which is now effective) of the sacramental structure and the judicial form of penance. This superimposition of a sacramental structure and a judiciary form—the complete realization of the judicial form through the sacramentalization of penance—was evidently a very important development; and it posed a series of problems that I do not have the time to go over, but that you can well imagine. It was essentially from all this that the great problems of moral theology were presented to the Church. It was also very significant because, in this episode of juridification by sacramentalization, you see that the Church established a juridical model, a judicial model of the relationship between man and God, at the heart of its organization. This introduced an idea that would have been unimaginable to an early Christian: that the relationship between God and man was of a legal nature, that the relationship could assume the order of a tribunal, that the relationship could be like the fault [and] the sanction; that between man and God, the scene was a judicial scene. This, indeed, was one of the Church's great accomplishments of the twelfth and thirteenth centuries.

This was evidently tied, on the one hand, to the entire debate, all the difficulty, all the conflicts regarding the Church's exercise of a certain type of temporal power. It was also tied, of course, to the problem of the redistribution of judicial powers within feudalism. It was also tied to the problem of defining spheres of action, of influence, and of sovereignty, of the exercise of power, between the Church and newborn monarchies. In any case, the Church became—and this is the essential point, in my opinion—the institution within [which] the relationships between God and man became fundamentally juridified.* With this begins or develops the great forgetting of Saint Augustine, as well as the beginning of an entire series of effects and consequences that were precisely those against which the Reformation would organize itself. And the Reform, with Luther and Calvin, was of course a tremendous effort to de-juridify the relationships between man and God—this juridification that had been the great work of the Church of the twelfth and thirteenth centuries.[25]

But you see as well, by way of conclusion, that in this superimposition of the sacramental and judicial forms, at the very center of the edifice,

---

* Foucault said "the relationship between God and the Church."

holding together these two elements ([these two pieces] whose juxtaposition posed so many theoretical and practical problems), we find, precisely, avowal. The avowal which developed, then, through an extraordinarily advanced technology. The avowal that had to constitute, in this *confessio oris*, in this "oral confession," one of the absolutely essential pieces of the ritual of penance.

This avowal had to begin with an act of faith, which shows well, for that matter, the articulation between the two great obligations of truth: truth with regard to faith, and truth of the self.

Second, this avowal had to begin by an avowal that took the form of free association or, in any event, of spontaneous unfolding: the penitent had to say what was in his heart and his conscience, remembering it as best he could and as he wished.

Then the confessor had to subject him to a questionnaire, a questionnaire whose structure was preestablished. Raymond of Penyafort,[26] the great theoretician or, I would say, the great technologist of penance in the thirteenth century, gave a long list of the seven capital sins and their derivative forms—a total of forty-three—that served as a grid for confession. But someone like Escobar,[27] for example, proposed as a framework for the confession a series of grids that were superimposed on one another; and the confessor could choose one of the grids, follow all of them, or propose some of them. There was the grid of the ten commandments of God, of the seven deadly sins, of the five senses of the body, of the twelve articles of faith, of the seven sacraments of the Church, and of the seven acts of mercy; and one had to perform the general examination of the life of the individual through, once again, one or more or all of these grids. You see that we have here a form of veridiction that was, then, entirely different from both *exomologēsia* and *exagoreusis*. It was no longer a question of telling one's every thought, nor of demonstrating one's state as a sinner. Rather, it was a question of verbally responding to a questionnaire that was defined by preestablished grids.

Finally, the form of avowal was determined by a series of characteristics of the enunciation itself that typified confessional avowal. These were the famous qualities of confession according to Raymond of Penyafort—the list has, for that matter changed, but in general the elements have remained the same. The confession had to be prompt; it had to be frequent; it had to be bitter, that is, accompanied by tears; it had to be integral; it had to be voluntary; it had to be faithful, that is, rooted in the faith; it had to be pure, in the sense that it could not be mixed with vanity (one could not be proud of the sins one had committed); it had to be *nuda*, naked, that is, it had to be done face to face; it had to be *morosa*, that is, done slowly (one must not, Raymond of Penyafort explained, list one's sins like an accountant would count sums); it had to be accusatory, that is, one had to show how one was guilty; it had to be *propria*, that is, concerned with the self and not with one's neighbor; it had to be true; and it had to be discrete, that is, each sin had to be isolated one from the other.

We have here, then, this *confessio oris*: you see that the manifestation of truth is now entirely verbal and entirely juridical.

I said "entirely verbal," but this is not wholly true because a certain number of residual traces of the old *exomologēsia* remained there, enveloping the verbal element that had become essential. They served as accompaniments; it is interesting, however, to recount them. During the course of the oral confession, a certain attitude was required of the penitent. If it was a man, he needed to take off his hood so the confessor could clearly see his face—you will see why in a moment. On the other hand, if it was a woman or a young boy, one needed to lower the hood so that one could not see the face, which a text described as the burning wind of the desert; in some cases, even, the woman or young boy was to stand in profile so that the confessor could not see them face forward, in order to avoid seduction. All of this was very important, and later on would develop a great deal: it captured the entire problem of the verbal act of confession as a medium for the contamination of sin and impurity—as a kind of transfer. In these physical rituals surrounding the confession, you surely know as well, there was a rule until the sixteenth century that confession would not take place in a confessional; the confessional did not exist before the sixteenth century.[28] But the confession was not even to take place in a dark or secluded area of the church; everyone needed to see the one who confessed with his or her confessor, precisely to prevent the verbal act . . . from conveying evil between the sinner and the confessor.

So there was a kind of marginal, accompanying importance within these physical rites—but you see that we are very, very far from that great ritual of *exomologēsia*. The importance of the physical, the necessity of seeing (on the part of the confessor) the one who was confessing, also had [. . .] another justification: it should also allow the confessor to decipher, through the attitude of the one who was confessing, what eventually he might have been hiding or what he was ashamed of telling; it allowed the confessor also to see if he was truly ashamed, if he felt contrition, or if he was indifferent to his sins or even happy to have committed them. There is a very significant text by Alain de Lille[29] in the *Liber poenitentialis* that reads: "One must understand the interior through the exterior. The face is *animi signaculum*. When the face is lowered and the tears are abundant, it is the sign of true internal contrition. If the face is held high and shows no sadness, the contrition is less intense."[30]

So there was a complex and carefully considered [. . .] organization of this verbal act—of this verbal act for which we can now understand why there needed to be so many precautions: because it was the essential piece. It was the essential building block as much for the judicial form as for the sacramental structure of the edifice. It stood, in a certain way, at the juncture. For what had the penitential avowal become now? In the words of Saint Thomas, it was the core matter of penance: it was the basis on which the act of absolution that would be formulated by the priest rested. And so, what would happen? In this act of confession and in the absolution that followed, two things could happen that would distort or rig the procedure. Either the penitent hid certain sins or did not express their full weight, or he did not feel contrition in pronouncing them when he sought penance. On the other hand, on the side of the words of absolution—of this *speech act*, of this performative act that consisted of saying "I absolve you"—there could also be deception if, for example, the priest may not have had the necessary power to hear the confession (he may not have been a priest; he may have been excommunicated—there are many reasons why this act might be rigged or manipulated). And yet, if on the side of the one who was confessing there was voluntary forgetfulness, or the absence of contrition, what should happen? The sacrament would not have taken place. That is, the matter proposed for sacrament was inadequate. Consequently there was no sacrament at all, no matter what the legitimacy of the priest's powers, no matter the sincerity (or rather the correctness) of the priest's words of absolution. [But if], to the contrary, [. . .] there was something wrong with the priest, something that was not quite right, something that prevented a legitimate interaction? If indeed the penitent was aware of it, then as in the previous case there was no sacrament. But if the penitent was absolutely in good faith—if he truly believed that the priest had the necessary power to accord him absolution, even if he didn't have these powers—it was sufficient and absolution was effectively given.

We see, as a result, that the essential element in this juridico-sacramental operation was indeed the verbal act through which the penitent announced his sins—as long as the act of avowal was an act of truth, that is, as long as one stated with appropriate contrition all of the sins of which one was conscious. I believe that the expression "*actus veritatis*"—act of truth—emerged quite late in fifteenth-century texts; but it defines extremely well what was then essential to the ritual of penance: at the very heart of the ritual of penance, all things being equal (that is to say, when all the rules had been respected by the one who spoke, who did so sincerely), the verbal act, the act of avowal, the *actus veritatis*, became the essential element of the procedure.

So we have here, I believe, the moment when avowal—taking place in a sacramental structure and in a fully juridified form—took its place as the fundamental element of penance. In my next lecture I will try to show you—much more rapidly—a parallel phenomenon in the forms of civil jurisdiction, the forms of civil justice, during approximately the same period, and then explore its effects on the history of penal law.*

[NOTES]

1. Cf. Irénée Hausherr, *Direction spirituelle en Orient autrefois* (Rome: Pont. Institutum Orientalium Studiorum, 1955), pp. 152–53; English edition, Irénée Hausherr, *Spiritual Direction in the Early Christian East*, trans. Anthony P. Gythiel (Kalamazoo, MI: Cistercian Publications, 1990), pp. 155–57:

> What is essential is to show the spiritual advisor not one's sins but one's thoughts (*logismoi*). . . . What the spiritual father needs to know and the spiritual child ought to reveal to him are one's actual dispositions which can be inferred from the "movements of the heart" (*mouvement des esprits*), without any need to stir up the past, a too detailed remembrance of which might do more harm than good. . . .
>
> What is important for the director to know and even more for the disciple to reveal are "movements of the heart" (of the mind), suggestions, inner promptings. When such an impulse or inner prompting develops into an outward deed, into consent of the will, it would be too late to show all this to the director. One must then go to a confessor, and resolve not to wait next time. The psychology of the ascetics, even before Augustine, differentiated between moments of temptation. There is the *prosbolē* (suggestion in thought), which is free from blame (*anaitios*). . . . Next follows the *syndiasmos* (coupling), an inner dialogue with the suggestion (temptation), then *palē* or struggle against it, which may end

---

* Foucault addresses the audience: "Well, thank you. Do you have any questions? No?"

with victory or with consent (*synkatathēsis*), actual sin. When repeated, such acts produce a *pathos* (passion) properly speaking, and in the end, a terrible *aichmalōsia*, a "captivity of the soul," which is no longer able to shake the yoke of the Evil One.

The proper object of *exagoreusis tōn logismōn* (revelation of thoughts) is the first stage of this process, the *prosbolē*. One must crush the serpent's head as soon as it appears. To massacre the children of Babylon from their tenderest age; to uproot the plant before it grows strong roots—these are classical metaphors in the matter. All this is done through an entire strategy: *nēpsis* (vigilance), watchfulness, the guarding of the heart (*custodia cordis*) and the mind, prayer, especially the invocation of the name of Jesus, and so forth.

An essential part of this war is specifically recourse to the spiritual father. . . .

2. Cf. Hausherr, "La pratique de la manifestation des pensées" in *Direction spirituelle en Orient autrefois*, p. 217, cites, among other illustrations, a letter of Saint Barsanuphius; English edition, Hausherr, *Spiritual Direction*, trans. Gythiel, p. 228:

Brother, do not rush into the discernment of thoughts that come to you. You are not qualified for this. If you continue, they will agitate you at will like someone who knows nothing of their deceptions. If they bother you, say to them, "I do not know what species you are. God who knows will not let you confound me." Turn over your powerlessness to God, by saying, "Lord, I am in your hands. Come to my help, and deliver me from their hands." But mention the thought that lingers in you and wages war upon you to your abba, and he will heal you through God.

3. Cf. Hausherr, *Direction spirituelle en Orient autrefois*, pp. 213–14; English edition, Hausherr, *Spiritual Direction*, trans. Gythiel, p. 225:

One should always stand guard at the door of one's heart or mind, and ask every suggestion that presents itself, "Are you one of ours, or from the opposing camp?" And precisely because one knows, by hypothesis and from experience, that one is often unable to tell the wolf from the sheep—the devil transforming himself into an angel of light—one will never run out of questions to ask the spiritual director, thanks to this unceasing attentiveness.

4. Cf. Hausherr, *Direction spirituelle en Orient autrefois*, p. 161; English edition, Hausherr, *Spiritual Direction*, trans. Gythiel, p. 164:

Together with the need for discernment (*diakrisis*), what also compels the revelation of thoughts is that basic precept of striving for perfection: the *abneget semetipsum* ("let one deny oneself"). In the common language of the Eastern ascetics (and of Saint Benedict), the self to be denied is one's own will (*voluntas propria*). *Ekkopē tou oikeou thelēmatos*, the cutting out of one's own will, is one of the sovereign mottos of monasticism.

5. Cf. Hausherr, *Direction spirituelle en Orient autrefois*, p. 165; English edition, Hausherr, *Spiritual Direction in the Early Christian East*, trans. Gythiel, pp. 168–69:

The only *raison d'être* of spiritual fatherhood is to lead from the stage of slavery to the freedom of the children of God, according to a very ancient division of the three ways: slaves, faithful servants, and sons. This blessed transformation takes place only when the human will is utterly replaced by the will of God.

6. Regarding the concept of the obligation of truth, see Michel Foucault, *Du gouvernement des vivants: Cours au Collège de France, 1979–80*, ed. Michel Senellart (Paris: Gallimard/Seuil, 2012), especially lectures of February 6 and March 26, 1980.

7. Foucault is apparently citing this text from memory. It is taken not from the Rule of Saint Benedict, but from Saint Ambrose of Milan. See Ambrose, *De officiis*, ed. and trans. Ivor J. Davidson, vol. 1 (Oxford: Oxford University Press, 2001), book 3, chapter 22, section 132, pp. 432 (Latin) and 433 (English): "Solatium quippe vitae huius est ut habeas cui pectus aperias tuum, cum quo arcana participes, cui committas secretum pectoris tui . . ." (It really is a comfort in this life to have someone to whom you can open your heart, someone with whom you can share your innermost feelings, and someone in whom you can confide the secrets of your heart . . .).

8. Ibid.

9. Ibid.

10. The Rule of Saint Donatus, established around 655, is one of the two rules created for women in Gaul. It comprised seventy-seven chapters, forty-three of which were directly inspired by the rule of Saint Benedict, while the others drew from the rule of Saint Cesar and those of Saint Columbanus. On this point see Michèle Gaillard, "Les origines du monachisme féminin dans le nord et l'est de la Gaule (fin VIe siècle—début VIIIe siècle)," in C.E.R.C.O.R., *Les religieuses dans le cloître et dans le monde des origines à nos jours: Actes du Deuxième Colloque international du C.E.R.C.O.R., Poitiers, 29 septembre–2 octobre 1988* (Saint-Etienne: Publications de l'Université de Saint-Etienne, 1994), p. 50. For an English translation see "The Rule of Donatus of Besançon," trans. Jo Ann McNamara and John Halborg, in Jo Ann McNamara, *The Ordeal of Community* (Toronto: Peregrina, 1985), pp. 35–77.

11. "Inter caeteras regulae observantias hoc magis super omnia tam juniores quam etiam seniores monemus sorores, ut assidue et indesinenti studio tam de cogitatu, quam etiam de verbo inutili, vel opere, seu aliqua commotione animi, confessio omnibus diebus, omnibus horis, omnibusque momentis semper donetur; et matri spirituali nihil occultetur (. . .). Ergo nec ipsa parva a confessione sunt negligenda cogitata, quia scriptum est: Qui parva negligit, paulatim defluit (Eccl., xix)," quoted in "Sancti Donati Vesontionensis Episcopi Regula Ad Virgines," caput XXIII ("Qualiter ad confessionem omnibus diebus veniant"), *Scriptorum ecclesiasticorum qui in VII sœculi secunda parte floruerunt opera omnia, ordine chronologico digesta, juxta memoratissimas editiones*, tomus unicus, accurante Jacques-Paul Migne, Petit-Montrouge, Bibliothecæ Cleri Universe, sive Cursum Completorum in Singulos Scientiæ Ecclesiasticas Ramos, Editore, 1851, p. 282.

12. Gregory of Nazianzus, *Oratio*, 2, 16. See *Nicene and Post-Nicene Fathers*, second series, vol. 7, trans. Charles G. Browne and James E. Swallow, ed. Philip Schaff and Henry Wace (Buffalo, NY: Christian Literature Publishing, 1894), available online at www.newadvent.org/fathers/310202.htm (accessed June 20, 2012). The quoted excerpt is commented on by Brian E. Daley, S. J., *Gregory of Nazianzus* (New York: Routledge, 2006), pp. 54 and 207 n. 234. On the behavior of souls as the art of arts and the science of sciences in Gregory of Nazianzus, see Christopher A. Beeley, *Gregory of Nazianzus on the Trinity and the Knowledge of God: In Your Light We Shall See Light* (Oxford: Oxford University Press, 2008), pp. 241–47. According to Beeley, Gregory of Nazianzus called *tekhnē* "a distinctive art or craft with its own method and sense of expertise, a science or profession based on a discreet body of knowledge (*episteme*)" (ibid., p. 242). He explains in the note that in ancient Greek, *episteme* usually refers to a practical or professional ability and the understanding that goes with it, rather than to knowledge in general. The latter meaning was developed by Plato and Aristotle, referring to scientific knowledge as opposed to doxa that designates an opinion (ibid., p. 242).

13. Gregory of Nazianzus, *Oratio*, 2, 28–30. See *Nicene and Post-Nicene Fathers*, available online at www.newadvent.org/fathers/310202.htm (accessed June 20, 2012).

14. The works of Saint Colombanus (ca. 600) were assembled in 1626 by Patricius Fleming and published by Jacques-Paul Migne (*Patrologia Latina*, 80, 209); the *Pénitentiel* was published for the first time in 1667, and for a second time in the *Patrologia Latina* (80, 223). English edition, John T. McNeill and Helena M. Gamer, *Medieval Handbooks of Penance: A Translation of the Principal* Libri poenitentiales *and Selections from Related Documents* (New York: Columbia University Press, 1938), pp. 250–65. The text is divided into two parts: the first relates to the sins of monks, and the second discusses the sins of clerics and laymen.

15. McNeill and Gamer, *Medieval Handbooks of Penance*, p. 252:

1. If a cleric commits homicide and slays his neighbor, he shall do penance for ten years in exile. Thereafter he shall be admitted to his own country if he has well performed his penance on bread and water and is approved by the testimony of the bishop or priest with whom he has done his penance and to whom he was committed, that he may make satisfaction to the parents of whom he slew, offering himself in place of their son and saying, "Whatever you wish I will do unto you." But if he does not make satisfaction to the man's parents he shall never be admitted into his own country, but shall be like Cain a vagabond and a fugitive upon the earth.

16. Ibid., p. 255:

21. If one of the laymen sheds blood in a quarrel or wounds or incapacitates his neighbor, he shall be compelled to make restitution to the extent of the injury. But if he has not the wherewithal to make a settlement, he shall do his neighbor's work as long as the latter is sick, and he shall provide a physician, and after the injured man is well he shall do penance for forty days on bread and water.

17. We are unable to locate this reference.

18. Canon XXI explains that once the faithful of either sex has attained the "age of discretion," he or she must confess their sins at least once a year to his or her own priest and complete the assigned penance to the best of his or her ability, receiving respectfully the sacrament of the Eucharist at least at Easter, unless there is a good reason, according to the priest, to abstain from receiving it for a period of time. The penalty for not doing so over the course of one's life is that of being excluded from the Church (excommunicated) and, at death, deprived of a Christian burial. Whoever wishes to confess his sins to another priest must first be authorized by his own priest; without this authorization, the other priest cannot grant absolution. The same canon recommends that the priest act as if he were a clever doctor, carefully investigating the circumstances of the sin in order to understand the nature of the opinion he must give and the appropriate remedy to heal the sick. It insists on the secrecy of the confession: the priest must keep it without betraying the sinner or revealing the sinner's identity in any way whatsoever. Any priest who would dare reveal a sin confessed to him in the confessional must be deposed and sent to a monastery until the end of his days. See *Disciplinary Decrees of the General Councils*, text, trans., and commentary by Rev. H. J. Schroeder (St. Louis and London: B. Herder, 1937), pp. 259–60.

19. Alexander of Hales was born in Hales in the Gloucestershire ca. 1185 and died in Paris in 1245. A philosopher and theologian, he was first one of the secular masters of the University of Paris. Roger Bacon explains that in 1210 he was *Magister regens* at the Faculty of Arts before entering the Faculty of Theology in 1220. In 1231 he entered the Franciscan order, but continued his university teaching. His most important work is the *Summa universæ theologiae*,

which he began ca. 1231 and left incomplete. It is the first *summa* in which Aristotle's treatises of physics, metaphysics, ethics, and logic are used systematically, as well as those of some of Aristotle's Arab commentators such as Avicenna. In this sense, Alexander of Hales opened the way for Thomas Aquinas. See William Turner, "Alexander of Hales," *The Catholic Encyclopedia*, vol. 1 (New York: Appleton, 1907), available online at www.newadvent.org/cathen/01298a .htm (accessed June 20, 2012).

20. The Council of Trent began in 1545 and included twenty-five sessions over eighteen years. During the fourteenth session it established that venial sins could be omitted without fault during confession and could be expiated by other means. On this point see *Disciplinary Decrees of the General Councils*, text, trans., and commentary by Rev. H. J. Schroeder, pp. 260–61 and n. 23 ("This evidently means all mortal sins, otherwise the declaration of the Council of Trent that venial sins may be omitted in confession without guilt and be expiated by many other remedies, would be unintelligible").

21. On Lanfranc, see Antoine Charma, *Lanfranc: Notice biographique, littéraire et philoso-phique* (Paris: Hachette, 1840); Margaret Gibson, *Lanfranc of Bec* (Oxford: Oxford University Press, 1978); Herbert J. Cowdrey, *Lanfranc: Scholar, Monk, and Archbishop* (Oxford: Oxford University Press, 2003). Theologian born ca. 1010 in the region of Pavia, Lanfranc died in 1089 in Canterbury. He was a monk and prior first at the Abbey of Bec and then at the Abbey of Caen. After 1066, William the Great (the Conqueror) brought him to reform the English church. In 1071 Lanfranc became archbishop of Canterbury after William deposed his predecessor on the pretext of simony. In 1075 he betrayed the secret of the confession by warning William of a plot against him by the Count of Norfolk, Ralph Guader, and the Count of Hereford, Roger de Breteuil. Waltheof, Count of Huntingdon, Norhampton, and Norhumbrie, who had confessed to him, was executed.

22. Lanfranc, "De celanda confessione libellus," in Lanfranc, *Œuvres*, ed. Dom L. d'Achéry (Paris: 1648), pp. 379–82, cited in M. A. Charma, *Lanfranc: Notice biographique, littéraire et phi-losophique*, p. 62.

23. Peter Lombard (Petrus Lombardus, also refered to as *Magister Sententiarum*) was born ca. 1100 and died in 1160. He was a scholastic theologian who knew Peter Abelard and studied and taught in Paris. He was the author of *Libri quatuor sententiarum*. See Marcia Colish, *Peter Lombard* (New York: E. J. Brill, 1994); see also PhilippW. Rosemann, *Peter Lombard* (New York: Oxford University Press, 2004); and Philipp W. Rosemann, *The Story of a Great Medieval Book: Peter Lombard's "Sentences"* (Peterborough, ON: Broadview Press, 2007).

24. Matthew 6:14–15 (King James version).

25. According to John Bossy, writing in "The Social History of Confession in the Age of the Reformation," *Transactions of the Royal Historical Society*, Fifth Series, vol. 25 (1975), p. 26, Luther made a clear distinction "between sins which upset the community—'adultery, murder, fornication, theft, robbery, usury, slander, etc.'—and 'the secret sins of the heart,' by which he seems chiefly to have meant interior sexual motions which had no overt consequences." Against the partisans of the psychologizing of sin and the sacrament of penance, he held that this was only an affair of the individual and God, and not a matter of confession. This doctrine, writes Bossy, "left intact the traditional annual and private confession to the priest, but confined it to offences of a community-disturbing character, principally considered as arising out of hatred." Ibid. at p. 27. According to Bossy, this makes Luther more traditional than revolutionary. Ibid., p. 26 ("Luther appears a radical or perhaps utopian traditionalist rather than a revolutionary").

26. On Raymond of Penyafort, who was born in Catalonia ca. 1175 and died in 1275, see Pierre Michaud-Quantin, *Sommes de casuistique et manuels de confession au Moyen-Âge (XII–XVI siècles), analecta mediævalia namurcensia* (Louvain: Nauwelaerts, 1962), pp. 34–43. Doctor in civil law and canon law at the University of Bologna, where he taught for three years,

he became a Dominican in 1222. During his novitiate he was charged with drafting a *summa* on the cases of penitence, the *Summa de casibus poenitentiæ* or *Summa de poenitentia*, the first compilation of this type. Gregory IX gave him the task of codifying canon law and preparing an official compendium of the *Décrétales*, a task that occupied him until 1234. After returning to Spain, he became superior general of the Dominican order in 1238, but resigned quickly to dedicate himself to the conversion of Jews and Muslims through debate and discussion; he recommended that clerics learn Hebrew and Arabic and base their argumentation on Talmudic and Koranic sources. He also invited Thomas Aquinas to write the *Summa contre Gentiles*.

According to Michaud-Quantin, the *Summa*, which contains three books in the first edition and four in the second, gathered "under one rubric, the last of book 3, which was extremely long"—70 paragraphs and 130 columns, or "a little more than one tenth of the total volume for the first three books"—the substance presented in the first manuals of confession. The doctrine and the practice taught under this rubric are very similar to those of Alain de Lille and the authors who followed him. The *Summa* examines the three constitutive elements of the sacramental form: contrition, confession, and satisfaction; it recommends a methodical examination of conscience "in the context offered by the seven capital sins"; and it calls for a proportional penance based on the gravity of each sin. Moreover, it challenges the perspective the authors of manuals of confession had adopted up to that point. On the one hand, "the old professor of Bologna intended to create an exposé of an essentially juridical character." Thus, of the twenty-four rubrics that make up the first two books, twenty-three carry the same title as the rubrics of the *Décrétales*; the *Summa* ignores the problem of internal faults such as envy, pride, and acedia, focusing instead on judicial duels, tournaments, and the use of ranged weapons (*Sommes de casuistique et manuels de confession au Moyen-Âge*, pp. 36–37). On the other hand, it "only judges the external act according to the motives, the intention, and the circumstances that surround it because the sentence pronounced is indeed a 'judgment of souls' that is located on the spiritual level. There is sin or there is not sin and the general formula that is used in the *Imputatur ei* shows that it is essentially a question of intimate and personal responsibility." Ibid., pp. 38–39. The method of "cases" or "cases of conscience" corresponds to this conception of the moral element of the fault.

27. On Andrés Dias de Escobar (also known as Andrés de Lisboa, Hispano, or Español), born in Lisbon in 1348 and deceased in 1450, see Michaud-Quantin, *Sommes de casuistique et manuels de confession au Moyen-Âge* (1962), pp. 71–72; Thomas N. Tentler, *Sin and Confession in the Eve of Reformation* (Princeton, NJ: Princeton University Press, 1977), pp. 38–40; see also the third chapter of Gustave A. Arroyo, *Les manuels de confession en castillan dans l'Espagne medieval* (Montréal: Université de Montréal, Faculté des arts et des sciences, Institut d'études médiévales, 1989), www.fordham.edu/halsall/projects/arroyo/man13.htm (accessed November 16, 2011). Benedictine, in 1408 named bishop of Ciudad Rodrigo, then Tabor, Ajaccio, and Megara, he participated in the Councils of Constance (1414–18), Basle (1431–37), and Ferrara-Florence (1437–39). He was the author of numerous works including two smaller complementary works: the *Lumen confessorum*, written for priests, and the *Modus confitendi*, sometimes called the *Confessio generalis*, written for the faithful. The first delineates penitential jurisdiction, recalls the sacramental doctrine, summarizes the indications given for the examination of conscience in the *Modus confitendi*, and gives directives for the satisfaction or rejection of absolution or the abstention from communion. The second offers the canvas for a detailed examination of one's conscience in a context limited by the commandments of God, the capital sins, and the faults committed through the five senses. See Michaud-Quantin, *Sommes de casuistique et manuels de confession au Moyen-Âge*, p. 71.

28. On the "invention" of the confessional that consecrates the psychological conception of sin and the confession, see Bossy, "The Social History of Confession in the Age of the Ref-

ormation," pp. 28–31. The norms for the construction of the confessionals were defined by
Charles Borromée, archbishop of Milan (1564–84).

29. On Alain de Lille, see Michaud-Quantin, *Sommes de casuistique et manuels de confession au Moyen-Âge*, pp. 14–19, as well as *Liber poenitentialis*, tome I: *Introduction doctrinale et
littéraire*, ed. Jean Longère, *Analecta mediævalia namurcensia* (Louvain-Lille: Éditions Nauwelaerts et Giard, 1965). According to Longère, Alain de Lille was born between 1117 and 1130
and died in 1203; he taught in Paris and Montpellier, where he was involved in the doctrinal
disputes against Catharism before entering the Cistercian order. Various indicators suggest
that the *Liber poenitentialis* was written after 1191. Longère emphasizes the mixed nature (at
once medical and juridical) of the relationship established in penance:

> The priest must act in *fidelis medicus* focusing on making a good diagnosis, distinguishing
> with precision between different sins and "their circumstances," all without appearing to
> be indiscrete (*indiscretus*). The priest must choose the best solutions among those offered
> by the penitentials and know "that everyone cannot be weighed in the same balance
> even if everyone is tied down by the same vices." That he forget not to be misericordious
> (*miséricordieux*) as it is written by the Word, but that he be severe (*districtum judicium
> debet judicare*) for those who continued in their wrongdoing.

And Longère continues:

> Of course, there is nothing very original in these words. One can see, however, and that
> is what is of particular interest in these preliminary developments, that they insist on
> the role of the priest and the importance that he has not only as a minister of the sacra-
> ments, but as a doctor (*fidelis, sapiens medicus*) who must, in order to heal his patient,
> know him and his illness and remain master enough of the remedy he must administer.
> This is already a question of situating what will be given to the penitents and 'relativizing'
> their tariffs.

Liber poenitentialis, p. 161. Michaud-Quantin locates the *Liber poenitentialis* in relation to
the "*pénitentiels*" of the earlier period, and the resurgence of the medical model next to fixed
penance:

> From the end of the patristic period in the twelfth century, a penance was a tariff, a
> barometer, that gave a list of the possible sins . . . indicating the importance, nature, and
> duration of the public penance that was to be imposed on the guilty. It was characterized
> by a great disorder in the presentation and at root by a notable severity—in principle, all
> mortal sins required seven years of penance. Above all, they are striking for their auto-
> matic nature; the priest who uses them does not play any personal role in their appli-
> cation or their prescription. He doesn't even have the latitude of appreciation that the
> modern codes leave to the judges in the establishment of punishment. Already, at the be-
> ginning of the eleventh century, Burchard of Worms in his canonical collection . . . called
> for the personal initiative and judgment of the priest. The *Decretum Gratiani* put into bold
> relief in the first half of the twelfth century the principle of *poenitentiæ sunt arbitrariæ*;
> the imposed penance was to be determined in each case by the confessor *ad arbitrium*,
> according to his appreciations, which demanded by consequence that he be informed of
> the objective and subjective circumstances that surrounded the avowed fault . . . The first
> preoccupation, which was certainly not foreign to Alain de Lille, was the anti-sacramental
> and anti-clerical debate of the Cathars which was expressed in a long initial prayer-

exhortation and an equally developed conclusion containing precepts and remedies under the heading of "Remedies appropriate for medicine of the soul" ("Quels sont les remèdes qui conviennent au médecin des âmes"). Indeed, the author essentially considered the confessor to be a doctor of spiritual life, and this comparison dominated the directives that governed his attitude and actions.

Sommes de casuistique et manuels de confession au Moyen-Âge, pp. 15–17.

30. See Alain de Lille, *Liber poenitentialis*, cap. XX, tome II: *La tradition longue*, ed. J. Longère, *Analecta mediævalia namurcensia* (Louvain-Lille: Éditions Nauwelaerts et Giard, 1966), p. 32: "Considerandus est etiam corporis gestus, vel faciei habitus, ut per exteriora comprehendantur interiora, quia cum vultus sit quasi animi signaculum, et figura, per vultum potest perpendi quae sit voluntas interna; quia si vultus est in terra demissus, fletibus irriguus, internos significat cruciatus; si vero facies fuerit erecta, nulla tristitiae gerens vestigia, minor videtur esse poenitentia."

SIXTH LECTURE

May 20, 1981

Juridification in ecclesiastical and political institutions. • From God as judge to a state of justice: sovereignty and truth. • Avowal, torture, and inquisitorial tests of truth. • Avowal, torture, and legal proofs. • Avowal, sovereign law, sovereign conscience, and punitive engagement. • Auto-veridiction, evidence, and penal dramaturgy. • Hetero-veridiction, examination, and legal psychiatry. • Relating the act to its author: the question of criminal subjectivity in the nineteenth century. • Monomania and the constitution of crime as psychiatric object. • Degeneration and the creation of the criminal as object for social defense. • From responsibility to dangerousness, from the rights-bearing subject to the criminal individual. • The question of criminal subjectivity in the twentieth century. • Hermeneutics of the subject and the meaning of crime for the criminal. • Accident, probability, and indices of criminal risk. • Veridiction of the subject and the breach in the contemporary penal system.

What I would have liked to have done, since I had tried to show you how the practice of avowal had formed within Christian institutions, is to continue by showing you how the recourse to avowal took on an increasingly important role in medieval judicial practice. This important role—of greater and greater importance—of avowal in the judicial institutions of the Middle Ages, of course, was the result of the contamination by the penitential practice, whose importance I tried to emphasize last time and which had itself become juridified. But I also

199

think that the increasing importance of avowal in the judicial practice of the Middle Ages resulted from modifications within the institutions of justice themselves. And it is this integration, this development, this solidification of the practice of avowal in judicial institutions of the Middle Ages that I would have liked to present to you. I then would have liked to explore the paradoxical effects of the introduction and development of this practice of avowal on modern and contemporary [. . .] penal theory and practice, and the introduction of what one might call the avowing subject through the development of this practice of avowal. I believe that these effects were so paradoxical that they have unsettled in part the penal machine that we now know, or at least introduced a series of impasses that, I believe, we are far from overcoming.

Indeed, it seems to me — and this is the point that I would like to come to — that by introducing the avowing subject, it was no doubt believed that it could bring about the fortunate coincidence between the author of the crime and the subject who had to account for it. And, in fact, I believe that a third party was introduced — or let's just say that a new order of reality was introduced that could not be assimilated into penal practice or even the theory behind it. This new object, the avowing subject, showed itself to be a cumbersome figure in that it was both indispensable to the functioning of the penal machine and at the same time somehow in excess — a third party constantly solicited to say what was asked of him, yet always saying less than what was expected, always saying something other than what would allow the machine to function properly; such that this character of the one who tells the truth, who tells the truth of his crime, far from being the keystone of the penal system — as had no doubt long been hoped for — instead, I believe, opened an irreparable breach in the penal system.

But in saying this, I do not want to give you the impression that in my view the penal institution somehow carelessly introduced a little foreign element into its own mechanism, which then ultimately caused it problems. Avowal was not the black sheep in the sheepfold of penality: avowal had been a cultural form; it had been and remains a social practice outside of the judicial institution. This cultural form, this social practice did not remain stable across the centuries. And it is no doubt the transformation, the evolution of the very practice of avowal, the very practice of the avowing subject, that no doubt produced a certain number of countereffects on penal practices within which the penal machinery itself got caught and became obstructed. If avowal, or rather what is said in and through avowal, has caused such problems for penal justice, it is not because avowal is in itself a nasty and perverse little machinery: it is because the status and the forms of veridiction of oneself have been profoundly modified in our societies. And if the avowal—let's say the one that was introduced in the Middle Ages, or in any case institutionalized in the Middle Ages in penal practice—if that avowal no longer functions today, it is no doubt because it is an entirely different avowal, within an entirely different penal machine.

Such is the broad arc of what I had hoped to present: on the one hand, the institutionalization of avowal in judicial practice, and on the other, the disordering of the penal machine through the impact of the practice of avowal—let's say there is an upward and a downward arc. But my rather clumsy organization of the lectures up to this point, and the fact that I have dragged my feet recounting stories about the young monks of early Christianity and a whole set of histories that enchanted me and perhaps bored you, but in any case have slowed us all down—all of that means that now I must choose between a discussion of the upward or downward arc: I must either show how the practice of avowal was inscribed and solidified in penal law from the Middle Ages on, or show how the veridiction of the subject has introduced a crisis into penal law since the nineteenth century from which, it seems, we have yet to escape. And since I was invited here by the institute of criminology (and I thank them for this invitation), it seemed to me that it would be perhaps more appropriate, given what may be expected of me, to insist on the second aspect, that is to say, to study more closely the appearance of the criminal—of the avowing criminal— as a destabilizing factor in punitive institutions: to study, if you will, the crisis of the regime common to the punishment of crime and the manifestation of the criminal. This, then, will be the focus of tonight's lecture.

However, before moving on to this, I would nonetheless like to take a few moments to offer a rather schematic outline of what should have been another lecture on the institutionalization of avowal in medieval criminal justice. I would have liked to show you, in effect, that the privileging of avowal in penal practices was inscribed, in a general manner, in a sort of broad juridification of Western society and culture in the Middle Ages, a juridification that could be perceived—as I tried to show you last time—in the institutions, the practices, the representations that were part of Christianity. We saw it precisely with regard to penance: how penance became at once a sacrament, and received the value and the meaning of a sacra-

ment by taking on a more juridified form. I evoked this process as well
with regard to the new dividing lines that were so carefully and laboriously
drawn between penitential jurisdictions and disciplinary jurisdictions in
the Church. It could also be seen, of course, with regard to the infinite
debates between ecclesiastical and civil jurisdictions. It could be seen as
well with regard to the Inquisition, which represented a considerable advance in this juridification of ecclesiastical practices. It could also be seen
with regard to the set of representations through which one tried to define
and manifest the relationships between God and men: God as judge, God
sitting on his throne at the head of his tribunal, the last judgment. Of
course, these were all very old themes that did not stem from Christianity
itself, but were inherited from Judaism; however, they are themes that re-
emerged with renewed intensity as of the twelfth century, and then were
accompanied by the appearance of other themes that were entirely new—
such as, for example, the theme of purgatory or the system of indulgences.

All of this juridified, if you will, the whole set of relationships between
man and God. This juridification, which can be felt so acutely in the ecclesiastical institutions and religious representations, can equally be felt
throughout the Middle Ages, especially as of the twelfth century, in political institutions. Without going into detail, let's just briefly say that the affirmation and growth of monarchical power in the context of feudal institutions, this affirmation and this growth were built on the exercise and
development of judicial power. It was in his capacity as judge, as arbiter,
as the one called upon to settle legal disputes, or as the one who himself
chooses cases to judge, that the king established his power on top of feudal power or within the interstices of feudal power. It was through a jurisdictional form that the king made and enforced his decisions. In short,
according to a well-known formula, the first form of the modern state was
a state of justice.

And yet, as political and jurisdictional power thus interpenetrated,
the forms of juridical procedures, of course, were undergoing change. In
particular, the accusatory procedure through which someone—whether
it was the victim or someone representing the victim—[. . .] accused another of having wronged him, this procedure, as you know well, centered
the entire penal mechanism on the confrontation between two adversaries or two partners. And these two, the accuser and the accused, then
had to settle their litigation according to rules and sometimes through
arbitration, or eventually they had to pursue their vengeance in a private

war. And as you well understand, this particular way of resolving a dispute raises issues that could no longer be posed in the same terms once it was the sovereign who intervened, either at the behest of a complainant or by intermediary of one of his prosecutors. The problem was no longer simply one of allowing the two adversaries who confronted one another to settle or end their conflict according to a given number of rules that needed to be respected. Once it was up to the sovereign to settle the dispute, the problem was one of establishing the truth and of determining a sanction based on the established facts. The necessity of a veridiction was inscribed in the displacement that had the effect that penal justice would rise, if you will, from a resolution of a conflict in the form of a struggle between two individuals to a resolution of a conflict in the form of a decision by a sovereign court or by a decision of the sovereign himself. Recourse was thus made, for the establishment of this truth, to means of inquiry more or less akin to those that were used at that time—and that had been for some time, for that matter—in administrative and fiscal inquiries. And as soon as the establishment of truth became an essential element of the procedure, the affirmation of the truth by the accused himself would become an important element. Avowal became—or rather, became again, because in fact, throughout Roman law, proof by avowal was recognized and admitted, but this type of procedure had almost disappeared, or in any case had declined in a massive way from the seventh or eighth centuries on—the establishment of the truth through the avowal of the culprit became once again an important piece of the procedure.

Yet it is interesting and, I think, noteworthy in this history that avowal was not simply called upon as a privileged form of testimony in the process of inquiry during this period. Avowal was not simply an element of proof that would be all the stronger because it was provided by the very one who committed the crime. The importance of the role of avowal came from the fact that it was located on the boundary between traditional accusatory procedures and the new procedures of inquisition. You will remember that one of the means used in accusatorial procedure was precisely the test [*épreuve*], the test that was proposed either by the accuser to the one he accused or by the judge. It was the ordeal of water, of fire, the judicial duel, that allowed one to determine, not exactly what was the truth, but rather who should be considered the victor in this confrontation, in this struggle, in this joust, between the two partners.

And yet the extortion of an avowal came to constitute in the inquisitorial procedure—and [. . .] in that particular form of inquisitorial procedure that can be found precisely in the Inquisition itself—[. . .] a sort of strange mix between the establishment of an element of proof [and] the establishment of a truth by means of a system of demonstration: as it happens, the testimony of the subject about himself was both the establishment of a truth and at the same time a test. The torture that allowed the truth to be extracted should be envisaged not at all as the most rapid means to arrive at the truth. It should be understood, in reality, as a test: "If I subject you to the test of torture, if I subject you to such and such suffering, will you win or lose, will you give in or, to the contrary, will you be able to resist by saying nothing, like the one who is not burned in the ordeal of the red-hot iron, like the one who does not drown in the ordeal of water, like the one who wins the judicial duel?" We see clearly why avowal became intimately tied to torture, or to the threat of torture, and remained so for such a long time in inquisitorial procedure: it was one of the remnants of the accusatory procedure that was transferred into the inquisitorial procedure—obtaining the truth by a test of avowal that was obtained by torture, this torture to which one could resist, to which on the contrary one could cede. Avowal under torture could produce the element of truth that was necessary for the new inquisitorial procedure; and it allowed it to be produced as a sort or at the end of a sort of judicial test, almost of a duel, though admittedly one with an obvious inequality between the accused and one who tortured him, that is to say the one who represented the power that pursued him. The extortion of the avowal was, at bottom, what could be called the inquisitorial test of truth. And I think that [if we understand correctly] this particular role that the avowal played at that precise moment, when it reintroduced itself within criminal procedure, I believe that we can, at that precise moment, understand well the broad traits of this practice.

On the one hand, of course, the importance it had in the Inquisition. The fact as well—and this must be remembered—that it was not at all an untamed practice, but rather a well-regulated one: as opposed to the torture as it may be practiced by our police today, torture in the Inquisition, torture in that type of procedure did not employ any and all means possible to extract from an individual the truth that he might know. It was in reality a well-defined exercise, in which the judge had the right to employ such and such torture with such and such an instrument during a certain period of time; beyond that, he could do no more, and he needed to stay strictly within the given framework, to stay within the prescribed tests. This explains the fact that the accused himself could in some sense win if he resisted the test. And if he resisted the test—so, according to the types of procedures, it varied; I will pass over the details, but roughly speaking, if he resisted the test—he was cleared and the prosecutor was forced to abandon his pursuit. I say this once again, keeping in mind that there was a whole series of other modifications; but in general, when one resisted torture, it was the prosecutor who lost, which clearly shows the test-like structure of this avowal.

This also explains, I think, the difficulty of situating exactly such a test within the inquisitorial procedure. What exactly was the status of the truth of an avowal obtained in this way? What value as proof could be given to this declaration that had been extracted through avowal? There was here a whole series of difficulties that jurists discussed often and at great length. So it was considered that an avowal obtained through torture had no legal value and could not have any effect unless it was repeated without torture, as if it were testimony that had been given by the individual about himself. Of course, when the individual denied an avowal obtained through torture and his new testimony did not correspond to what he had said under torture, then he was tortured again, so that the threat of torture might. . . . In the end, things were complicated, but I think it is interesting to note [. . .] the significance of torture in this procedure of avowal, its place within the confines and at the interface [. . .] of accusatory procedures (with the practice of the test) and of the inquisitorial procedure (with the inquiry and the search to establish the truth).

I will say nothing of the evolution, displacements, and decline of this practice of extracting an avowal in criminal justice in the period leading up to the eighteenth century, because I must move on. I will only mention, first, the fact that this procedure went through a period of decline and then it reappeared. In particular, the practice of extracting an avowal through torture reappeared in the sixteenth and seventeenth centuries with the development of the great state structures. As examples, I would point to the *Constitutio criminalis carolina* of Charles V at the end of the first third of the sixteenth century, and various criminal ordinances in France—that of Francis I, as well as that of 1670.[1]

I would also like to mention that the system of avowal was tied to a curious system referred to as legal proofs—it was within the system of legal proofs that the avowal needed to take place. This system of legal proofs defined exactly the relative weight of each element of proof within the total quantity of proof considered necessary for establishing perfect certainty. This is what was called a complete proof. So you had—until the middle of the eighteenth century and even at the end of the eighteenth century—an entire table on how one could establish the truth of an infraction, with a certain number of principles, some of them well known, but whose consequences were rather curious and oftentimes paradoxical. For example, there was the principle that two eyewitnesses of a fact constituted a complete proof, but that one eyewitness, contrary to the principle of Roman law, constituted not an absence of proof but a half-proof, and a half-proof corresponded to being half guilty, such that a fact established by half of a proof would entail half the punishment. This was a very complicated system in which there were what were called complete proofs, what were called semi-proofs, there were indices, there was a whole series of graduated elements of proof, signs of the capacity to produce a proof that were different from each other and that one had to add together to arrive at a complete proof. Once again, if the sum did not amount to a complete proof, this did not mean that the proof had not been established and therefore one could not condemn: rather, it authorized the judge to impose a condemnation that was proportional in its gravity to the quantity of proof that had been produced. And avowal played an essential role in this, evidently; it had a privileged position insofar as avowal was obviously a proof of great value. But it is noteworthy that this avowal could never be entirely sufficient in itself, and that there needed to be at least one supplementary sign that confirmed the avowal. In short, there was a whole calculus that bound the judge, in a way, and that allowed him to compute the judicial value, the judicial truth that he needed.

If I have emphasized these two aspects that characterize, I believe, the practice of avowal in judicial institutions from the Middle Ages to the eighteenth century—these two aspects, namely its connection with torture and its privileged place in the bizarre system of legal proofs—if I emphasized these two aspects, it is because these two elements would disappear from the juridical system, legal codes, and penal practice in the second half of the eighteenth century, in general, or in some cases at the beginning of the nineteenth century. And yet, [in spite of the disappearance of] these two elements which sort of accompanied and served as the context to the practice of avowal—torture and the system of legal proofs—in spite of this disappearance, the importance of avowal was not undermined. To

the contrary, avowal would acquire an importance, and a decisive importance, in an unprecedented way, in these new legal codes that are the modern codes and whose structure, frame, and general architecture remain in
place today. And this, for several reasons.

The first, which is the most implicit, is also without doubt the most important. It has to do with the general meaning of the penal system, the
very foundations of the right to punish exercised through this penal system. For in modern and contemporary legal codes, as you know, the foundation of the law is or is supposed to be the will of all, which is supposed
to express itself in this law, decided and validated by an act of the legisla-
tive body in its capacity as a sovereign body. So what serves as the foundation of the law is the will of all. And, as a consequence, one of the most
frequent and most essential themes in the penal theory of the eighteenth
century, but also in contemporary penal theory, is the principle that when
someone has committed a crime, he himself punishes himself—through
the law to which he is supposed to have consented or that he is supposed
to support of his own free will—and punishes himself through the institution of the tribunal that delivers the sentence in conformity with the law
that he supposedly has willed. In the modern penal system, the one who
commits a crime is, in a certain way, the one who punishes himself. This
fiction that you must recognize yourself in the law that punishes you—
which is equally, for that matter, a necessity—this fiction explains both
the symbolic and the central role of avowal. Why, at bottom, is the avowal
there? Not only so that the individual might say, "Well yes, I committed
such and such a crime," but so that in saying this, he manifests in a way
the very principle of the penal law; he takes on the role of the guilty party
and recognizes through his avowal the sovereignty both of the law and of
the tribunal that will punish him and in which he recognizes himself. In
the modern system, avowal consists not simply of recognizing one's crime,
[but] at the same time recognizing, through the recognition of one's crime,
the validity of the punishment that one will suffer. In this sense, avowal is
a rite of sovereignty by means of which the guilty party provides a foundation for his judges to condemn him and recognizes his own will in the decision of the judges. Avowal is in this sense the reminder of the social contract, it is its restoration—such that through these words of avowal, the
guilty party can at the same time (and in the strict terms of the law, not
by any means in psychological terms) seal the punishment that separates
him from the social body or deprives him of his rights; and at the same

time, the avowal marks the first step of his reintegration (since through avowal, one recognizes that one has broken the fundamental pact, but in recognizing this, one takes the first step, one makes the first move, in the direction of this reintegration). Avowal, from this perspective, is an act that draws its meaning from the very root of the punitive system. It is a theoretical and functional act. It is an act that must manifest in truth the exercise of the right to punish. This is the first reason why avowal is so important in the modern and contemporary penal systems.

The other reason why avowal is important is the regime of truth to which both the inquiry and the sentence must be subjected. The system of legal proofs had more or less disappeared by the second half of the eighteenth century. [. . .] This meant that since then, it has been up to the judge to look deep within himself in order to determine what is probative and what is not probative among the elements of proof that are submitted to him, whether by the prosecutor, the accused, or those who defend him. The probative value is not determined by a prior code; it is simply the conscience of the judge or the juror that—by itself, of its own authority, in its own sovereignty, whether Cartesian or empirical, as you wish—has to decide that in effect, this constitutes proof, that this establishes a truth that is absolutely irrefutable and evident. It is no longer a question of that calculus that adds up the elements of proof that had been previously measured; it is accepted—and it has been accepted, for that matter, for political reasons, for philosophical reasons also, and equally because of institutional motivations—that truth can no longer be weighed according to units of measurement that had been defined in advance, that we are dealing with (and must deal with) a sort of indivisible truth in penal practice that cannot be calculated according to criteria proper to juridical practice, that the truth operative in penal practice is a matter that is common to everyone. Every citizen, as long as he is of course an adult, that he is reasonable—and, depending on the period and its codes, as long of course as he is a man—every citizen must be able to recognize what is true or false in his soul and conscience: it is a question of the sovereignty of any conscience in relation to sovereignty. From this emerges, as you can well understand, the importance of avowal as irrefutable proof that serves as an equivalent of evidence in penal matters. As soon as it is no longer a question of adding calculable fragments of truth, but of producing a truth that can be perceived by all—and in particular, by the judges and the jurors—avowal becomes the most sought-after form of proof.

Finally, the third reason why avowal became so important is that punishment took on the dual function in these new codes of punishing, of course, but also of making amends and correcting. That is to say, it is a question of ensuring, by means of the punishment, that the subject be transformed in relation to the offense committed and thanks to the punishment to which he is subjected. The subject is to be transformed with regard to the offense committed; transformed as well in relation to the possible offenses he might commit. The punishment thus needs to be corrective—and avowal, as a means of recognizing oneself to be guilty, constitutes the first element or, let us say, if you will, the first pledge of the punitive pact: "By avowing, I receive the punishment as something that is just and I agree to participate in the corrective process that the judges expect of my punishment."

In sum, and to synthesize all this, you see that avowal first recalls and restores the implicit pact upon which is founded the sovereignty of the institution that judges. Second, avowal constitutes a sort of contract of truth that allows the one who judges to know with indubitable knowledge. Third and finally, avowal constitutes a punitive engagement that gives meaning to the imposed sanction.

We can easily surmise, on this basis, the extent to which the modern legal codes and the penal institutions, throughout the nineteenth and twentieth centuries, were in need of and still today need avowal. Avowal by the guilty party has become—besides, of course, all the ease and conveniences it provides the inquiry, which naturally should not be neglected—avowal by the guilty party has become a fundamental need of the system. And when I say "fundamental," it is not for mere rhetorical emphasis; rather, it is because the very foundations of the system were put on the table in the case of avowal, and they called for avowal. The Romans used an expression to celebrate a case that was as simple as one in which the accused avowed: "*habemus reum confitentem*."[2] For us, we need an accused who confesses. We need an avowal for the system to function to its fullest. It is true that avowal can resolve some uncertainties and complement missing knowledge; avowal thus plays a very important role in the procedure of inquiry. But it serves as well—and, I believe, above all—to fulfill the punitive system in general, the penal system in general. It plays an important role in ensuring that jurisdiction—the fact of pronouncing the sentence—is carried out to its fullest.

I am familiar, of course, with the resonance of the word "symbolic." And perhaps one might be tempted to say that avowal plays a symbolic role with regard to the penal system. But it seems to me that in fact something slightly different is taking place, because avowal does not refer to anything else than what effectively takes place in that judicial scene. It exerts its effect on, within, through, and in that judicial scene—and to that extent, I do not think it is a symbolic element. Should one then say that it is a performative element—that is to say, a verbal act constitutive of a modification defined in reality? I don't think this is exactly right either. There is indeed a performative element in the penal procedure, but it is, for example, when the court declares that the accused is guilty and constitutes him, from the point of view of the law and the institutions, as effectively guilty. There is performativity when the court declares that someone is condemned, because indeed, after that moment, he is condemned. To the contrary, when the accused declares his guilt, it is more than symbolic, if you will, and it is not performative: the accused who declares his guilt does not thereby transform himself into the guilty party. And yet avowal is, I think, essential in this whole system. Neither performative nor symbolic, I would suggest instead, in changing the usual meaning slightly, that avowal is of the order of drama or dramaturgy. If one understands the "dramatic" not as a mere ornamental addition, but as every element in a scene that brings forth the foundation of legitimacy and the meaning of what is taking place, then I would say that avowal is part of the judicial and penal drama. It is an essential element of its dramaturgy, in the full sense of the term. And if we accept that there cannot be degrees of the symbolic or the performative, while dramaturgy—the dramatic—is, on the other hand, susceptible to various intensities, we could say that avowal is one of the most intense elements of the judicial drama and one of the most necessary. The appetite for avowal—the appetite for veridiction of the crime by its perpetrator—is central to our criminal jurisdiction. And you remember, perhaps, the anecdote with which I began, or that I evoked in any event, in the very first lecture that I presented to you: that story of a magistrate who, interrogating the culprit, asked him, "Well, in the end, who are you?" And since the accused did not respond, the tribunal, the presiding judge asked him: "But how do you expect us to judge you if you will not tell us who you are?" The need for avowal, I believe, is absolutely fundamental to the penal system: one cannot judge—that is to say, the judicial dramaturgy cannot be fully realized—if the accused does not avow in some way.

In fact, the moment the need for avowal was renewed—created, to some extent, or in any case renewed—by the modern systems, those of the eighteenth century and the early nineteenth centuries, [. . .] the renewal and the permanence of this need for avowal made the entire penal system deviate toward something completely different from what it aimed for when it established itself or tried to refound itself on rational and universal foundations in the eighteenth century—and for which, for that matter, it had recourse to avowal. It was as if there were a trap of avowal within the modern and contemporary system.

To show some of the effects of this need for avowal in modern criminal jurisdiction, I would like to take as my guiding theme, somewhat paradoxically, what takes place, or what we see happen, or better, what impasses and derailments are produced when this need for avowal is not satisfied and when something escapes within this very procedure—when, to the question we pose to the one who has committed his crime, he cannot respond or gives a different response than the one we expect.

We might say, as a general matter, that this need for avowal was experienced early on and soon recognized, in fact, to be so essential and so fundamental that, in a certain number of cases to which I will now return, where avowal was impossible or could not fill the required function which it was asked to fulfill, [. . .] it was necessary to substitute or to double the deficient or insufficient avowal with something else. And this other thing that was substituted for the auto-veridiction of the subject—this sort of hetero-veridiction, if you will—was the examination: the psychiatric examination, the psychological examination of the criminal, which was substituted for the avowal, filled its lacunae, filled the white or black spaces left by the avowal, and tried to bring forward the truth of the criminal that the criminal himself was not capable of formulating. And it seems to me that through the process by which the psychiatric and psychological examination of the criminal developed in the nineteenth century, we can see, as if we were looking through a magnifying glass, what was present but half-hidden in the need for avowal that had been inscribed in the legal codes put in place in late eighteenth and early nineteenth centuries. It seems to me that we see emerge here [. . .] the point of diffraction that would derail the entire system: in asking the subject to avow, in fact, we were not simply trying to make appear the legal subject who was asked to account for the infraction committed, but we were also trying to have emerge a subjectivity that maintained a significant relationship to his crime. It is from this moment, I think, that the question of the knowledge of the subject as a criminal subject begins; and this is what derails avowal and blocks the contemporary penal system.

How was the question of criminal subjectivity posed? It was posed at the beginning of the nineteenth century in connection with a series of cases that all had about the same form and that took place between 1800 and 1835. The first case, which took place in Germany and for which I have few details, for that matter, really constitutes the *princeps* case and was briefly reported by Hoffbauer.[3] It is the story of a servant who took a little girl to the market in her little cart and, during the course of her errands, killed the little girl. Metzger recounted another case.[4] It is the story of a retired officer who lived a solitary life in a lodging house and who became very attached to his landlady's child. And then, one day, to cite Metzger, "without motive, without any passion such as anger, pride or vengeance, he threw himself onto the child and stabbed, without killing, the child twice with a knife."[5] The third affair is that of Sélestat, which took place in 1817 in Alsace during a harsh winter that threatened famine. A peasant woman took advantage of her husband's absence, while he had left for work, to kill their little daughter, cut off her leg, put it in a kettle, and cook it with cabbage.[6] In Paris, in 1827, a servant named Henriette Cornier went to find the neighbor of the family with whom she was staying. She asked insistently that the neighbor leave her young daughter in her care so she could look after her.[7] The neighbor hesitated and finally consented because she had work to do and needed the help. When she returned a short while later to collect the child, Henriette Cornier had just killed the little girl, cut off her head, and thrown it out the window. In Vienna, not long after, a woman named Catherine Ziegler killed her illegitimate child, explaining that she was driven by an irresistible force.[8] She was acquitted on grounds of insanity and released from prison, but she declared that it would be better to keep her in prison because she would certainly do it again. And indeed, ten months later, she gave birth to a baby and killed it immediately, declaring at the trial that she had become pregnant for the sole purpose of killing her child. She was then sentenced to death and executed. In Scotland, a certain John [Howison] entered a home where he killed an old woman whom he did not know. He left without stealing anything and without even hiding, and when he was arrested he denied against all evidence. The defense argued that it was a case of insanity because it was a crime without motive.[9] [Howison] was executed, and it was considered in retrospect a sign of madness that he had said to a civil servant who was present that he wanted to kill him. I will end this enumeration of cases, each one of which had its own importance and repercussions during the period of [thirty]* years from 1805 to 1835, with a case from the United States. In New England a certain Abraham Prescott killed, in plain sight, his foster mother, with whom he had always maintained a good relationship.[10] He returned home, began to cry in front of his foster father, who then asked him why, at which point Prescott without hesitation avowed his crime. He explained afterwards that he was overcome by a sudden acute toothache and that he remembered nothing. Prescott was condemned to death, but the jury at the same time asked for his commutation. He was executed nonetheless.

These cases, a few others of the same type, but these cases as the *princeps* cases, became the themes of reference, the reference cases for psychiatrists and penal specialists of the period. Among the psychiatrists were Metzger, Hoffbauer, Esquirol, Georget, William Ellis, and Andrew Combe.[11]

The problem or first question: Why, among all the crimes committed, were these crimes understood to be of such importance? Why were these cases objects of endless discussion among doctors and jurists? Why were these the cases that forced the system of penal justice to call itself into question and dislodged it from the rational structure within which it had developed at the end of the eighteenth and beginning of the nineteenth centuries? First, I think it should be noted with regard to all these cases that they presented a very different picture from the one that had hitherto constituted the jurisprudence of criminal madness. Let's say that up to the end of the eighteenth century, the problem of madness had indeed been raised in penal law, but the question of madness was raised in precisely those cases, and almost solely in those cases, where civil or canon law raised [the question] as well—that is to say, in cases where madness took on the form either of dementia and of imbecility, or where it took on the form of rage; and in both cases, whether it was a question of a definitive state or of a momentary explosion, madness was only proven and was only admitted by the court when it was accompanied by a whole series of numerous signs that were easily recognizable and, in any case, external to the crime itself. Madness had to be proven outside the criminal act. And yet what is important in all of the cases I just discussed is that the subject

* Foucault said "twenty."

gave almost no sign of madness outside of the actual crime itself. So the problem could not simply be resolved by asking: "Had the subject in fact shown any earlier sign of madness that could lead one to suppose [. . .] that he was not responsible for his crime?" Now, we were presented with cases in which madness was suspected solely because, first, the crime was committed for no reason—there was no motive, calculation, or passion—and second, because the subject was incapable of telling anything whatsoever about his crime. The subject is, in a sense, mute in relationship to his crime.

So, first of all, these are crimes without reason. This is, I believe, why they were of interest and what they had in common. They are crimes without passion, without motive, without interest. They are not even driven by a delirious illusion. In all of the cases I mentioned, the psychiatrists and judges struggled with the fact that there was no relationship between the partners of the tragedy, between the one who killed and who was killed, or the one who killed and the parents of the child who was killed—because it is also interesting to note that in almost every case, or at least quite often, they were stories about murdering children. Between the partners of the tragedy, there was no relationship that would make it possible to render the crime intelligible. In the case of Henriette Cornier, for example, who had decapitated her neighbor's young daughter, there was a long inquiry to find out if, by chance, she had not been the father's mistress and thus acted out of vengeance. And they discovered that there was no connection. In the case of the woman from Sélestat—you recall, the one who boiled her daughter's thigh with the cabbage—the important element of the discussion had been: "Was there a famine during this period? Was the accused poor or not, famished or not?" And the prosecutor said: if she had been rich, then, there was no material interest for her to eat her daughter (since she could have purchased meat from the butcher), so she could have been considered deranged [aliénée]. But she was miserably poor, and, as a result, in these times of famine, she must have been hungry; and since she was hungry, cooking her daughter's leg with the cabbage was a motivated act; and since it was a motivated act, it was reasonable behavior; and since it was reasonable, she was mad.* [12]

---

* The audience laughs. Foucault's spoken words, faithfully reproduced here, differ from the other published versions of this scene, in which Foucault consistently concluded: "She was not mad." For a discussion of this discrepancy, see infra p. 231 n. 12.

To play on words, I would say that these crimes—and this is the other aspect—these crimes without reason were crimes without avowal. They were crimes about which one could say nothing, in the following sense. They were, of course, perfectly flagrant crimes. All of the possible proof of guilt was gathered. The authors, in most cases, recognized their crime. There was only one case in which the guilty party tried to deny the crime; all the others recognized their crime easily. So, juridically speaking, if avowal were simply the material confirmation of a truth that was otherwise established, it should have sufficed and satisfied the judges. And yet the avowal was made, but it is clear that this was not what the judges were seeking; what they demanded was that the guilty party say something about his crime—that he say why he committed his crime, what meaning he gave to his gesture. And if he could not say anything about it, if the accused could say nothing about his crime, this is where the difficulty began. This is where the penal machine began to stumble and to jam.

In this type of case, we see clearly that the avowal, in all of its materiality, is insufficient: we demand an avowal that fulfills the dramaturgical role that I spoke of earlier. And we see clearly that here, the recognition by the sick person or by the criminal who states, "Yes, I committed this murder. Period. That is all I have to say," does not function properly. The avowal does not function within the dramaturgy that is demanded.

I am not at all suggesting that this series of cases that I have cited—and this series is interesting because the cases took place in Germany, Austria, England, France, the United States, and their similarity shows that it was the same type of problem that was being encountered everywhere—I am not in any way suggesting that these cases created the situation I am about to analyze. Let's simply say that they brought out, through their singularities and their paradoxes, an entire series of questions that were implicit in the functioning of penal justice. They brought to light the question of the criminal subject behind the author of the crime and behind the juridically legitimate mechanisms of imputation. They brought out, from behind or rather interlaced between them, the discursivity of the inquiry that sought to establish the truth of the fact and the discursivity of the examination that sought to establish the truth of the criminal. Let us say that the judge essentially told the accused: "Don't simply tell me what you did, without telling me, at the same time and through this, who you are." Finally, this series of cases brought forward the need for another type of knowledge than the one that allowed them to establish the facts. I have done nothing more here than indicate a vague point of departure, from an historical-anecdotal point of view, of a vast shift that we can now see develop. My aim was simply to show the general roots and the historical emergence of the problematic through which modern penal law entered, I believe, its endless labyrinth. The doubling of avowal and its opening onto another type of questions—that is to say, the questions of subjectivity— are, I believe, inscribed here.

An analysis that stopped here, of course, would be entirely insufficient to account for everything that took place in the nineteenth century concerning the principle of this truth-telling on subjectivity. And in order to project two spotlights on two periods, on two important moments in this history, I would like to take, in the middle of the nineteenth century— more exactly, at the end of the first half of the nineteenth century—the question of monomania and of the constitution of crime as a psychiatric object. Then I will place myself at the end of the nineteenth century and speak briefly about the notion of degeneration and of the constitution of the criminal as object for social defense.[13]

First, monomania and the constitution of crime as a psychiatric object. As you know, the psychiatrists responded to the question raised by these great crimes that I described for you earlier—these great monstrous and mute crimes, these crimes without motive and without avowal—with the notion of monomania, of homicidal monomania.[14] This is a strange notion since, for psychiatrists, the peculiarity of this illness resided in the fact that it had practically only one visible symptom: the crime itself. At the same time, it was a strange notion from the point of view of penality because the crime was entirely devoid of motivation, interest, or passion; its only raison d'être was the illness itself, an illness consisting of nothing but having committed the crime. "Crime-madness"—this is the paradoxical notion that the doctors of the 1830s through the 1850s [put forward]. In fact, the notion began to fall out of usage in the 1850s and then reappeared briefly before, let's say, the 1870s. Well, let's say that for about thirty to forty years, this notion of homicidal monomania as "crime-madness," as crime that was entirely equivalent to madness and madness that was entirely equivalent to a crime, this notion was central, I believe, to the question of the criminal subject or of the crime as an object for a psychiatric science of the subject: a crime that was entirely madness, madness that was nothing other than a crime.

It is out of the question, of course, to retrace the theoretical background of the notion, or the reasons why this notion developed. I would simply like to pose the question of why this great fiction of homicidal monomania became the key notion in the proto-history of criminal subjectivity. I believe that one must start by searching for the reason why doctors proposed, as it were, this notion of monomania to the judicial institution — why did they thus hold out their hand to the judicial institution? I believe that the reason is tied, [in the end], to the role and to the definition of psychiatry at that particular period. At the beginning of the nineteenth century, the task of psychiatry was essentially to define its specificity within the realm of medicine and to gain scientific recognition among the other medical practices. Why did they attempt to intervene in the domain of justice, and of penal justice, at the moment when mental-health medicine was trying to establish its own scientific grounding and to define its specificity and its own domain with regard to all the other medical disciplines?

I do not think that we should try to explain this attempt, this temptation, this move to penetrate penal practice, by some vague form of imperialism on the part of psychiatrists seeking to annex a new domain; we should not seek to explain it by a dynamic that was internal and specific to medical knowledge, trying to rationalize this confused domain where madness and crime mixed. If crime became at that precise moment such an important matter for psychiatrists that they sought to enter, to push open the door of the judicial institution, it is, I believe, because it was less a field of knowledge to be conquered than a modality of power — than the modality of their own power that had to be guaranteed and justified.

Indeed, if psychiatry became so important in the nineteenth century, it was not simply because it applied a new medical rationality to mental and behavioral disorders. The importance of psychiatry at the beginning of the nineteenth century was that it functioned as a sort of public hygiene. The development in the eighteenth century of demography, of urban structures, the problem of industrial manpower, among others — all this had raised the biological and medical question of human populations, including their conditions of existence, of habitation, of nutrition, and the question of birth and mortality rates. The social body ceased to be in the nineteenth century, I believe, a simple juridico-political metaphor and became instead a biological reality as well as a field of medical intervention. The doctor from that moment on became a technician of the social body, and medicine became a public hygiene. And if psychiatry, at the turn from the eighteenth to the nineteenth century, established its autonomy and assumed at the same time such prestige, it was because psychiatry was able to inscribe itself within the framework of a medical discipline that was conceived as a reaction to apparent or potential dangers inherent in the social body. The psychiatrists [aliénistes] of the period could discuss ad infinitum the organic or psychic origin of mental illnesses, they could propose physical or physiological therapy; through their theoretical and practical differences they were all conscious of treating a social danger, whether they considered madness the result of unhealthy living conditions (many psychiatrists argued that overpopulation, promiscuity, urban life, alcoholism, sexual debauchery were all at the origin of mental illness) or whether they perceived madness itself as a source of danger for oneself, for others, for one's company, for one's descendants through the path of heredity. In any case, the psychiatrists were conscious that by manipulating madness they were manipulating of course an illness, but above all a danger. And what authorized them to intervene in this dangerous situation was, of course, that they could give this danger the status of illness.

Psychiatry in the nineteenth century, or in any case at the beginning of the nineteenth century, seems to me to have been far less a medicine of the individual soul than a medicine of the collective body. We can understand, from this point of view, why psychiatry was so driven to demonstrate the existence of something as fantastic as homicidal monomania, this surprising madness that would only manifest itself in the crime. We can understand from this perspective, I believe, how this notion remained operative for a period of thirty to forty years in spite, evidently, of its weak theoretical justification. For homicidal monomania, if indeed it existed—what did it show us? It was the living proof—or deadly proof, I should say—that in some of its more extreme and intense forms, madness could become entirely crime, and nothing but crime. So, at least at the furthest edges of madness, there was crime—and thus madness and crime belonged to one another essentially, they were cousins, there was an essential kinship. Homicidal monomania revealed, moreover, that madness was capable of leading not only to behavioral disorders, but also to the ultimate crime, the one that broke all of the laws of nature and society: murdering children, murdering one's own child [. . .] .*

---

* This break corresponds to a change in the audiovisual tape. As there is no original typescript of this course, there is no way of filling this lacuna.

: : :

They resisted it, of course: there was a whole series of very interesting discussions. But nonetheless, through these refusals and these hesitations, they did not entirely reject this notion and slowly let themselves be convinced. One cannot say that they were violated by the discipline of medicine: they finally made, with more or less good will, this notion of homicidal monomania function within their practice. Why did they ultimately accept it? It is because of the new codes—and above all, the reforms of these new codes, with the mitigating circumstances and all the modulations of punishment which they were to administer themselves within these new codes (all these measures concerning mitigating circumstances, you know, well, these reforms dating from about the 1830s and 1840s). Well, from the moment they began to manage the punishments, the quantity if not the nature of the punishments, as a function of something that was not simply the crime but the criminal—well, at that point, with these psychiatric notions, they had an instrument at their disposal. Neither the great theoreticians, such as Beccaria and Bentham, nor those who actually had written the new penal legislation had sought to elaborate anything resembling the knowledge of the subject. But as soon as the reform of the penal system had proposed around the 1830s these modulations concerning the application of punishment, they needed to equip themselves with a new instrument. Hence the fact that while the legal code, in France in particular, the Napoleonic Code only had the famous article 64, that is to say simply dementia or rage, magistrates began in the 1840s—after the period 1835 to 1840, since mitigating circumstances were added in 1832 [. . .]—to accept the usage of this notion of madness, of homicidal monomania. And as a result, they found themselves faced not only with a new notion, but also a new subject, that is to say the criminal subject. They no longer simply had to punish a crime, they had to treat, that is, they had to manipulate, they had to index their judicial practice not only on the crime, but on the criminal individuality.

What begins to be put into place in the 1840s took on an infinitely greater importance and breadth in the last years of the nineteenth century and the first years of the twentieth. What happened between these two periods, roughly between the years 1840 and 1850 and the years 1880, 1900, and 1910? The notion of monomania was abandoned by psychiatry proper. It was abandoned for two reasons: first, because the negative idea of a partial madness that only touched upon a given point and only broke out in certain moments was replaced by the idea that a mental illness was not necessarily a breach of thought and conscience, but could also attack the sentiments and emotions, the instincts, behaviors, et cetera. Second, monomania was also abandoned for another reason, which is that the idea of mental illnesses with a complex evolution came of age: the idea that mental illnesses could present one particular symptom or another at one stage or another of their development, and this, not only at the level of the individual, but also at the level of generations. In other words, the idea of degeneration.

Once it was possible to define this vast evolutionary tree, there was no longer any need to oppose the great, monstrous, and mysterious crimes that could be ascribed to an incomprehensible and essential violence of madness against the minor criminality that was too frequent and too familiar to necessitate recourse to the pathological. From then on, whether it was a question of these incomprehensible massacres of which Henriette Cornier and others had provided examples at the beginning of the century, or whether it was a question of little misdemeanors concerning property, sexuality, et cetera, in either and any case there was now an instrument—an instrument that allowed one to suspect a more or less serious disruption of one's instincts or the development of an uninterrupted march toward illness. And it is in this manner that we see appear, in the field of forensic psychiatry, new categories such as necrophilia, which first appeared around 1840; kleptomania, around 1860; and exhibitionism, in 1876; as well as the consideration by forensic psychiatry of behaviors like pederasty, which will be called homosexuality after 1869; sadism, et cetera. We have then, at least in principle, a sort of psychiatric and criminological continuum along which it is possible to interrogate in medical terms any and all degrees on the penal scale. The psychiatric question was no longer simply confined to the pinnacle of criminality. It was not located, it was not posed simply with regard to a few great crimes. Even if it called for a negative response, one could legitimately pose the question in every case across the entire domain of infractions: between a woman who steals lingerie in a store and a mother who cooks her daughter's thigh in a cauldron, in the end one must, in either case—or one may in one case as in the other—pose the question: "Is there not madness here?"

Now this clearly had extremely important consequences for the juridical theory of responsibility. In the conception of monomania, the suspicion of pathology arose precisely when there was no reason for an act. Madness then appeared to be the cause of that which made no sense, and the lack of responsibility established itself within that gap. But with this new analysis of instinct and emotions, there arose the possibility of a causal analysis of all conduct, whether criminal or noncriminal and whatever its degree of criminality. At this point, the juridical and psychiatric problem of crime entered an infinite labyrinth: if an act was determined by a causal nexus that the analysis of the criminal subject could uncover—if, then, an act was determined by such a causal nexus, could it be considered to be free? And, in that case, could the responsibility of the subject be recognized? And was it necessary, in order to be able to condemn someone, that it be impossible to restore the causal intelligibility of the act?

So you see that behind this new way of posing the problem, we can recognize the impact of a certain number of transformations that were its conditions of possibility. In order for the problem of the continuous and multiform relationship between psychiatry and criminality to be able to establish itself, in order to be able to suspect that there is madness across behaviors that are even the most simple and the least intensely criminal, it was first necessary for there to be an intensive development of a police network [*quadrillage policier*] in most European countries; which entails in particular a new organization and surveillance of urban space, which also entails a far more systematic and efficient pursuit of minor delinquency. We should also add [. . .] the social conflicts, the class struggles, the political confrontations, the armed revolts—whether of the revolutionaries of 1848, of the communards of 1870, of the anarchists of the last years of the century, including all the violent strikes—all of these social conflicts prompted the authorities to assimilate political infractions with common-law crimes in order to better discredit them. And gradually an image was constructed of an enemy of society: an enemy of society who could be the revolutionary just as he could be the assassin, since, after all, revolutionaries do sometimes kill. In response to this, there was an extraordinary development throughout the second half of the century of a literature on criminality (I mean literature in the largest sense, including local crime stories in the newspapers, as well as detective novels and all the romanticized writings that developed around crimes): glorification of the criminal, of course, but also confirmation that criminality was omnipresent, that it was a constant threat and a menace of which one could find worrisome traces throughout the entire social body.

The general fear of crime, the dread of this danger that seemed to be as one with the social body itself [was] thus perpetually inscribed in the conscience of each and everyone. And Garofalo, in his preface to the first edition of *Criminology*—his treatise, his text entitled *La criminologie* and published in 1887—evoked the nine thousand murders that were recorded annually in Europe, not counting Russia, and declared: "Who is the enemy that has so greatly devastated this region?"—Europe. "Who is the enemy that has wrought such great destruction? It is an enemy who has remained mysterious and unknown in history up until now: his name is the criminal."[15]

And to this, another element must clearly be added: namely, the continuing and incessantly reported failure of the penitentiary system. As you know, the eighteenth-century reformers and the philanthropists of the following period dreamed that incarceration, provided that it be rationally organized and directed, would serve as a penal therapy. The correction of the condemned was supposed to be the result of the punishment. But, as you know, from early on it was observed that the prison led to precisely the opposite result, that the prison was on the whole a school of delinquency, and that even the most refined methods of the police and judicial apparatus, far from ensuring a better protection against crime, led, to the contrary, through the medium of imprisonment, to a reinforcement of the criminal milieu.

There was, then, for a whole series of reasons, a situation that gave rise to a very strong social and political demand to respond to crime and to repress it. And this demand concerned a criminality which, in its totality, could be thought of in juridical and medical terms. Yet the central piece of the penal institution since the Middle Ages—namely, responsibility and the practice of avowal as being an enunciation by the individual that he effectively accepted this responsibility—all this seemed, in effect, inadequate to think through the vast and thick terrain of medico-legal criminality.

This inadequacy became apparent both at the conceptual and at the institutional levels in the conflicts of the 1890s and 1900s that opposed what was called the school of criminal anthropology and the association for penal law. Confronted with the traditional principles of criminal legislation, the Italian school (or the anthropologists of criminality) sought nothing short of exiting the realm of law. They called for a veritable depenalization of crime through the creation of an apparatus that was entirely different from the one prescribed by the legal codes. I would say, in very schematic terms, that criminal anthropology aimed to completely abandon the juridical notion of responsibility, to pose as the fundamental question not at all the degree of the individual's liberty, but rather the level of danger that the individual constituted in society. For criminal anthropology, it was a question of emphasizing that the accused whom the law recognized as lacking responsibility (because they were ill, mad, abnormal, or victims of irresistible impulses) were precisely those who were the most dangerous in reality. It was a question of insisting that what was called the penalty did not have to be a punishment, but rather a mechanism for the defense of society; and, then, of noting that the relevant difference was not between those who were responsible and needed to be condemned and those who were not responsible and needed to be released, but between subjects who were absolutely and definitively dangerous and those who could cease to be so after certain treatments. In sum, it was a question of concluding that there had to be three main types of social reaction to crime, or rather to the danger constituted by the criminal: definitive elimination by death or confinement in an institution, provisional elimination with treatment, or a sort of relative and partial elimination such as sterilization or castration.

We see clearly the series of displacements that the anthropological school called for: from the crime to the criminal, from the act committed to the danger that is potentially inherent in the individual, and from a modulated punishment of the guilty party to the absolute protection of others.[16] We entered at that precise moment, I believe, an entirely different regime: that of security. All of these displacements implied quite clearly an escape from a universe of penal law that was in fact centered on the act itself: an escape from a universe of penal law in which the essential piece was the imputability to a rights-bearing subject of acts that had been committed and which breached the law. Neither the criminality of an individual nor the index of his dangerousness, neither his potential or future conduct nor the protection of society in general from these possible perils—all of these things that had now become so essential in this society of security, in this society with securities: none of this could be integrated as such into the system of juridical principles and notions around which the legal codes of the end of the eighteenth century and beginning of the nineteenth century were organized. And the judges, magistrates, or jurors, if they had to use these notions, were incapable of determining how they could articulate them within the institutional system that gave them the right to punish. These notions of the criminality of the individual, of dangerousness, of potential criminal conduct could be made to function in a rational way only within something that was entirely different from a juridical code, only within a technical knowledge [*un savoir technique*]: a technical knowledge that was able to characterize what a criminal individual was in himself and in some sense beneath his acts.[17] What was needed was a form of knowledge capable of measuring the degree of danger present in an individual. What was needed for all this was a form of knowledge that could determine the protection that was necessary and sufficient in the face of this danger that was represented by an individual.

Hence, there emerged the idea that crime should not be handled by the judges—or could not be the sole responsibility of judges unless the jurisdiction effectively exercised by the judge be doubled by an entirely different type of veridiction from the one obtained and defined either through inquiry or through the avowal—in the sense which I discussed with you and which functioned so intensely in the codes of the early nineteenth century. Knowledge became a necessity: the subject and its truth required a type of competence [*connaissance*], a type of knowledge [*savoir*], a type of experience, and a type of exchange and of dialogue that could only come from psychiatry, criminology, psychology.

And I believe that we [see] here—having arrived at the moment when the notion of social defense began to emerge,[18] a notion that would be so important throughout the twentieth century—we see appear at this very moment an entirely different form of the truth of the subject, or of the veridiction of the subject, that was far removed from the one that was associated with the traditional veridiction of avowal. And it seems to me that we can grasp the effects of this new demand for a knowledge of the subject that is of an entirely different type from the one that could manifest itself in avowal—that we can grasp the manner in which this new demand inscribed itself in penal law and the manner in which it continues to function today—by recalling two things that, fittingly, did not so much come from the internal history of penal law as from transformations produced elsewhere.

The first took place at the end of the nineteenth century, at the moment when—within penal law and for the reasons that I just told you about, that is to say the necessity to defend society—what I referred to last time as a hermeneutics of the subject was constituting itself, or perhaps reconstituting itself: a hermeneutics of the subject that clearly was, in its forms and in its objectives, extremely different from what we found in the practice of Christian spirituality. In the practice of Christian spirituality, you will remember, the hermeneutics of the subject consisted essentially in bringing to light the secrets of conscience—the *arcana conscientiae*—through the process of the permanent examination of oneself and of the exhaustive verbalization in the direction of another. Through a whole series of efforts in which, naturally, Freud and psychoanalysis occupied a central place, the hermeneutics of the subject opened itself at the end of the nineteenth century to a method of analysis far removed from the practice of the permanent examination and exhaustive verbalization about which I spoke to you regarding ancient Christianity. A hermeneutics of the subject opened up, weighed down or burdened, having as its instrument and method principles of analysis that bore a far greater resemblance to the principles of textual analysis. This hermeneutics of the subject, which took the form of deciphering a text, was supposed to make it possible to root the behaviors of a subject in a meaningful whole.

Once the hermeneutics of the subject took this form, crime would emerge as a meaningful act. This new practice of the subject was clearly very different from the one that could be delineated in criminal anthropology or in the pathology of degeneration—but from the point of view of penality itself, this new practice did not and still does not resolve the problem of these notions, even if the [latter] have been abandoned. Rather, this new practice doubled [the problem] because, with the hermeneutics of the subject, penal practice itself would internalize the problematic relationship between the responsibility of the act and its intelligibility. The relationship was transferred into penal practice itself, since it showed that the relationship between the act and the subject was not simply a question of imputing responsibility with a more or less determined notion of causality, but that it was also, at the same time, a question of giving meaning. The causal relationship dispossessed the judge, whereas the relationship based on meaning [*signification*] restored the judge's hold, but in an equally ambiguous way: what should be done with the meaning of a given crime? This was the first axis of transformation, outside of penal practice, but that weighed and still today weighs on contemporary penal practice.

The other mutation can be located, I believe, within the juridical system, but with regard to the notion of responsibility in civil law. It seems to me—and here again I am going to be very schematic—that there was a very important transformation in civil law at the end of the nineteenth century and beginning of the twentieth. This transformation revolved around the notion of accident, of risk, of responsibility.[19] In a general way, I would say it is important to underscore the salience of the problem of the accident, especially at the end of the nineteenth century and not only in the realm of law for that matter, but also in the economic realm—the problem of the accident, of its probability, of how to reduce its probability, how to compensate for its effects, et cetera. With the development of the wage system, of industrial techniques, of mechanization, of means of transportation, of urban structures, two very important things appeared. First, the risks that were imposed on third parties: the employer exposed his salaried workers to work-related accidents; carriers exposed not only their passengers to accidents, but also innocent bystanders. Next, there was the fact that these accidents could often be linked to a sort of error, but a minimal error—such as inattentiveness, lack of precaution, negligence—committed, moreover, by someone who might be in a position neither to carry the civil liability nor to assure the payment of the ensuing damages (the type of situation, if you will, that involves the negligence of an employee who brings about a mine disaster or a railroad accident).

Now, all this implied that the notion of civil liability had to be elaborated anew. It was necessary to erase the heritage of Roman law that was still present—this idea that responsibility was necessary to assign fault and that the payment of damages should constitute a sort of civil penalty. It was necessary to de-penalize, to remove guilt from civil responsibility, to cut it off from any reference to a subjective fault, to release it from the burden of having to demonstrate the existence of a personal fault.[20] Concretely, in the case of a work accident, it was necessary that the workers who were affected by a work accident could be compensated without having to prove that their boss had committed a specific fault in violation of a law or of a precise regulation. In sum, the problem was to establish in law the concept of no-fault responsibility. This was the effort of Western jurists—and especially German jurists, who were pressed by the demands of Bismarckian society, a society not only of discipline but of security. And it seems to me that this arrangement of a responsibility without culpability was, along with the new hermeneutics of the subject that opened with psychoanalysis—or let's say, more generally, with psychiatry or with psychology—the other great mutation that allowed for the question of criminal subjectivity to be posed in new terms.

In a rather strange way, this extraction of culpability [*déculpabilisation*] from civil liability would constitute a model for penal law—on the basis of the very propositions formulated by criminal anthropology. After all, what does it mean to be a born criminal, what is a degenerate, what is a criminal personality, if not someone who, according to a causal chain that is difficult to reconstruct, has a particularly high level on a criminal probability scale? Someone who is, deep down, a risk of crime? Just as one can determine civil responsibility without establishing fault, but solely by estimating the possible risk against which one must defend oneself without being able to remove it entirely—in the same way, one can render an individual responsible as a matter of penal law without having to determine if he was acting freely and thus whether there was fault, but rather by tying the act that was committed back to the risk of criminality that his very personality constituted. He is responsible since, by his sole existence, he is a creator of risk, even if he is not at fault because he did not choose evil over good of his own free will, even if he did not choose to be neurotic or psychotic over being healthy. The purpose of the sanction, therefore, will not be to punish a rights-bearing subject who voluntarily broke the law. Its role will be to diminish as much as possible—either by elimination, by exclusion, or by various restrictions, or again through therapeutic measures—the risk of criminality represented by the individual in question.

This represents an important moment in the history of penal thought: it is the moment when the need for avowal—this dramaturgical piece that was so essential and whose role was so fundamentally stamped into the codes of the eighteenth and the beginning of the nineteenth centuries—found itself replaced and doubled by a demand of a different type. It was no longer a matter of the judge stating what he implicitly stated at an earlier time: "Tell me whether, indeed, you committed the crime of which you are accused. Tell me if, indeed, you recognize deep within your will the soundness and the legitimacy of the condemnation that I will pronounce against you." Now, the judge implicitly posed the following question to the one who was accused: "Tell me who you are, so that I may make a judicial decision that will have as its measure both the crime that you have committed, of course, but also the individual that you are."

Let's return to the dialogue that I evoked at the beginning of these lectures, the dialogue in which the judge asked the accused to speak of himself: "Tell me why you raped those girls. Tell me why you wanted to kill them. Tell me who you are, so that I may judge you." This demand of an

avowal—not at the level of the act, nor at the level of the justification and
the foundation of jurisdiction, but at the level of the very being of criminal
subjectivity—is, I believe, something absolutely fundamental. It is something that poses a question in the penal law that has, I believe, remained
whole. And if so many difficulties, so many obstacles, so many contradictions—not only in penal theory, but also within penal practice itself—
arise and are felt today, it is in large part because and to the extent that
this question of subjectivity, of truth-telling of criminal subjectivity, has
come to double and extend its shadow, in a way, over the simple question
of avowal that was: "Did you indeed commit the crime of which you are accused? Do you really consent to being punished for it?"

This other question of the veridiction of the subject has been the thorn,
the splinter, the wound, the vanishing point, the breach in the entire penal
system. Let me recount one final anecdote.[21] It is an argument that was
recently used by a French lawyer whom I will not cite by name, not out
of discretion but because he played a crucial role in the campaign against
the death penalty. It is an argument that he used in a case involving the
kidnapping and assassination of a child. This argument—what I am going
to say carries no polemical nuance whatsoever, nor any polemical intent,
I simply would like to make apparent, as [one] of the paradoxes of reason, what I might call the paradox or antinomy of penal reason in our
contemporary system. So he was pleading on behalf of someone who had
kidnapped and killed a child. The case—perhaps some of you remember
it—had a tremendous impact, not only because of the seriousness of the
crime, but also because the use of the death penalty or, it was hoped, its
abolition, was hanging in the balance in this trial—or, in any event, people
thought so. The lawyer—who did not so much plead for the accused as
plead against the death penalty—deployed a certain number of arguments
on behalf of the accused. Among them there was one that struck me. He
turned toward the jurors and said to them: "But in the end, the accused,
of course, he acknowledged his crime. He confessed. But what did he tell
you about this crime? What information did he give you about his crime,
about the reasons for his crime, about who he is? You have no idea. He
could tell you nothing. Nothing of this could show through, either in the
interrogations that he was subjected to during the course of the investigation or in the psychiatric examinations, or even today when he appeared
before you in criminal court. He did not say anything. He did not want to
say anything. He could not say anything. In any case, you, you know noth-

ing about him." And he concluded with this reflection that I find, once again, astonishing, but astonishing because it is so indicative of the antinomy of our penal reason. He concluded his closing statement on this precise point, he closed with this sentence: "In the end, can you condemn to death someone whom you do not know?"

Thank you.

[NOTES]

1. On the *Constitutio criminalis carolina* of 1532 during the reign of Charles V, see Friedrich-Christian Schroeder, *Die peinliche Gerichtsordnung Kaiser Karls V und des Heiligen Römischen Reichs von 1532* (Stuttgart: Reclam, 2000); Clive Emsley, *Crime, Police, and Penal Policy: European Experiences 1750–1940* (New York: Oxford University Press, 2007), pp. 18–20; and Yves Cartuyvels, *D'où vient le code pénal? Une approche généalogique des premiers codes pénaux absolutistes au XVIIIe siècle*, preface by Françoise Tulkens (Paris-Brussels: De Boeck Université, 1996), pp. 27–32. Regarding the criminal ordinance of 1670, see Adhémar Esmein, *Histoire de la procédure criminelle et spécialement de la procédure inquisitoire depuis le XIIIe siècle jusqu'à nos jours* (Vaduz-Paris: Topos-Duchemin, 1969; new edition Paris: Éditions Panthéon-Assas, 2010).

2. The Latin expression, which is more commonly known in Anglo-American jurisprudence as *habemus optimum testem, confitentem reum*, means "We have the best witness, a confessing defendant." Henry Campbell Black, *Black's Law Dictionary*, 5th ed. (St. Paul, MN: West Publishing, 1979), p. 639.

3. Johann Christoph Hoffbauer (1766–1827) was principally a philosopher of natural law and ethics, though he was interested in psychology as well. He was the author of *Untersuchungen über die Krankheiten der Seele und der verwandten Zustände* (Halle: Trampen, 1802–7), in three volumes, as well as the treatise *Médecine légale relative aux aliénés et aux sourds-muets, ou les lois appliquées aux désordre de l'intelligence*, trans. Antoine M. Chambeyron, annot. Itard et Esquirol (Paris: J.-B. Baillière, 1827). Foucault makes reference to Hoffbauer, as well as to other psychiatrists discussed in the passages that follow—Johann Daniel Metzger, Jean-Étienne Esquirol, Étienne-Jean Georget, William Ellis, and Andrew Combe—in his course summary in *Psychiatric Power: Lectures at the Collège de France, 1973–74*, English series ed. Arnold I. Davidson, trans. Graham Burchell (Hampshire, UK: Palgrave Macmillan, 2006), p. 338 (Hoffbauer and Esquirol); as well as in a paper given at the Law and Psychiatry Symposium at York University, Toronto, October 24–26, 1977, entitled "About the Concept of the 'Dangerous Individual' in 19th-Century Legal Psychiatry," trans. Alain Baudot and Jane Couchman, *International Journal of Law and Psychiatry* 1:1–18 (1978), pp. 2–5; also reprinted in Michel Foucault, *The Essential Works of Foucault, 1954–1984: Power*, vol. 3, pp. 176–200, series ed. Paul Rabinow, ed. James D. Faubion, trans. Robert Hurley and others (New York: The New Press, 2000), pp. 179–80 (Hoffbauer, Metzger, Esquirol, Georget, Ellis, and Combe). Robert Castel discusses Hoffbauer, Esquirol, and others in his essay "The Doctors and Judges," pp. 250–69 in Michel Foucault, ed., *I, Pierre Rivière, Having Slaughtered My Mother, My Sister, and My Brother . . .* trans. Frank Jellinek (New York: Pantheon, 1975), p. 254 et seq. For detailed annotations on Hoffman, Esquirol, and these other psychiatrists, see Jacques Lagrange's copious notes to Foucault's lectures in *Psychiatric Power* (especially in the English translation, pp. 225–31 and 263–64). On the history of the profession of psychiatry in the

nineteenth century, see Jan Goldstein, *Console and Classify: The French Psychiatric Profession in the Nineteenth Century* (Cambridge: Cambridge University Press, 1987).

4. Johann Daniel Metzger (1739–1805) was a doctor, psychiatrist, and professor at the University of Königsberg. He was the author of *Gerichtlich-medicinische Beobachtungen* (Königsberg: J. Kanter, 1778–80), 2 vols.

5. Foucault discussed this case presented by Metzger in his lecture "About the Concept of the 'Dangerous Individual' in Nineteenth-Century Legal Psychiatry," in *Power*, p. 179.

6. The case from Sélestat was first reported in an article by Dr. Reisseisen entitled "Examen médico-légal d'un cas extraordinaire d'infanticide," which appeared in *Annales d'hygiène publique et de médecine légale* 8, no. 1: 397–411 (translated by the psychiatrist Charles Chrétien Henri Marc [1771–1841], this text originally appeared in German in the eleventh volume of the *Annales de Médecine Politique* [*Jahrbuch der Staatsartzneikunde*, 1817] of J. H. Kopp). Reisseisen's text was reproduced in its entirety by Charles C. H. Marc in his work *De la folie considérée dans ses rapports avec les questions médico-judiciaires* (Paris: J.-B. Baillière, 1840), pp. 130–45, and then elaborated upon, along with the cases of Henriette Cornier and Pierre Rivière, by Marc in the pages that followed. As Foucault explains in his lectures, the Sélestat case was also analyzed by Jean-Pierre Peter in his article "Ogres d'archives," *Nouvelle Revue de psychanalyse* 6 (1972): 251–58. See Foucault, *Abnormal: Lectures at the Collège de France 1974–1975*, English series ed. Arnold I. Davidson, trans Graham Burchell (London: Verso, 2003) p. 102 and p. 107 n. 38. Foucault interprets the Sélestat case in *Abnormal*, lectures of January 22, 1975, p. 62; January 29, 1975, p. 102; February 5, 1975, p. 110–12; and February 12, 1975, pp. 137–42; as well as in his lecture "About the Concept of the 'Dangerous Individual' in Nineteenth-Century Legal Psychiatry," in *Power*, p. 179.

7. The Henriette Cornier case is perhaps the case Foucault discussed the most often after Pierre Rivière. Foucault introduces and interprets the case in his lecture of January 22, 1975, in *Abnormal*, p. 62, and then discusses it extensively as a foil to the later "new psychiatry" of the 1960s represented by the case of Charles Jouy. See Foucault, *Abnormal*, pp. 109–18, 293–98, and 300–303; see also "About the Concept of the 'Dangerous Individual' in Nineteenth-Century Legal Psychiatry," in *Power*, p. 179. The case of Henriette Cornier first appeared in the works of C. C. H. Marc, who was asked by Henriette Cornier's lawyer for a medical-legal consultation. The consultation is reproduced in its entirety in the treatise of Marc, *De la folie considérée dans ses rapports avec les questions médico-judiciaires*, pp. 71–116 (Paris: J.-B. Baillière, 1840); see also Étienne Jean Georget, *Discussion médico-légale sur la folie ou aliénation mentale, suivie de l'examen du procès criminel d'Henriette Cornier, et de plusieurs autres procès dans lesquels cette maladie a été alléguée comme moyen de défense* (Paris: Migneret, 1826), pp. 71–130 (a new edition, edited by Jacques Postel, was published by L'Harmattan, Paris, in 1999). The note by Valerio Marchetti and Antonella Salomoni in *Abnormal*, p. 135 n. 4, offers additional references for an analysis of the case: "N. Grand, *Réfutation de la discussion médico-légale du Dr Michu sur la monomanie homicide à propos du meurtre commis par H. Cornier* (Paris, 1826). There are also excerpts from the medical legal reports in the series of articles that the *Gazette des tribunaux* dedicated to the trial in 1826 (February 21 and 28; June 18, 23, 25)."

8. Foucault introduced and discussed the Catherine Ziegler case in his lecture "About the Concept of the 'Dangerous Individual' in Nineteenth-Century Legal Psychiatry," in *Power*, p. 179.

9. Foucault also discussed the John Howison case in "About the Concept of the 'Dangerous Individual' in Nineteenth-Century Legal Psychiatry," in *Power*, p. 179.

10. Foucault also discussed the Abraham Prescott case in "About the Concept of the 'Dangerous Individual' in Nineteenth-Century Legal Psychiatry," in *Power*, p. 180.

11. Jean-Étienne Dominique Esquirol (1772–1840) was a renowned nineteenth-century psychiatrist and is considered one of the founders of the French psychiatric hospital. He is

the author of a number of important works, most notably *Des Maladies mentales considérées sous les rapports médical, hygiénique et médico-légal* (Paris: J.-B. Baillière, 1838), 2 vols; English edition, Jean-Étienne D. Esquirol, *Mental Maladies: A Treatise on Insanity*, trans. E. K. Hunt (Philadelphia: Lea and Blanchard, 1845). Étienne-Jean Georget (1795–1828) was a student of Jean-Étienne Esquirol and Philippe Pinel. He was a psychiarist and author of many treatises on psychopathology, most notably *De la Folie: Considérations sur cette maladie* (Paris: Crevot, 1820), new edition edited by Jacque Postel (Paris: L'Harmattan, 1999); and *Examen des procès criminels des nommés Léger, Feldtmann, Lecouffe, Jean-Pierre et Papavoine, suivi de quelques considérations médico-légales sur la liberté morale* (Paris: Migneret, 1825). Sir William Charles Ellis (1780–1839) was also a psychiatrist and worked in an asylum in England in the nineteenth century. He is the author of *A Treatise on the Nature, Symptoms, Causes, and Treatment of Insanity, with Practical Observations on Lunatic Asylums* (London: Samuel Holdsworth, 1838). Andrew Combe (1797–1847) was a Scottish doctor and phrenologist who studied in France under Jean-Étienne Esquirol. He is the author of many treatises including *Observations on Mental Derangement: Being an Application of the Principles of Phrenology to the Elucidation of the Causes, Symptoms, Nature, and Treatment of Insanity* (Boston: Marsh, Capen & Lyon, 1834).

12. Foucault's spoken word at Louvain ("She was mad") differs from all the published texts in which he discussed this passage. See Foucault, "About the Concept of the 'Dangerous Individual' in Nineteenth-Century Legal Psychiatry," in *International Journal of Law and Psychiatry* 1 (1978), p. 5, and in *Power*, p. 182 ("to cook the leg with the cabbage was interested behavior; she was therefore not insane"); "L'évolution de la notion d''individu dangereux' dans la psychiatrie légale," in *Déviance et Société*, 1981, vol. 5, no. 4, p. 407, and in *Dits et écrits*, III, n. 220, p. 448 ("faire cuire avec des choux la jambe était une conduite intéressée; elle n'était donc pas folle." Given the consistent published versions and the context of the passage, we could have corrected this sentence. However, there is another possible interpretation of this passage that can be derived from the primary materials that Foucault relied on, namely the "Examen médico-légal d'un cas extraordinaire d'infanticide" by Dr. Reisseisen of Strasbourg, in the eleventh volume of the *Annales de Médecine Politique*, translated by Dr. Marc and reproduced in the *Annales d'hygiène publique et de médecine légale* 8, no. 1, pp. 397–411. In the proceedings, the jury determined that the accused had murdered the child, but added that the act "was committed by the effect of delirium, so she was acquitted and returned to the competent authority." The doctors called to give their expert opinion agreed that she had committed the act during an attack of mania; one of the doctors added that he had had a hard time identifying, at the time of the crime, a fit of rage or a fit of melancholy, but, Reisseisen wrote, "he felt obliged, *for the honor of humanity*, to consider the accused as having been deprived of her reason." In his commentary, Reisseisen discusses whether poverty or hunger might have caused the act, before considering whether the accused had shown signs of melancholy or other "kinds of madness." In both cases, the answer was negative. Hence a first conclusion: "When [. . .] we consider the circumstances surrounding the murder, and the fact that either before nor after the act, there was not a trace of mental disorder, it becomes difficult to square this series of revolting acts with such a condition." That first conclusion is immediately followed by a second: "We are thus forced," he writes, "to consider the act as the product of a combination of insanity [*aliénation mentale*], despair, and an instinctive propensity. However, as the law admits only insanity as an excuse for a crime, the forensic doctors naturally had to declare that, at the moment of the crime, the accused had acted out of delirium, in order to get the judges to exclude, for the honor of humanity, the imputation of such a horrendous crime. '*Indignum est crimina atrocitate defendi.*'" It is possible that it is this reasoning—to commit such an act without being mad, one had to be mad, or at least we would have to suppose "for the honor of humanity"—that Foucault summarized when he said: "And since it was reasonable, she was mad."

13. Foucault developed these themes in "About the Concept of the 'Dangerous Individual' in Nineteenth-Century Legal Psychiatry," in *Power*, p. 190 et seq., where he goes into greater detail on this period marked by the first Congress of Criminal Anthropology in 1885 and the publication of Adolph Prins's work *La Défense sociale*. Ier Congrès international d'anthropologie criminelle (Rome, November 1885), *Actes du congrès* (Turin: 1886); Adolph Prins, *La Défense sociale et les transformations du droit pénal* (Brussels: Misch et Thron, 1910; reedited with an introduction by Françoise Tulkens, Geneva: Editions médecine et hygiène, 1986). See also the writings published in connection with the research seminar Foucault directed at the Université Catholique de Louvain in 1981, collected in Françoise Tulkens, ed., *Généalogie de la défense sociale en Belgique: Travaux du séminaire qui s'est tenu à l'Université catholique de Louvain sous la direction de Michel Foucault* (Bruxelles: Story-Scientia, 1988).

14. Foucault began examining the notion of monomania in his research on the *Pierre Rivière* dossier, and he treats the issue at length in his lectures in *Psychiatric Power* and *Abnormal*. See, e.g., *Psychiatric Power*, pp. 206, 249, and 272; *Abnormal*, pp. 119, 142–44, and 284–85; Foucault, foreword to *I, Pierre Rivière*, p. ix; Castel, "The Doctors and Judges," in *I, Pierre Rivière*, pp. 255–69. As Foucault explains in *I, Pierre Rivière*, the concept of monomania, advanced by Esquirol in 1808, began to be resisted strenuously by lawyers, judges, and doctors by 1827; so by the time of the Pierre Rivière case in 1835, references to monomania had become "extremely discreet." Foucault, *I, Pierre Rivière*, p. ix. Foucault also, naturally, treats the issue at length in "About the Concept of the 'Dangerous Individual' in Nineteenth-Century Legal Psychiatry," in *Power*, p. 182 et seq. For a detailed treatment, see the chapter "Monomania" in Jan Goldstein, *Console and Classify*, pp. 152–96. Jacques Lagrange, in his notes to Foucault's lectures in *Abnormal*, p. 263 n. 45, draws attention to three other works on the history of the concept of monomania: Raphaël Fontanille, *Aliénation mentale et criminalité (historique, expertise médico-légale, internement)* (Grenoble: Allier Frères, 1902); Paul Dubuisson and Alexandre Vigouroux, *Responsabilité pénale et Folie: Étude médico-légale* (Paris: Alcan, 1911); and Alessandro Fontana, "The Intermittences of Rationality," pp. 269–88, in *I, Pierre Rivière*.

15. Raffaele Garofalo, *La Criminologie* (Paris: Félix Alcan, 1905), p. ix; Raffaele Garofalo, *Criminology*, trans. Robert Wyness Millar (Boston: Little, Brown, 1914), p. xxvii ("And in sinister climax, it reveals to us the author of these scenes of desolation—an enemy mysterious, unrecognized by history;—we call him the CRIMINAL"). Foucault develops his analysis of Garofalo in "About the Concept of the 'Dangerous Individual' in Nineteenth-Century Legal Psychiatry," where he refers to the "Garofalo principle": "Criminal law had only two terms, the offence and the penalty. The new criminology recognizes three, the crime, the criminal and the means of repression" (*Power*, p. 178).

16. This movement is analyzed by Pasquale Pasquino in "Naissance d'un savoir spécial: La criminologie," in "Michel Foucault. Surveiller et punir: La prison vingt ans après," *Société & Représentations* 3 (November 1996), pp. 173–86; translated as Pasquale Pasquino, "Criminology: The Birth of a Special Knowledge," pp. 235–250, in *The Foucault Effect: Studies in Governmentality*, Graham Burchell, Colin Gordon, and Peter Miller, eds. (Chicago: University of Chicago Press, 1991).

17. On these questions, already studied at the Université Catholique de Louvain prior to 1981, see Christian Debuyst ed., *Dangerosité et justice pénale: Ambiguïté d'une pratique* (Geneva: Masson/Médecine et Hygiène, coll. Déviance et Société—Bibliothèque de la Faculté de droit de l'Université Catholique de Louvain, 1981).

18. On the notion of social defense, see Adolph Prins, *La défense sociale et les transformations du droit pénal*, as well as the texts produced for the seminar that Foucault held at Louvain, collected in Françoise Tulkens, ed., *Généalogie de la défense sociale en Belgique*. For background and context on Prins, see also Pasquale Pasquino, "Criminology: The Birth of a Special Knowledge," in *The Foucault Effect*.

19. Foucault discusses the theme of risk and responsibility in his lecture "About the Concept of the 'Dangerous Individual' in Nineteenth-Century Legal Psychiatry," and pursued his analysis in his lectures in *Security, Territory, Population* in 1978 and in *Birth of Biopolitics* in 1979. The theme was developed by François Ewald in *L'État Providence* (Paris: Bernard Grasset, 1986); by Robert Castel in *La Gestion des Risques: De l'anti-psychiatrie à l'après-psychanalyse* (Paris: Éditions de Minuit, 1981); and by Jacques Donzelot in *L'invention du social* (Paris: Fayard, 1983).

20. For an analysis of the way in which this problem was posed and resolved from a comparative law perspective, see Geneviève Schamps, *La mise en danger: Un concept fondateur d'un principe général de responsabilité* (Paris: LGDJ, 1998).

21. The reference here is to the Patrick Henry case that was pleaded by Robert Badinter. See Robert Badinter, *L'Abolition* (Paris: Fayard, 2000) pp. 41–123; English edition, *Abolition*, trans. Jeremy Mercer, (Boston: Northeastern University Press, 2008), pp. 27–80. Badinter wrote: "I evoked the limitations of psychiatric knowledge, the uncertainty of the experts. Nobody really knew who this young man was. Not them, the people judging him, not any more than those experts did. But it was they who were being asked to kill him. So, that is what the death penalty was, a judicial sacrifice made amid the shadows of ignorance." Ibid. pp. 76. Foucault made reference to this anecdote in his lecture "About the Concept of the 'Dangerous Individual' in 19th-Century Legal Psychiatry," in *Power*, pp. 177–78, and in "L'angoisse de juger" (entretien avec R. Badinter et J. Laplanche), *Le Nouvel Observateur*, no. 655 (May 30–June 6, 1977, pp. 92–96, reprinted in M. Foucault, *Dits et écrits*, III, no. 205, pp. 282–97.

INTERVIEW WITH ANDRÉ BERTEN

May 7, 1981

Michel Foucault has been invited by the Faculty of Law and the School of Criminology at the Catholic University of Louvain to give a series of lectures entitled "Wrong-Doing, Truth-Telling," on the function of avowal in justice. I would like to ask you a few questions to introduce you to our listeners. Of course, you are very well known. You teach at the Collège de France and have published a series of works since the History of Madness— The Birth of the Clinic, The Order of Things, The Order of Discourse, The Archaeology of Knowledge, *and* Discipline and Punish—*and you are in the process of writing a* History of Sexuality. *Most of these works are well known, some more than others, and some have at times incited passionate debate. But I think it would be interesting if you could tell us something about your path through this series of problems and questions. Why did you become interested in the history of psychiatry, the history of medicine, the prison, and now the history of sexuality? Why are you interested in the history of law today? What was fundamentally your itinerary? What has been the guiding thread in your reflection, if it is possible to answer such a question?*

You have asked a difficult question. In the first place, because one can hardly discern the guiding thread until the end of the process—that is to say, at the moment one has or is going to stop writing. And also because, as you know, I consider myself neither a writer nor a prophet. I work, it is true, [. . .] often according to circumstances as they arise, outside requests, or various situations, and I have no intention of imposing strict rules on

235

myself. It seems to me that if there is a certain coherence in what I do, it is perhaps tied more to a situation that we all share, one and other, of which we are all a part, than to any [. . .] fundamental intuition or systematic reflection. It is true, if you will . . . it seems to me that modern philosophy, perhaps since Kant asked the question "What is Enlightenment?"—that is to say, "What is our current situation? What is happening around us? What is our present?"—it seems to me that at that moment, philosophy acquired a new dimension, or it opened itself up to a certain task that it had ignored or that had not previously existed, which is to state who we are, to explain our present, what it is, today. This is very clearly a question that would have been meaningless to Descartes. It is a question that acquired meaning for Kant when he asked what the Enlightenment was. In one sense, it was Hegel's question as well: "What is the now?" It was also Nietzsche's question. I believe that philosophy, among the different functions that philosophy can and should have, also has this one, of asking itself who we are in our present and in our current situation. [I would say that] it is in one sense around all this that I have posed the question—and to that extent, I am a Nietzschean, or Hegelian, or Kantian from that perspective.

So how did I come to pose these kinds of questions? To offer a quick historical account of our intellectual life [. . .] in Western Europe after the war, one could say the following. [On the one hand,] in the 1950s we had at our disposal a perspective, a mode of analysis that was profoundly influenced by phenomenology; I would say that this was, in one sense, the dominant philosophy during that period. I do not mean "dominant" in a pejorative sense: there wasn't any kind of dictatorship or despotism in this mode of thinking. But in Western Europe and France in particular, phenomenology was something like a general style of analysis. It was a style of analysis that claimed as one of its fundamental tasks the analysis of the concrete. And to the extent that the concrete to which phenomenology referred was—how shall I say it?—somewhat academic and scholarly, it was quite certain that from that point of view, we were also somewhat unsatisfied. There were the privileged objects of phenomenological description, which were either lived experiences or the perception of a tree through an office window . . . OK, I am being a little severe, but the field of objects that phenomenology explored was, I would say, a bit predetermined by a philosophical and academic tradition that needed to be opened up somewhat. Secondly, another important and dominant realm of thought was obviously Marxism, which made reference to an entire realm of historical analysis upon which, in a way, it was stuck. While the reading of Marxist texts and the analysis of Marxist concepts was an important task, the historical content or the historical knowledge to which these concepts should have made reference, and for which they were operational, was left somewhat unexamined. In any case, Marxism or a concrete Marxist history was not, in France in any case, very well developed. And then there was a third current that was very distinct in its development in France, which was the history of science with figures such as Bachelard, Canguilhem, et cetera, and Cavaillès before the war. The problem here was that of understanding [whether] there is a historicity of reason, and [whether] one can tell the history of truth.

If you will, I would say that I situated myself at the crossroads of these different currents and problems by asking myself, with regard to phenomenology, the following question: Rather than describe the interior of a lived experience, should one not or can one not analyze a certain number of collective and social experiences? As Binswanger and Kuhn demonstrated, it is important to describe the consciousness of someone who is insane. But, after all, is there not a cultural and social structuring of the experience of madness, and shouldn't it be analyzed? This led me to reconsider a historical problem, which was to know if one can . . . if one wants to describe the social and collective articulation of an experience such as madness, what is the social field and what is the set of institutions and practices that must be analyzed historically, and concerning which a Marxist analysis offers something of a one-size-fits-all approach to these developments? And thirdly, through this—through the analysis of historical, collective, and social experiences tied to a specific historical context—how is it possible to write the history of knowledge [*d'un savoir*], the history of the emergence of knowledge [*d'une connaissance*]; and how can new objects emerge in the domain of knowledge [*de la connaissance*], and how can they present themselves as knowable objects?

If you will, in concrete terms, I came to the following: Is there or is there not an experience of madness that is characteristic of a given society or a type of society such as ours? How could this experience of madness be constituted, how could it emerge? And, through this experience of madness, how could madness be constituted as an object of knowledge for a medical discipline that presented itself as a mental health discipline? Which means, roughly: Through what historical transformations or what institutional modifications could an experience of madness be constituted in which there was both the subjective pole of the experience of madness and the objective pole of mental illness?

Such was, if not the itinerary, at least the point of departure. And to return to the question you asked, "Why did you choose those objects?" I would say that it seemed to me . . . and this is perhaps a fourth current, the fourth reference point in my trajectory or my inching forward—which included, if you will, more literary texts that were less integrated into the philosophical tradition (I am thinking of writers like Blanchot, Artaud, and Bataille, who, I think, were extremely important for people of my generation)—was the question of limit experiences. Those forms of experience that, instead of being considered central and positively valorized in a society, were considered limit experiences, those borderline experiences that put into question the very things that were considered ordinarily acceptable. So in one sense, to turn the history of madness into an interrogation of our system of reason . . .

As an experience . . . madness as a limit experience . . .

That's right. For example, what is the relationship between medical thought, knowledge of illness and life—what is this with regard to the experience of death? And how was the problem of death integrated into this knowledge? Or how was this knowledge indexed at this moment, at the absolute point of death? The same thing stands for crime in relationship to law. Instead of interrogating the law itself and how it could be founded, take crime as the point of rupture with regard to the system, and then take this point of view to ask: What is the law then? Take the prison as something that will clarify for us what the penal system is, rather than investigating the penal system from within, to know how it was established, how it was founded and justified, in order to deduce from that what the prison is.

You have presented the contemporaneity of philosophy (since Kant) as posing a question that, I think, concerns us all and that allows for man to question his situation in history, society, and the world. It seems to me that in everything you have written from the History of Madness *up to the* History of Sexuality, *there is a perception of this reality, or at least there is a perception of an element of this reality that seems to interest you in particular and that concerns what we might call techniques of confinement, surveillance, and control—in short, the manner in which individuals in our society have increasingly been controlled. Do you think that this is an element that has for some time already, since the classical period, been essential for understanding modernity?*

Yes, that's true. If you will, this was not a problem that I asked myself from the beginning. It was little by little, by studying a certain number of things, like psychiatry, medicine, and the penal system that all of these mechanisms—confinement, exclusion, surveillance, individual control—became very interesting and very important to me. I would say that perhaps I asked those questions in a rather brusque way at one point, at the moment when I realized their importance. I believe that one must separate out the issues and the kinds of problems that one can pose with regard to such things. It seems to me that in most analyses—either analyses of a properly philosophical type or a more political or Marxist analysis—the question of power had been relatively marginalized . . .

Simplified . . .

Or, in any case, simplified. It was either a question of knowing what juridical foundations could legitimize political power, or it was a question of defining power as a simple function of the conservation or renewal of relations of production. It was the philosophical question of the foundation or the historical analysis of the superstructure. This struck me as insufficient for a certain number of reasons. First of all, because I think—and a certain number of things in the concrete domains that I tried to analyze show this—that power relations are implanted far more deeply than on the simple level of the superstructure. Second, the question of the foundation of power is important, but—I'm sorry—power does not function on the basis of its foundation. There are powers that lack foundation and that function very well, and powers that seek a foundation, indeed find a foundation, and then ultimately fail to function. So, if you will, the problem I asked myself was: Can't we study the way in which power actually functions?

When I say "power," it is absolutely not a question of finding an authority or some sort of force that is there, hidden or visible—whichever—and that noxiously radiates out through the social body or that fatally extends its network. It is not a question of power—or something like "power"—throwing out a vast net that slowly tightens, strangling society and individuals. It is not this at all. Power *is* relations. Power is not a thing. It is a relationship between two individuals, and a relationship that allows one individual to conduct the conduct of another or to determine the conduct of another—to determine their conduct voluntarily according to a number of objectives that are his own. In other words, when one examines what power is, one sees that it is the exercise of something one could call government, in the broadest sense of the term. Society can be governed, a group can be governed, a community can be governed, a family can be governed, someone can be governed. And when I say "govern someone," it is simply in the sense of determining their conduct on the basis of strategies, using a certain number of tactics. So, if you will, it is governmentality in the broadest sense, understood as the set of relations of power and techniques that allow these power relations to be exercised—this is what I tried to study. How have we governed the mad? How did we pose the problem of governing the sick? And once again, I put the word "government" in quotation marks, giving it at once a vast and rich meaning—how did we govern the sick; what was done with them; what status did we give them; where did we put them, in what system of treatment, of surveillance as well, of caretaking, of philanthropy; in what economic field was care brought to the sick . . . I think that all of this should be explored.

It is clear that this governmentality became increasingly strict, from a certain point of view, as time went on. In a political system like the one that existed in the Middle Ages, power understood as the government of some by others was relatively slack: the problem was to extract the fiscal resources that were necessary, useful, or desired. How people conducted themselves in their daily lives was not very important for the exercise of political power, though it was no doubt important for the ecclesiastic pastorate. And then a new moment came for political power when it was suddenly extremely important—and today, for example, to take a very simple example, types of individual consumption have become something that is economically and also politically important. And it is true that the number of objects that become objects of a governmentality that is deliberately thought through within even liberal political frameworks has increased considerably. But I also don't think that this governmentality must necessarily take the form of confinement, surveillance, and control. Through a whole series of interventions, which are often very subtle, we are able, in effect, to conduct the conduct of others, or to conduct oneself, in such a way that the conduct of others does not have the harmful effects that we fear. It is this vast field of governmentality that I wanted to study.

To study this object, or these different objects, you have employed a historical methodology. But what appears clearly today—and moreover, what is an essential part of the innovation in your analysis, not so much from the point of view of the content, but from the point of view of method—is that you have displaced the historical method to some extent. That is to say, it is no longer a history of science, an epistemology, or a history of ideologies; it is not even a history of institutions. One has the impression that it is all of these at once, but that in order to think about the work of psychiatry, for example, or what criminologists do today (since you were invited by criminologists), or think about institutions such as prisons or asylums, you were forced to transform profoundly the way in which we conceive of history. For example, does the opposition between knowledge and science that appears in your work—primarily in a number of methodological writings—seem very important to you from the point of view of the historical genre that you propose?

I do indeed think that the type of history that I do bears a certain number of marks or handicaps, as you wish. To begin with, what I would say is that, once again, the question that serves as my point of departure is: What are we, and what are we *today*? What is this moment that is ours? So, if you will, it is a history that takes the present as its point of departure. Second, by posing concrete problems, I necessarily start from—and what seems interesting to me is to take or to choose—areas that seem particularly fragile or sensitive in our present situation. That is to say, I can hardly conceive of a history that would be strictly speculative, if you will, and whose field was not motivated by what is happening at present. What interests me is not to follow what is happening and to follow the current fashion, as we say—for example, once one has written ten books on death, and very good ones at that, one is not going to write an eleventh book on the same subject under the pretense that it is *the* current question. It is a question . . . the game is to try to detect, among those things that we haven't yet spoken about, what are those things that currently introduce, show, and give more or less diffuse indications of the fragility of our system of thought, our mode of reflection, or our practice.

In the period around 1955, when I was working in psychiatric hospitals, there was a kind of latent crisis, if you will—something that we felt was falling apart. It had not been spoken about very much, and yet it was being lived rather intensely. The most obvious proof that this was being lived was that right next to us in England, without ever having any relationship with one another, people like Laing and Cooper were confronting similar problems. So it is a history that is constantly referring to a present situation. It is the same for the problem of medicine. It is true that the question of medical power—or in any case, of the institutional field within which medical knowledge functioned—was a question that began to be posed, and widely so, in the 1960s, but didn't enter the public domain until 1968. It is thus a history of the present as it is taking form.

Yes, but with regard to the present, the way you develop history seems very original. It seems to me fundamentally that history, for you, is structured by the very object you are analyzing. It is because of these moments you perceive as fragile, as key problems in our society, that you are pushed to reconsider their history in order to clarify them, of course, but also to rewrite history in a specific way . . .

As far as the objectives that I set when I write this history, often people have read what I have done as a kind of complicated and slightly obsessive analysis that leads to the kind of results where one ultimately says, "My God, we are so imprisoned in this system we live in, look at how tightly we are bound and how difficult it is to undo these knots that history has tied around us!" When in fact I am doing precisely the contrary! For when I tried to study something like madness or the prison . . . take, if you will, the example of the prison. When we were discussing with others, even just a few years ago—let's say, toward the beginning of the 1970s—the reform of the penal system, I was struck by something. It was that, for example, we asked, of course, the theoretical question of the right to punish. Of course, we also posed the question of knowing how the penitentiary system should be arranged. But the basic assumption, if you will, that depriving people of liberty was fundamentally the most simple, logical, and reasonable, the most equitable way to punish someone because he had committed a crime—this was not generally questioned. And what I wanted to do was show how this equation of punishment with the deprivation of liberty—which was so clear and simple for us—was in reality something that was fairly recent. Something that was recent: it was an invention, a technical invention, whose origins were distant, but which was truly integrated into the penal system and made part of penal rationality from the end of the eighteenth century onward. And I tried to examine the reasons why the prison had thus become a kind of obvious element of our penal system.

It was a question, then, of making things more fragile through this type of historical analysis, or rather showing at once why and how those things could be constituted in this way, but at the same time showing that they were constituted through a precise history. It is necessary to show at once the logic of things—or if you will, the logic of the strategies within which things were produced—and, at the same time, to show that that they were only strategies and that, as a result, by changing a certain number of things, by changing strategy, by looking at things differently, what appeared evident is no longer so. Our relationship to madness is a relationship that has been historically constructed; and if it is historically constituted, it can be politically destroyed. I say "politically," giving the word "political" a very large meaning. In any case, there are possibilities for action, because it is through a certain number of actions and reactions—through a certain number of struggles, of conflicts, to respond to a certain number of problems—that we chose those particular solutions. I wanted to reintegrate things that seemed self-evident in our practices into the very historicity of those practices. As a result, I sought to strip them from their self-evident status in order to give them the mobility that they once had and that they must still have in the field of our practices.

In your current lectures you use the term "veridiction," which refers to a "truth-telling" and touches on a problem of truth. In your method and everything that you have just said concerning at once your interest in the present and the manner in which you envisage history, as well as in one sense the very constitution of the present, you call into question what one might think of as the foundations of such and such a practice. You have said to us with regard to power that fundamentally power does not function from its foundation—but there are indeed always justifications or philosophical reflections that seek to ground power. Your historical method, which is a method that calls for a kind of archaeology or genealogy—depending perhaps on the object or the development of your thought—seeks to show that there is not a foundation for practices of power. Would you agree with the statement that from a philosophical point of view and in your general development, what you are aiming for is also to deconstruct any enterprise that would provide a foundation to power?

But I think that the activity of providing a foundation to power, the activity that consists of interrogating [. . .] that which grounds the power I exercise or [. . .] that grounds the power that is exerted on me, I think that is an important question. It is essential. I would say it is the fundamental question. But the foundation that is given in response to this question has a very relative place within the historical field of which it is a part. That is, one does not find the foundation, but it is very important that in a culture like ours, the question is to know whether one can find it elsewhere or not; in other cultures, on that point I have no idea. But it is very important that for us, not only for centuries but even millennia, a certain number of things, and the exercise of political power in particular, questioned itself or was questioned by those who asked: "But on what are you founded? What makes you legitimate?" There is here a work of critique . . .

What you consider important is precisely the critical aspect of this question that comes back time and again, and that interrogates the truth . . .

That's it, that comes back constantly. It has been two thousand years that we have asked the question of the foundation of political power; and when I say two millennia, I actually mean two and a half. It is this questioning that is fundamental.

Fundamentally, the type of history that you have pursued is indeed an analysis, you said, of strategies, but also an analysis of the way in which a certain number of practices have searched for their own foundation.

Absolutely. Absolutely. I would say that it is the history of—I am going to use a barbaric word, but words are only barbaric when they do not say exactly what they mean, to such an extent that many familiar words are barbaric because they say a lot of things at the same time and say nothing at all, whereas, on the other hand, certain technical words that are bizarrely constructed are not barbaric if they express rather clearly what they mean. I would say that I pursue a history of problematizations: that is to say, a history of the way things pose a problem. How and why and according to what particular mode did madness become a problem in the modern world? And why did it become an important problem? Such an important problem that a certain number of things, for example psychoanalysis—which, God knows, has been diffused throughout our culture—

grew out of a problem that was completely internal to the relationship one could have with madness. It is the history of these problems. According to what new mode did sickness—which obviously had always been seen as problematic, but which, it seems to me, was subject to a new mode of problematizing illness after the eighteenth and the nineteenth centuries . . .

So indeed, it is not the history of theories, ideologies, or even the history of mentalities that interests me. It is the history of problems. If you will, the genealogy of problems interests me: why a given problem and why such and such a problem, why did such a mode of problematization appear at a certain moment in a certain domain. For example, with regard to sexuality, it took me a long time to begin to see how one could respond to this. What was the new problem? You see, with regard to sexuality, it is not only a question of knowing or repeating indefinitely the question: Let's see, was it Christianity, was it the bourgeoisie, or was it industrialization that led to a repression of sexuality? The repression of sexuality is only interesting to the extent that it makes a certain number of people suffer, still today. It's also interesting because it has always taken diverse forms but has always existed. What I think is important to bring forward is how and why did this relationship to sexuality or this relationship to our sexual behaviors pose a problem, and under what forms did they pose a problem. For they always posed a problem, but it is certain that they did not pose a problem in the same way for the Greeks of the fourth century BC, the Christians of the third and fourth centuries, in the sixteenth and seventeenth century, and now. It is this history of problematizations: [. . .] how, within human practices, there is a moment when, in one sense, what is obvious becomes muddied, the lights go out, evening comes, and people begin to perceive that they are acting blindly and that, as a result, a new light is necessary. A new light is necessary, a new lighting, and new rules of behavior. And here a new object appears: an object that appears as a problem. Voilà.

I would like to pose one last question. You have been invited by the Faculty of Law and you seem to be particularly interested now in law and juridical phenomena. Could you explain briefly where this interest in law comes from and what you hope to draw from it?

Listen, I think that I have always been interested in law. As a layman; I am not a specialist of the law, nor am I a jurist. But whether it be on questions of madness, crime, or the prison, I have encountered the problem of law, the problem of the law. And the question that I always asked was that of knowing how the technologies of government—how these relationships of power, understood in the sense that I discussed earlier—how all of this could take form within a society that claimed to function according to law and that, at least in part, functioned according to law? I would like to study the connections, the relationships of cause and effect, as well as the conflicts, the oppositions, and the irreducibilities between the functioning of law and this technology of power. And it seems to me that questioning juridical institutions, interrogating the discourses and the practice of law from the perspective of technologies of power, is of particular interest— not at all in the sense that it could entirely transform the history and the theory of law, but it seems to me that this could simply throw a certain light on relatively important aspects of judicial practice and theory. Thus, it seems to me that investigating the modern penal system through practices of punishment and correction, through the whole series of technologies used to model or modify, et cetera, the individual criminal, probably brings a certain number of things forward. Thus, if you will, I encounter law constantly without making it a particular object of investigation. And God willing, after madness, illness, crime, sexuality, the last thing I would like to study would be the problem of war and the institution of war within what one might term the military dimension of society. And there again I will surely encounter the problem of law, both in the form of the law of people and international law, et cetera, as well as the problem of military justice and, finally, what makes it possible for a nation to ask someone to die for it.

Well, we all hope that God will be willing . . .

I don't wish it upon him.

. . . so that we may be able to continue to read your histories, these multiple histories that have been so enriching for us. I thank you.

INTERVIEW WITH CHRISTIAN
PANIER AND PIERRE WATTÉ

May 14, 1981

Are there certain things that an intellectual of the left does, in his capacity as actor in a social movement, that only he can do?

I confess that I do not subscribe to the idea of the intellectual intervening or assuming the role of someone who gives lessons or advice regarding matters of political choice—it doesn't sit well with me. I think people are grown-up enough to choose for themselves who they vote for. To say: "I am an intellectual and I vote for Mr. So-and-so, and therefore you should vote for Mr. So-and-so," strikes me as a rather astonishing attitude, a kind of arrogance of the intellectual. On the other hand, if for any number of reasons an intellectual thinks that his work, his analysis, his reflections, his way of acting or thinking about things can shed light on a particular situation, social domain, or conjunction of circumstances, and that he can bring to bear his theoretical and practical contributions on them, then in that case one can draw political consequences by taking, for example, the problem of penal law or of justice . . . I think that if he wants to, the intellectual can contribute important elements to the perception and critique of things, from which certain political choices would then naturally follow, if people are so inclined.

Even if it is not necessarily a question of being the bard for a political choice or being a flag bearer, and even if the specific contribution of the intellectual allows people, perhaps, to make a more informed political choice, there are still certain moments and certain problems where you have been directly or are actively involved. What comes, then, of the link between the function of the intellectual that you have just defined and this more concrete engagement, more directly involved in current affairs?

When I was a student, I was struck by the fact that during that period we were in a profoundly Marxist atmosphere where the problem of the link between theory and practice was absolutely at the center of all theoretical discussions.

It seems to me that there was perhaps an easier way, or I would say a more immediately practical way, of posing the question of the relationship between theory and practice correctly, and that was to carry it out directly in one's own practice. In this sense, I could say that I have always insisted that my books be, in one sense, fragments of an autobiography. My books have always been my personal problems with madness, the prison, and sexuality.

Second, I have always insisted that there take place within me and for me a kind of back and forth, an interference, an interconnection between practices and the theoretical or historical work I was doing. It seemed to me that I was all the more free to reach deeper and farther into history because I also tied the questions I was asking to practice, in an immediate and contemporary way. It was because I spent a certain time in psychiatric hospitals that I wrote *The Birth of the Clinic*. With regard to prisons, I began to do a certain number of things, and then I wrote *Discipline and Punish*.

I also took a third precaution: during the period when I pursued these theoretical and historical analyses exclusively in relation to the questions that I had specifically asked myself, I always insisted that this theoretical work not dictate rules with regard to contemporary practice, and that it pose questions. Take the book on madness, for example: its description and analysis end in the years 1814 to 1815. Thus, the book did not appear to be a critique of contemporary psychiatric institutions, but I knew their functioning well enough that I could question their history. It seems to me that the history I wrote was sufficiently detailed for it to pose questions for those who currently live in the institution.

These questions are often felt to be attacks by those concerned. How useful are they in that case?

It is not my fault—or perhaps it is my fault at some level, in which case I am happy to have committed it—if psychiatrists felt or truly experienced the book as an assault on them. On many occasions in speaking of my book, I met psychiatrists who were so tense and nervous that they called it—this was in some sense avenging for me, perhaps too avenging—suggestively, "In Praise of Folly." When they said "In Praise of Folly," I am not at all suggesting that they took me for Erasmus; there would be no reason to do so. In reality, they took it as a kind of choice in favor of the mad and against them, which was absolutely not the case.

In the same way, the book on prisons stops in 1840 and I have often been told: "This book constitutes such an indictment of the penitentiary system that we don't know what to do once we have read it." To tell the truth, it is not an indictment. My question simply consists in saying to psychiatrists and to the personnel of the penitentiary: Are you capable of enduring your own history? Given that history and what it reveals for the system of rationality, the type of proof, the postulates, et cetera, the ball is now in your court." And what I would like would be for them to tell me, "Come work with us," instead of hearing people say, as they sometimes do, "You are keeping us from our work." No, I am not keeping you from your work. I am asking you a certain number of questions. So let's try now to work together to elaborate new modes of critique, new modes of questioning, to attempt something else. This is my relationship to theory and practice.

Now, there is the other side of the question regarding the role of the intellectual. When you do this work, you initiate an analysis that has not been done. That is to say, you put in question the political power within a society in which you show that its functioning does not in fact have all the legitimacy that it claims. If I were to present the way I understand you somewhat schematically, it seems to me that in your analysis of madness, as in your analysis of the prison or of power in the first volume of the History of Sexuality, *you lay the groundwork for restituting the place of the political as a means and not as an end. I have in mind a text by the Swedish writer Myrdal, who said: "If a Third World War were to break out, it would be the fault of intellectuals who were the purveyors of a commonly held, false clear conscience." In the context of such a statement, do you perceive your work as a contribution to a demystification of power?*

I am not familiar with that statement by Myrdal, which I find at once very beautiful and very worrisome. It is very beautiful because, indeed,

I think that a commonly held clear conscience wreaks havoc in the order of politics, as it does within the moral order. So I subscribe to this statement. What worries me, though, is the way he somewhat lightly, it seems to me, makes intellectuals responsible for this. I would say: What is the intellectual, if not the one who works to prevent others from having such a clear conscience? So all I can say is that perhaps they didn't do their job well enough. I wouldn't want Myrdal's statement to be understood in the following terms: "As intellectuals and because they are intellectuals, they contribute to a commonly held clear conscience."

It was a denunciation.

Well if that is what he meant, then I agree completely. This is precisely what I have tried to do on specific points. I pursued my studies between 1948 and 1952 to 1955; this was a period when phenomenology was still very dominant within European culture. The theme of phenomenology was, of course, to reexamine what was perceived as evident. While I distanced myself from phenomenology, if possible, I willingly recognize — and naturally one recognizes this with age — that ultimately one never escapes the fundamental question posed by the very things that make our youth. Not only have I not escaped, I have incessantly asked the question: Should what is obvious in fact be so obvious? Should we not look beneath what appears so evident, even that which is the most obvious? This is what it means to fight against one's familiarities, not just to show how much of a foreigner you are in your own land, but to show to what extent your country is foreign to you and to what extent everything that surrounds you and appears to be part of an acceptable landscape is, in fact, the result of a whole series of struggles, conflicts, dominations, postulates, et cetera.

Perhaps we might turn now to more specific questions on power and the subjectivity-society relationship. As for power, my question is the following, and it remains somewhat in the direction of what Myrdal was saying. Should one not only distinguish between power and political power, but also, within the political form of power — that is, within the steady concentration of political power in the state — should one not distinguish between the base and the top? Aren't there different forces at play at these two levels? Freud said that states were tormented by the instinct for death. When we look at what is happening today on the international scene, we do indeed see that the highest reaches of

state power are a game of life and death, even for a state as small as the Vatican.
Wouldn't this provide some kind of explanation that would be complementary
to your study of germinations? Aren't there different phenomena there?

I think that your question is a very good one and is very important. When
I began to develop, more explicitly, an interest in power, it was not at all
to make power into something like a substance or a fluid that was more or
less evil and spread through the social body, with the intention of knowing
whether it came from above or below. I simply wanted to propose a general
question, which was: What are power relations? Power is essentially relations; that is to say, what brings individuals, human beings, into relation
with one another, not only in the form of the communication of meaning,
not only in the form of desire, but also in a specific form that allows them
to act on one another—if you will, in the broadest sense of the term, to
"govern" each other. Parents govern their children, a mistress governs her
lover, a professor governs, et cetera. We govern each other in a conversation, through a whole series of tactics. I think that this field of relations
is very important, and this is what I tried to pose as a problem. How does
this happen, through what instruments, and, since I am in one sense a historian of ideas and science, of what effect are these relations of power in
the order of knowledge? That is our problem.

I once used the formula "Power comes from the bottom." I immediately
explained it but, of course, as always in cases like this, the explanation was
cut off. It became: "Power is a horrible malady. You must not think that it
takes you by the head when, in fact, it comes up through the bottom of
your feet." Obviously, that was not what I meant. I have already explained
myself elsewhere, but let me return to this explanation. Indeed, if one
poses the question of power in terms of relations of power, if one readily
admits that there are relations of "governmentality" between individuals,
a crowd, a complex network of relations, then the broad forms of power
in the strictest sense—political power, ideological power, et cetera—are
necessarily in these types of relation; that is to say, in relations of government, of conduction that can be established between men. And if there is
not a certain type of relations like these, then there cannot be other types
of overarching political structures.

Broadly speaking, democracy, if we view it as a political form, can only
exist to the extent that there are, at the level of individuals, families, and
everyday life, if you will, governmental relations—a certain type of rela-

tions of power that are produced. This is why democracy cannot take just anywhere. The same thing is true of fascism. The fathers of German families were not fascist in 1930, but for fascism to take, among many other conditions—I am not saying these were the only conditions—one had to pay attention to relations between individuals, to how families were constituted, to how teaching was done; there had to be a certain number of these conditions. Having said this, I do not in any way deny the heterogeneity of what one might have called these different institutions of government. I mean that they simply cannot be located in the apparatus of the state or be derived entirely from the state. The question is much larger.*

* The recording is interrupted at this point. The rest of the interview, as a result, cannot be published.

INTERVIEW WITH JEAN FRANÇOIS AND JOHN DE WIT

May 22, 1981

You are currently giving a series of lectures on avowal at the Catholic University of Louvain in Belgium. What is of interest to you in this problematic, and what place would you give it more generally within your work?

Broadly speaking, I have consistently pursued the problem of knowing how truth comes to things and how it comes about that a certain number of areas are slowly integrated into the problematic and search for truth.

I tried to pose this question with regard to the individual human being and, in particular, to human conduct. I also tried to pose it with regard to madness, for example. Social and religious reactions to madness—regulated reactions—had been established for a long time. But that the behavior of someone who was considered mad, that his thoughts, desires, and the reasons for his behavior could be an object of study in the search for truth, and that a domain of medical knowledge could be constituted in relation to it—this has had a relatively recent and short history. We must know how the question of madness became a question that was integrated into general problems of knowledge. How did the insane enter into the field of the search for truth? This is a problem. I also tried to pose this question with regard to language, work, and natural history. This is what I was pursuing in *The Order of Things*. I also tried to pose the question around the issue of crime. Traditionally, we've always opposed to crime a certain number of reactions that were institutionally regulated. But from a certain point on, this practice was coupled with an interrogation that was not simply a legal interrogation on legitimate punishment, but a question of truth: What is a criminal? Similarly, with regard to sexuality, my problem was not that of knowing what series of forms were imposed in order to regulate sexual behavior, but how it was that sexual behavior became, at a given moment, not only the focus of practical preoccupations but also a theoretical preoccupation. This sends us back to a question that is older than the prison and madness. The question of the truth of madness was posed between the seventeenth and the nineteenth centuries. For sexuality, one must go back to the Christianity of the first centuries. It is during this period that we encounter an important practice in our culture, one that I think was decisive in the history of sexuality: avowal. The institutional practice through which the question of truth formed with regard to madness was confinement or hospitalization—the question of the history of madness lay in the relationship between exclusion and truth. In the case of criminality, the problem was the institution of the prison in that it was not only an exclusion but also a corrective procedure. And yet it was through the project of reform, or amending the detainee, that the question of truth was posed. In the case of sexuality, it was through the practice of confession that the question of truth was posed. Exclusion-madness-truth, correction-prison-truth, sexual behavior-avowal-truth. These form three series.

I have the impression that in Discipline and Punish *the question of knowing the truth of the criminal was not terribly present, while the question of the truth of the insane was more thematized in* History of Madness.

It is true that on the prison, or rather on the construction of the question of truth with regard to criminality, I should have placed more emphasis on the second half of the nineteenth century. But I realized that the practice of imprisonment was historically rather poorly known, and that often the institution of the prison was confused with the practice of punitive imprisonment. The prison existed in the Middle Ages and in antiquity, of course. My problem was to bring forth the truth of the prison, to see within which system of rationality, which program of governing individuals and delinquents in particular, the prison was thought to be an essential means. But in fact, I have in mind a project on criminal psychiatry that would be at the crossroads of the history of madness and the history of punitive imprisonment and would show how the question of the truth of the criminal was posed. My work on avowal also contributes to making progress on this question.

Is the seminar we are organizing with you at the School of Criminology that focuses on social defense important for this attempt to combine the fields of madness and crime?

Yes, certainly. With the doctrine of social defense, we thought we found what we were seeking for decades: a way of making a legal system and a system of truth function simultaneously. This is one of the problems that touches upon everything I have tried to do. How does a society such as ours find itself perpetually confronted with a challenge that it consistently takes up, but that it is unable to overcome — that is, the challenge of making a system of law and a system of truth work together? This is true with regard to madness, crime, and sexuality. One cannot get outside of it.

Do you intend to publish a work on avowal? What place does it hold within this set of questions?

Currently, I hesitate to publish on this question because, in one sense, the study of avowal is purely instrumental for something else. I first encountered this question within the history of psychiatry for a period that followed the one I studied in my book. It was after 1830 that the question of avowal appeared in psychiatry; I recounted it through the case of Leuret. It was then that we began to listen to the discourse of the madman by asking him: "What are you saying? What do you mean? And who are you — you who want to say what you say?" The question of avowal was equally important for the functioning of modern penal law. The question appeared very clearly in the years 1830 through 1850, when there was a shift from avowal, which was an avowal of an offense, to a supplementary demand: "Tell me what you did, but above all, tell me who you are." The history of Pierre Rivière was, in this context, extremely significant. In that case there was a crime that no one understood, and the examining judge in 1836 had the idea of saying: "Fine, it is obvious that you killed your mother, your sister, and your brother, but I cannot understand why you killed them. Write it down." Here Pierre Rivière obeyed the request for an avowal, but in a way that was so enigmatic that the judge did not know what to do with it. And then, one encounters the question of avowal even more in the case of sexuality. Avowal is an instrumental element that I come across constantly. I hesitate between writing the history of avowal in itself as a kind of technique with its different aspects, and only treating it in the context of studies of different domains where it is put into play, that is to say, with regard to sexuality or criminal psychiatry.

But isn't the question of avowal fundamental to the question of the truth of the subject?

Absolutely. This is what makes me wonder if I should not have written the history of avowal in itself. Here, indeed, one finds something that is rather fundamental in terms of how we are tied to what I call the obligations of truth. By "obligations of truth" I mean two things. First, there is the obligation to believe, admit, or postulate, whether it be in the order of religious faith or in the order of accepting scientific knowledge; and second, the obligation to know the truth of ourselves, as well as to tell, manifest, and authenticate it. The problem is that of knowing if this connection to the truth of who we are has a form that is proper to Western Christianity. This question does not simply touch upon the history of psychiatry or the history of sexuality. It touches upon the history of truth and the history of subjectivity in the West. I am wondering if I shouldn't write a history of subjectivity-truth.

Nonetheless, I think that to do it effectively, it is necessary to show these relationships at work in each domain. Indeed, I believe that there is thinking not only where thought thinks about itself, in the form of philosophy or reflection on the self. There is dense and important thinking that serves as a support and a condition of existence, as well as a condition for the functioning of a whole series of practices. In a psychiatric institution there is thought that must be investigated. This is why I am not interested in a lot of easy denunciations of medical, oppressive, ideological discourse. What seems interesting to me is to pull out the profound and serious thought that engages our historical destiny in the institutions that nonetheless give the impression of merely speaking the language of barbarism, archaism, and institutional idiocy. There is thought in a prison, no matter how stupid the prison is.

Where are you in the completion of your project on the history of sexuality? You had announced that it would consist of six volumes . . .

I realized that, like many, I had incorrectly subscribed to the idea that the history of sexuality and the modern repression of sexuality had begun around the seventeenth and eighteenth centuries with the great campaign on the sexuality of children. The famous texts of doctors of the eighteenth and nineteenth centuries on child masturbation, that are currently portrayed as absolutely typical of bourgeois morality, are in some cases translated directly from Greek medical texts. You find, for example, in the texts of the first centuries a description of the effects of exhaustion due to the excesses of sexuality, and a warning against the social dangers of this exhaustion for the entire human race. When we see that these texts had an existence—more or less intense, or more or less discreet—between the first and eighteenth centuries, and that they were translated in the eighteenth century, one can no longer pursue an analysis in terms of the modern repression of sexuality, bourgeois mentality, or industrial necessity. This repression appeared in an entirely different context. It is already visible in ancient texts. It is necessary, then, contrary to what I thought, to go back far deeper. And indeed, I found a mass of Christian and even older texts concerning masturbation, imagination, fantasizing, et cetera.

Did this observation modify your analysis of the creation of the apparatus of sexuality?

Partly yes, partly no. Of course, it is more and more clear that one cannot use the idea of a mechanics of repression as a key for understanding the history of the relationship between sexuality and truth. I have already said this, but not enough, no doubt. When I say that we must throw off the schema of repression, this does not mean, as some have suggested, that I am claiming that sexuality is not repressed. Repression seems to me to be the global effect. In each period there is a profile of repression, a repressive schema, a line of repression. This is not the very principle of the transformation. It would be dangerous to see the very principle here. For example, you have historians who, haunted by the idea of a repressive schema—that is, of the code, the forbidden—still say that homosexuals were burned in the eighteenth century. It is indeed in the legal codes, but how many were there in all of Europe in the eighteenth century? There weren't even ten, I think. On the other hand, you see homosexuals arrested by the dozens, hundreds, each year in Paris in the Luxembourg Gardens or the Palais Royal. Repression? It is not law, in any case, that allows one to understand the system of arrests. They are arrested generally for twenty-four hours. What does this mean? What is happening here, in fact? A new kind of relationship is being established between homosexuality and political power, at the levels of police and administrative power.

Was the articulation you presented between the creation of the subject and the production of an apparatus of sexuality modified by your discovery of the ancient texts?

We need to throw out the schema of repression and substitute some other explanatory principle. When I was consulting the ancient texts that I'll tell you about, my attention was increasingly drawn to what I call the techniques or the technologies of the self. It seems to me that in society, outside of the techniques of the production of objects and outside the procedures of communication with others, there are also procedures of formation and transformation of the self. At some point, sexuality became a very important issue in society and the techniques of the self were organized around it. It became the privileged object of the self.

The problem that haunted ancient moral texts was anger, not sexual behavior. One asked how to avoid reacting violently toward another. The problem was how to maintain self-mastery. As for sexual behavior, of course a certain number of rules were given, but this was obviously not what was most important: one senses very clearly that the general ethical problem did not turn around the issue of sexuality. The problem of anger shifted, and this was due in large part to the impact of Christianity, and monasticism in particular. One sees two problems appear that were tied to one another: the problem of gluttony and the problem of sexuality—how can one not eat too much, and how can one control that thing that is not even, in the monk's case, a sexual relationship with another, but something that is sexual desire, sexual phantasmagoria, sexuality as a relationship of the self to the self, with such manifestations as imagination, reverie, masturbation, et cetera. Around these techniques of the self, which were manifestly related to monasticism, one sees sexuality take precedence over the problem of anger, which was a social problem—it was a problem that was typical of a society in which jousting with others, competition with others within social space was very important.

By tracing the history of the techniques of the self, one has a much clearer understanding of the valorization of sexuality and the mix of interest, anxiety, and preoccupation that sexual behavior elicited. The problem is to understand why, after the seventeenth and the eighteenth centuries especially, these techniques of the self that concerned sexuality played a role outside of monasticism. To better understand the state of the modern apparatus of sexuality, they must be tied into the history of the technologies of the self. The schema of repression is unsatisfactory; a different key is necessary. I had already sketched all of this in my first book on the history of sexuality, but no doubt it was too negative. The interdiction of masturbation, for example, was certainly the interdiction that was most often repeated, the most unrelenting in the modern education of children. However, forbidding masturbation did not suppress it. One might even imagine that it was never so important or so desirable as it has become since children have lived in a culture of restriction, curiosity, and solicitation. One cannot understand such a profound relationship to masturbation as a fundamental question within sexuality by saying that it was forbidden. I think that it is tied to a technology of the self.

It seems to me that previously you linked the creation of the apparatus of sexuality, disciplinary technologies, and different substances like the delinquent, the homosexual, et cetera. Now you seem more inclined to associate the creation of the apparatus of sexuality and such substances (objects and labels) with techniques of the self. Is this how it developed, in your view?

I put a certain emphasis on discipline because I realized while studying the prisons that there was what I call a technique of government of individuals, a means of controlling their conduct, and that this mode of governing individuals constituted a coherent technique whose form we find, with some variation, in prisons, schools, workshops, et cetera. It is obvious that this was not the only technique for governing individuals, and that currently, for example, the construction of an insurance-bound horizon of existence and security is a situation in which the [conduct]* of individuals is insured, but along very different lines from those of the disciplines.

* The original transcript reads *"conduction."*

Technologies of the self are also different, or at least partially, from disciplines. Controlling sexual behavior does not at all have the disciplinary form that one can find, for example, in schools. There is something else going on here.

Is it still a question of a kind of production of sexual labels through the disciplinary mode?

This is a long story. The Greeks and the Romans did not have a notion like sexuality. Nor did the Christians. You might argue that just because they did not have the notion does not mean that the reality was not organized along these lines. Nonetheless, I think the ideational field is very important. [. . .]* For the Greeks and the Latins, sexual acts were designated by a word: it was *aphrodisia*. *Aphrodisia* were sexual acts, though it is difficult to determine whether or not it was necessarily a question of relations between two individuals, penetration. In any case, it did consist of sexual activities, but nothing like a sexuality that was constantly present in the individual, with its bonds and its demands. With the Christians there was something else: there was flesh and concupiscence, which indicated the presence of a permanent force [*puissance*] within the individual. But flesh was not exactly sexuality.

Rather than studying what I imprudently planned to study in my first book, I would like to define what these different experiences are—*aphrodisia* for the Greeks, flesh for Christians, and sexuality for modern man.

Might one argue, then, that for you the creation of the subject, the sexuated individual, emerged with the appearance of sexuality and the creation of the apparatus of sexuality?

Yes, that's exactly right. In Greek culture, where *aphrodisia* existed, the idea that there was someone that was homosexual in substance and identity absolutely did not exist. There were people who performed decent *aphrodisia*, in line with common practice, and others who performed *aphrodisia*

---

* A sentence was lost in the original transcription. Only the beginning and the end of the sentence are legible: "When we analyze the manner in which things [*two unreadable words*], we also see that they did not have an experience of sexuality."

that were not good; but the idea of identifying someone according to their type of sexuality was inconceivable. And effectively, once there was what I call the apparatus of sexuality—that is, a set of practices, institutions, and knowledges that constituted sexuality as a coherent domain, and which turned sexuality into that absolutely fundamental dimension of the individual—it was at that point that the question "Who are you sexually?" became indispensable.

On this point I have not always made myself well understood by certain movements for sexual liberation in France. In my opinion, as important as it may be, tactically speaking, to say at a given moment, "I am a homosexual," over the long run, in a wider strategy, the question of knowing who we are sexually should no longer be posed. It is not then a question of affirming one's sexual identity, but of refusing to allow sexuality as well as the different forms of sexuality the right to identify you. The obligation to identify oneself through and by a given type of sexuality must be refused.

What was your involvement in the movements for the emancipation of homosexuality in France?

I never participated in any kind of movement for sexual liberation. First, because I am not part of any movement whatsoever, and second, because I reject the idea that an individual could be identified with or by his sexuality. On the other hand, I have made a certain number of occasional and specific interventions with regard to abortion, for example, as well as specific cases of homosexuality or the more general problem of homosexuality. But it was never within any kind of ongoing activism. Here we come upon a problem that I wanted to address and that I am addressing, which is extremely important for me regarding one's way of life. Even though I resist the idea that one may be identified by one's actions or one's belonging to a group, there is still for me the problem of knowing how to define, for oneself and the people immediately around oneself, a concrete and real way of life in which sexual behavior and all the pleasures that are associated with it can be integrated in a way that is at once transparent and as satisfying as possible. For me, sexuality is a question of a way of life. It is a technique of the self. Never to hide anything about one's sexuality, never to entertain the question of secrecy—this seems to me to be a rule of life, but that does not coincide with the principle of a proclamation. The proclamation does not seem indispensable to me—I would even say that I often find it dangerous and contradictory. I want to be able to do what I want, and I do it. But don't ask me to proclaim it.

Should this refusal to be identified according to and by one's sexuality be an indication of a more general refusal on your part of any obligation to identify oneself through and by one's behavior and appearance?

This is indeed a fundamental choice for me.

You are often associated in the Netherlands with Hocquenghem and his work Homosexual Desire, *among others. Hocquenghem insists that there can be no solidarity between the proletariat and the subproletariat that has a homosexual desire requiring a certain way of life. What do you think of this thesis? This split that was such a great problem throughout the nineteenth century would seem to repeat itself within the leftist movements with regard to movements for sexual liberation . . .*

There are a lot of interesting things in Hocquenghem, and I think, in general, we agree on a certain number of points. But I would prefer not to discuss his book, because I would need to reread it to have a clearer sense.

This split is indeed a great historical problem. The tension between the so-called proletariat and the so-called subproletariat clearly characterized the end of the nineteenth century. I am not sure that the proletariat or the subproletariat exist. But it is true that there were dividing lines in society and in individual consciousness. It is also true that in France and many other countries in Europe, a certain type of leftist thought lined up alongside the subproletariat, while others were on the side of the proletariat. It is true that ideologically speaking, there have been two great families that never got along—on the one hand there were the anarchists, and on the other the Marxists. There was also a similar division between the socialists: still today, one senses that the attitude of socialists concerning drugs or homosexuality separates them from the communists. But I think that this opposition is currently eroding. What separated the proletariat from the subproletariat is that some were working and others were not. This boundary is threatened with extinction by the expansion of unemployment. This is probably why these somewhat marginal, quasifolkloric themes like sexuality have become more general problems.

During the reform of the penal code in France, you commented on the question of rape and argued that it should no longer be considered a crime. What exactly is your position on this question?

I was never part of any commission on penal reform, but there was such a commission and some members asked that I be heard as a consultant on legal problems of sexuality. I was surprised by how interesting the discussions were. During the discussions, I tried to pose the following problem. On the one hand, can sexuality truly be structured through law? Shouldn't everything that has to deal with sexuality be taken out of the legal realm? But in that case, if anything of a sexual order is to be removed from law, what should be done about rape? That was the question I posed. During a dialogue with Cooper,* I simply said that there was a problem that had to be discussed and to which I did not have an answer. I am discomfited, that's all. But, perhaps because of the difficulties of translation or lack of real understanding, an English journal screamed that I wanted to decriminalize rape, that I was some sort of horrible *phallo* . . . No, excuse me, these people didn't understand a thing. I simply said what kind of dilemma we could find ourselves in. And it is not by throwing out violent condemnations against those who pose problems that they can truly be resolved.

You said in an interview in 1973, I think, that you were opposed to popular tribunals. You made reference to the example of China. One could also speak today of Iran, where the Ayatollah Khomeini no longer even knows how many people must be executed. What do you think of these tribunals?

Indeed, I had an interview with a Maoist on popular tribunals—an interview that was reproduced in *Les Temps modernes*.† This was a period when many people in France were calling for a form of popular justice in oppo-

---

* Editors' note: Foucault is referring to a dialogue with David Cooper and others, originally published in French in 1977, that was translated and republished as Michel Foucault, David Cooper, Jean-Pierre Faye, Marie-Odile Faye, and Marine Zecca, "Confinement, Psychiatry, Prison," pp. 178–210 in Michel Foucault, *Politics, Philosophy, Culture: Interviews and Other Writings 1977–1984*, ed. Lawrence D. Kritzman (New York: Routledge, 1990); in French, it appears as "Enfermement, psychiatrie, prison," in *Dits et Écrits* III, no. 209, pp. 332–360.

† Editors' note: Foucault is referring to a debate with Benny Lévy and André Glucksmann in 1972 on popular justice. The debate was translated and republished as: "On Popular Justice: A Discussion with Maoists," pp. 1–36, in Michel Foucault, *Power/Knowledge: Selected Interviews and Other Writings, 1972–1977*, ed. Colin Gordon (New York: Vintage, 1980); in French,

sition to and against institutionalized and bourgeois justice, by taking as an example what happened in France during the Revolution. In their estimation, there was a desire for justice in the people, and popular tribunals were made to express and manifest this need for justice.

That's why I critiqued the idea of a popular tribunal. In these emotionally intense movements that require a strong intervention on the part of people, there is no need for justice; there is a need for vengeance. These people want to fight. Those against whom they hold something, they are their enemies. There is a background of social war that is still very present when, spontaneously, people want to lynch someone, sometimes someone who has done nothing more than steal. He is perceived as a social enemy, and he is to be done away with as such.

People who wish to establish popular tribunals on what is in fact a war are doubly wrong. Either they do not do what people want and they don't make war, or they do what people want and they do not perform justice. I'll even say this more crudely. You know perfectly well that if we created juries that were entirely popular, the death penalty would be applied to everyone, even the most minor thieves. So there is this background of social warfare: he who steals wages war; he who is robbed fights the one who stole. This should not be forgotten. So it is necessary to have the courage to say that justice serves to prevent this rather than to translate it. The popular tribunal translates it. Khomeini is precisely this. Once again, this discussion was misunderstood. People saw an apology for this form of justice that is not even a kind of popular tribunal, but rather the cutting of throats. No, no.

In The Order of Things, *you spoke of the death of man. Does this mean that humanism does not serve as a reference for your activism? Do you reject any engagement in the name of human rights on the grounds of the death of man?*

Both the context in which I wrote that sentence and its meaning must be kept in mind. You cannot imagine to what extent we were swimming in preachy humanist sermons in the postwar period. Everyone was a humanist: Camus was a humanist, Sartre and [. . .] were humanists, Stalin was a humanist. There was not a single discourse with a moral or political philo-

---

it appears in Dits et Écrits II, no. 108, pp. 340–69. We discuss this theme in "The Louvain Lectures in Context," in this volume.

sophical pretension that did not feel obliged to place itself under the sign of humanism. I would not be so cruel as to remind you that Hitler's followers also referred to themselves as humanists. This does not compromise humanism; it simply means that during this period we could no longer think within those categories. I could no longer pose as the objective of my thought the idea of being a humanist, because it was ensconced in total intellectual confusion.

More generally, the problem was not to build on the immediate and absolutely acceptable conception of the subject that the philosophical tradition had given itself up to that point. Even for a philosophy as radical as phenomenology, the subject considered as the founding subject was a sort of given. Putting into question the subject was, I think, something that was common to many people at that time, people who were labeled under the entirely inadequate term of structuralism. Take for example the case of psychoanalysis. It was solely in the name of humanism, in the name of the sovereignty of the human subject, that many phenomenologists, at least in France, such as Sartre and Merleau-Ponty could admit the unconscious, or only admitted it, as a kind of shadow on the margins, a surplus, because consciousness could not be relieved of its sovereign rights.

The renewal of psychoanalysis was indeed just that; the unconscious cannot be understood to be a shadow or a surplus of consciousness. This was also the case for linguistics. It was so important at that period because it allowed us to say that it was too simple or inadequate to try to make sense of what people said simply by keeping in mind the subject's intention. The idea of an unconscious and the idea of a structure of language incited us to reconsider—from the outside, so to speak—the question of the subject. What some were doing with linguistics, I tried to do a little with history. Is there not a historicity to the subject? Can one admit the subject as a kind of meta- or trans-historical invariable?

I am wondering if it is possible to reconcile the movement in favor of human rights and what you have said against the humanist subject. Fundamentally, what is the rationale behind your political engagements, your activism, as you call it?

I try to consider human rights in their historical reality while not admitting that there is a human nature. Human rights were acquired in the process of a struggle, a political struggle that posed a certain number of limits on governments and that attempted to define general principles that no government should break. It is very important to have clearly defined frontiers against governments—no matter which governments—that incite indignation, revolt, and permit struggle when they are crossed. So, as a historical fact and as a political instrument, human rights appear to me to be something important. But I do not associate them either with human nature or the essence of the human being in general. Nor do I associate them with any form of government; for by definition, no form of government has, as a vocation, to respect human rights—they have, to the contrary, a vocation not to respect them. I would go so far as to say that human rights are the rights of the governed.

What is the coherence of the different modalities of your activist engagement?

I would say that I am not looking to establish any coherence. I would say that the coherence is the coherence of my life. I have fought for certain issues, it's true: these are fragments of my experience, fragments of my autobiography. I had a certain experience in psychiatric hospitals; I had, for other reasons, experiences with the police; and I have, in relation to sexuality, a certain experience as well. That is my biography.

I try to fight when I perceive a logical connection, implication, or coherence between one element and another. But I do not understand myself as a universal combatant for a humanity suffering in all of its different forms and aspects. I also remain free with regard to the struggles with which I have associated myself.

I would say that the coherence is strategic. If I am fighting for such and such an issue, it is because, indeed, it is important to me in my subjectivity. I completely realize that the foundation and coherence pass through there as well. But on the basis of these choices that are drawn from a subjective experience, one can move on to other things in such a way that there is a real coherence, a schema, or a point of rationality that does not take as its foundation a general theory of man.

You insisted earlier that you refused the idea of being identified with and identifying someone through and by their sexuality. Is it not possible to see a key to your engagements in this refusal to be identified and located by power? The death of man is above all the rejection of a substantialist and ahistorical conception of man . . .

Yes, yes, yes ...

In a sense, could one say that Foucault is a libertarian?

In a certain sense, if you will. But in one type of libertarian ideology there is often a deliberate call for the "fundamental needs," of "true nature" and all that. I would not situate myself in that perspective. What I seek is a permanent opening of possibilities. For example, what is called sociobiology consists of descending from biology to the most extreme consequences of biological determinations on the structuring of human conduct. In my historical analyses, which I hope have a political meaning, I try to reach back *up* as far as possible to grasp all of the contingencies, events, tactics, and strategies that have brought forth a certain situation that should not be considered definitively acquired, even if it truly exists. It was constituted, and thus can be unconstituted, by politics. Yes, it is the movement of reaching back historically, with a projection on the space of political possibilities: this is the move I am making.

What do you think of the current change that is taking place in France? Well, I don't know if it is a great change ...

No, but that's precisely the point, no one knows. That is what is interesting. Not only does no one know, but there is nothing there yet. That is, everything remains to be done. It is possible that nothing will be done. The situation is open. It is open because the Socialist Party has been sensitive to a certain number of problems. This is where its strength lies, but also from the fact that a whole group of people, who had never been in politics up to the present and who distrusted politics, suddenly recognized themselves in the candidacy of Mitterrand, or rather in Mitterrand's victory. This attitude should not be looked down upon. These people were battling on different fronts: ecology, feminism, antinuclear, housing, a whole number of things. They were fighting, and they had no horizon of common victory. They found themselves in this victory, which is more of a possibility than an outcome. This is the victory of a possibility. The victory of Giscard would have been the victory of an impossibility, the defeat of a possibility.

It seems to me that your questions on psychoanalysis have varied at different times. In Maladie mentale et personnalité, *you seemed to be against it and*

you appeared to be more behaviorist. However, the point of view that you devel-
oped in the History of Madness, *in* The Birth of the Clinic, *and even in* Discipline and Punish *was entirely different. In* The Order of Things, *on the other*
hand, you wrote of psychoanalysis as a counter-science, especially in its Lacan-
ian version. What do you think about psychoanalysis presently?

Maladie mentale et personnalité is a work that I completely set apart from
what I did afterwards, even though it was a point of entry. I wrote it at a
period when the different meanings of the word alienation—in the philosophical, historical-sociological, and psychiatric sense—were conflated in
a phenomenological-psychiatric-Marxist perspective. These things have
now become completely foreign to one another, but this was not the case
during this period. I tried to debate these points, and to that extent, *Maladie mentale et personnalité* is indeed the indication of a problem to which
I did not bring a solution at that time. Nor did I later on, but I moved on.
I took up the problem differently, by asking: "Let's take things as they
present themselves, see how people were effectively treated, instead of
doing this giant slalom back and forth between Hegel and psychiatry while
passing through neo-Marxism. Let's try to make a historical point and
study the effective and real manipulation of the insane." So if my first text
on mental illness was coherent, it certainly is not with the others. Let's
leave it aside then.

Yes, but what do you think now of the function of psychoanalysis?

In *The Order of Things*, it was a question of taking the types of scientific
discourse, or those that claimed to be scientific, and seeing what their
transformations and reciprocal relationships were. I tried in this case to
understand the rather curious role psychoanalysis could play with regard
to these areas of knowledge.*

How is it possible to explain that psychoanalysts reject the idea that psycho-
analysis can figure among the techniques of subjectification? Isn't this sur-
prising?

---

* The original transcription reads: "Interruption, missing a part of the interview that
focused on the nonscientific character of psychoanalysis and that psychoanalysis is above all a
technique of the self, which the psychoanalysts refuse to admit. This should be completed."

That they reject this idea is a fact. Why? You know, it is important in the history of a discipline, or an area of knowledge or practice, to accept its history no matter how humiliating it may be. I have, in any case, noticed that psychiatrists do not appreciate it when we try to rethink the history of their knowledge through the practices of the asylum. On the other hand, I have noticed that Einstein could say that physical causality was once rooted in demonology without it bothering physicists. Why would a psychiatrist be offended where a physicist is not, if not because one is a true savant who has nothing to fear for his science, and the other lives in fear that the fragile scientific status of his knowledge could be compromised by history? So when psychoanalysts calm down about the history of their practice, I will have much greater confidence in the truth of what they tell.

Has Lacanianism brought forth a profound change in psychoanalysis?

"No comment," as the civil servants of a department of state say when they are posed an embarrassing question. I am not familiar enough with the modern psychoanalytic literature, and I understand far too little of the texts of Lacan to say anything about them. In a purely impressionistic way, I would say that I have the impression that there is a considerable transformation. But I can't say anything more.

THE LOUVAIN LECTURES
IN CONTEXT

Fabienne Brion and Bernard E. Harcourt

. . . avowal has become, in the West, one of the most highly valued techniques for producing truth. We have become a singularly avowing society. Avowal has diffused its effects far and wide: in justice, in medicine, in education, in family relations, in love relationships, in the ordinary and quotidian, and in the most solemn rituals. We avow our crimes; we avow our sins; we avow our thoughts and our desires; we avow our past and our dreams. . . . We admit to ourselves, in pleasure and in pain, avowals that would be impossible to tell others, and concerning which we write books.

—Michel Foucault, *The History of Sexuality: The Will to Know* (1976)[1]

In a promising footnote on the very same page of the French edition of *La Volonté de savoir*, Foucault elaborated the relationship between the legal confession and torture in the ancient world, before adding: "These questions will be taken up in *The Power of Truth*."[2] That pregnant sentence was never translated into English and, as a result, Foucault's reference to that broader project and larger framework was not retained in the English edition of *The History of Sexuality: Volume I*.[3] Neither did *The Power of Truth* make it onto the list of the six-volume series announced on the back cover of the original French edition of *La Volonté de savoir*[4] and much discussed on both sides of the Atlantic—an absence which seems natural given that the book would have been transversal to Foucault's more specific histories of sexuality, madness, and the prison. As we all know, *The Power of Truth* never appeared in print, nor in manuscript form, and there was therefore practically no trace of it in the English language—perhaps, one could say, until today with the publication of *Wrong-Doing, Truth-Telling.*

These Louvain lectures—or rather this book, because the text reads like a completed work—trace a history of avowal since the Homeric era and explore the power of truth-telling in justice. On one reading, it is a book that explores precisely the power of truth and the ethical and political consequences for us, as truth-telling subjects. It sets forth a genealogy of the juridical confession—of the legal confession in our modern criminal justice practices. And, together with Foucault's 1973 lecture series delivered in Rio de Janeiro, "Truth and Juridical Forms," it constitutes Foucault's most direct intervention into criminal law and criminal justice.

Foucault pursued the question of truth—of its production and power, of its relation to the self and subjectivity, and of the implications for politics and ethics—throughout his writings and throughout his political engagements. In an interview with two Belgian criminologists immediately following the Louvain lectures, he emphasized: "Broadly speaking, I have consistently pursued the problem of knowing how truth comes to things and how it comes about that a certain number of areas are slowly integrated into the problematic and search for truth."[5] Foucault worked on these questions steadily in his theoretical and historical writings and his political practice—which, he maintained, were deeply interconnected. As he explained in another interview while at Louvain, "I have always insisted that there take place within me and for me a kind of back and forth, an interference, an interconnection between practices and the theoretical or historical work I was doing."[6]

To situate these Louvain lectures in their context, then—to articulate the set of problematics and struggles from which they emerge and the directions in which they lead—is to explore how Foucault integrated avowal into the larger project on the power of truth. There are, naturally, various possible readings of *Wrong-Doing, Truth-Telling,* but ours is guided by this overarching project, and it can be articulated by means of a set of questions: What are the tasks that Foucault assigned to critique? How did he weave together politics and ethics in his writings and in his practice? What did it mean, for Foucault, to be a thinker engaged in the present? What could it mean to speak of the courage of truth? To address this set of questions, we will examine how Foucault problematized the power of truth in the various cycles that frame the Louvain lectures, and sketch some of the consequences—epistemological, political, and ethical—that could possibly be drawn. We will proceed along three dimensions.

First, we situate the Louvain lectures in a series of texts on criminal law and criminal justice—texts in which Foucault explored what he referred to as "repression" in 1971 or "techniques of domination" in 1981. Broadly speaking, Foucault inscribed this series of texts within the second of what he would call "three domains of possible genealogies," and defined the second of these domains as the historical analysis of how individuals work on themselves and on others through complex relations of power, as he had done in *Discipline and Punish*—or more formally, as he would say, the "historical ontology of ourselves in our relations to a field of power through which we constitute ourselves as subjects acting on others."[7] Within this domain, avowal is a means of producing truth in the legal context, and more specifically in the realm of criminal law. Beyond avowal, though, Foucault is examining "a whole technology of truth production that scientific practice and philosophical discourse have bit by bit eroded and disqualified," and exploring different models of judicial truth production, from agonistic practices in ancient Greece to modern judicial procedures, in order to show how a "truth-test in the order of the event" has come to take the form of a "truth-finding in the order of knowledge."[8]

Second, we situate the Louvain lectures in the context of Foucault's analysis of techniques of the self. This analysis is located at the threshold between the second and third domains of genealogy, the third being the "historical ontology in relation to an ethics through which we constitute ourselves as moral agents."[9] The task here is to study how, above and beyond repression, the subject himself, through his own work on himself, produces his own subjection. Like the aphrodisiacs mentioned in Foucault's 1981 lectures at the Collège de France, *Subjectivity and Truth*, avowal is a "refracting surface"[10] on the basis of which the historical modalities of the relation to the self can be examined from four angles: as ethical substance, as a mode of subjection, as a practice of the self, and as *telos*.[11]

The third dimension situates the Louvain lectures in relation to the project of a critical philosophy—a question that Foucault had already addressed in 1966 in *The Order of Things* and to which he would sketch the outline of a solution in 1984 in *The Courage of Truth*. Along this third dimension, the Louvain lectures represent a movement toward a new form of critique—what could be called, following Foucault, an "alethurgical" form of critique—that builds on and completes his archaeological and genealogical methods. Through a history of the forms of the production of avowal, Foucault focuses at Louvain on the form of subjectivity-truth. This represents a return to the debate with Kant that, as the editors of Foucault's *Introduction to Kant's Anthropology* suggest, nourished Foucault's entire trajectory. It is the question, woven through and through: If truth "is not observed, but produced,"[12] then to what can or must critical philosophy aspire? The Louvain lectures intimate the outline of a response, one that Foucault would first propose in his inaugural lecture: "a *counter-positivism* that is not the opposite of positivism but rather its counterpoint."[13]

On Repression and Its Objects

The first dimension, then, is how politics and ethics are linked in Foucault's writings on criminal law and criminal justice, and relatedly how the question of the power of truth presents itself in that domain. To sketch an answer to this question, it is important to recall that Foucault himself observed that his research was often influenced by "circumstances as they arise"—in other words, by the political circumstances which surrounded him and the political struggles that he engaged.[14] It is equally important to remember, as Gilles Deleuze would remind us, that for Foucault practice was "a set of relays from one theoretical point to another, and theory was a set of relays from one practice to another."[15] This suggests the importance of returning, briefly, to the political situation of the early 1970s, to Foucault's struggles alongside members of the French militant organization, the Gauche prolétarienne (GP), and to his work with the militant prisoner organization he helped found, the Groupe d'information sur les prisons (GIP)—in order not so much to explain his writings from his biography, but rather to discover what the ethics of a critical philosophy demanded, in his view.

The Circumstances

The circumstances included, first, the repression of the student movements of May 1968. In Tunisia, where Foucault had taught since 1966, the student protests were brutally repressed and dozens of student activists were imprisoned. Foucault hid students who were sought by the police, and communicated information to their lawyers. After their trial, in September 1968, Foucault requested that the French government terminate his appointment in Tunisia and reassign him.[16] In France, where Foucault returned, twelve nonparliamentary leftist organizations had just been outlawed, and by 1970 the pressure was mounting against the GP, a Maoist group headed by Benny Lévy, among others, which included militants from two previously prohibited organizations.[17] Meanwhile, in February 1970 sixteen miners were killed in a mining explosion at Fouquières-lez-Lens in the northern Pas-de-Calais region of France; shortly thereafter, Molotov cocktails were thrown at the mining company's headquarters and nine GP militants were put behind bars—as were the editors of the GP's newspaper, *La cause du peuple*.[18] On May 27, 1970, the GP itself was banned on the basis of a new law against violent organizations and private militias.[19] A few days later, on June 9, 1970, another new law "aiming to repress new forms of delinquency" imposed a form of collective responsibility that included a potential sentence of two years in prison even for nonviolent participation in a banned gathering.[20] Almost two hundred militants were imprisoned, partly on the basis of the new law, but also for trying to reconstitute a prohibited and dissolved organization—an offense that the sale of *La cause du peuple* was enough to establish.[21]

The circumstances were shaped, secondly, by the GP's particular reaction to the government repression. Prohibited, the organization continued its struggle in a number of ways and on a number of different fronts. To begin with, the GP enlarged the resistance movement[22] and opened a democratic front.[23] It mobilized certain intellectuals whose notoriety protected them from the risk of being arrested and convicted. On June 9, 1970, Simone de Beauvoir and Michel Leiris filed the charter for "The Friends of *La cause du peuple*";[24] a few days later, Jean-Paul Sartre, who had become the newspaper's editor, called for the reconstitution of another organization, the *Secours rouge*, for the defense of the imprisoned militants.[25] In addition, the GP initiated alternative mechanisms of justice—what were called measures of "popular justice." While the militants accused of having thrown the Molotov cocktails were tried (and acquitted) by the French government in December 1970, the GP organized its own popular tribunal to try the owners and managers of the mines in Lens. Sartre served as prosecutor and argued for the criminal responsibility of the state and the company's management in the deaths of the sixteen miners. His closing argument was based on an independent counterinquiry conducted by doctors and engineering students.[26] Finally, the GP militated to obtain the status of political prisoner for its incarcerated members. Within the prison walls, the imprisoned militants led a hunger strike to obtain the right to assemble, access the press, communicate with their organization, and denounce repression; outside the prison walls, the "Organization of Political Prisoners" (OPP), a cell of the GP led by Serge July and Benny Lévy, took on the task of "turning their trials into a political forum in keeping with the Leninist tradition."[27]

A third and important circumstance was that Daniel Defert, who was a member of the GP at the time and had joined the OPP at the invitation of Jacques Rancière, invited Foucault to organize a commission of inquiry like the one at Lens, but focused this time on prison conditions.[28] Foucault agreed and threw himself completely into the endeavor—but what he proposed was different from what the GP expected. From the outset, Foucault sought to integrate theory and practice; more specifically, he placed the problem of repression in relation to the question of blindness—or willful blindness. The fact was that May 1968 had marched right past the prisons without seeing them, and the militants, who confronted repression, opted for strategies that left the common-law prisoners in the shadows.[29] Despite the fact that the student protesters were some of the most politicized, well educated, and engaged anarchist, Marxist-Leninist, and Maoist thinkers, the prison and the plight of the common criminal had completely escaped their view. Perhaps this was the product of well-intentioned intellectuals being trapped in a dominant criminological discourse, despite their ardent desire to be the "consciousness and eloquence" and to tell "the truth to those who could not yet see it and in the name of those who could not yet say it."[30] Whatever the cause, the effects were clear: the political movements had sidestepped the problem of the prison.

Foucault did not, however, reproach them for this blindness. As Deleuze would remark several years later, for Foucault it was not a question of "the manner by which a subject sees: the seeing subject is himself a space within visibility, a function derived from visibility."[31] For Foucault, the blindness itself was a key dimension of the problem and of the relations of power produced by the repression of those with whom he had allied himself. Their blindness represented the invisibility of the visible, or to go even further, the invisibility of this invisibility—of which Foucault had observed, writing about Blanchot in 1966, that it was precisely that which fiction must reveal.[32] "What intellectuals have discovered since the recent events," Foucault explained to Deleuze in 1972, "is that the masses do not need them to know; they know perfectly well, clearly, much better than they, and they say it exceedingly well. But there exists an entire system of power that bars, prohibits, and invalidates their discourse and their knowledge."[33] Foucault would then add: "The intellectuals themselves are part of this system of power; the very idea that they are agents of 'consciousness' and discourse is itself part of the discourse."[34]

The Two Duties of the Intellectual

Two imperatives would immediately follow—imperatives that would determine the form of Foucault's engagement alongside the members of the GP and the OPP. The first was a negative, though active, duty. It was negative in the sense of an injunction: the role of the intellectual, Foucault would contend, "is not to place himself 'a little ahead or slightly to the side' to tell the silent truth to everyone."[35] Therefore, a popular tribunal was out of the question, especially one prosecuted by intellectuals—and so was a commission of inquiry. Foucault would eschew these forms of truth production, of "jurisdiction," of the telling of justice. But this would not by any means imply any form of quietism. There was, importantly, an *active* element to this negative imperative: it was important to engage the struggle actively in order to allow those who had acquired firsthand the type of experience, knowledge, and consciousness that could be shared to disseminate their knowledge and information.[36]

And so, on February 8, 1971, at a press conference concerning the hunger strike of the imprisoned militants, Foucault read and distributed the manifesto of the Groupe d'information sur les prisons (GIP). The acronym, Foucault confided to Defert, evoked that of the GP "with this iota of difference that the intellectuals had to introduce."[37] The GP militants had allied themselves with renowned intellectuals; by contrast, the GIP would appeal to "specific intellectuals" ready to "subvert their own positions within power relations and their power within knowledge" to assemble and diffuse testimonials of incarcerated prisoners.[38] The first "intolerance inquiry" was conducted in March and April of that year.[39] It brought together "hundreds of people"—doctors, lawyers, social workers, prisoners, and their loved ones—all of whom had firsthand experience of the prison in one manner or another.[40] The resulting information was diffused in brochures produced by the GIP.[41]

The second duty of the intellectual was a positive imperative, also active and transformative in terms of theoretical practice. The role of intellectuals was, as Foucault emphasized, "to struggle against forms of power right where they [intellectuals] are both the object and the instrument: in the order of 'knowledge,' of 'truth,' of 'consciousness,' and of 'discourse.'"[42] Here the trouble was that the GP militants were too "full of knowledge," to borrow an expression Foucault would use in 1972 in his lecture "The Knowledge of Oedipus."[43] The militants were full of knowledge, but they could not see. What were the truths that blinded them—that gouged their eyes out, as Oedipus had done to himself? The militants were also full of will—of good will. So what were their interests, what were their "investments" (to borrow a term from Deleuze)[44] that made them complicit in their own blindness? And how could one speak, write, or act so as to avoid this and more effectively shape one's practice? These questions all pointed to another: How does one conduct oneself in struggle, especially when the struggle itself demands a transformation of the self? For Foucault the answer would call not for psychoanalysis, but rather for a linking of politics and ethics, in both practice and theory.

Foucault's first lecture series at the Collège de France—which spanned December 9, 1970, to March 17, 1971—can be read between the lines as addressing this fundamental question. On one reading, it may be interpreted as an encrypted dialogue with the GP. The central question is that of the will to know—or, more exactly, the doublet of the will to truth (as Foucault would say, the "central episode"[45] in the history of the will to know in our civilization) and the elision of desire or, more precisely, of the subject of desire (an elision that for Foucault, as we will see, was paradoxically a condition of truth in philosophical and scientific discourse).

In those first lectures, Foucault began by suggesting that what characterizes and defines philosophy, at least since Aristotle, is pushback against "the sophistic or Socratic-sophistic question, 'Why does one desire to know?'"[46] He described how, in ancient Greece, law and truth were first linked through the form of the test (épreuve), a binary form involving performative statements in the context of agonistic rituals, and were later linked in the ternary form of findings (constat), involving descriptive statements in the context of rituals that substitute the agonistic competition or struggle with the telling of justice (juridiction). By means of a commentary on Sophocles's Oedipus Rex, Foucault then showed how the act of excluding the criminal—the act that defined the city of Thebes in an effort to purify it—replicates the act of exclusion by the Sophist and the disqualification of the subject of desire, which, according to Foucault, defined what philosophy and science are said to be or must be at their very essence.

Exploring the spectrum of notions from *discrimen* (that which divides, discerns, distinguishes, discriminates) to *crimen* (an accusation, a reproach, a charge), and from *crimen* to repression (in all senses of the term), Foucault showed that the system of truth and falsity had historically served in Western societies — and continues to serve — a function of exclusion analogous to that of the system of prohibitions, analogous also to the type of oppositions (for instance, between madness and reason) that he had studied since the *History of Madness*;[47] and that these could be articulated in relation to systems of domination. As we saw earlier, in his militant practice Foucault struggled not only on behalf of the self-identified "political prisoners," but for all prisoners. In a similar fashion, beyond his immediate audience at the Collège de France, and also beyond the members of the GIP, Foucault may have targeted a much larger set of interlocutors in his *Lessons on the Will to Know*: all those who want to know without wanting to know about their own desire to know; all those who, under pretext of truth, avoid the question of desire that holds them in its clutch.

In this sense, Foucault wove together the theoretical and practical dimensions associated with the two duties of the intellectual: the "intolerance inquiries," in the register of practice, would be embedded within archaeological and genealogical investigations in the realm of theoretical activity. We see prisons without seeing them, we tolerate the intolerable, we accept the unacceptable: the task, then, must be to return "to the system of acceptability, analyzed on the basis of relations of knowledge-power"—what Foucault would refer to as "the level of archaeology."[48] It must also involve destabilizing those evident truths on the basis of which the intolerable is tolerated: to show, "no matter the blinding strength of the mechanisms of power or the justifications that have been elaborated," that it has not been rendered acceptable "by any originally existing right"—what Foucault would refer to as the level of genealogy.[49]

"The prison as an institution is, for many, an iceberg," Foucault stated in March 1971. "The visible part is the rationale: 'We need prisons because there are criminals.' The hidden part is the biggest, the most fearsome part: the prison is an instrument of social repression. . . . Here are two statistics that give food for thought: 40 percent of prisoners are in pretrial detention, about 16 percent are in immigration detention."[50] Asked about his plans at the Collège de France in an August 1971 interview, Foucault replied: "There is a problem that has interested me for a long time: it is that of the criminal justice system. . . . So I will probably do a series of lectures on this subject during the twenty-seven years I have left at the Collège de France. I'm not saying I will spend twenty-seven years on the topic, but certainly a good number. With some friends . . . we have formed a kind of small group; what shall I call it? A group for intervention and action on justice, on the criminal justice system, the penal institutions in France, and we have launched an investigation into the conditions of prisoners in France. . . . That's what I am dedicating myself to right now, perhaps for the months and years to come."[51] And when his interlocutor perceptively observed that since the beginning Foucault had "subordinated the discourse of logic to the discourse of morality," and that it would lead not to a metaphysics but to an ethics, Foucault remarked: "I am simply trying to see, to reveal, and to transform into legible discourse, legible to all, that which may be unbearable for the most disadvantaged classes in our current system of justice."[52]

Justice and Truth

For Foucault, then, the situation in the early 1970s presented the following problem: resistance to the criminal justice system was, in his words, "an important struggle,"[53] but it was particularly difficult because of the question of truth—of the power of truth. And to address this difficulty, Foucault would explore the problems of criminal justice in relation to the larger question of "the conditions of existence, functioning, and institutionalization of scientific discourses."[54] Foucault would tie the problems of criminal justice to the question of the production of scientific truth. Already, in April 1971, he had begun to explore the relationship in his "Lecture on Nietzsche," delivered at McGill University. Nietzsche, Foucault argued, saw truth as an effect: one that a knowledge, "subservient, dependent, interested," produces by "the game of an initial falsification, repeatedly reiterated, that poses the distinction between true and false."[55] If this is correct, of course, it would also apply to criminal justice and judicial decision-making, given that justice represents but another mode for the production of truth, in the Nietzschean sense of the word. As Foucault remarked in his debate with Maoists "On Popular Justice," judicial decisions are made by judges deemed neutral with respect to the parties involved, "according to a certain standard of truth and a number of ideas about right and wrong," after a ritual—an inquiry, an examination—designed to "establish the 'truth' or to obtain an 'avowal.'"[56] Judicial practices have the power to transmute force into law, and to convert resentment about police violence into assent to the evidence and necessity of the prison. For the consciousness of the arbitrary, they substitute the illusion of necessity. And if this is correct, it is because the juridical procedures have effects of truth. As a result, in order to struggle against passivity and blindness in the face of a repressive criminal justice system, it would be necessary first to explore and ferret out the very mechanisms that produce truth.

Foucault's second series of lectures at the Collège de France, *Penal Theories and Institutions*, explored precisely the development of the inquiry (*enquête*) as a form of truth production, as well as the forms of social control that developed from the sixteenth century onward and that would give rise to the method of the examination (*examen*). These lectures were inscribed within the project outlined in the *Lessons on the Will to Know*, which was to "follow the formation of certain types of knowledge from the juridical and political matrices that gave birth to them, and which serve as their support."[57] Foucault would take up the matter again the following year, in May 1973, in a series of lectures delivered at the Pontifical Catholic University of Rio de Janeiro, titled *Truth and Juridical Forms*. As Foucault indicated in Rio, he was interested not in an internal history of truth but in an external one: to study truth, not as it is self-consciously conceived in the history of science, but where, unthought, it informs practices and ideas. Judicial practices, he said, are practices on the basis of which whole areas of knowledge are formed, and they reveal "new objects, new concepts, new techniques" and "completely new forms of subjects and subjects of knowledge."[58] Foucault continued in Rio to develop the comparison between different juridical forms for the production of truth, elaborating further on the contrast between the binary structure of agonistic settlements of disputes, the introduction of a third party who gives justice through a process of inquiry, and the development of modes of examination that produce the truth of a criminal.

Discipline and Punish followed suit in 1975, proposing a "genealogy of the present scientific and judicial complex where the power to punish finds its support, receives its justification and its rules, extends its effects and masks its exorbitant singularity."[59] Foucault showed how, in the first half of the nineteenth century, the criminal justice system sought to uncover, beyond the truth of the crime, the truth of the offender—or, more precisely, the truth of "the criminal," who the prison had substituted for the offender, and who was related to his crime by a whole series of determinations (biological, psychological, social, etc.). "A whole corpus of knowledge, techniques, 'scientific' discourses form and intertwine with the practice of the power to punish," he wrote.[60] Thus penal practice took on a new form: we judge the act, to be sure, "but we also judge at the same time passions, instincts, anomalies, infirmities, maladjustments, the effects of environment or heredity."[61] Other characters emerge and participate: doctors, psychiatrists, criminologists, and of course the delinquents themselves. If the repression goes unnoticed, it is because the truth of "the criminal" is the veil, woven with the appearance of science; and penal moderation is the veil of the veil, woven into the appearance of law. As Foucault explained, "By an analysis of penal leniency as a technique of power, one might understand both how man, the soul, the normal or abnormal individual have come to duplicate the crime as objects of penal intervention; and in what way a specific mode of subjection was able to give birth to man as an object of knowledge for a discourse with a 'scientific' status."[62] The courts and prisons are factories where facts continuously are transformed into truths, and delinquents are fabricated on the basis of the detained. These institutions keep busy an arsenal of practitioners and theorists of a knowledge deemed true and of a power deemed right: people who are not always entirely deceived by the illusions they produce, but who may be constrained to forget them if they prefer to remain ignorant of the benefits they extract.

To this body of work the Louvain lectures added in 1981 the element of avowal—already identified as important in 1972.[63] Avowal had intrigued Foucault for many years. Since at least 1975 he had expressed astonishment that in most legal systems "what one says against oneself could constitute proof."[64] Surely, he suggested, it would not be difficult to imagine "that someone might take responsibility for something to exempt another person or to exempt themselves from another fault"; moreover, torture and other coercive techniques are bound to result in some false confessions.[65] And yet the juridical confession thrived in the eighteenth and nineteenth centuries, and continues to do so today. Some of the questions that this would raise and that Foucault would ask at Louvain echoed his *Lessons on the Will to Know*. For instance, if conformity with reality was not necessarily the condition of truth in avowal, then when and how is an avowal taken to be true, and what purpose is served by believing it to be true? These questions problematized the relationship between language, reference, and the function of avowal in justice. Other questions extended those of *Discipline and Punish*. If we punish "aggressions, but through them aggressivity; rape, but at the same time perversions; murders that are at the same time impulses and desires"[66]—if indeed the criminal has replaced the offender and must confess not only what he did but who he is (or what he must be in order to have done what he did), could it then be that avowal is "the thorn, the splinter, the wound, the vanishing point, the breach in the entire penal system?"[67] This question would problematize the human subject who, through avowal, is constituted as a correlative to truth. It problematizes the couplet subjectivity-truth.

Beyond developing these themes, the Louvain lectures also open new directions and raise larger questions about the function of avowal beyond its function in "societies that banish (Greece), societies that arrange a compensation (Germanic), societies that mark (Western societies until the late Middle Ages), or societies that confine, like ours," as Foucault would say in *The Punitive Society* in 1973 and continue to develop at Louvain.[68] The lectures raise questions about the function of avowal in the singular process of veridiction that is Foucault's own work, as well as about its function in that lengthy series of subjects who, from Pierre Rivière to Patrick Henry, confess to having killed without being able to explain themselves or explicate what caused them to act, despite their best efforts (recall that Pierre Rivière did indeed try hard, in a desperate face-to-face with himself, at a time when there remained nothing left for him but death). These are, no doubt, puzzles; but if we accept that Foucault was at times enigmatic, perhaps for some of the same reasons that he ascribed to Lacan—namely, that he wanted "the work necessary to understand him to be work that had to be done on oneself"—the questions may constitute a key to deciphering how, beyond his engagement against the criminal justice system, Foucault's critical philosophy tied together politics and ethics.[69]

On Knowledge and Its Subject

What role, then, does avowal play in Foucault's work? A short answer would be that it serves as a bridge between what he calls in *The Subject and Power* the second and third parts of his project—namely, between the study of "the objectivizing of the subject in what I shall call 'dividing practices,'" a process that turns the subject into an object and separates him from others, and the study of subjectification, "the way a human being turns him- or herself into a subject."[70] This calls for the study of the relationship between two series: the first series being the object, its divisions (such as mad/sane, diseased/healthy, and criminals/"good boys"),[71] and the associated techniques of domination; the second series consisting of the subject, subjective division, and techniques of the self. Or, to push this further, it would call for the study of subjection insofar as it proceeds first on an objective plane and then on a subjective one—in other words, studying subject making at the precise point where, because of that doubling, servitude may become voluntary. This is a critical space that has the potential of opening a passage for resistance—a passage that makes possible the "ability to loosen one's hold on oneself"[72] or, possibly, that leads back from docility to reflective indocility, from servitude to voluntary unservitude.

A Demanding Task

To articulate the link between object and subject—or, more precisely, to problematize their articulation in knowledge and to interrogate at once what Foucault calls "the form of knowledge" and "the 'subject-object' norm"[73]—was a task Foucault pursued consistently at least since his *History of Madness* in 1960 and his *Introduction to Kant's Anthropology* in 1964. And given that his larger critical project targeted not simply repression or domination in the criminal justice system but the broader philosophical tradition and the discourse of science, the stakes were high—as would be the resistance to the project. As a genealogist, Foucault sought to highlight not only the historicity of the "mentally ill" and of "the criminal," but also that of the human subject more generally, of the subject of knowledge. Naturally, that kind of critical project would produce pushback in philosophical and scientific circles. As he noted in Rio in 1973, psychoanalytic practice and theory had already "re-evaluated in a most fundamental way the somewhat sacred priority granted to the subject that had established itself in Western thought."[74] Still, "in the field of the theory of knowledge, of the history of epistemology, of the history of science, or of the history of ideas," the way in which the subject was conceived at the time was "still very philosophical, very Cartesian, very Kantian."[75] Moreover, as he often observed, there was also a "certain academic or university tradition of Marxism that had not yet overcome this traditional philosophical conception of the subject."[76] It is to this task that Foucault would turn his attention — to the task of reelaborating a theory of the subject — and it is within this second dimension as well that the Louvain lectures contribute importantly and should be situated.

This is, naturally, a demanding task. It would not be sufficient to assert or even establish that "the subject's relationship with truth, or simply the relationship of knowledge, is disturbed, obscured, veiled by conditions of existence, by social relations, or by political forms imposed on the subject of knowledge from the outside," which in certain Marxist analyses would translate into the "negative element of ideology."[77] Nor would it be enough to maintain that the notion of a "subject endowed with a consciousness in which he forms freely or freely recognizes the ideas he believes" is the product of an "ideological apparatus," as Althusser might have asserted.[78] To deploy the apparatus of ideology was to suggest that there is both a subject prior to knowledge and an object, and between them a veil that can be removed; it was to assert that, parallel to one's false consciousness, there are other consciousnesses that can be revealed to be true. What Foucault aimed to show, instead, was that "the political and economic conditions of existence are not a veil or a barrier for the subject of knowledge, but rather that within which subjects of knowledge are formed, and thus relations of truth as well."[79] This was evidently a return to Nietzsche: besides truth, the challenge was to do a history of the subject presupposed by the discourse of science; to do a genealogy of this event that is consciousness; and to reveal (contra Althusser) the historicity of what makes and divides a subject — the historicity of what the subject remembers and forgets, of what the subject is conscious of, and unconscious.

On this delicate terrain, Foucault edged forward cautiously. At the root of knowledge, he said in his "Lecture on Nietzsche," there is a will to power of which the subject is the point of emergence — the subject as this "system of deformations and perspectives," as this "principle of dominations" that receives from the object "the very mark of its identity and reality."[80] The lesson Nietzsche taught is that in knowledge, the relationship of the will and truth is conditioned not on liberty (liberty of truth and liberty of the will), but on violence. And the lesson Foucault taught, reading Nietzsche, is that there is not "in the violence of knowing, a constant, essential, or prior relationship that the activity of knowledge would both deploy and effectuate."[81] The relationship of subject to object that serves to found the activity of knowing is in truth "the product" and "the first illusion"; and the same is true of "all its derivatives, such as the *a priori*, objectivity, pure knowledge, the constituent subject."[82]

For those who identify more with the subject of the philosophical tradition and scientific discourse, this argument could amount to a "tremendous narcissistic injury"—to borrow the term Foucault used to describe the wound inflicted by Pasteur on doctors in *Psychiatric Power*.[83] For the way in which the subject is conceived may also be the way in which subjects conceive themselves: it may indeed be difficult for intellectuals who dream of being agents of "conscience and eloquence"[84] to accept that the subject of this aspiration is nothing more than an illusory effect of that "singular form of power-knowledge that is expertise [*la connaissance*]."[85] It might not come as a surprise that, following Descartes, they might cling to evidence; not surprising that they might not surrender without resistance. And so, to address this, Foucault's first weapon was terminological precision. Early on, he tried to "fix the vocabulary":[86] the term *connaissance* came to refer to the "system that makes it possible to give a unity in advance, a mutual belonging, and a naturalness to desire and knowledge [*savoir*]"; and the term *savoir* would refer to that which had to be "torn from the interiority of knowledge [*connaissance*] to rediscover the object of a will, the end of a desire, the instrument of a domination, the stake of a struggle."[87] But terminological precision was not enough, even if it was necessary. It was important not only to say, but to do—to tear at the traces of the *agōn* between a will to power and the object it gives itself. To pose the question of the subject, then, Foucault took up again a theme from the *Lectures on the Will to Know*, namely the theme of the truth-test with its binary structure, and of truth-finding with its ternary structure—as a way, in other words, to investigate the subject in relation to the question of truth.

"For a long time and still today in large part," Foucault said in 1974, "medicine, psychiatry, criminal justice, and criminology have been confined to a manifestation of truth in accordance with the norms of knowledge [*connaissance*] and a production of truth in the form of the test [*épreuve*]; the latter always tending to hide behind the former and to seek to be justified by it."[88] Based on the example of psychiatry, Foucault would show how the production of truth expanded in the nineteenth-century psychiatric hospital—a field not only of "diagnosis and classification," but also of a struggle, of "a joust, an institutional field where it is a question of victory and submission."[89] To mark the point, Foucault here introduced Doctor Jean-Martin Charcot, the great master of the Salpêtrière hospital. Charcot served to reveal how, "at the request of medical power-knowledge," certain phenomena such as lethargy or catalepsy were produced and ultimately turned hysteria into an object of science;[90] how, too, with the help of nosography, the relations of power that represented its very condition of possibility vanish in the peculiar symptomatic trait of suggestibility;[91] and finally, how the status of pure subject of knowledge was conferred on it by being thus formed as an object.

Foucault took this question up anew in *Discipline and Punish* in relation to criminal justice and criminology. But here, despite the repetition, the object's relation to knowledge would eerily resemble the criminal's relationship to repression: it was the tip of the iceberg that otherwise remained invisible. From the writings that analyzed the "practices that divide," Foucault's readers mostly would retain the concept of knowledge-power, paying less attention to the subject born of that "singular form of power-knowledge."[92] Even though they may well have remembered the remarkable characters produced by the "dividing practices"—the mad, the delinquent, the criminal—there may not have been sufficient attention paid to the role of the sovereign subject in the production of those truths, that sovereign subject reflected in the mirror of Velázquez's *The Maids of Honor*.[93] And when Foucault pointed to the subject of the philosophical tradition and the discourse of science—whatever its modality, whether the *cogito*, the subject of the representation, or consciousness—his project seemed to meet with even more pushback.

Reluctance

It is relatively easy, naturally, for a philosopher to accept that crises in criminal justice or in criminology and psychiatry—disciplines that have made a specialty of *crimen* and of *discrimen*—"call into question their limits and uncertainties in the field of knowledge."[94] It is somewhat less easy to take the position that such crises "put in question knowledge, the form of knowledge, the 'subject-object' norm."[95] But it is far more daunting—perhaps it calls for *parrhēsia*, for the courage to tell truth—to question, beyond the objects these disciplines have disseminated, the divided subject itself; to put in question the unity of the subject that philosophy and science presuppose; to reveal desire within the subject of knowledge; or to show once again (recall that he had discussed this in his *Lessons on the Will to Know*) that if in the philosophical tradition and the discourse of science "the subject of desire and the subject of knowledge are but one,"[96] it is because "desire is elided."[97] To reveal the subject and its schism, and their invisibility, and the invisibility of their invisibility—that is a tall order not only for the speaker, but also for those who would listen.

Foucault explored these themes in the first volume of the *History of Sexuality*, published only a year after *Discipline and Punish*. After considering the title *Sex and Truth* [*Sexe et Vérité*],[98] Foucault opted for *The Will to Know*, a title he had already given to his first set of lectures at the Collège de France. As he would write eight years later in his introduction to *The Use of Pleasures*, "The notion of desire or of the desiring subject constituted if not a theory, at least a generally accepted theoretical theme";[99] and it was by means of this "generally accepted" theme that Foucault began to historicize the sovereign subject. The project, he wrote, is to "understand how, in modern Western societies, something like an 'experience' of 'sexuality' came into being, a familiar notion that however would only appear around the early nineteenth century."[100] This would necessitate a genealogy of desire and of the desiring subject—which, Foucault would emphasize in 1984, did not mean "doing a history of successive conceptions of desire, lust, or *libido*," but rather "analyzing the practices by which people were brought to pay attention to themselves, to decipher themselves, to recognize and avow themselves as subjects of desire, making room for a certain relationship to themselves that would allow them to discover in desire the truth of their being, whether natural or fallen."[101]

In a crucial chapter titled "Scientia Sexualis," Foucault returns to the distinction between the truth-test and truth-finding. All along the nineteenth century, Foucault suggests, sex seemed to have been inscribed on different registers of knowledge—reproductive biology on the one hand, the medicine of sex on the other[102]—with no real exchange between the two. Foucault then pins the theme of blindness, "the refusal to see and to hear,"[103] on the form of the truth-test. Charcot again makes an appearance, placing a baton on the ovaries of a patient, G., thereby provoking at will the appearance and disappearance of hysterical spasms. But the doctor has G. removed as soon as she "calls for the stick-sex in words that, by contrast to his, carry no metaphor."[104] The operation produces two new series, combining previous ones in new ways: on the one hand, the series of truth-finding, of the subject of knowledge, and of this "immense desire to know that fueled the institution of scientific discourse in the West"; on the other hand, the series of the truth-test, of the subject of desire, and of this "determined will to not know" that doubles expert discourse like a glove, producing both "ageless credulity" and "systematic blindness."[105] The first series is represented by the signifiers of biology and reproduction, the second by medicine and sex.

But Foucault does not limit himself to showing that Charcot wants nothing to do with desire. As a physician, Charcot is intimately familiar with the discourse of medicine and sex. He also knows well the biology of reproduction—it is on her ovaries, after all, that he places his baton. Does the metaphor here signal that the two series must be superimposed, as they are in his practice? Charcot, a subject of knowledge bound by a scientific discourse, is also a man of passion and desire; G., the object of knowledge, is also a desiring woman. It matters not that his desire does not match hers. It matters not that, to Charcot, it is a desire for knowledge and power that comes in place of what, for G., is a sexual desire: in the relationship of knowledge, there is a meeting of these misperceived desires at work. It is desire that arcs the body that Charcot and his disciples watch, fascinated; it is also desire that engenders the illusion that brings them together. Desire is at the source: for him, of the accumulation of knowledge and power, and for her, of a delusional complacency.

Several lessons ensue. The first is that both the subject and the object of knowledge are subject to desire. They are subject *to* desire, not subjects *of* desire: if the conduct of Charcot and G. is guided by a will, that will does not take the form of a choice or decision by an individual subject. It is, as Foucault said of power relations, intentional but not subjective.[106] A second lesson: it is desire that is the relay, if not the cause, of the blindness; however, as shown by the example of the hysterical contracture, it is also desire that makes up for it. A third lesson is that Charcot is, in truth, linked to his patient—and vice versa.[107] By giving him what he wants or needs to see and know, G. becomes an accomplice to the power that exercises itself through her.

Could one describe this as a return to the theme of subjectivity? Not entirely, since there is neither a real choice nor a decision by an individual subject. On the other hand, it is G.'s desire that motivates the episode. This is not yet enough for Foucault to speak of "voluntary servitude," but enough for him to deploy the term "docility." Between the protagonists of the scene, the relationship of domination passes through the production of an identity, one that Charcot attributes to G.; and the condition of its actualization is the validation by G. of the identity that she is assigned.

One further lesson: Notice that Charcot receives the hysterical body "in full knowledge and full ignorance,"[108] and that neither he nor G. know where it will lead. Power reaches the body without first having been internalized in the conscience; the relations of power need not be relayed through representation in order to be effective.[109] Final lesson: Recall here that it is in psychiatric hospitals in the second half of the nineteenth century that the "hysterical outbursts" manifested themselves, and that they constituted a "backlash of the very exercise of psychiatric power."[110] The historicity of desire, of which Charcot and G. are themselves subject, acts as a relay of the power exercised.

This exposes the subject and its schism: the subject and object of knowledge symbolize the conscious part, the part that the philosophical tradition and scientific discourse remember, while the man and woman of desire symbolize its unconscious, repressed, and forgotten part. In these relations of, on the one hand, man of desire and subject of knowledge, and on the other hand, woman of desire and object of knowledge, it is the element of desire that affects and commands both the doctor and the patient. The element of desire represents not so much a secret to decipher, but more an effect of the discourse that produces the individual as subject—or, perhaps, the effect of practices that aim to decipher it and thereby not only decipher but link it to what, in this operation or truth-test, is constituted as its truth—a truth given in the form of a proper identification of what it would be in reality (a truth-finding). The aim of the work is to do a history of the process, its results, and each term of the equation of the subject—including desire.[111] The idea, in essence, is "to investigate how people were brought to practice on themselves and on others a hermeneutics of desire of which their sexual behavior was doubtless the occasion, but certainly not the exclusive domain."[112] But along this path, Foucault soon discovered the need to engage—after the study of games of truth in their relations to each other and to relations of power—the study of "games of truth in the relationship of self with self and the constitution of oneself as a subject."[113] The *History of Sexuality* is also, in this sense, a history of the subject.

Politics and Ethics

What then is the relationship to politics? With "Scientia Sexualis" at the center of the analysis, *The Will to Know* offered a new approach to the study of power. Repression has the heuristic virtue of revealing "the social contours that determine it,"[114] but for the most part, that is by no means the only mechanism of power in the West. At the juncture of a political anatomy of the body and a bio-politics of the population, sexuality reveals another modality of power: relations of power pass not only through interdictions, but also through the obligation to speak. More precisely, power may also pass through the obligation to tell ourselves and another our "truth"—or the truth of our desire, or of what in the ritual of a test has been constituted as such; and this produces an effect, in return, on ourselves as subjects. It can have, for instance, an effect of confining the subject to an identity that has been assigned—as perhaps was the case for G. We say, with passion, that we are repressed; yet it is not only through repression that we are governed, but also through truth claims. This gives rise to the need to develop a different analytics of power, one focused more on a strategic model than on a juridical one. The argument, of course, is not that repression does not exist, or that one should not oppose it. It is rather that the mechanisms of power have been transformed: the question focuses now on our own truth-telling, and it is now our "docility"—our complacency or our cowardice—that takes center stage and becomes the locus of politics.

As for the link to ethics, let us propose a hypothesis. As we know, Foucault's writings pursued a conversation not only about power and knowledge, but also about the subject. In this vein, *The Will to Know* continued to elaborate the problem of blindness—a theme already present in the "Lecture on Nietzsche" (just recall this passage from *The Dawn*: "Why does man not see things? He finds himself in the way; he hides things").[115] This elaboration would require a discussion of the dialectic of master and slave (as Hegel developed it in the *Phenomenology of Spirit*) and could be read as a reaction against Althusser's view of subjection (as a challenge to his distinction, in "Ideology and Ideological State Apparatuses," between "'bad subjects' who on occasion provoke the intervention of one of the detachments of the [repressive] State apparatus," and "the vast majority of [good] subjects" who "work all right 'all by themselves,' i.e. by ideology [whose concrete forms are realized in the Ideological State Apparatuses]").[116] But if God is dead and so is ideology, then how can one proceed on these questions?

An indication had come a few years earlier. In a lecture delivered in 1969 entitled "What Is an Author?" Foucault had directly examined the problem of the "author-function"—the formulation of which he borrowed from Samuel Beckett ("'What does it matter who is speaking?' someone said; 'What does it matter who is speaking?'").[117] Exploring the author-function, Foucault suggested, might allow us to introduce a "typology of discourses" and to "reexamine the privilege of the subject."[118] And in order to do that—to reexamine the privileged place of the subject, to "remove from the subject its originary and foundational role, and to analyze it as a complex and variable function of discourse"—Foucault proposed asking the following set of questions: "How, under what conditions, and in what form can something like a subject appear in the order of discourses? What place can it occupy in each type of discourse, what functions does it exercise, and following what rules?"[119] On the basis of these questions it might be possible to identify a certain structure of discourses in the case, for example, of Charcot and his patient G.—a structure of discourse that might account for the different modalities of subjectification, and for the different modalities in the relationship of a subject to its desire. These might include the discourse of the master, of the hysteric, of the teacher and savant. It might then be possible to compare these discourses and their structure to the types of truthful speech—the *veridictions*—that Foucault later defined in *The Courage of Truth*: a comparison, as it were, of the discourses of psychiatric power and of *parrhesiastic* truth-telling.

The study of avowal at Louvain would fit neatly here. By tracing a genealogy of avowal and exploring different forms of truth-telling over the past two centuries, the Louvain lectures once again take up the theme of the production and manifestation of truth, with a focus on the subject. In the realm of knowledge, avowal serves as proof; in the realm of the event it serves as a test. *Juridiction*, the telling of justice, is a continuation of agonistic competition through other means which are centered on the subject. But the Louvain lectures go further; they allow us to discover, under the mask of neutrality that those who profess truth are wont to wear, "the forms and transformations of the will to know that is instinct, passion, the relentless inquisitor, cruel refinement, and meanness."[120] The Louvain lectures also displace the issue of subjection into the field of penal law and criminal justice. This is a strategic move: what it does is to hand over to the disciplines that study the *crimen* and the *discrimen* the opportunity to study how an individual constitutes himself as subject. It is to those disciplines—criminal law, criminology, criminal justice, and the psychological sciences—that Foucault offers the challenge of exploring, as he said in his inaugural lecture in Louvain, "governing through truth," which raises both the political question of "how the individual finds himself tied, and accepts to be tied, to the power exerted over him," and the epistemological question of "knowing how subjects are effectively tied within and by the forms of veridiction in which they engage."[121]

From Governing Through Truth to the Courage of Truth

What then is really at stake in the lectures from the period 1980–81? According to Foucault himself, lecturing at Dartmouth and Berkeley, the goal was to produce a theoretical analysis that also has a "political dimension" insofar as it related to "what we are willing to accept in our world, to accept, to refuse, and to change, both in ourselves and in our circumstances."[122] The objective, then, is threefold. The first objective is to conduct an analysis of the ways in which an individual constitutes himself and is constituted by others as a subject telling truth—to analyze in effect forms of veridiction. The second is to build from there "a genealogy of the subject"—which is a way both to write "a history of what we have done" and to pose "a diagnosis of what we are."[123] And from there, the third is to to develop a critical philosophy whose goal is to determine not the conditions under which "a subject in general may understand an object in general,"[124] but rather "the conditions and the indefinite possibilities of transforming the subject, of transforming ourselves."[125]

From Critique to *Aufklärung*

Two texts are of particular importance here: a lecture delivered in 1978 titled "What is Critique?" and the 1980 lectures *On the Government of the Living*. At the threshold between governing through truth and the courage of truth, the Louvain lectures elaborate the answer Foucault had sketched three years earlier in "What Is Critique?" The anchor for the work to come would be his definition of critique: in the face of increased governmentalization of society and individuals, critique could be thought of as the "art of not being governed quite so much"[126] or, as he would say, "how not to be governed *like that*"[127]—an art form that developed "as a counterpart, or rather as a partner and adversary at the same time, to the arts of governing."[128] More precisely, from the moment that governing begins to produce subjected individuals "through mechanisms of power that claim truth," critique becomes the "art of voluntary unservitude" or a form of "reflexive disobedience" whose function is "de-subjection [désassujettissement] in the game that might be called, in a word, the politics of truth."[129]

Three points should be clarified. First, as Foucault himself observed, this definition of critique is not far removed from the one Kant gave of the Enlightenment in his brief essay of 1784, *Was ist Aufklärung?*"[130] For Kant, as we know, critique is a question posed to knowledge: "Do you know up to what point you can know?"[131] The corollary, naturally, is that the Enlightenment itself is a call to courage: the courage to leave the state of voluntary minority, that condition characterized by the inability to make use of one's own understanding without direction from another. Like voluntary unservitude, then, the Enlightenment implicates and calls for a transformation of the self. It is necessary to dare to know—this is, after all, its motto. But dare to know what? For Foucault, the challenge goes beyond simply knowing the limits of knowledge and reason. For him, the challenge is to know "who we are in our present and in our current situation,"[132] and this requires "that we see under what conditions . . . we can apply this question of the Enlightenment at any time in history, that is, the question of the relationships between power, truth, and the subject."[133]

Second, who we are in our present and in our actuality is intimately related to the subject of knowledge, and it has both a political and an epistemological aspect. The nineteenth and twentieth centuries offered certain objects for critique: scientific positivism and the rationalization of state power. In Germany, from Hegel to the Frankfurt School, "to dare to know" would come to mean daring to ask whether there is "something in rationalization or perhaps in reason itself that is somehow responsible for the excesses of power."[134] In France it would take phenomenology and the philosophy of sciences of Bachelard, Cavaillès, and Canguilhem for the question of the Enlightenment to return, and to do so in two symmetrical forms: to dare to know "how [it is] that rationalization leads to the furor of power" and, conversely, "how this rationality is formed on the basis of something that is entirely other."[135] But in addition to phenomenology and the philosophy of sciences in France, one could add what Foucault referred to as "our history for over a century": for, as Foucault explains, "by dint of repeatedly telling ourselves that our social or economic forms of organization lacked rationality, we found ourselves face-to-face with either too much or not enough reason, but in any case surely facing too much power."[136] And by the same token, "by dint of repeatedly opposing the ideologies of violence and the real scientific theory of society, of the proletariat, and of history, we found ourselves faced with two forms of power that were as alike as two brothers: Fascism and Stalinism."[137]

Third and last: the question of the Enlightenment has most often been raised in terms of knowledge and of what knowledge has become with the advent of modern science. From this perspective, to be critical has been — "since Kant, because of Kant"[138] — to question the legitimacy of what Foucault called "the historical modes of knowing,"[139] and to ask about them the following questions: "What misconceptions has knowledge formed about itself and to what excessive use has it been exposed? To what domination has it therefore been linked?"[140] In contrast to this approach, Foucault engaged the question of the Enlightenment from the angle of power. To the inquiry into legitimacy, he proposed that we substitute a test — what he referred to as *"une épreuve d'événementialisation"*[141] — covering a set of elements wherein it might be possible to identify the connections between knowledge (procedures and effects of knowledge acceptable in one area at a particular time) and power (the "mechanisms susceptible of inducing behavior or speech").[142] The analysis would have to be simultaneously archaeological, genealogical, and strategic: these dimensions are all necessary to recover the conditions of acceptability of singularities whose intelligibility, Foucault explained, "is established by identifying the very interactions and strategies within which they are integrated."[143]

This is where Foucault's 1980 lectures *On the Government of the Living* come in. From the very first, Foucault advances two hypotheses: on the one hand, "it is probable that no hegemony can be exerted without something like an alethurgy;"[144] on the other hand, "what we call knowledge, that is to say the production of truth in individual consciences through logical-experimental processes," is "merely one of the possible forms alethurgy can take."[145] It is important to note here that by hegemony he meant "the fact of finding oneself leading others, conducting them and conducting their conduct,"[146] and that by alethurgy — a neologism derived from the word *alēthourgēs*, truthful — he meant "the set of verbal and nonverbal processes by which one manifests what is postulated as true as opposed to the false, hidden, inexpressible, unpredictable, forgotten, et cetera."[147] The aim of the 1980 lectures is to further elaborate the notion of "government by truth."[148] It is a question, Foucault explained, of "shaking up the by-now well-worn theme of power-knowledge," a theme that had itself served as "a way to shake up the pervasiveness of analyses in the field of intellectual history that were centered around the notion of a dominant ideology."[149]

Let's return, for a moment, to the question of ideology. From as early as *The Punitive Society* and *Truth and Juridical Forms*, Foucault had refused to analyze "man's thought, behavior and knowledge" through the lens of ideology.[150] One reason was that the notion of ideology is "tied, at least implicitly, [. . .] to the opposition between truth and falsehood, reality and illusion, the scientific and the non-scientific, the rational and the irrational."[151] By contrast, Foucault focused on knowledge in order to get beyond these distinctions and to call our attention instead to the practices that constitute the domains structured by them. Another reason was that ideological analysis is blind to mechanisms of subjection: in talking about power, Foucault tried to move the analysis from the system of dominant representations to the techniques and procedures by which power is effectively exercised. *On the Government of the Living* added to this a third shift, this one regarding the subject. Foucault there inverted the "politico-philosophical question."[152] He went beyond the examination of a subject capable of voluntarily entering a relationship of knowledge in terms of what he "can say about, in favor or against the power that subjects him against his will."[153] Instead, he explored how the problematization of power itself can shed light "on the subject of knowledge and on the relationship to truth to which he is involuntarily held."[154]

This represented a new take on the question Foucault had tackled in "What is Critique?" It rested less on a thesis than on an attitude—an attitude of doubt resembling less the *epochē* of the skeptics than a political version of the methodical doubt by which Descartes deduced the existence of a thinking subject conscious that he is thinking.[155] Foucault's version consisted of a doubt that no power "can be taken for granted" and that none deserves "to be accepted from the outset."[156] What determines power's legitimacy or illegitimacy cannot be a "critique of representations in terms of truth and error, truth and falsehood, ideology and science, rationality and irrationality."[157] Instead, "the movement to free oneself from power is what must reveal the transformations of the subject and his relationship to truth."[158] Foucault replaced the series "universal category-humanist position-ideological analysis"[159] with a new series: "refusal of universal categories-antihumanist position-technological analysis of mechanisms of power."[160] Needless to say, one of the universal categories he rejected was the subject that the former series presupposed.

To analyze the effects on the subject of power's "lack of a ground in right or necessity,"[161] Foucault introduced the notions of regimes of truth and of regimes of knowledge, along with that of alethurgy. Foucault explained that in common language, the word "regime" refers to the set of processes and institutions that bind individuals, or at least that compel them in a relatively pressing manner. If it is a political regime, they are forced to obey the decisions of a collective authority in the context of a territorial unity in which that authority exercises a right of sovereignty; if it is a penal regime, they are forced to obey general laws.[162] By "regimes of truth," Foucault made an analogy by which he meant "the set of procedures and institutions by which individuals are engaged and constrained to perform, under certain conditions and with certain effects, well-defined acts of truth."[163] These acts, which are obligations of truth, constitute part of an alethurgy "the subject has to carry out."[164] What Foucault meant by the notion of a "regime of knowledge" was the articulation of a regime of truth within a juridico-political regime. This established the subject as a nodal point in the relationship between the epistemological and the political: he is a subject "in both senses of the word, subject in a manifestation of truth and subject in a relation of power."[165]

The method, here, would be to engage in an "(an-)archeology of knowledge." Foucault sought not to conduct "a global study of relations of political power and knowledge or of scientific competences,"[166] but to examine how different regimes of truth constrain individuals to perform determinate acts of truth and how they tie "the manifestations of truth to the procedures and subjects that are their operators, their witnesses and eventually their objects."[167] Second, to clear away "the separation between science and ideology":[168] "Every regime of truth, whether scientific or not, involves more or less constraining methods that tie the manifestation of truth and the subject who engages in it."[169] Just as knowledge is simply "one of the possible forms of alethurgy,"[170] science—and the various games of truth to which this word refers—is but "one of the possible regimes of truth."[171] What is specific to science is that "the power of truth is organized in such a way that it is the truth itself that constrains."[172] The subject of a scientific discourse is "a subject that *makes* logic"[173] by subordinating the just to the true and the true to conformity with reality, just as in an apophantic assertion. In so doing, the subject grants "to the truth the right to say: you must accept me because I am the truth."[174]

This is a regime where—and this is the magic of logic—"the fact that it is a regime disappears, or at least does not appear."[175] This explains the political invisibility of those techniques of power that are articulated scientifically; and it also explains their necessity. If, in Western societies, hegemony is exercised through knowledge and power is founded on knowledge, what makes the unacceptable accepted is not just what is said on the topics about which truth is manifested; what also matters is the constitution of the subjects that are the operators or the witnesses of the alethurgy. Two paths are then available to critique. On the one hand, it can police the truth of statements; on the other, it can engage in a genealogy of the subject of scientific discourse and of the articulation of the juridico-political to the scientific. As a matter of fact, it is not enough to inquire why the relationship between government and truth has been defined since the eighteenth century in terms of a "certain reality that is the state or society"[176] and in terms of a "more or less objective knowledge of phenomena,"[177] whether this is done through the principle of rationality (Boreto), evidence (Quesnay), competence (Saint-Simon), general conscience (Rosa Luxemburg), or terror (Soljenitsyne).[178] Subjection and government by truth amounts to more than knowledge being put to political and social use. In our regime of knowledge, just as in others, the exercise of power goes through auto-alethurgies. The truth that emerges is constitutive of the subjects who tie themselves to it by avowing; it is actualized in their identities—which is also, possibly, where governing takes its hold.

From Techniques of Domination to Techniques of the Self

On a first reading, then, the lectures delivered during the period 1980–81 appear to open a passage from the techniques of domination to the techniques of the self. In his Dartmouth lectures in November 1980, *About the Beginning of the Self*, and in the Louvain lectures in 1981, Foucault distinguished, following Habermas, three types of techniques: the techniques of production, of signification, and of domination.[179] At Dartmouth he remarked that he had "insisted, I think, too much on the techniques of domination" when he was studying the asylum and the prison.[180] And he added, "Power consists in complex relations: these relations involve a set of rational techniques, and the efficiency of those techniques is due to a subtle integration of coercion-technologies and self-technologies."[181] At Louvain he explained that he had wanted to analyze "governmentality . . . understood as the set of relations of power and techniques that allow these power relations to be exercised"; and he added that he does not think "this governmentality must necessarily take the form of confinement, surveillance, and control."[182] As for discipline, it is certainly "a coherent technique whose form we find, with some variation, in prisons, schools, workshops, et cetera," but it is clear "that this was not the only technique for governing individuals and that currently, for example, the construction of an insurance-bound horizon of existence and security is a situation in which the conduct of individuals is insured, but along very different lines from those of the disciplines."[183]

The course summary for his 1980–81 lectures at the Collège de France, *Subjectivity and Truth*, sharpens the point. In tandem with the Louvain lectures, Foucault in Paris analyzed the techniques of the self, defined as "the procedures . . . proposed or prescribed to individuals in order to fix their identity, to maintain it or transform it according to a certain number of purposes and by means of relations of mastering of the self by the self or of knowledge of self by the self."[184] The project, he wrote, lies at the crossroads of the history of subjectivity and the analysis of forms of governmentality.[185] Previously, Foucault examined the "modes of objectification of the subject in realms of knowledge such as those dealing with language, labor, and life" and "the divisions operating in society in the name of madness, disease, delinquency, and their effects on the formation of a reasonable and normal subject."[186] Henceforth he would analyze "the development and transformation in our culture of the 'relations to oneself,' with their technical armature and their knowledge effects," as well as the "government of the self by oneself in its articulation with relations with others (such as one finds in pedagogy, counsels regarding conduct, spiritual direction, prescriptions for models of living, etc.)."[187]

On a second reading, though, it becomes clear that the goal is not only to shift the analysis from techniques of domination to techniques of the self, but also to compare their articulation in various auto-alethurgies and their effects on the constitution of the subject. The scene that opens the Dartmouth lectures opposes not Charcot to his patient G., but Doctor François Leuret—another French psychiatrist of the nineteenth century—to a patient called A., who is driven by repeated cold showers to recognize his own madness. Foucault saw in that scene an example of "the strange and complex relationships developed in our societies between individuality, discourse, truth, and coercion."[188] The idea then is to explore the interaction among the different techniques. According to Foucault, "if one wants to analyze the genealogy of the subject in Western civilization, one has to take into account not only techniques of domination but also techniques of the self. Let's say: one has to take into account the interaction between those two types of techniques—techniques of domination and techniques of the self."[189] What interests Foucault are the "the points where the technologies of domination of individuals over one another have recourse to processes by which the individual acts upon himself" or, conversely, "the points where the techniques of the self are integrated into structures of coercion or domination."[190] And the stakes are both philosophical as well as political: the project is to go beyond the philosophy of the subject by studying the history of the practices that gave birth to the modern concept of the self.

Though the framing is slightly different, the Louvain lectures borrow the same opening episode and reveal similar preoccupations. But what retains Foucault's attention, beyond the articulation of techniques of domination and techniques of the self, is also the integration of the technologies of the subject with regimes of veridiction. Penal practice and criminal justice are illuminated, he says, when placed in the context of technologies of government. Six years earlier, *Discipline and Punish* had linked the penitentiary system to disciplinary techniques and processes. At Louvain he would compare avowal to those other procedures that seek to tie the individual to telling his truth, notably in religious practices, and situate avowal within "the broader history of . . . the techniques through which the individual is brought, either by himself or with the help or the direction of another, to transform himself and to modify his relationship to himself."[191] To the criminologists who question him about the importance of this problem compared to that of the truth of the subject, Foucault responded that it "does not simply touch upon the history of psychiatry or the history of sexuality," but equally on "the history of truth and the history of subjectivity in the West."[192] And he then added, "I am wondering if I shouldn't write a history of subjectivity-truth."[193] A draft was delivered in these Louvain lectures.

Drawing on earlier analyses of the examination of conscience, the direction of conscience, and rituals of penance that he began to sketch at Dartmouth and Berkeley, Foucault reconnects the episodes at Louvain, as

Deleuze would say,[194] and invents a new series that stretches over twenty-eight centuries and weaves together the scenes discussed in the *Lessons on the Will to Know*, the practices and rituals discussed in *Subjectivity and Truth* and *Christianity and Confession*, the production of judicial truth he studied in Rio and in other lectures at the Collège de France, and the criminal justice episodes analyzed in "About the Concept of the 'Dangerous Individual' in Nineteenth Century Legal Psychiatry."[195] It is a heterogeneous series that shakes all of our "familiar ways of thinking"[196]—somewhat like Borges's taxonomy, which opened *The Order of Things*. It represents a break from the more traditional historians who study social processes and in doing so attribute to society the role of subject. It also breaks with those philosophers who prefer "a subject without history."[197]

From Avowal to *Parrhēsia*

The overarching project of the new series presented at Louvain is to question and unsettle the sovereign subject—thus laying the groundwork, in many ways, for *The Courage of Truth* three years later. Foucault takes up the concept and examines several "alethurgies," which he refers to as "ritual procedure[s] for bringing forth *alēthes*: that which is true."[198] In studying avowal, Foucault effectively identifies certain structural features on the basis of which he would later define *parrhēsia*, in terms both of the similarities between that form of truth-telling and avowal (especially in the relationship between the speaker and the listener) and of distinctions (especially in the relationship between the speaker and the statement).[199] At Louvain, Foucault explores the truth-telling of the prophet, the sage, and the man of *technē*—which he will later oppose to the veridiction in *parrhēsia*. He multiplies the different versions of the partner who listens or guides—the critical role of that "character very consistently presented as the indispensable partner, that necessary auxiliary in this obligation to tell truth about oneself," which he will compare later to the *parrhesiast*.[200] He highlights the effects of the structure of relations between this character, the partner of truth-telling, the avowing subject, and truth told—the effects of *alethurgical* forms—on the way in which individuals constitute themselves as moral subjects. And he studies various techniques of the transformation of the self—for instance, memorization of rules of conduct and examination of one's conscience—techniques that he will later describe as forms of *epimeleia heautou*, practices of the care of the self.[201]

The common element in avowal and *parrhēsia* is that "certain cost of enunciation,"[202] of which Foucault emphasizes two modalities in 1981. These would be associated, in 1984, to two modalities of courage: minimal and maximal.[203] The first modality involves putting at risk the relationship that unites the speaker to the listener. "For the declaration 'I love you' to be an avowal, the other must be able to accept, refuse, break out in laughter, slap the person, or say, 'I will speak about this with my husband,'" Foucault remarks, with tongue in cheek, at Louvain.[204] Three years later: "For there to be *parrhēsia*, . . . the subject must take a certain amount of risk, risk regarding the very relationship he has with the one he is addressing . . . We can see this clearly in *parrhēsia* as direction of conscience—for example, where there can only be direction of conscience if there is friendship, and where the use of truth in the direction of conscience puts at risk precisely this relationship of friendship that made the very discourse of truth possible."[205] The second modality is the risk of losing one's life.[206] At Louvain, Foucault discusses the example of the martyr in his analysis of penance, and, conversely, of the lapsed, those Christians who feared stating their conviction in the face of the danger of persecution. In *The Courage of Truth*, Foucault turns to the example of Plato, who, despite danger, goes to see Dionysius of Syracuse to give his opinion.[207]

As for the differences, Foucault says at Louvain that avowal "is not simply an observation about oneself. It is a sort of engagement, but an engagement of a particular type. It does not obligate one to do such and such a thing. It implies that he who speaks promises to be what he affirms himself to be precisely because he is just that."[208] Somewhat like a *speech act*, avowal gives birth to the avowing subject, who takes on as his own the truth told and binds himself to it, regardless of his liberty to speak or not, and regardless of the relationship between the truth told and reality. To be sure, *parrhēsia* is also a type of commitment, but it implies—to paraphrase Foucault—that the speaker commits to thinking and believing what he says he thinks and believes, precisely because he thinks and believes those things. Like the avowing subject, the *parrhesiast* "signs the truth he tells, binds himself to his truth, and obligates himself";[209] but if he does so, it is not because he said so, but because what he said is "his opinion, his thought, his belief,"[210] and he has chosen to speak at the risk of endangering his relationship to the other, or his very own life. In short, the avowal is a ritual of discourse in which the subject who speaks overlaps with the subject of the statement; in *parrhēsia*, the speaker seeks to overlap with the speaking subject.

At Louvain, Foucault explores the veridiction of the prophet, the sage, and the man of *technē*. Regarding the prophet, he will later explain in *The Courage of Truth* that he does not speak on his own behalf, but "articulates and utters a discourse that is not his."[211] He is located between the present and the future; he reveals, but his speech is unclear. This is the figure of Tiresias in the Louvain lectures, at least before, out of anger, he mixes prophecy with *parrhēsia*. The sage speaks in his own name, but on the condition of being "solicited by the questions of someone, or in an emergency by the city."[212] Unlike the prophet who says what will happen, the sage says what is. This is the figure of Seneca solicited by Serenus in the Louvain lectures. The man of *technē* has a duty to bestow upon others the wisdom of his knowledge and his competences. His veridiction creates a link that can be "that of common knowledge, heritage, or tradition" or "of personal recognition or friendship."[213] This is the figure of Oedipus in the Louvain lectures, at least before the plague comes upon Thebes. And *parrhēsia* is opposed, term by term, to these three forms of veridiction: the *parrhesiast* speaks in his own name about the present in the clearest possible way; he initiates and assumes his obligation to intervene "in the singularity of individuals, situations, and circumstances";[214] and his truth-telling creates the possibility—"structurally necessary," Foucault says—of "hatred and anguish."[215]

With regard to the avowing subject's partner, the Louvain lectures multiply the possibilities and characters. In *Wrong-Doing, Truth-Telling* it is no longer Charcot but numerous others who are introduced: Leuret, Menelaus, Tiresias, Jocasta, the shepherd of Cithaeron, Seneca, and, behind them, the long procession of specialists of *discrimen* and *crimen*: confessors, directors of conscience, inquisitors, psychiatrists, judges, and criminologists. All are involved in some alethurgy. All take part in a ritual by means of which an individual constitutes himself and is constituted by others as a subject telling truth about himself. But, as Foucault will remark in *The Courage of Truth*, their status is more or less institutionalized, and they practice different modes of truth-telling—with the effect, conversely, of multiplying the subjects constituted in these games of truth. Faced with the hand that Tiresias has dealt, for instance, Oedipus is nothing more than a toy of fate, and to this he resists. But faced with the truth-play that he himself imposes on the shepherd, Oedipus is able to recognize his own responsibility, to recognize that he, the man of *technē*, has been the cause of his own blindness.

No more than the prophet, the sage, or the man of *technē*, the *parrhesiast* does not confess. Like them, he tells truth. But his manner of telling truth makes him the partner of a very particular avowal and, beyond avowal, the partner of the care of the self. In *The Courage of Truth*, Foucault will say that he is "that other who is indispensable for truth-telling about oneself,"[216] who helps others in "their blindness about who they are, about themselves, and in consequence not of a blindness due to an ontological structure, but due to some fault, a distraction or moral dissipation, the consequence of an inattention, a complacency, a weakness."[217] He is indispensable because he offers his assistance in the form of a dialogue that is opposed—again, term for term—to the art of rhetoric. First, the *parrhesiast* binds together the speaker and the statement in a relationship of conviction, whereas the rhetorician unties it. Second, the *parrhesiast* puts at risk the relationship between the speaker and the listener, whereas the rhetorician assures it. Third, the *parrhesiast* proposes the link between the listener and the statement, whereas the rhetorician imposes it. The corollary to this is that the *parrhesiast* offers his interlocutor the possibility to constitute himself freely as a courageous subject—a subject with the courage of truth. He leaves him—and this is a sign of recognition—"the difficult task of having the courage to accept this truth, to recognize it, and to make it a principle of conduct."[218] In the Louvain lectures, this is the figure of Antilochus faced with Menelaus's challenge. It is also that of Oedipus when faced with the shepherd of Cithaeron—as is shown in *Oedipus at Colonus* by the heroic death of the blind tyrant at the end of the path where his daughter has guided him.[219]

To be sure, *Wrong-Doing, Truth-Telling* also examines techniques of examination and direction of conscience. By comparing these techniques as they existed in antiquity and in Christianity, the lectures explore the work and discourse through which, and the relations and auto-alethurgic procedures within which, subjects are formed—those subjects who want to loosen the grip of what dominates and governs them, or those subjects who submit to the desires of others without resistance by shutting down their preference for autonomy over obedience. In *The Courage of Truth*, by contrast, Foucault will highlight ancient ideas regarding the care of the self and *parrhēsia*. It is as if Foucault studied the forms of governing through truth in 1981 so as to better identify the formal conditions of the courage of truth in 1984. If that is the case, it becomes clear why the leading character of *Wrong-Doing, Truth-Telling* is the avowing subject, while the leading character of *The Courage of Truth* is the partner of the avowal—the *parrhesiast*, perhaps even the critical philosopher.

Telling-Truth, Loosening One's Hold on Oneself

In order to tie together the three dimensions we have thus far explored, it would be important at this juncture to show, first, how Foucault's analysis of auto-alethurgies in *Wrong-Doing, Truth-Telling* can contribute to the task of a genealogy of the subject presupposed by the discourse of science—as Foucault would explain in the first lecture of *The Hermeneutics of the Subject.*[220] Second, it would be useful to highlight what gives the truth its force in a scientific regime of truth, a regime in which the subject so often disappears. Third, it would be wise to emphasize the inseparably political and ethical dimensions of these questions—questions that lie at the crossroads of a politics of identity and a "politics of things"[221]—and to recall the questions Foucault raised during an interview in Louvain: How was fascism able to "take," given that "the fathers of German families were not fascist in 1930?"[222] How do democratic regimes tie together subjection and government?[223] Finally, it would be crucial to differentiate between two possible meanings of the term *ēthos*: on the one hand, the idea of an identity that results from a process of subjection, drawing on the common meaning of the word *ēthos* as a set of characteristics that individuals who belong to the same society have in common; and on the other hand, the idea of a process by which individuals undo the identities through which they are dominated and governed.

We will limit ourselves, though, in this conclusion, to a more modest task: to explore how *Wrong-Doing, Truth-Telling* contributes to the search for "the conditions and the indefinite possibilities of transforming the subject, of transforming ourselves."[224] By reading in parallel the Louvain lectures and *The Courage of Truth*, it may be possible to discern the distinction between the two critical philosophies Foucault evoked in 1981: first, the analysis of "epistemological structures," and second, the analysis of "alethurgic forms."[225] The question raised by the second is not to seek "under what conditions a statement is true,"[226] but rather to explore what a statement does and whether what it does can be undone. If, in order to situate his analyses, Foucault outlines at Louvain a "*counter-positivism that is not the opposite of positivism but rather its counterpoint*,"[227] this suggests that he may have been looking, beyond Kantian critique, for the conditions of the "courage of the Enlightenment."[228] How can we speak to meet the challenge of daring to know (truth-test) what we are (truth-finding), and in so doing open the possibility of transforming ourselves (truth-test)? How can we—much like Antilochus and Menelaus—take up the challenge to constitute ourselves as subjects of the courage of truth?

By the 1980s, Foucault was certainly not new to the question of how telling could not only inform, but also transform. We could look, for instance, at the description he gave of his book *History of Madness* in a 1978 interview, where he explained that the book had transformed the "historical, theoretical, moral and ethical relationship" that both he and his readers might have "to madness, to the mad, to the psychiatric institution and to the very truth of psychiatric discourse."[229] Foucault observed that the book functioned "as an experience [. . .], far more than as the chronicling of a historical truth."[230] This required, to be sure, that "what is said must still be true in terms of an academic and historically verifiable truth"; but "what is most crucial does not reside in these true and historically verifiable observations, so much as in the experience the book provokes. Yet this experience is neither true nor false. An experience is always a fiction. It is something that one constructs for oneself, something that does not exist beforehand and that does exist after."[231] Foucault spoke of *Discipline and Punish* in strikingly similar terms: "To a certain extent, it is a purely historical work. But those who loved or detested it did so because they felt that the book spoke about them, about the contemporary world, or about their own relationships with the contemporary world, as it is accepted by all."[232]

In a similar manner, *Wrong-Doing, Truth-Telling* and the other contemporary lectures can be interpreted as an effort to transform our historical, theoretical, and ethical relationship to the subject. Just like Oedipus, we do not always know that we are speaking about ourselves when we curse another and push him to the other side of *discrimen*'s border, into the barbarian lands of the *crimen*. Naturally, this raises a great difficulty: How can we speak so as to problematize what seems so evident and weaken the hold of identifications? How shall we proceed, and through what choreographed succession of linguistic acts? How can truth-telling materialize within a "set of operations" that would enable "veridiction to induce transformations in the soul," which is to say, have ethopoietic effects?[233] How can one speak, how can one write so that the subject "changes itself, transforms itself, displaces itself and becomes to some extent other than itself," as it does through the practices of the care of the self?[234]

A possible answer may emerge from what we have already suggested: if, at Louvain in 1981, Foucault analyzed how subjects fix their identities and shape and transform themselves by speaking and writing about themselves, it is undoubtedly because he turned to the study of the government of truth to uncover the conditions of the courage of truth. This hypothesis, though, must be completed: it is almost as if his project was to develop an auto-alethurgic practice capable of loosening one's hold on one's self. This transformation would be simultaneously ethical and political. It would amount to a clinical philosophical practice in which one turns and returns to philosophical texts to enrich and confront one's critical practice.

Austin asked, "How to do things with words?" Perhaps Foucault's question was: "How to undo things with words?" Like Austin, Foucault explored in *Wrong-Doing, Truth-Telling* the illocutionary and perlocutionary dimensions of language; like Austin, he challenged the privileged position, within the philosophical tradition and scientific discourse, of categoric statements and apophantic games of truth. That said, two differences are worth noting. First, the Louvain lectures not only examine different verbal performances and auto-alethurgies, but themselves take on the form of an alethurgy and a performance if they are analyzed in terms of their pragmatics.[235] Second, for Foucault, what words do and undo are the identities through which we are governed. What they do and undo is our identification with the subject "as he represents himself to himself and as he is recognized by others as a truth-telling subject" in an alethurgy.[236] If this is right, then how can one speak to undo the chains that tie the subject to the identities he has made his own—especially when those ties have the objective form of a logical predicate and the subjective form of "economic and unconscious" investments,[237] and are buttressed by myriad forms of self-interest and attachment?

We know well that for Althusser, what consitutes concrete individuals and subjects is an interpellation through which they recognize themselves—a process in which Althusser identified the function of ideology. Foucault reformulates the question: supposing that subjection is an effect of discourse and that different discursive practices produce different subjects, how then can one speak in such a way as to facilitate rather than

hinder or obstruct—for both the one who speaks and the one who is addressed—to get beyond the state of immaturity that so troubled Kant?
How should we formulate the relationship between the one who tells, the
one who hears, and what is said, in order to help constitute subjects as
enlightened or autonomous—that is to say, for them to be in a position
to make use of their own understanding rather than to depend on that of
another?

One might think that someone on this path—someone who effectively
is trying to help themselves or another overcome a certain blindness—
may need to be as reserved as Socrates.[238] Yet *The Courage of Truth* seems
to suggest, in certain passages, that this may not always be the best approach; that, in certain circumstances, the philosopher cannot merely "be
content with asking questions."[239] Perhaps, in working on ourselves, we
should "have access to the greatest possible share of what we are told is
inaccessible."[240] In any case, Foucault seemed to suggest at times that the
parrhesiast should not always leave the "difficult task of interpretation" to
those he addresses.[241] How then can the *parrhesiast* navigate between a reserved stance and an interpretive voice?

Foucault proposed an answer to this complex problem as early as 1971,
when he returned to Nietzsche, to genealogy, and to those series of me-
thodically diversified histories which are true "in terms of academic truth"
and are told in the mode of fiction.[242] As we know, a series is a set of elements, so that the meaning of an element does not stem from a correspondence between the sign and its objective referent, between the word
and the thing, but is produced instead by the other elements with which
an element is associated and by the system of differences the game establishes. If the philosopher stays reserved, it is that he does not tell those
he addresses what they should think. Yet if he also takes a lead in the in-
terpretative task, he gives them material to think about by making them
spectators of the series he has organized. He invites them to think about
what the present was for others: Every history provides information and
draws attention to moments and relationships that can then serve as
material, in the series, for further comparisons. He also invites them to
think about their own present. As the recounted histories are placed into
a series, their propositional contents and objective referents erode, while
sets of questions and transformations—of similarities, inversions, and
displacements—emerge. A new instrument also appears. While it appears
at first to be like a kaleidoscope, once the readers take it up, it resembles

more a telescope that allows them to see in and of their present what they had been unable to discern previously.[243]

The histories that Foucault told in 1981 in *Wrong-Doing, Truth-Telling* present characters who subject themselves, in both senses of the word: by telling who they are, they subject themselves to the power that is exercised by them or on them. The histories provide information, to those who listen, about prejuridical and juridical forms of dispute resolution, about ancient and Christian practices of examination and of direction of conscience, about *exomologēsis* and *exagoreusis*, about inquiry, examination, and expertise. And they allow those who listen to inductively discover categories and a set of questions with which to better see and read the present. The categories: modes of subjection, ethical substance, techniques of transformation of the self, and *telos*, among others. The questions: who is doing the speaking (the director or the directed), whether their relationship is temporary or unending, whether one becomes master of oneself or remains forever in obedience, et cetera. *Wrong-Doing, Truth-Telling* is in this sense a heterotopia, "capable of juxtaposing in a single real place several spaces, several sites that are in themselves incompatible."[244] In this place we see a succession of scenes that gives to each "her or his own little box for her or his own little personal decay."[245] The scenes seem to produce mirror-like effects on those who view them. They allow those who look to see themselves where they are not—a matter of seeing, of visibility—and to discover themselves absent from where they are, since they see themselves elsewhere.

It may now be possible to make better sense of Foucault's statement, in his 1978 essay "What is Critique?," that to make the Enlightenment—the courage of knowing—into the "central question" means to "fabricate a history, as if through fiction, that would be traversed by the question of the relations between the structures of rationality that articulate the true discourse and the mechanisms of subjection that are tied to it."[246] In the same way, it may be possible to make better sense of why archeology, genealogy, and strategy are not "successive levels that would be derived, one from the other," but rather "necessarily simultaneous dimensions of the same analysis."[247] To dare to know, it seems, one must engage in a historical-philosophical practice that Foucault insisted is neither philosophy of history nor history of philosophy. One must break the hold of that identification by which one becomes the subject presupposed by the discourse of truth.[248] And to do so, "one has to make one's own history."[249]

One must stage on the *theatrum philosophicum*[250] a series of episodes — a series of series — that manifests how truth is transformed into *ēthos* and *ēthos* into truth.[251] *Wrong-Doing, Truth-Telling* is one of these series.

This is, of course, a delicate matter. Insofar as Foucault seemed to make himself the partner of an avowal, it was an avowal in which the subject avows (or not) to himself in such a way that there is no opportunity to take hold of the subject. To those who listened, Foucault proposed the "moral task"[252] of courageously accepting a truth he only half-told them. This might explain Foucault's attraction to Sophocles's *Oedipus Rex*, which he so often returned to, from the *Lessons on the Will to Know* to *The Government of the Self and Others*, including in *Wrong-Doing, Truth-Telling*. Foucault would highlight two aspects of *Oedipus Rex*, among others: on the one hand, "the reconstitution of the story by the missing half" (this is what he described as the "double game of the symbolic mechanism," Oedipus being the symbol),[253] and on the other hand, the necessity of repetition, for Oedipus finally to be "able to recognize himself as the one who did what he did" and to say "I" (this corresponds to the three alethurgies in which a pair of characters each possess and tell half-truths).[254]

In the end, this leaves us free to guide ourselves by that "only kind of curiosity . . . that is worth acting upon with a degree of obstinacy: not the curiosity that seeks to assimilate what is proper for one to know, but that which enables one to loosen one's hold on one's self."[255] That curiosity, in other words, which might enable us to loosen ourselves from the engagements and interests that attach us to our identities, and from the fear that we will find ourselves naked if we undo these identities without daring, like Diogenes, to embrace our act. Foucault suggested that there is militancy in the Cynic life "that returns the beneficial sovereignty of the *bios philosophikos* into combative endurance."[256] If the study of governing through truth means examining the speech acts by which individuals constitute themselves as subjects and tie themselves to identities given as their truth, then to oppose the courage of truth to the power of truth may mean inventing a philosophical clinical practice of the subject that enables subjects to loosen themselves from the identities by which they are governed.

[NOTES]

An earlier version of this essay was presented by Fabienne Brion and Bernard Harcourt as "Le Pouvoir de la vérité. Trois lectures de *Mal faire, dire vrai*, de Michel Foucault," a series of lectures presented at the Collège Belgique, Académie royale des sciences, des lettres et des beaux-arts de Belgique, October 27–28, 2010, available at http://www.academieroyale.be /cgi?pag=1026&tab=146&rec=10279. Versions of the first and third part were presented in a seminar titled "Foucault on Ethics and Politics" led by Bernard Harcourt and Fabienne Brion at the University of Chicago (2010–11), and in a course on Foucault and criminology taught by Fabienne Brion and Véronique Voruz at the Catholic University of Louvain (2008–9, 2009–10 and 2010–11). An earlier version of the second part and of the conclusion was presented by Fabienne Brion in a course she taught on Foucault and criminology at the Catholic University of Louvain in 2011–12.

For the most part, the English translations of passages from Foucault's writings are our own, and this is indicated by the fact that the first reference in the note is to the French text; in those cases, we have provided citations to English editions and translations, and to the related pagination in English, where published translations are available. Where the citation reference is first to an English edition, we have relied on that preexisting translation; we also have tried to include the original French source reference.

Special thanks to Daniel Nichanian for comments on the English version of this essay and for assisting with certain portions of its translation, and to Daniel Henry for outstanding research assistance.

1. Michel Foucault, *La Volonté de savoir: Histoire de la sexualité 1* (Paris: Gallimard, 1976), p. 79; English edition, *The History of Sexuality, Volume I: An Introduction*, Robert Hurley, trans. (New York: Vintage Books, 1978), p. 59.

2. Ibid., p. 79 n. 1.

3. See Foucault, *The History of Sexuality, Volume I*, p. 59 n. 2.

4. The other five volumes of the *History of Sexuality* that were promised were called "2 *La chair et le corps*," "3 *La croisade des enfants*," "4 *La femme, la mère et l'hystérique*," "5 *Les pervers*," and "6 *Population et races*."

5. Michel Foucault, "Interview with Jean François and John de Wit," this volume, p. 253.

6. Michel Foucault, "Interview with Christian Panier and Pierre Watté," this volume, p. 248.

7. Michel Foucault, "À propos de la généalogie de l'éthique: Un aperçu du travail en cours," interview with Hubert Dreyfus and Paul Rabinow, reproduced in *Dits & écrits* IV (1980–88) no. 344, 609–31, p. 618 (Paris: Gallimard, 1994); English translation, "On the Genealogy of Ethics: An Overview of Work in Progress," 253–80, in *Ethics: Subjectivity and Truth: Essential Works of Foucault 1954–1984*, Paul Rabinow, ed. (New York: The New Press, 1997), p. 262.

8. Michel Foucault, "La maison des fous" ("La casa della folia," in F. Basaglia and F. Basaglia-Ongardo, *Crimini di pace*, Turin, Einaudi, 1975, pp. 151–69), reproduced in *Dits & écrits* II (1970–75), no. 146, 693–98, p. 694 (Paris: Gallimard, 1994).

9. Foucault, "À propos de la généalogie de l'éthique," p. 618; English translation p. 262.

10. Michel Foucault, *L'herméneutique du sujet: Cours au Collège de France. 1981–1982*, Frédéric Gros, ed. (Paris: Gallimard/Seuil, 2001), pp. 3–4; English edition, *The Hermeneutics of the Subject: Lectures at the Collège de France, 1981–1982*, Graham Burchell, trans., Arnold I. Davidson, English series ed. (New York: Picador, 2005), p. 2.

11. For a discussion of these four aspects of the relationship to the self, which the Louvain lectures explore without yet naming, cf. Foucault, "À propos de la généalogie de l'éthique: Un aperçu du travail en cours," in *Dits et écrits* IV, no. 326, pp. 394–97 and no. 344, pp. 619–21; English translation, "On the Genealogy of Ethics: An Overview of Work in Progress," at

pp. 263–64; as well as Michel Foucault, "Usage des plaisirs et techniques de soi" (*Le débat*, no. 27, November 1983, pp. 46–72), *Dits et écrits* IV, no. 338, pp. 556–57.

12. Foucault, "La maison des fous," p. 694.

13. Michel Foucault, "Inaugural Lecture," this volume, p. 21.

14. Michel Foucault, "Interview with André Berten," this volume, p. 235.

15. Michel Foucault, "Les intellectuels et le pouvoir" (interview with Gilles Deleuze, March 4, 1972, published originally in *L'Arc*, no. 49: *Gilles Deleuze*, 2nd trimester 1972, pp. 3–10), in *Dits & écrits* II, no. 106, 306–16, at p. 307 (Paris: Gallimard, 1994); English translation, "Intellectuals and Power," 205–17, in *Language, Counter-Memory, Practice: Selected Essays and Interviews by Michel Foucault*, Donald F. Bouchard, ed. (Ithaca, NY: Cornell University Press, 1977), p. 206.

16. See Daniel Defert, "Chronologie," in Foucault, *Dits & écrits* I (1954–69) (Paris: Gallimard, 1994), p. 33.

17. Benny Lévy, alias Pierre Victor or "Victor," is one of the two Maoists with whom Foucault would debate in 1972 on the question of popular justice; the other, "Gilles," was André Glucksmann (cf. Michel Foucault, "Sur la justice populaire: Débat avec les maos," *Les Temps modernes*, 310 *bis*; *Nouveau fascisme, nouvelle démocratie*, June 1972, pp. 335–66, in *Dits & écrits* II, no. 108, pp. 340–69; English translation, "On Popular Justice: A Discussion with Maoists," pp. 1–36 in Michel Foucault, *Power/Knowledge: Selected Interviews and Other Writings, 1972–1977*, Colin Gordon, ed. [New York: Vintage, 1980]). Lévy, a philosopher, was one of the leaders of the Gauche prolétarienne; he would serve as Jean-Paul Sartre's personal secretary from 1974 to 1980.

18. See Bernard Brillant, "Intellectuels et extrême-gauche: Le cas du Secours rouge," CNRS-IHTP, *Lettre d'information* 32 (July 1998), pp. 6–8; see generally Michael C. Behrent, "Accidents Happen: François Ewald, the Anti-Revolutionary Foucault, and the Intellectual Politics of the French Welfare State," *Journal of Modern History* 82:3 (September 2010), pp. 585–624.

19. See "Rapport n° 1622 sur les agissements, l'organisation, le fonctionnement, les objectifs du groupement de fait dit 'Département, protection, sécurité,'" established by B. Grasset, reporter to the commission of inquiry, submitted to the Assemblée nationale May 26, 1999. Accessed at www.assemblee-nationale.fr/dossiers/dps/r1622p03.asp (accessed January 1, 2012).

20. See "Loi n° 70–480 du 8 juin 1970 tendant à réprimer certaines formes nouvelles de délinquance," *Journal officiel de la République française*, June 9, 1970, p. 5324.

21. See Laurent Quéro, "Les prisonniers enfin: De l'indifférence à l'effet de souffle,'" in Philippe Artières and M. Zancarini-Fournel, eds., *68: Une histoire collective [1962–1981]* (Paris: La Découverte, 2008), p. 569; Daniel Defert, "L'émergence d'un nouveau front: Les prisons," in *Le groupe d'information sur les prisons: Archives d'une lutte, 1970–1972*, Philippe Artières, Laurent Quéro, and M. Zancarini-Fournel, eds. (Paris: Editions de l'IMEC, 2001), p. 316.

22. See Defert, "L'émergence d'un nouveau front: Les prisons," p. 315.

23. On this point, see Jacques Rancière, "La légende des philosophes: Les intellectuels et la traversée du gauchisme," in Rancière, *Les scènes du peuple: Les Révoltes logiques, 1975/1985* (Lyon: Horlieu éditions, 2003), pp. 295–98; Defert, "L'émergence d'un nouveau front: les prisons," p. 315; Quéro, "Les prisonniers enfin: De l'indifférence à l'effet de souffle,'" p. 570.

24. The association, considered "a leftist organization proposing to reconstitute a dissolved assocation," did not receive a charter. On this point, see François Luchaire, "La décision du 16 juillet 1971: Allocution devant le Conseil Constitutionnel," *Dossier thématique: Anniversaire de la loi de 1901 relative au contrat d'association*, 2001, available online at www .conseil-constitutionnel.fr/conseil-constitutionnel/francais/documentation-publications /dossiers-thematiques/2001-anniv.-loi-de-1901-relative-au-contrat-d-association/allocution

-de-monsieur-francois-luchaire.16461.html (accessed January 1, 2012); see also "Rapport no. 1622," *supra*.

25. See Jean-Paul Sartre, "Appel pour le Secours Rouge," (June 18, 1970) in *Fonds: Biblio-thèque nationale de France, Département des manuscrits, Fonds Sartre* (NAF 28405), box "Articles et conférences, 1944/73" (*Catalogue génétique général des manuscrits de Jean-Paul Sartre*, ITEM, ENS-CNRS, Paris, p. 2). For a discussion of this, see Brillant, "Intellectuels et extrême-gauche: Le cas du Secours rouge," CNRS-IHTP, Lettre d'information no. 32, juillet 1998, p. 2.

26. See Artières, Quéro, and Zancarini-Fournel, "Contexte," in *Le groupe d'information sur les prisons. Archives d'une lutte, 1970–1972*, at p. 15; Jean-Paul Sartre, "Sur les mineurs," décembre 1970, *Fonds: Bibliothèque nationale de France, Département des manuscrits, Fonds Sartre*, NAF 28405; see also, generally, Michael C. Behrent, "Accidents Happen: François Ewald, the 'Antirevolutionary' Foucault, and the Intellectual Politics of the French Welfare State," *Journal of Modern History* 82 (September 2010), pp. 585–624.

27. See "Déclaration des emprisonnés politiques en grève de la faim" (September 1, 1970), reproduced in *Le groupe d'information sur les prisons: Archives d'une lutte, 1970–1972*, p. 31.

28. See Defert, "L'émergence d'un nouveau front: Les prisons," pp. 315–16; and Quéro, "Les prisonniers enfin: De l'indifférence à l''effet de souffle,'" pp. 570–71. See generally Audrey Kiéfer, *Michel Foucault: Le G.I.P., l'histoire et l'action* (Université de Picardie Jules Verne d'Amiens, 2009).

29. See Defert, "L'émergence d'un nouveau front: Les prisons," p. 320; M. Perrot, "La leçon des ténèbres: Michel Foucault et la prison," *Actes: Cahiers d'action juridique* 54 (1986), p. 75.

30. Grégory Salle, "Mettre la prison à l'épreuve: Le GIP en guerre contre l''Intolérable,'" *Cultures & conflits* 55 (autumn 2004):71–96; Foucault, "Les intellectuels et le pouvoir," p. 308. When Foucault, in his debate "On Popular Justice: A Discussion with Maoists," tells Benny Lévy that the penitentiary system now functions to absorb the surplus populations, Lévy, the young leader of the GP and of the OPP, resists (ibid., pp. 352–53; English translation, pp. 18–19). Lévy has the same reaction when Foucault adds that, as a state apparatus, penal justice "has always functioned to introduce contradictions" in the population, and when he evokes the "ideological barrier (regarding the crime, the criminal, theft, the underworld, the degenerates, sub-humanity)" that constitutes a second wall around the prison (ibid., pp. 356 and 353; English translation, pp. 17 and 21). The principal rupture, Lévy retorts, "is between the minority of workers and the masses that are becoming proletarian: these masses, it's the worker who is migrating from the countryside, it is not the punk, the crook, or the hooligan" (ibid., p. 356; English translation, p. 21).

31. Gilles Deleuze, *Foucault* (Paris: Minuit, 1986), p. 64; English edition, *Foucault*, Seán Hand, trans. (Minneapolis: University of Minnesota Press, 1988), p. 57.

32. Michel Foucault, "La pensée du dehors," *Critique* 229 (June 1966), pp. 523–46 in *Dits & écrits* I, no. 38, p. 524: Foucault would write that "fiction consists then not in making us see the invisible, but in making us see how invisible is the invisibility of the visible."

33. Foucault, "Les intellectuels et le pouvoir," p. 308; English translation, "Intellectuals and Power," p. 207.

34. Ibid.

35. Ibid.; English translation, pp. 207–8.

36. Ibid., pp. 308–9; English translation, p. 208. This position was evidently different from that of Sartre; see generally Sartre, "Situation de l'écrivain en 1947," in Sartre, *Qu'est-ce que la littérature?* (1947) (Paris: Gallimard, Folio Essais, 1985), p. 239.

37. Defert, "L'émergence d'un nouveau front: Les prisons," p. 320.

38. Ibid., p. 318.

39. See Defert, "Chronologie," in *Dits & écrits* I, p. 33.

40. Michel Foucault, "Enquête sur les prisons: Brisons les barreaux du silence," interview by C. Angeli of Foucault et Pierre Vidal-Naquet, *Politique-hebdo*, no. 24, March 18, 1971, pp. 4–6, in *Dits & écrits* II, no. 88, p. 176.

41. They are all collected in *Le groupe d'information sur les prisons: Archives d'une lutte, 1970–1972*, Philippe Artières, Laurent Quéro, and M. Zancarini-Fournel, eds. (Paris: Editions de l'IMEC, 2001). A number of other intellectuals would coordinate and collaborate, including Gilles Deleuze, Hélène Cixous, Jacques-Alain Miller, François Régnault, and others. As philosophers, what they all had in common was critical thought, language, and the living word; recognizing the effects of discourse, they would approach their mission not only as academics, but as performers and psychoanalysts as well.

42. Foucault, "Les intellectuels et le pouvoir," p. 308; English translation, p. 208.

43. Michel Foucault, "Le savoir d'Œdipe," (lecture given at the State University of New York at Buffalo, in March 1972, and at Cornell University in October 1972), in Michel Foucault, *Leçons sur la volonté de savoir: Cours au Collège de France, 1970–1971*, Daniel Defert, ed. (Paris: Gallimard/Seuil, 2011), p. 240; English edition, "The Knowledge of Oedipus," in *Lessons on the Will to Know: Lectures at the Collège de France, 1970–1971*, Graham Burchell, trans., Arnold I. Davidson, English series ed. (New York: Palgrave, 2013), p. 229.

44. Deleuze, quoted in Foucault, "Les intellectuels et le pouvoir," p. 314; English translation, p. 215.

45. Foucault, *Leçons sur la volonté de savoir*, p. 6; English edition, p. 4.

46. Ibid., p. 16; English edition, p. 14.

47. Ibid., p. 4; English edition, p. 2.

48. Michel Foucault, "Qu'est-ce que la critique ? [Critique et *Aufklärung*]," lecture delivered at the Société française de philosophie, May 27, 1978), *Bulletin de la Société française de philosophie*, t. LXXXIV, 1990, 35–63, at p. 49; English translation, "What Is Critique?" pp. 41–82 in Michel Foucault, *The Politics of Truth*, Sylvère Lotringer, ed. (Los Angeles: Semiotext(e), 2007), p. 61.

49. Ibid.; English translation, p. 62.

50. Foucault, "Enquête sur les prisons: Brisons les barreaux du silence," p. 179.

51. Michel Foucault, "Un problème m'intéresse depuis longtemps, c'est celui du système pénal," interview with J. Hafsia, *La Presse de Tunisie*, August 12, 1971, in *Dits & écrits* II, no. 95, 205–9, p. 206.

52. Ibid., p. 208.

53. Foucault, "Sur la justice populaire. Débat avec les maos," at p. 358; English translation at p. 23.

54. Michel Foucault, "Réponse à une question" (*Esprit*, no. 361, May 1968), in Foucault, *Dits et écrits* I, no. 58, p. 688.

55. Michel Foucault, "La volonté de savoir," *Annuaire du Collège de France, 71e année, Histoire des systèmes de pensée, année 1970–1971*, 1971, pp. 245–49 in *Dits et écrits* II, no. 101, p. 243; English translation, "The Will to Knowledge: Course Summary," pp. 11–16 in *The Essential Works of Michel Foucault, 1954–1984, Volume 1: Ethics: Subjectivity and Truth*, Paul Rabinow, ed. (New York: The New Press, 1997).

56. Foucault, "Sur la justice populaire. Débat avec les maos," pp. 346 and 341; English translation, pp. 2–3 and 6.

57. Michel Foucault, "Théories et institutions pénales," *Annuaire du Collège de France, 72e année, Histoire des systèmes de pensée, année 1971–1972*, 1972, pp. 283–86 in *Dits & écrits* II, no. 115, p. 389; English translation, "Penal Theories and Institutions: Course Summary," pp. 17–22, in *Essential Works: Ethics: Subjectivity and Truth*, p. 17.

58. Michel Foucault, "La vérité et les formes juridiques" (lectures delivered at the Pontifical Catholic University of Rio de Janeiro May 21–2, 1973, J. W. Prado Jr., trans., *Cadernos da*

P.U.C., no. 16, June 1974, pp. 5–133), in *Dits & écrits* II, no. 139, p. 539; English translation, "Truth and Juridical Forms," pp. 1–89 in Michel Foucault, *Power: Essential Works of Foucault, 1954–1984, Volume III* (New York: The New Press, 2000), p. 2.

59. Michel Foucault, *Surveiller et punir: Naissance de la prison* (Paris: Gallimard, 1975), p. 27; English edition, *Discipline and Punish: The Birth of the Prison*, Alan Sheridan, trans. (New York: Vintage, 1979), p. 23.

60. Ibid.

61. Ibid., p. 23; English edition, p. 17.

62. Ibid., pp. 28–29; English edition, p. 24.

63. Foucault, "Sur la justice populaire: Débat avec les maos," p. 341; English translation, p. 2.

64. Michel Foucault, "Michel Foucault: Les réponses du philosophe" ("Michel Foucault: El filosofo responde," interview with C. Bojunga and R. Lobo, P. W. Prado Jr., trans.), *Jornal da Tarde*, November 1, 1975, in *Dits & écrits* II, no. 163, p. 810.

65. Ibid.

66. Foucault, *Surveiller et punir*, at p. 23; English edition, p. 17.

67. Foucault, "Sixth Lecture," this volume, p. 228.

68. Michel Foucault, "La société punitive," *Annuaire du Collège de France, 73e année, Histoire des systèmes de pensée, année 1972–1973*, 1973, pp. 255–67 in *Dits & écrits* II no. 131; English translation, "The Punitive Society: Course Summary," pp. 23–39 in *Essential Works: Ethics: Subjectivity and Truth*, p. 23.

69. Michel Foucault, "Lacan, le 'libérateur' de la psychanalyse" ("Lacan, il 'liberatore' della psicanalisi," interview with J. Nobécourt, trans. A. Ghizzardi), *Corriere della sera*, vol. 106, no. 212, September 11, 1981), in *Dits & écrits* IV, no. 163, p. 205.

70. Michel Foucault, "The Subject and Power," pp. 208–26, in Hubert Dreyfus and Paul Rabinow, *Michel Foucault: Beyond Structuralism and Hermeneutics*, 2nd ed. (Chicago: University of Chicago Press, 1982), p. 208.

71. Ibid.

72. Michel Foucault, "Le souci de la vérité" (interview with François Ewald) in *Dits & écrits* IV, no. 350, p. 675.

73. Michel Foucault, "Le pouvoir psychiatrique," *Annuaire du Collège de France, 74e année, Histoire des systèmes de pensée, année 1973–1974*, 1974, pp. 293–300), in *Dits & écrits* II, no. 143, p. 675; English translation, "Psychiatric Power: Course Summary," pp. 39–50 in *The Essential Works of Michel Foucault, 1954–1984, Volume 1: Ethics: Subjectivity and Truth*, Paul Rabinow, ed. (New York: The New Press, 1997), p. 39.

74. Foucault, "La vérité et les formes juridiques," p. 540; English translation, p. 3.

75. Ibid.

76. Ibid.

77. Ibid., p. 552; English translation, p. 15.

78. Louis L. Althusser, "Idéologie et appareils idéologiques d'État (Note pour une recherche)," *La Pensée: Revue du rationalisme moderne*, no. 151 (June 1970), pp. 3–38, p. 27; English translation, "Ideology and Ideological State Apparatuses (Notes towards an Investigation)" in Louis Althusser, *"Lenin and Philosophy" and Other Essays*, Ben Brewster, trans. (New York: Monthly Review Press, 2001), p. 113.

79. Foucault, "La vérité et les formes juridiques," pp. 552–53; English translation, p. 15.

80. Michel Foucault, "Leçon sur Nietzsche: Comment penser l'histoire de la vérité avec Nietzsche sans s'appuyer sur la vérité," lecture delivered at McGill University in Montreal in April 1971, pp. 195–213 in Foucault, *Leçons sur la volonté de savoir: Cours au Collège de France, 1970–1971*, Daniel Defert, ed. (Paris: Gallimard/Seuil, 2011), p. 240; English edition, "Lecture on Nietzsche," pp. 202–23 in *Lessons on the Will to Know: Lectures at the Collège de France,*

1970–1971, Graham Burchell, trans., Arnold I. Davidson, English series ed. (New York: Palgrave, 2013), p. 212.

81. Ibid., p. 202; English translation, p. 210.

82. Ibid.

83. Foucault, "Le pouvoir psychiatrique," p. 677; English translation, p. 41.

84. Foucault, "Les intellectuels et le pouvoir," p. 307; English translation, p. 207.

85. Foucault, "Le pouvoir psychiatrique," p. 686; English translation, p. 49.

86. Foucault, *Leçons sur la volonté de savoir*, p. 18; English translation, p. 17.

87. Ibid.

88. Foucault, "Le pouvoir psychiatrique," p. 675; English translation, p. 39.

89. Ibid., p. 679; English translation, p. 43.

90. Ibid., p. 680; English translation, p. 44.

91. Ibid., pp. 680–81; English translation, p. 44–45.

92. Ibid., p. 686; English translation, p. 49.

93. Cf. Michel Foucault, *Les mots et les choses: Une archéologie des sciences humaines* (Paris: Gallimard, 1966); English edition, *The Order of Things* (New York: Vintage, 1970), p. 3.

94. Foucault, "Le pouvoir psychiatrique," p. 675; English translation, p. 39.

95. Ibid.

96. Foucault, *Leçons sur la volonté de savoir*, p. 19; English edition, p. 18.

97. Ibid.

98. Michel Foucault, "Le jeu de Michel Foucault," in *Dits & écrits* III, no. 206, p. 312 (Paris: Gallimard, 1994).

99. Michel Foucault, *L'usage des plaisirs: Histoire de la sexualité 2* (Paris: Gallimard, 1984), p. 11; English edition, *The Use of Pleasure: Volume 2 of The History of Sexuality*, Robert Hurley, trans. (New York: Vintage, 1985), p. 5.

100. Michel Foucault, "Histoire de la sexualité," in Foucault, *L'usage des plaisirs*, slip page included in the original edition.

101. Foucault, *L'usage des plaisirs*, p. 12; English edition, p. 5.

102. Foucault, *La volonté de savoir*, p. 73; English edition, p. 54.

103. Ibid., p. 74; English edition, p. 55.

104. Ibid., p. 75; English edition, p. 56 and n. 1.

105. Ibid., p. 74; English edition, p. 55.

106. Ibid., p. 124; English edition, p. 94.

107. Michel Foucault, "Les rapports de pouvoir passent à l'intérieur des corps," in *Dits & écrits* III, no. 197, p. 228.

108. Ibid.

109. Ibid.

110. Ibid.

111. Foucault, *L'usage des plaisirs*, p. 10; English edition, p. 4.

112. Ibid., p. 11; English edition, p. 5.

113. Ibid., p. 12; English edition, p. 6.

114. Michel Foucault, "Les mailles du pouvoir" ("As malhas do poder," P. W. Prado Jr., trans.; lecture delivered at the department of philosophy at the University of Bahia, 1976, *Barbarie*, no. 4, summer 1981, pp. 23–27), in *Dits & écrits* IV, no. 297, p. 198.

115. Foucault, "Leçon sur Nietzsche," p. 199; English translation, p. 206.

116. Althusser, "Ideology and Ideological State Apparatuses," p. 123; "Idéologie et appareils idéologiques d'État," p. 35.

117. Michel Foucault, "Qu'est-ce qu'un auteur?" *Bulletin de la Société française de philosophie*, 63e année, no. 3, juillet–septembre 1969, pp. 73–104 (also in *Dits & écrits* I, no. 69,

p. 792); English edition, *What Is an Author?*, pp. 377–91 in *The Essential Foucault*, Paul Rabinow ed. (New York: The New Press, 2003), p. 377.

118. Ibid., p. 810; English translation, pp. 389 and 390.

119. Ibid., pp. 810–11; English translation, p. 390.

120. Michel Foucault, "Nietzsche, la généalogie, l'histoire" (*Hommage à Jean Hyppolite*, Paris, P.U.F., coll. Prométhée, 1971, 145–72) in *Dits & écrits* II, no. 84, p. 155; English translation, "Nietzsche, Genealogy, History," pp. 351–69 in *The Essential Foucault*, Paul Rabinow ed. (New York: The New Press), p. 366.

121. Foucault, "Inaugural Lecture," this volume, p. 20.

122. Michel Foucault, "About the Beginning of the Hermeneutics of the Self: Two Lectures at Dartmouth," *Political Theory*, vol. 21, no. 2 (May, 1993), pp. 198–227, p. 224 n. 4.

123. Ibid.

124. Foucault, "Inaugural Lecture," p. 20.

125. Foucault, "About the Beginning of the Hermeneutics of the Self: Two Lectures at Dartmouth," p. 224 n. 4.

126. Foucault, "Qu'est-ce que la critique? [Critique et *Aufklärung*]," p. 38; English translation, p. 45.

127. Ibid., p. 38; English translation, p. 44.

128. Ibid.

129. Ibid., p. 39; English translation, p. 47.

130. Foucault discusses the essay in his "What is Enlightenment?," pp. 32–50 in Paul Rabinow, ed., *The Foucault Reader* (New York: Pantheon Books, 1984).

131. Foucault, "Qu'est-ce que la critique?," p. 41; English translation, p. 49.

132. Foucault, "Interview with André Berten," this volume, p. 236.

133. Foucault, "Qu'est-ce que la critique?," p. 47; English translation, p. 57.

134. Ibid., p. 42; English translation, p. 51.

135. Ibid., p. 44; English translation, p. 54.

136. Ibid., p. 44; English translation, p. 54.

137. Ibid., pp. 44–45; English translation, p. 54.

138. Ibid., p. 47; English translation, p. 58.

139. Ibid.

140. Ibid., pp. 58–59.

141. Ibid., pp. 47–48; English translation, p. 59.

142. Ibid., p. 48; English translation, p. 59.

143. Ibid., p. 52; English translation, p. 65.

144. Michel Foucault, *Du Gouvernment des vivants: Cours au Collège de France, 1979–1980*, Michel Senellart, ed. (Paris: Gallimard/Sevil, 2012), p. 8.

145. Ibid, pp. 8–9.

146. Ibid, p. 8.

147. Ibid.

148. Ibid, p. 12.

149. Ibid.

150. Ibid., p. 74.

151. Ibid., p. 13.

152. Ibid., p. 75.

153. Ibid.

154. Ibid.

155. Ibid.

156. Ibid.

157. Ibid. This highlights just how surprising the question is that Robert Badinter asks the jury during the trial of Patrick Henry: "Can you sentence to death someone you do not know?" Foucault ends *Wrong-Doing, Truth-Telling* on this question, which he had already cited in "The Evolution of the Notion of 'Dangerous Individual' in the Legal Psychiatry of the 19th Century," *Dits et écrits* III (1976–79), no. 220, p. 444. In the latter, Foucault explains that this question is surprising because it reveals the "antinomy of penal reason" (ibid., p. 227).

158. Foucault, *Du Gouvernement des vivants*, p. 76.

159. Ibid., p. 78. The series includes a fourth element: "programming of reforms."

160. Ibid. The fourth term of this series is the "postponing of the moments of non-acceptance," which relates to the critical theme of the acceptance of the inacceptable and of the system of acceptability acceptance depends on.

161. Ibid.

162. Ibid., p. 85.

163. Ibid., p. 92.

164. Ibid., p. 79.

165. Ibid.

166. Ibid., p. 98.

167. Ibid.

168. Ibid.

169. Ibid.

170. Ibid., p. 9.

171. Ibid., p. 98.

172. Ibid.

173. Ibid., p. 95.

174. Ibid. This discussion picks up on the arguments made by Michel Foucault in *Leçons sur la volonté de savoir*, especially pp. 64–67.

175. Ibid., p. 96.

176. Ibid., p. 18.

177. Ibid.

178. Ibid., p. 16.

179. Foucault, "About the Beginning of the Hermeneutics of the Self: Two Lectures at Dartmouth," p. 203; Foucault, "Inaugural Lecture," p. 23.

180. Foucault, "About the Beginning of the Hermeneutics of the Self: Two Lectures at Dartmouth," p. 204.

181. Ibid.

182. Foucault, "Interview with André Berten," this volume, p. 240.

183. Michel Foucault, "Interview with Jean François and John De Wit," this volume, p. 259.

184. Michel Foucault, "Subjectivité et vérité," *Annuaire du Collège de France, 81e année, Histoire des systèmes de pensée, année 1980–1981*, 1981, pp. 383–89 in *Dits & écrits* IV, no. 304, p. 213; English translation, "Subjectivity and Truth: Course Summary," pp. 87–92 in *The Essential Works of Michel Foucault, 1954–1984, Volume 1: Ethics: Subjectivity and Truth*, p. 87.

185. Ibid., p. 214; English translation, p. 88.

186. Ibid.

187. Ibid.

188. Foucault, "About the Beginning of the Hermeneutics of the Self: Two Lectures at Dartmouth," p. 201.

189. Ibid., p. 203.

190. Ibid.

191. "Inaugural Lecture," this volume, p. 24.

192. Foucault, "Interview with François and De Wit," this volume, p. 256.

193. Ibid.

194. Gilles Deleuze, *Foucault* (Paris: Minuit, 1986), p. 125; English edition, p. 117.

195. Michel Foucault, "About the Concept of the 'Dangerous Individual' in 19th Century Legal Psychiatry," *Journal of Law and Psychiatry* 1 (1978), pp. 1–18.

196. Michel Foucault, *Les mots et les choses: Une archéologie des sciences humaines* (Paris: Gallimard, 1966), p. 7; English edition, *The Order of Things* (New York: Vintage, 1970), p. xv.

197. Foucault, "About the Beginning of the Hermeneutics of the Self: Two Lectures at Dartmouth," p. 202.

198. Foucault, "First Lecture," this volume, p. 39.

199. Cf. Foucault, "Inaugural Lecture," pp. 15–17.

200. Michel Foucault, *Le courage de la vérité: Le gouvernement de soi et des autres II. Cours au Collège de France. 1984.* Frédéric Gros, ed. (Paris: Gallimard/Seuil, 2009), p. 6; English edition, *The Courage of Truth: The Government of Self and Others II: Lectures at the Collège de France, 1983-1984,* Graham Burchell, trans., Arnold I. Davidson, English series ed. (New York: Palgrave, 2011), p. 5.

201. Foucault, *L'herméneutique du sujet*, pp. 12–13; English edition, pp. 10–11.

202. Foucault, "Inaugural Lecture," p 15.

203. Foucault, *Le courage de la vérité*, p. 13; English edition, pp. 11–12.

204. Foucault, "Inaugural Lecture," p. 17.

205. Foucault, *Le courage de la vérité*, p. 13; English edition, p. 11.

206. Foucault, *Le courage de la vérité*, p. 13; English edition, p. 12.

207. Ibid., pp. 57–59; English edition, p. 61.

208. Foucault, "Inaugural Lecture," p. 16.

209. Foucault, *Le courage de la vérité*, p. 12; English edition, p. 11.

210. Ibid.

211. Ibid., p. 16; English edition, p. 15.

212. Ibid., p. 18; English edition, p. 17.

213. Ibid., p. 24; English edition, p. 24.

214. Ibid., p. 26; English edition, p. 25.

215. Ibid.

216. Ibid., p. 8; English edition, p. 6.

217. Ibid., p. 17; English edition, p. 16.

218. Ibid., p. 17; English edition, p. 16.

219. Thank you to Daniel Wyche for this important observation.

220. On this topic, see Foucault, *L'herméneutique du sujet*, pp. 16–31.

221. Jean-Claude Milner, *La politique des choses* (Paris: Navarin, 2005).

222. Foucault, "L'intellectuel et les pouvoirs," in Foucault, *Dits et écrits*, IV, no. 359, p. 751; in this volume, p. 252.

223. Ibid.

224. Foucault, "Subjectivity and Truth," in *The Politics of Truth*, p. 153.

225. Foucault, *Le Courage de la vérité*, p. 5; English edition, p. 3.

226. Foucault, "Inaugural Lecture," this volume, p. 20.

227. Ibid., p. 21.

228. For more about this opposition, see Foucault's "What is Critique?"

229. Michel Foucault, "Entretien avec Michel Foucault" ("Conversatione con Michel Foucault," interview with D. Trombadori, Paris, *Il Contributo* 4, no. 1 [January–March 1980], pp. 23–84), in Michel Foucault, *Dits & écrits* IV, no. 281, p. 45.

230. Ibid.

231. Ibid.

232. Ibid., p. 47.

233. Foucault, *Le Courage de la Vérité*, p. 61; English edition, p. 65.

234. Foucault, *L'Herméneutique du sujet*, p. 17; English edition, p. 15.

235. We are transposing here the perspective Foucault adopted in *L'Usage des plaisirs*, p. 15.

236. Foucault, *Le Courage de la vérité*, p. 4; English edition, pp. 2–3.

237. Foucault, "Les Intellectuels et le pouvoir" (entretien avec G. Deleuze), p. 314.

238. Foucault, *Le Courage de la vérité*, p. 27; English edition, p. 27.

239. Ibid.

240. Michel Foucault, "Est-il important de penser?" (interview with D. Eribon, originally published in *Libération*, no. 15, May 30–31, 1981, p. 21) in M. Foucault, *Dits et écrits* IV, no. 296, p. 182.

241. Foucault, *Le Courage de la vérité*, p. 17; English edition, p. 16.

242. Foucault, *Language, Memory, Counter-Practice*, p. 161.

243. In his response to Jacques Derrida's objection to his reflections on the role and status of madness and dreams in the development of Cartesian doubt, Foucault identifies a point of resistance to doubt, a "de facto" resistance "to the effectuation of doubt by the subject who is meditating *in actuality*." It is with an eye to defeating this resistance that Descartes talks about madness and dream in his first *Meditation*. Indeed, both "force doubt regarding the subject's system of actuality." First comes madness: "The mad live in illusion regarding their actuality: They believe they are dressed when they are naked, kings when they are poor." But this language is too strong, since calling the subject mad disqualifies him and assumes him incapable of "reasonably conducting his meditation through doubt and toward a potential truth." Hence the turn to dreams, which constitute the subject as both "*really doubting* his own actuality, and *continuing a valid meditation* that discards anything that is not a manifest truth (Michel Foucault, "Mon corps, ce papier, ce feu," in Michel Foucault, *Histoire de la folie à l'âge classique*, pp. 595–97). *Mal faire, dire vrai* is in a twofold relationship with Descartes's text. On the one hand, Foucault conducts a genealogy of the Cartesian subject and of that exclusion of madness that constitutes him as a thinking subject. On the other hand, it is as if these "series of series," these "concerted carnivals," were themselves exercises meant to cast doubt on the subject's system of actuality, just like madness and dreams in the first *Meditation*. The role of these exercises would then be to bring the readers to cast real doubt; that which, since Descartes, constitutes their subject's actuality, which is to say to doubt the Cartesian *cogito*. Having done so, they can then pursue a meditation on the way in which they are tied to the truth, without "leaning on the truth" nor giving themselves the guarantee that the medicating Descartes had given himself. Cf. text at n. 59, "Fourth Lecture," this volume, p. 161.

244. Foucault, "Of Other Spaces," *Diacritics* 16, no. 1 (Spring 1986), p. 25.

245. Ibid.

246. Foucault, "What is Critique?," in *The Politics of Truth* (Los Angeles: Semiotext(e), 1997), p. 56.

247. Ibid., p. 65.

248. Foucault, *Leçons sur la volonté de savoir*, p. 45; English edition, pp. 43–45.

249. Foucault, "What is Critique?" in *The Politics of Truth*, p. 56.

250. Foucault, "Theatrum philosophicum," pp. 75–99. Foucault wrote about "philosophy-theater," by which he meant "not a reflection on theater, nor theater overloaded with significations, but rather philosophy that has become a stage, characters, signs, the repetition of a unique event that will never again be reproduced." Michel Foucault, "Arianne s'est pendue" (published originally in *Le Nouvel Observateur*, no.229, March 31–April 6, 1969, pp. 36–37), in Michel Foucault, *Dits et écrits*, I, no. 64, pp. 767–71.

251. On this notion of a series of series, see Foucault, *L'archéologie du savoir*, pp. 15 and 19, as well as Defert, "Situation du cours," in Foucault, *Leçons sur la volonté de savoir*, p. 269; English edition, p. 268.

252. Foucault, *Le Courage de la vérité*, p. 17; English edition, p. 16.

253. Foucault, "Le savoir d'Œdipe," p. 240; English edition, p. 235.

254. Ibid. See also Foucault, *Leçons sur la volonté de savoir*, p. 191 (English edition, p. 191); and *Wrong-Doing, Truth-Telling*, "Second Lecture," this volume, p. 67.

255. Foucault, *The Uses of Pleasure*, p. 8.

256. Foucault, *Le Courage de la vérité*, p. 261; English edition, p. 284.

Acknowledgments to the French Edition

We are indebted to Daniel Defert, François Ewald, Françoise Tulkens, and Jean-Michel Chaumont for their guidance and generosity in the preparation of the French edition, as well as to many colleagues whom we would like to sincerely thank, including:

At the Catholic University of Louvain, Bernard Coulie, professor in the department of philosophy and letters, who was at the time of these lectures chancellor of the university; Henri Bosly and Damien Vandermeersch, professors in the law school; Vincent Francis and Martin Moucheron, assistant professors; Jean-Philippe de Limbourg, assistant; and several masters and doctoral students, including Laure Kervyn de Meerendre and Emmanuel Picardi;

At the University of Chicago, Arnold Davidson, professor in the department of philosophy; several doctoral students, including Daniel Nichanian, Tuomo Tiisala, Lyubomir Uzunov and Daniel Wyche; and Margaret Schilt and Greg Nimmo, research librarians at the D'Angelo Law Library;

Emmanuel Francis, researcher at the Centre for the Study of Manuscript Culture at the University of Hamburg; Elisabeth Geoffroy at the University of Paris II; Claire Lechevallier, assistant professor at the University of Caen; Stephen Sawyer, professor of history and chair of the department of history at the American University of Paris; and Claude Terreaux, professor in Paris.

Thank you to Philippe Artières, director of research at the CNRS, who provided us with the texts that we requested, as well as Michel Senellart, professor at the École normale supérieure in Lyon, who generously put at our disposition the text of the lectures delivered by Foucault at the Collège de France in 1979–1980, *On the Government of the Living*, which Michel Senellart edited.

Thank you to Colin Gordon, to Eric Heilmann, professor at the University of Burgundy, and to Véronique Voruz, professor at the Université de Leicester, for their generous rereadings of all or parts of the course context.

Fabienne Brion and Bernard E. Harcourt

Acknowledgments to the English Edition

It has been an immense pleasure to work closely with Stephen Sawyer on the English translation of the lectures that Foucault delivered at Louvain. I am deeply grateful to Steve for his tireless work and for producing a translation of the lectures that is so faithful to the critical, philosophical, political, and ethical interventions that Foucault made at Louvain, while at the same time being so elegant and pleasant to read.

In our work on the English edition, we sought counsel and received generous guidance first and foremost from Arnold Davidson at the University of Chicago, and I thank him sincerely for his generosity, collegiality, friendship, and for our many collaborations, past, present, and future. Richard Helmholz at the Law School and Margaret Mitchell at the Divinity School at the University of Chicago, Danielle Allen at the Institute for Advanced Studies at Princeton University, Adriaan Lanni at Harvard Law School, and Mariana Valverde at the University of Toronto also generously provided guidance and expertise at critical junctures of the translation. I sincerely thank them for their advice. Frances Spaltro at the University of Chicago provided priceless assistance with the Greek and Latin, for which I am deeply grateful as well.

The English edition benefited greatly from close readings and extensive comments by Daniel Nichanian, Tuomo Tiisala, Lyubomir Uzunov, and Daniel Wyche, four outstanding doctoral students at the University of Chicago. It benefited as well from extensive and generous comments by two anonymous readers for the University of Chicago Press. Daniel Wyche, Gabriel Mathless, and Christopher Berk at the University of Chicago provided selfless assistance in researching and preparing the English notes and comments, and Daniel Henry provided excellent research assistance. Margaret Schilt and Greg Nimmo of the University of Chicago Library were invaluable in tracking down rare and sometimes difficult sources, and I am deeply grateful to them, as well as to Zachary Togami, Samantha Geloso, and Claire Merrill for exceptional administrative assistance.

John Tryneski at the University of Chicago Press shepherded this translation through to publication and I thank him dearly for his guidance and encouragement. Renaldo Migaldi provided outstanding copyediting and I am deeply grateful to him as well.

Bernard E. Harcourt

Index of Notions and Concepts

Index of Proper Names